ORIGINS
OF THE
GODS

"*Origins of the Gods* presents nothing less than a grand unified theory of the Other that finally gives the paranormal the respect it has long been due but has rarely received. With clear-eyed objectivity and scholarship, this book fearlessly covers a vast array of subjects within the 'jigsaw of paranormality'—highlighting sacred knowledge and shamanism's role in the origins of civilization and linking it all back to quantum reality and transdimensional intelligences. An important book and instant classic."

LYNN PICKNETT & CLIVE PRINCE, AUTHORS OF
WHEN GOD HAD A WIFE AND *THE FORBIDDEN UNIVERSE*

"*Origins of the Gods* explores evidence for shamanistic contact with divine consciousness more than 400,000 years ago in the newly excavated Qesem Cave in Israel. We see the actual origins of divine contact—the earliest forms of multidimensional communication. Power places like Qesem Cave are portals to divine beings because of potent plasma light manifestations triggered by high tectonic stress. These forces enabled our ancestors to link with beings in other dimensions, so they venerated these sacred sites and enhanced their power. This remarkable book, which includes little-known Native American sites, traces the journeys of our ancestors to these power places over a few millions years to explore how contact with the gods triggered human evolutionary leaps. It is a must-read for students of shamanism, transdimensional contact, and the secrets of our ancient origins."

BARBARA HAND CLOW, AUTHOR OF
AWAKENING THE PLANETARY MIND

"For years I have marveled at these two explorers and their passion for digging deeper into the mysteries surrounding the dimensions of life with its familiar and alien entities that live throughout. Their discoveries combined with an innate understanding of the paranormal have lifted us from our finite terrestrial consciousness into an infinite wondrous awareness. In this latest volume they chronicle the evolution of life in all its manifestations. An enlightening, fascinating, and astonishing read."

JOHN VAN AUKEN, DIRECTOR OF EDGAR CAYCE'S
ASSOCIATION FOR RESEARCH AND ENLIGHTENMENT (A.R.E.)

"Collins and Little reveal extraordinarily unique and deeply meaningful patterns and information that have long been overlooked, and they accomplish their objective by looking where so many others have failed to look. These authors just may have shaken loose the formerly forbidden fruit from the true lost tree of knowledge."

BRENT RAYNES, EDITOR OF
ALTERNATE PERCEPTIONS MAGAZINE

"Reading *Origins of the Gods* has inspired me to take a road trip to visit the Great Sand Dunes in southern Colorado, Skinwalker Ranch in Utah, and Jewel Cave in the Black Hills of South Dakota. Maybe take a side trip to Israel and Egypt? Only I'll be leaving my iPhone, Kindle, Apple Watch, and other EMF-producing devices home for the holiday so that I can better tap into Earth's ambient frequency. Thanks to this pair of intrepid researchers and fellow writers, I'll be trying to recapture the mystery and magic of planet Earth, as did our ancient ancestors, whose mystical experiences—communicating with an intelligence greater than their own—is at the root of divine revelation."

SIDNEY D. KIRKPATRICK,
NEW YORK TIMES BESTSELLING AUTHOR OF
A CAST OF KILLERS AND *EDGAR CAYCE*

ORIGINS

OF THE

GODS

Qesem Cave, Skinwalkers, and Contact with Transdimensional Intelligences

ANDREW COLLINS and GREGORY L. LITTLE

Bear & Company
Rochester, Vermont

Bear & Company
One Park Street
Rochester, Vermont 05767
www.BearandCompanyBooks.com

Bear & Company is a division of Inner Traditions International

Cataloging-in-Publication Data for this title is available from the Library of Congress

ISBN 978-1-59143-409-2 (print)
ISBN 978-1-59143-410-8 (ebook)

Printed and bound in the United States by P. A. Hutchison Company

10 9 8 7 6 5 4 3 2 1

Text design and layout by Debbie Glogover
This book was typeset in Garamond Premier Pro with Belda and Gill Sans MT Pro used as display typefaces

Image Credits
For "Part 1—All Things Are Connected": Gregory L. Little, plate 1, figures 2.2, 2.3, 2.4, 12.1; Lora Little, plates 2, 3, figures 1.1, 1.2, 1.3, 1.4, 3.2; Licensed from Big Stock Photo, figures 3.1, 7.1; Duncan Long, figure 6.1; Edgar Cayce Foundation, Photography Collection, 11.2.

For "Part 2—Contact with the Outside": Ran Barkai/Tel Aviv University, plates 4 and 5, figures 18.3, 18.4, 21.4; Andrew Collins, plates 6, 7, 9, 10, 11, 12, 13, 15, 16, 17, 18, 20, 21, 22, 23, 24, 26, 28, 29, 32, 33, 34, figures 18.1, 18.2, 20.1, 21.2, 21.3, 22.1, 22.2, 22.4 (map), 25.1, 34.1, 34.2, 36.5, 37.4, 38.1, 38.2; Wikipedia Creative Commons Agreement 2.0, plate 8 by ЧуваевНиколай, plate 25 by Flavio Grynszpan, figure 36.1 photographer unknown; Rodney Hale, plates 18, 19, figure 23.1; Lora Little, plates 30, 31; Russell M. Hossain, plate 35, figure 37.2; Google Earth maps, figures 18.1, 20.1, 22.2, 23.1, 25.1, 34.1, 34.2, 37.4, 38.1, 38.2; Nick Burton, figures 22.3, 22.4 (Dragon Man skull outline and finished sketches), 35.1, 35.2, 36.3, 36.4.

All other illustrations and plate pictures are either from the author's personal collection and are copyright Andrew Collins or Gregory L. Little, or they are out of copyright and in the public domain. Original sources of noncopyright images are indicated in the caption. Every attempt has been made by the authors to clarify the ownership of illustrations used in this book. Any oversights or omissions will be corrected in future editions.

To send correspondence to the authors of this book, mail a first-class letter to the author c/o Inner Traditions • Bear & Company, One Park Street, Rochester, VT 05767, and we will forward the communication, or contact the authors directly: Andrew Collins at **www.andrewcollins.com** and Gregory L. Little at **www.freedom2change.org**.

To the memory of John Keel (1930–2009)
Someone who understood the true nature of contact
with the outside and helped set the current authors
on their course of discovery.

Also to Richard Ward and Erich von Däniken
for their help and contributions to this book.

CONTENTS

PART TWO

CONTACT WITH THE OUTSIDE

by Andrew Collins

FOREWORD

Erich von Däniken

Archaeology is a noble and also conservative science. It searches for the development of cultures, arranges ruins and artifacts, determines dates, and draws its conclusions. This is how a model of our past was created: from prehistoric man to Stone Age cultures. Everything went its natural, evolutionary way.

However, hard facts on ancient ruins show that the archaeological model cannot be correct in many areas. Beside the Stone Age people, who hunted in furs and searched for berries, something like a spiritual elite must have existed. Grandiose buildings and complexes from every period prove it. Yet conservative archaeology remains trapped in its model.

In their new book *Origins of the Gods,* authors Andrew Collins and Greg Little, two leading figures in the field of speculative science and explorative archaeology, convincingly argue that transdimensional beings have been influencing humankind since the earliest beginnings of the human species as much as two million years ago. This has been especially so, they say, at locations with intense electromagnetic anomalies that today we might describe as earth portals, vortex sites, and window areas. At such places, which include Skinwalker Ranch in Utah, the authors propose that these nonhuman intelligences are able to more easily interact with human beings, shamans in particular, through altered states of consciousness and contact with manifesting light beings.

Through such contacts, the evolutionary process takes place, as can be seen from evidence emerging right now from sites like the 400,000-year-old

Qesem Cave in Israel, today considered the birthplace of shamanism. There the early human inhabitants quickly grew to become among the most advanced peoples on the planet, the presence of shamanism and the regular appearance of mysterious lights in the same area almost certainly contributing to these advancements.

All these findings are natural extensions of the questions I posed as far back as 1968 with the publication of *Chariots of the Gods*. There I suggested that human civilization, and the incredible monuments we have fashioned, from Egypt's Great Pyramid to Stonehenge in England and the Nazca Lines of Peru, might well have been inspired by the arrival of extraterrestrial beings from the stars.

Andrew Collins and Greg Little continue this tradition, arguing that these intelligent beings could be transdimensional in nature and exist usually beyond normal space-time. Collins and Little use cutting-edge scientific understanding and quantum theory to explain the nature of these beings, and how, through the processes of entanglement and the presence of plasma environments, they are able to communicate with humankind and, through this, accelerate human evolution.

Perhaps we have here, finally, new answers to the nature of some UFOs and the light beings so often associated with them—beings that in the past have been interpreted under many different names, such as the fairies of folklore and the angels of Jewish mysticism.

In my own books, I examine how the stories of the Bible seem to contain accounts of firsthand encounters with extraterrestrials and the vehicles they use to reach Earth. Most obviously, we speak about the strange craft seen and described by the prophet Ezekiel or how Moses encountered Yahweh as a blinding light on Mount Sinai.

Taking the matter further, Collins and Little argue that Moses was inspired to construct the Ark of the Covenant following information received from transdimensional intelligences manifesting as plasma light. Were similar technologies being given to our ancestors in other parts of the world, and, if so, did this alter the course of human history? I have always believed this to be the case.

The authors, in this new book, use their combined knowledge to both critique and support the findings of classical archaeology. With their analytical minds, they point out inconsistencies, show cross-cultural connections, and prove that our previous thinking has innumerable gaps. This book is a milestone. Here it is proven as clean as a whistle that many a finding that was considered certain has to be revised. *Origins of the Gods* should become a textbook and compulsory reading in all schools.

ERICH VON DÄNIKEN
INTERLAKEN, SWITZERLAND

ERICH VON DÄNIKEN is a Swiss author who challenges the way we view the rise of human civilization. In books such as his 1968 superseller *Chariots of the Gods* he has asked important questions regarding the source of human technology and innovation, proposing that some of the greatest monuments of the ancient world were inspired by contact with visitors from the stars.

Although his views have met with considerable criticism from the scientific community, von Däniken's books have inspired generations of young people to consider the possibility that contact with extraterrestrial intelligences occurred in humanity's past and still continues today. His thought-provoking ideas were directly responsible for the birth of the History Channel's ever-popular TV series *Ancient Aliens*, which regularly features von Däniken's theories and views. He has also appeared as a guest on the show.

Von Däniken is the co-founder of the Archaeology, Astronautics and SETI Research Association (AAS RA), and in 2003 created the Mystery Park (now called Jungfrau Park), a theme park in Interlarken, Switzerland, built to educate visitors on the concept of ancient astronauts in Earth's history. Von Däniken lives in his native Swizerland where he regularly hosts the *Chariots of the Gods* podcast. His website is www.daniken.com.

ACKNOWLEDGMENTS

As usual, there are certain individuals without whom the book might never have existed, or certainly not in the form we find it. They are Richard Ward and Debbie Cartwright, whose unique insights into every facet of the mysteries inspire me always; Rodney Hale, my associate on everything technical and experimental, something my work needs to keep it grounded; Greg Little, for whom I have been able to create half a book that hopefully complements his own quite brilliant contribution to this project, and Erich von Däniken, for the fantastic foreword, which is much appreciated (his bestselling book *Chariots of the Gods* ([1968] 1969) was an inspiration to me when I was just a youth). New to the list of acknowledgments is Helena Reznor, whose friendship, enthusiasm, and deep understanding of the inner sciences behind portal locations and contact with the outside has constantly caused me to pursue areas of this subject I might otherwise have left alone, making the book that much better in the final mix.

There are many other people who have contributed to my life during these dark times as I have attempted to keep safe and get down to writing and researching the book. They include Hugh Newman, J. J. Ainsworth, Marinus van der Sluijs, Lora Little, Michael Staley, Lisa Weaver, Kerry Ann Dar, Yuri Leitch, Paul Weston, Bob Brown, Erik Bard, Jan Summers, Rob Macbeth, Leela Bunce, Buster Todd, Abbie Todd, Darcie Todd, Joan Hale, Yvan Cartwright, Graham Phillips, Renee Goulet, Moira Brown, Alicia McDermott, Catja de Lorenzo, Özgecan Berdibek, Damla Selin Tomru, Fatih Aslan, Santha Hancock, Rowan Campbell Miller, Storm Constantine,

Jim Willis, Jim Hibbert, Eileen Buchanan, Roma Harding, Ioannis Syrigos, Joanna Gillen and all at Ancient Origins, and David Silver and Erik Pinkston and all at Prometheus Studios.

Special thanks also go out to Nick Burton for his wonderful illustrations, the briefs for which must have come across as mind-bending upon first presentation; George Hernandez for his sketches of the Dragon Man skull; Catherine Hale, Caroline Wise, and Debbie Cartwright for line reading; and Russell M. Hossain, not only for his cover artwork suggestions but also for his Navajo skinwalker and Qesem Cave "First Shaman" illustrations.

Additionally, I would like to thank archaeologists Ran Barkai and Avi Gopher of Tel Aviv University for sharing the extraordinary discoveries being made right now in Israel's Qesem Cave and for letting me explore this extraordinary site; Ramon Zürcher, secretary to Erich von Däniken, for his help in securing the book's foreword, and Graham Hancock, for his continued support and encouragement. Thanks go out also to Paul Sinclair for guiding me around Bempton, Britain's Skinwalker Ranch, and Brandon Fugal for allowing me to explore the real thing in Utah's Uintah Basin.

Beyond this, I do also want to thank everyone at my publisher, Inner Traditions, for continuing to believe in me and for always being patient and understanding. That is so important to a project like this one.

ANDREW COLLINS

I want to express my deepest appreciation to my wife, Lora, who for over 40 years has been an integral part of this journey and quest. I could not have done what I did without her help and support. Thanks are also expressed to Brent and Joan Raynes, who have been on the same quest and whose friendship and support have been a blessing. Thanks also to Andrew Collins for his friendship and allowing me to share in his research. Finally, many thanks to the staff of Inner Traditions, who have performed an outstanding job in making our work so much better.

GREGORY L. LITTLE

RITE OF THE FIRST SHAMAN

By Andrew Collins

Our destination is just beyond the eastern limits of the Mediterranean Sea. The age in geological terms is the Middle Pleistocene, and the date sometime around 330,000 years ago. The climate is pretty much as it is today, although the river valleys saddled between the deep rocky hills are much more verdant, much more fertile in nature.

Some little way inland, the topography starts to rise toward the east, its distant horizon crowned with low mountain peaks. Two mountains in particular are like the horns of some enormous landscape beast, and for some reason, these draw the eye for longer than is necessary.

As the light gradually fades and the full moon is seen to rise from the direction of the twin peaks, the ear now catches the slowly rising sound of a bizarre vocal cacophony. It seems to be a mixture of high and low guttural chants produced by the deepest parts of the human windpipe in a manner that would disturb even the most accomplished Mongolian throat singers.

This constant noise seems to be coming from within a steep rocky cliff, in particular from beyond the opening of a large cave entrance. Inside burns a fierce fire lit somewhere close to the center of the large cavern. From the flames comes a thick pungent smoke that immediately invades the throat, causing a violent reaction to this unwanted intrusion into the body. Yet very quickly, the effects of the smoke become tolerable as the interior of the cave starts to become a little hazy.

From out of the smoke appears a strange figure, just over five and half feet tall, with dark, swarthy skin, deep-set eyes, a heavy brow ridge, and a mass of coarse, dark hair. He is a man of some power who crouches slightly as he rhythmically stomps on the ground around his feet. A loincloth made of hanging cords and dried reeds cover his genitals, while a tuft of tall white feathers stick almost vertically up from his centrally parted shock of hair.

The figure's near-naked body is daubed with white paint to create a series of dots, lines, and rectangles. In his hands are bundles of dry plants that he throws on the fire to create even more thick pungent smoke, which now becomes intoxicating beyond belief.

He is also not alone. As the smoke wafts around the cave in ever-rising waves, it becomes apparent that behind him, a little away from the fire and in the semidarkness, are a dozen or so similar individuals. Males and females are present, and, like him, they are also slightly crouched in their stance. They sway and sing in unison to create the bizarre vocal cacophony that provides the energy necessary for what the central figure is trying to achieve.

His focus is now fixed on concentric rings of stones laid out before him. These are both spherical and polygonal in shape and are about the right size to fit tightly in a human hand. They are light in color and made from limestone. At the center of the circle is another polyhedron, slightly smaller in size and blue-grey in color. This one is made of flint and appears important to this strange ceremony.

As the vocal cacophony intensifies still further, the shaman—for that is what he clearly appears to be—takes hold of a swan's wing bone and clenches it tightly in one hand. Still dancing rhythmically on the spot, he cries out above the other voices before entering into a trance state and staring into nowhere. He looks to be possessed by some kind of animating spirit that has taken control of his bodily functions, allowing his mind to be elsewhere.

It is what the shaman experiences next that now compels us, for from his body emerges the vision of a magnificent swan that flaps its wings to rise into the air and out through the cave roof. Free at last, his soul spirit is able to fly at will, encircling about the local hills before heading toward the rising full moon and the twin mountains off in the distance.

This is a fictional account, a confabulation inspired by the discoveries being made right now at one of the most exciting archaeological sites in the world. I speak of the Qesem Cave, near Tel Aviv, in modern-day Israel. There evidence has emerged of extraordinary and quite innovative technological firsts for very early humanity. They include the earliest "canned food," a unique means of preserving the precious and highly nutritious marrow from inside deer leg bones; the earliest "freezers," a unique method of using fire ash to store fresh food and animal hides for extended periods of time; the earliest known mass production of precision-made blade tools; the first sustained use of fire within a permanent hearth; the first use of fire to temper and soften stone materials, and the earliest "school of rock," where pupils were taught the art of stone knapping and tool manufacture.

Perhaps more significantly, from the same cave, comes the earliest evidence anywhere in the world for the existence of shamanistic activities. This realization stems from the discovery of a single swan wing bone sequestered for use in what appears to have been animistic practices. Most obviously, these activities involved an individual, someone whom we might call the First Shaman, adopting the guise of this great white bird to achieve soul flight. (See plate 35 for an artist's impression of Qesem's first shaman.) The purpose of this action would have been the attainment of otherworldly wisdom from the inhabitants of an invisible realm that, as we shall see, was thought to coexist with the world of the living.

The incredible thing is that the highly talented inhabitants of the Qesem Cave did not belong to one of the archaic human populations that are known to have occupied Africa and the Eurasian continent at this time. Instead, what slim anatomical evidence we have about the Qesem people, as we shall call them, is that they may well constitute the earliest form of pre-dispersal modern humans, the forerunners of anatomical modern humans; that is, *Homo sapiens* like ourselves.[1]

Since they also appear to have been the earliest known exponents of shamanism and their community suddenly rose to become arguably the most advanced on the planet at this time, this is all strangely coincidental, to say the least, and raises important questions. Were they among the first people in the world to benefit from communications with otherworldly denizens? Did these communications, achieved through shamanistic activities like those described above, start to provide the inspiration that allowed the Qesem people to develop new technologies and formulate ideas on such profound matters as the meaning of life and death, the nature of the soul, and even their connection with the stars?

OF STARS AND STRANGE REALMS

These earliest shamans at places like the Qesem Cave were clearly trying to access higher powers, powers that the ancients would come to terms *the gods.* Across time complete mythologies developed around these powerful supernatural figures. They could control the violent forces of nature, cause changes in the weather and in the oceans, and even shake the earth itself. Other elements of these mythological traditions reflected ontological and even cosmological beliefs indicating that the earliest ancestors of these prehistoric peoples came from the stars. More disturbingly, our ancestors came to believe that the inhabitants of stars and strange realms could appear as physical beings here, *in this world.* Sometimes these beings were invisible and seen perhaps only during altered states or in dreams, while at other times they could appear in what can only be described as material form.

All this might sound like the start of an episode of *Ancient Aliens,* and there is a very good reason for that. This ever-popular TV show—first broadcast on the History Channel in April 2010, with new episodes being made every year—has asked important questions concerning the true source of the knowledge and wisdom that has inspired the rise of civilizations worldwide and the nature of the supernatural beings that have coexisted with humankind for many thousands of years.

How *did* ancient man come to build Stonehenge and the pyramids of Egypt? Why exactly *were* Peru's Nazca Lines created, and most important of all, why did so many ancient cultures and indigenous peoples come to believe that their earliest ancestors came from the stars? Where did all this knowledge originate? Was it purely a product of random beliefs and ideas accumulated across tens of thousands or even hundreds of thousands of years? Or has there been a slow drip of knowledge coming through to humanity from very real otherworldly intelligences? Is this what our most distant ancestors came to understand themselves? If so, are such intelligences contactable, not just through shamanistic practices but also in the knowledge that certain locations around the globe appear to produce mysterious lights and other strange phenomena on a regular basis? Are these same sites—portals or points of contact, as they might be described—somehow able to trigger transformative experiences in those most in tune with their inherent energies? Have these transformative experiences changed humankind's spiritual views of life and perhaps even triggered the foundations of major religions, including those of a monotheistic nature?

As we will see in part 1 of this book, written by my colleague Greg Little, all these ideas were common to Native American peoples, right through to the arrival among their tribes and communities of the first European ethnographers in the eighteenth and nineteenth centuries. These enlightened Native peoples would have been able to provide suitable answers to all the questions posed here, explaining how much of their knowledge and wisdom came from otherworldly beings—spirits, ancestors, tricksters, and even the somewhat eerie "little people" who bear some semblance to the alien Greys of today. This is where these people said they gained the knowledge that helped inspire not just their natural sciences, which included an understanding of hundreds of different plants and medicines, but also the development of their spiritual worldview. It seems to have been a belief that inspired the creation of unimaginably large earthen mound complexes, many of which are aligned to the sun, moon, and stars.

Greg Little will make it clear that we ignore at our peril the lessons of these indigenous peoples of the North American continent, since they can provide the key to understanding exactly what our earliest ancestors really did believe about the supernatural world that was thought to surround them at all times. In part 2 of this book, I will provide the earliest evidence of these beliefs, which might well have begun at places like the Qesem Cave in Israel as much as 400,000 years ago. Moreover, and most important of all, we reveal the true nature of those "ancient aliens" that we all so long to understand. What we find is that their existence is almost certainly linked, not just with entities existing at the very edge of the electromagnetic spectrum but even with such matters as plasma consciousness, quantum realities, and multidimensionality. This line of investigation, as we shall see, will provide us with compelling and quite mystifying evidence for the true origins of the "gods" who are strongly believed to have guided humanity since the beginning.

PART I

All Things Are Connected

By Gregory L. Little

All things are connected.

ATTRIBUTED TO CHIEF SEATTLE

1

SEEKING THE SOURCE OF THE PARANORMAL

November 8, 2019—it was early on a cold, clear-skies Friday morning as we began the 100-mile drive from our motel in Farmington, New Mexico, to the Hovenweep National Monument, located in the extreme southeastern corner of Utah. The ruins are attributed to the Ancestral Puebloan people (commonly called the Anasazi). The building of the impressive stone constructions at Hovenweep began sometime around CE 750. The name Hovenweep means "deserted valley" in the Ute language.[1]

The large, three-story-tall stone towers at Hovenweep were made around CE 1000. Abandonment of the site began around the year 1250, and within 100 years it was completely abandoned due to prolonged drought.[2] But even today it remains a very impressive complex of stone construction. In short, Hovenweep was a place my wife, Lora, and I really wanted to see *again* and was high on our agenda during a nine-day exploration of ruins and culture located on the massive Navajo Nation reservation. On the way to the site, we talked about how our visits to many sites, including Hovenweep, had gone full circle after a more than 30-year quest.

THE QUEST TO FIND THE SOURCE

Some 31 years earlier, we had visited the remote Hovenweep site while I was writing the book *People of the Web* and gathering information for a planned encyclopedia of Native American mound sites. *People of the Web* came out in 1990 and was supposed to be the follow-up to my first book, *The Archetype Experience,* which was released in 1984. *The Archetype Experience* was about Carl Jung's ideas on the UFO phenomenon, abductions, contactees, synchronicity, and other archetypal and paranormal experiences. It was clear to me that psychological processes were involved in all of those phenomena, but also that there was something *physically real* happening. The inclusion of archaeological material in my investigations into the paranormal and the UFO phenomenon was not something I expected. It just happened that way, as it has to many others.

While awaiting the publication of my first book, I became fascinated with Native American mounds. In 1983, I began a quest to visit every significant mound site known in the United States. I also sought to understand Native rituals, how mounds and earthworks were employed in these rituals, and whether there was anything other than explainable psychological processes involved in the outcome of rituals. In particular, I had read a few Native American myths indicating that spiritual beings would, at times, physically manifest during some rituals and ceremonies. Like many others, I wanted to identify the ultimate source of all of it: UFOs, abductions, paranormal phenomena, and strange beings that walk out of a landed saucer and tell the startled witness that they are from Venus, Mars, or some other planet.

Back in 1988, we were in a hurry, and Hovenweep was just one of dozens of sites we planned to visit. We took a hectic 14-day trip that took us to mound and archaeology sites in twelve different states. We rushed from site to site, taking photos and seeing as much as possible from sunup to sunset. But we never spent much time at any site—even at Hovenweep.

EARTH SPIRIT AS THE SOURCE

I first became aware of the Hovenweep ruins in Jim Brandon's 1983 book, *The Rebirth of Pan,* and I still retain a tattered and worn copy of the book in my now culled-down collection. Brandon's book is a compilation of nearly everything unexplained and weird in America. It covers cryptocreatures, mounds and earthworks, mysterious inscriptions, significant numbers, UFOs, and the humanoid entities associated with UFOs. Brandon suggested that all of these phenomena were interrelated and tied together by a subtle earth energy interacting with human consciousness. According to Brandon, we humans have an important relationship to a powerful "Earth Spirit," but he added that the relationship was an "incomplete mosaic, something like a paint-by-numbers dot pattern of an unknown image, in which we have only a portion of the necessary reference points."[3] In addition, Brandon's book was, for me, one of the first books (along with several John Keel books) that somewhat convincingly linked together Native American mounds with UFOs. Today, there is increased interest in earth spirit energy and the paranormal, as evidenced by the hit video series *Hellier*.[4]

HOVENWEEP AND ARCHAEOASTRONOMY

Brandon related that Hovenweep was one of many "collections of towers, 'forts,' and lofty ramparts. . . . Supposedly a production of the fabled Anasazi Indians."[5] He also noted that several astronomical alignments were built into the stone towers.[6] I was especially intrigued by the stone towers, some of which were three stories tall, with their small openings oriented to the solstices as well as several proposed alignments to stars (see fig. 1.1). In the early 1980s, American archaeoastronomy was in its infancy and was controversial in mainstream archaeology. However, many people knew that the alignments that ancient sites had to certain stars had an importance we didn't really understand.

When we visited Hovenweep in 1988, we arrived in the very late afternoon after traveling over what can barely be called roads. The unmarked dirt road into the site often vanished, and we drove across desert and flat rock formations not really knowing if it led there. When we reached the end of what we thought was the road, it was apparent we had arrived, as a canyon loomed right in front of us. There was no one else there, and it was strangely quiet. Back then I did not understand the significance of the profound silence. We quickly walked everywhere around the site and took photos of the towers, but as the sun started going down, we needed to leave. I was then in a frenetic search for something I didn't quite grasp. But the alignments that ancient sites like Hovenweep supposedly had to stars were enigmatic and very intriguing. I knew that the shamans and medicine people who lived at Hovenweep had connected with something, but I wasn't sure what it was.

In the 1980s, it was becoming clear that ancient Native Americans were carefully charting the movements of the moon, sun, and various stars. It is

Fig. 1.1. The Hovenweep "Castle" today. It is one of many stone structures along the canyon walls. Note the many small window openings (each only a couple inches square) used for viewing astronomical alignments.

accurate to say that archaeologists attributed virtually all of the astronomical alignments to marking the seasons for planting, harvesting, and holding seasonal celebrations. In brief, all of the alignments supposedly served as a calendar. It is obvious that ancient cultures were focused on the solstices and equinoxes for planting and harvesting, but what they were doing was far deeper than that. Why they pinpointed stars at certain times of the year has long been a great mystery. Of course, archaeoastronomy has come a long way since the 1980s, due in large part to the work of alternative writers and researchers who are not part of the mainstream archaeology community.

HOVENWEEP IN 2019

The drive from Farmington, New Mexico, to Hovenweep winds through mountains and desert in New Mexico, Colorado, and Utah. Just before we

Fig. 1.2. Boulder along Highway 41 in Colorado depicting ancient
rock carvings, including animals, the moon, and spiritual beings.
Note all the modern initials and graffiti.

crossed into Utah from Colorado's two-lane Highway 41, we were surprised to
see a huge boulder along the side of the road that was covered in petroglyphs
(see fig. 1.2). I stopped the car, backed up, and Lora got out and scrambled
up an embankment to take photos. Just then a Colorado State Police car flew
by us and immediately screeched to a halt. The officer watched us for a few
moments, and when Lora got back in the car, he left in the opposite direction.
When I looked at one of the photos I was astonished at the ancient carvings.
But I was also saddened by the large amount of graffiti made by modern people. The destruction of the Native American culture is pathetic and continues
to this day. I'm fairly confident that the police officer stopped to make sure we
weren't defacing the rock.

When we reached the entrance road to Hovenweep, we were surprised at
the major improvements there. There were prominent signs and a paved road
that led to a modern visitors' center. Other than a couple staff members, we
were the only people there. After checking in, we began a short walk to the
main ruins, just one of six different groupings of pueblo constructions associated with the site. Only the occasional sound of a crow could be heard. We

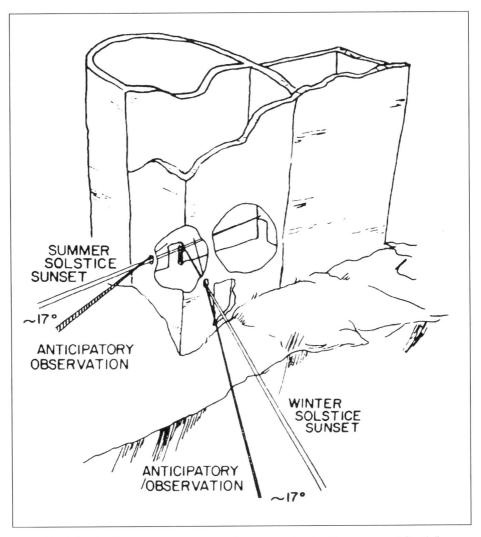

Fig. 1.3. Display at the site shows the portals in the Hovenweep "Castle"
aligned to the solstice sunsets.

stopped several times and just listened—to nothing at all. It is difficult to really describe what it feels like to be outside and surrounded by utter, complete silence, and the significance of it is probably lost to most people, yet it is important in subtle ways. The silence was profound, but it was eventually interrupted by the sounds of other visitors arriving, walking, and talking. Those sounds reverberated everywhere. We walked through the main site (called Square Tower Canyon, see plate 1), took a lot of photos and video, and then drove to several other associated Puebloan people sites some miles away. But we

Fig. 1.4. View of "Cutthroat Castle" and other stone structures
around the canyon rim at Hovenweep.

felt a lot different during that brief time of silence and complete calm in the
environment. Silence can be deafening.

LIVING IN NATURE IN
A DARK AND QUIET WORLD

Hovenweep is also known for its spectacular nighttime views of the sky, and
as I have written many times in the past few years, the sky has lost its significance for many of us. When the majority of people walk outside at night now,
all they can see are the most prominent stars. Even that will soon change as
SpaceX gradually puts up their planned 42,000 low-Earth-orbit Starlink satellites that, in all probability, will be the brightest lights in the night sky over

many areas.[7] However, because of modern lights and pollution, the Milky Way is already obscured nearly everywhere.

To most people, the implication of an obscured view of the night sky is unimportant. We typically live our lives as far away from nature as we can. But it's not just the sky we are insulating ourselves from, it also is all of nature. We spend most of our daily 24 hours inside—inside a house, a building, a car, or another vehicle. We typically drive or ride in what is basically an insulated metal container and walk on pavement. We avoid walking on soil or dirt, and if we do so, we usually wear shoes that insulate us from the ground. We spend most of our nighttime inside. If we are outside at night, there are usually lights in the area. The vast majority of our time, we are surrounded by concrete, wood, metal, bricks, and lots of electrical wiring and cables. We are also immersed in a swirling mass of electromagnetic fields (EMFs) and electric fields that few people really understand or care about. But electromagnetic energy is probably the key to understanding some intriguing mysteries. For those who have been spending their lives in a quest to understand the paranormal or UFOs or any other kind of psychic phenomena, electromagnetic energy is a key.

So here is a huge clue to understanding the people of the ancient world. They lived every moment of their lives in the Earth's ambient EMF and did so without the noise of modern society. There were virtually no human-produced EMFs in existence then. Changes in their ambient EMF were the result of natural processes such as water movements, rock formations, earthen embankments, earthquakes, underground tectonic strain, and weather phenomena such as thunderstorms. This will be mentioned again in later chapters, but for the moment it is important to understand that the Earth serves as a huge electrical circuit with a surrounding electromagnetic shield, or bubble, consisting of extremely-low-frequency wavelengths that vary in a regular pattern. However, the fundamental frequency, which can be described as the ambient frequency of the Earth's EMF, is 7.83 hertz (Hz). It is known scientifically as the Schumann resonance.[8] (There are three Schumann resonances, all multiples of 7.83 Hz, but the ambient, fundamental frequency is 7.83 Hz.)

All life-forms on Earth evolved within the Schumann resonance and incorporated it into their evolving neurological and biological processes. For example, the transition point between the brain's theta waves and alpha waves, as measured by an electroencephalograph, is 8 Hz—essentially at the cusp of the ambient Schumann resonance.[9] Alpha waves are produced when you are awake but relaxed, while theta waves are characterized by profound relaxation and meditation states. So one piece of the puzzle being put together in this book is that attuning oneself to this ambient frequency makes you more amenable to certain profound experiences. That is especially true for paranormal experiences that create balance and harmony in one's life. This is one reason why people find lying by the ocean, sitting on a mountaintop, or immersing oneself in nature so relaxing and beneficial. As modern technology continues to produce more and more electromagnetic frequencies leaking into the environment, attuning to the ambient Schumann resonance is becoming increasingly difficult.

WE NOW LIVE IN AN ELECTROMAGNETIC CESSPOOL

As I sit typing these words in a densely populated urban area of Memphis, Tennessee, I check how many Wi-Fi signals I am receiving. There are twenty-one signals available. I'm picking up my own Wi-Fi devices, those of neighbors, a hotel, and I even get signals from the FBI, Homeland Security, and the Coast Guard, which are located a few hundred yards away on the other side of a small harbor. Each of those Wi-Fi routers sends out bursts of ultra-high-frequency electromagnetic waves continually. Some of these signals are powerful and extend for some distance, while others are weaker and localized. There also are cell towers all around that broadcast countless bursts of electromagnetic waves every few moments. These waves aren't small, confined beams, as most people conceptualize them, but are emitted as gigantic electromagnetic bubbles covering wide areas. They are designed in the most efficient manner to maximize their coverage. They are becoming increasingly powerful and emitting ever-increasing frequencies. For example, 5G wireless technology is already partly installed here in Memphis and is being rapidly put in place everywhere. In addition, countless cell phones are continually sending out high-frequency electromagnetic energy bubbles to keep in contact with the towers. And far above us, satellites—both civilian and military—use electromagnetic beams to transmit their signals. What does all that mean?

Back in the early 1990s, I corresponded with British author Albert Budden, who was working on a theory that I was also working on, albeit both of us had our different twists to the idea.[10] Budden, a UFO skeptic, wrote a series of books on the theory that the entire range of paranormal phenomena and UFOs were related to EMFs and electrical energy fields that naturally emanated from the Earth. Of course, lots of researchers have proposed similar ideas, including Paul Devereux, Greg Long, neuropsychologist Michael Persinger, and a several others. In his 1998 book *Electric UFOs,* and a 1994 book, *Allergies and Aliens,* Budden proposed that UFOs and related phenomena were electrical in nature and speculated that many health issues were emerging from so much EMF and electrical pollution being generated in our increasingly industrialized society.[11] Budden mentioned a controversial modern ailment called electromagnetic sensitivity, characterized by an individual experiencing a host of ill-defined symptoms attributed to exposure to modern electromagnetic fields. Budden's theory asserted that the energies involved were both natural and man-made and had no intelligence or sentience of their own.[12] In essence, they are simply overlapping energy or radiation fields that can affect human neurological processes in strange ways.

In 1994, both Budden and I speculated that the mineral magnetite, which was first discovered in the hippocampus of the human brain in 1992, was perhaps the primary way that EMFs affected brain processes.[13] Budden asserted that electromagnetically induced hallucinatory experiences accompanied by occasionally visible electrical phenomena in the atmosphere provided the entire explanation of UFOs and paranormal phenomena. According to that view, there is no other source or intelligence behind them. That represents one very major point in which we differed.[14] However, in recent years, it has become clear that electromagnetic pollution is very real and may have significant and unknown health consequences. There have been many studies that show that some levels of EMF radiation do, in fact, have harmful effects on human physiology. If you read the precautions in the last pages of the tiny-print manual that came with your cell phone, you will see that your phone is supposed to be kept away from your body. Of course, just about no one does that. But we are constantly assured that the EMF levels that all of our modern technology produces are *within the acceptable ranges* as long as you don't use it too much or hold it too close. That's accurate in some ways, especially if you don't keep your cell phone on your body and you stay away from the back of your microwave oven. However, the effects of EMFs on mental health and subtle neurological processes are less clear and are virtually unresearched in any meaningful way.

The internet is rife with articles linking a wide range of mental disorders to EMF pollution, but in general, technology companies consistently deny the validity of such reports. The World Health Organization relates that there are many anecdotal reports that make a tenuous link between EMFs and various mental health conditions such as anxiety, depression, headaches, sleep disturbances, and even epileptic seizures.[15] A 2018 study published in the *Lancet* journal refers to EMF proliferation as "electrosmog" and relates that there is an urgent need to do adequate research on the effects of so much EMF radiation in the environment on both mental and physical health.[16] Many other scientific articles plead for such research to be conducted, but funding for such research is scant. In short, it is not in the interests of technology development firms to restrict their expansion, and some health effects may be viewed as acceptable, especially if only mental health issues are affected. If it's true that only mental health issues are affected, it is likely to be very difficult to scientifically prove this. And the government makes a lot of money by selling EMF wavelengths to telecom companies. As the 5G technology continues with its unstoppable rollout, all that can reasonably be said is that we are all in the midst of a large experiment. In addition, there is one more piece to this that remains totally unacknowledged and unresearched. It appears that no one has thoroughly studied what 5G frequencies or other cellular frequencies do to viruses or bacteria. However, we do know that EMFs can cause bacteria to rearrange their DNA and mutate.[17] In sum, we live in a swirling EMF cesspool. The world we live in today has a very different electromagnetic background than the ancient world had. And we have no definitive idea if there are or might be consequences to it.

2

UNDERSTANDING THE
ANCIENT MINDSET

A Psychological Near Impossibility

One major point in discussing the remote, quiet, and relatively EMF-free site of Hovenweep in the first chapter along with the modern proliferation of EMF-producing technology is likely lost on many readers. Recall that the way we live our lives today—relatively insulated from nature—was also mentioned. So here is the point.

Many of us try to understand the ancient world. That includes how ancient people lived their lives and why they erected the amazing mounds, earthworks, and countless megalithic stone structures found nearly everywhere around the world. We want to know what their spiritual lives and rituals were like, why they focused so much on the stars, and how shamans and medicine practitioners engaged with a realm many of us call the paranormal. We want to know if so-called paranormal phenomena are *real* or if they are simply the result of mind tricks or hallucinations, as most skeptics argue. We want to know if the ancients were really tapping into some sort of alternative reality or communing with an unknown intelligence when constructing their incredible sacred sites. Or were they deluded by their own misunderstandings of the natural world? Are ideas of ancient gods, visiting aliens, supernatural forces, and spiritual entities intruding into our world just superstitious ways to explain the forces of nature? Or might there really be some other reality at work? There are likely some legitimate answers we can get to these questions. But gaining a true understanding of the ancient mindset is a far more difficult task than most of us realize. Think for a moment about just one ancient anomaly found in America.

THE NEWARK, OHIO, EARTHWORKS

Around 2,100 years ago, a group of mound builders (commonly called the Hopewell culture) began construction of a set of geometric earthworks in what is today Newark, Ohio (see fig. 2.1). Even now the formations boggle the mind and defy verbal description.[1] Over several miles in extent, a complex of several circular and square earthworks enclosing 20 to 30 acres were connected to a

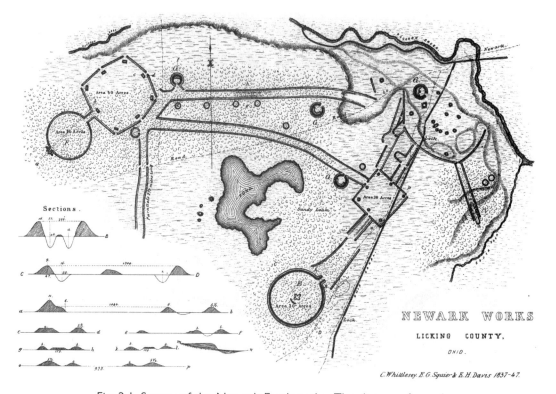

Fig. 2.1. Survey of the Newark Earthworks. The distance from the circle-and- octagon formation on the left side to the square on the right side is over 1 mile (1.6 kilometers). The formation was constructed on flat land. The walls of earth forming the circle and octagon are 8 to 14 feet (2.4 to 4.2 meters) in height. The circle encloses 20 acres and the octagon encloses 50 acres. The walkways between the sites were formed from parallel linear lines of earth about 3 feet (1 m) in height with a 175-foot (53.3 meters) width (from Squier and Davis 1848).

Fig. 2.2. This photo shows the connection point between the Newark octagon and circle today. In the center, curving to the right and around to the upper left, the 20-acre circle's outer wall can be seen.

50-acre octagon formed by high walls of earth (see fig. 2.2). Pyramid shaped, truncated mounds were erected at each of the eight points of the octagon's walls. Long walkways, a uniform 175 feet (53.3 meters) wide and enclosed by linear walls of earth on both sides, extended from the earthen circles and octagon formations leading to other square earthworks and smaller circles formed from walls of carefully piled earth. Many of these walled walkways were miles in length. One walled walkway extended some 56 miles (90 kilometers) south to a set of almost identical earthworks at Chillicothe, Ohio.

In 1982, one purpose of the octagon and its connected circular earthwork was figured out by a pair of college professors—Robert Horn and Ray Hively, a philosopher and an astronomer.[2] The octagon served as a physical, permanent observation mechanism to directly point to the moon's key movements on its 18.61-year lunar standstill cycle. In brief, it took its builders at least 18.61 years to complete the design of this colossal structure and perhaps another 18.61 years to check the accuracy of it as a lunar observatory. It's known how it was done, and we know why it was done: it was built by forming large earthen mounds and geometrically shaped walls from basket loads of earth piled in specific locations and in accordance with a plan overseen by *someone.* It was created to chart the movements of the moon over 18.61 years so that the lunar cycle and eclipses could be predicted in the future (see fig. 2.3). Obviously, the builders conducted rituals related to the moon at specific times. So that is the simple explanation of how and why it was done. But what was the mindset that motivated it? What was the belief system that propelled so many people to engage in backbreaking work for such a long period of time? How did the difficult lifestyle of hunter-gatherers, nomadic tribes engaged in limited agriculture methods, enable them to remain organized and focused on such long-term construction activities?

My conclusion has long been that it's a nearly impossible task for most of us to truly comprehend the world, beliefs, motivations, and mindsets of ancient people. *They lived in nature every moment of their lives.* They became one with nature. I think it's true to assert that no one reading this can say the same for themselves. Ancient Native Americans had intimate relationships with plants, animals, insects, waterways, the weather, the sky, and the landforms they interacted with every day. They touched the earth constantly. They saw the night sky in all of its splendor every night. And they lived in a very quiet world completely free of EMF pollution.

We, on the other hand, can only try to comprehend how the ancients lived and interacted with their world. The differences between *then* and *now* are so vast they can be seen as incomprehensible. People assume that by spending a week camping, hiking, or sitting in a wilderness or on a mountain to meditate they can make the same connections that the ancients did. But psychologically, that's simply not really true. You might get a momentary *glimpse* of what the ancients were immersed in, but you can't really experience it the same ways they did. One big difference is this: You were not raised in that natural world. Even if you stay in nature for any length of time, you know you are going to go back to your insulated home or shelter when you are done. You know that you are going back to your world and life. Another important difference is more subtle: *You aren't tuned to the Earth's natural EMF resonance, and you live in a world swirling with human-produced EMFs.*

We evaluate and make judgments about *everything* based on how we perceive the world now, and we use our current knowledge and beliefs to evaluate how we *assume* it was back then. Our perceptions and beliefs are formed and shaped by what we experience in our day-to-day lives, whether it is by observa-

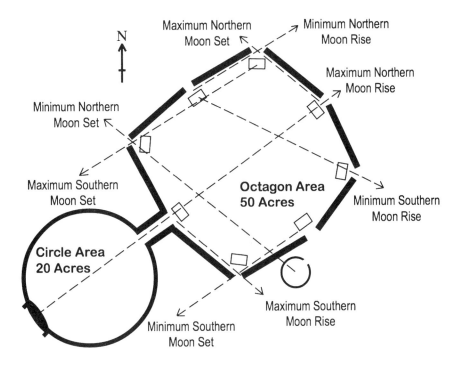

Fig. 2.3. Schematic showing how the circle and octagon earthworks at Newark, Ohio, were used to chart the movements of the moon over 18.61 years, based on the work of Ray Hively and Robert Horn. They also found similar visual alignments at other Newark earthworks as well as at Chillicothe, Ohio.

tion, through education, reading books, or via other influences we encounter. Learning about and manipulating the world we live within creates a powerful, built-in perceptual bias related to humans' remarkable ability to adapt and survive. We have adapted our mindset to a world where we have created our own lifestyle, which is insulated from nature, and that's not necessarily a bad thing. We have insulated and protected ourselves as much as we can from a world that has a chaotic nature. It's a natural world of sunrises and sunsets, floods, earthquakes, thunderstorms, other weather phenomena, interacting with dangerous animals, interacting with plants, and dealing with the basic human condition all at the same time. Some of it is predictable, while other parts of nature are seemingly chaotic. The ancients spent their entire lives in that natural world and understood it in ways many people today belittle as animism, superstition, and being downright savage and primitive in nature.

These ancient people understood that they were connected to the natural world in mind, spirit, and body. They were one with the natural world, and their shamans and healers connected to nature to provide understanding, power, and even control. A few very attuned people today are able to connect with the forces of nature and understand what lies at its core, and a few can enter that state of connectedness at will. I'm not one of them, but the long quest I've been on has given me a few glimpses of that connectedness, and I've been able to sort out some of the important ideas that drove the ancient people to do the things they did.

ALL THINGS ARE CONNECTED

Back in 1990, I titled my book *People of the Web* from a deeply held belief that has been expressed by many Native Americans from many different tribes and eras. A quote that expressed this belief is attributed to Chief Seattle, a Suquamish chief who lived in what is now Washington State. He died in 1866, but a 1972 film script re-created a speech or letter supposedly formed from Seattle's own words. It related, "All things are connected. Whatever befalls the earth befalls the sons of earth. Man did not weave the web of life; he is merely a strand in it. Whatever he does to the web, he does to himself."[3]

Fig. 2.4. The entrance sign at Kolomoki Mounds in Georgia displays the fundamental Native American belief system.

The interconnection of all things means every part of creation is like a portion of a spider's web. If you pull on any strand of the web, it affects all the other strands. Vibrate one part of the web and all of it vibrates. But the idea of the world as a *web* has a far deeper meaning, because the web is weaved by a spider, a creature that has intelligence and a plan. The spider is often symbolically seen as a weaver of all of life (a creator), but it is also a trickster in some Native American lore. The trickster is an element in nature that causes disorder and chaos and has been cited as "the original trouble-maker."[4] And it weaves traps that can be beautiful and alluring. The web is both creation and chaos occurring simultaneously. We are all people of that web.

3

CARL JUNG, TRICKSTERS, AND JOHN KEEL

I became aware of the trickster during the late 1970s when I was studying the UFO speculations of Carl Jung. Jung's 1959 book *Flying Saucers* has been one of the most misunderstood UFO-related books of all time.[1] His concept of archetypal manifestations in the sky appearing at the same time as the Cold War (synchronicity) served as the underlying basis of his ideas on UFOs. Most people who have read Jung's UFO works generally conclude that Jung believed that the phenomenon was psychological in nature. For example, Ron Story's *Encyclopedia of Extraterrestrial Encounters,* in which I wrote several sections (but not the entry on Jung), summarized Jung's ideas about UFOs by inaccurately stating that "they are purely mental and have no existence outside the mind of the observer. He [Jung] regarded the UFO phenomenon as a visionary rumor and as a psychological projection of man's hopes and fears in an uncertain world."[2] That's partly accurate, but it is clear Jung believed that something very real was behind the phenomenon. It was *not* all in the mind of the observer, but that's what most people incorrectly believe about Jung's conclusions. It is the *interpretation* of what was observed that comes from the mind of the witness. And the "something" that was observed interacts with the mind of its witnesses. Jung also asserted that what was often interpreted as a UFO by witnesses was usually something deceptive. It was trickster-like.

ARCHETYPES AND THEIR PSYCHOID NATURE

Jung's writings cast a large net over the concept of the trickster, citing it as a mythological creature and archetypal symbol found in virtually all cultures. The trickster is a personification of the disruptive forces of nature—a mechanism to explain chaos. It usually appears in an animal-like or humanlike form. It was an archetypal figure that adapted its physical appearance to the beliefs, expectations, and mythology of different cultures in specific times and specific places throughout history. So it's probably important to define what Jung meant by the term *archetype*.

Few people are aware that Jung's "beliefs about archetypes evolved and changed over the course of his lifetime."[3] Archetypes are commonly thought of as symbols that are consistently found in all cultures. For example, to Jung, apparitions of the Virgin Mary, fairies, disc-shaped objects, circular patterns, and even angels and demons are included in the vast range of archetypal symbols. They all have an underlying symbolic meaning. Symbols that are found again and again through time and across cultures he called archetypes. The word *archetype* "essentially means the original model after which others are copies."[4] Archetypes typically come in polar opposites: male-female, wise man-fool, light-dark, God-Satan, angel-demon, trickster-helper. Only one archetype, the *mandala* (a circular or disklike image), represented wholeness, balance, and harmony.[5] This is why Jung saw the emergence of the flying saucer era in the late 1940s as a mechanism for the masses to look for alien intervention to assist humanity at a time when nuclear obliteration was a very real possibility. The circular objects being reported as UFOs (mandalas) were interpreted as a type of divine intervention, salvation from possible destruction. In essence, Jung theorized that something real was seen in the skies and that our psychological hopes for salvation were mentally projected on the round, disklike objects. That is, we gave the objects the meaning we wanted and needed. Jung repeatedly stated, "Something is seen, one doesn't know what."[6] In essence, when we don't know what the "something" is, we attribute a meaning to it based on our own beliefs and our unconscious needs. But it's important to keep in mind that, with the exception of the mandala, Jung related that archetypes exist in opposites. In essence, the array of archetypes categorized as opposites are "splinters" from the original whole. In 1984, I theorized that all of the archetypes were created through the initial act of creation itself, in that the oneness of all things

was splintered apart into opposites.[7] However, Jung's speculations about archetypes were not confined to mental images and symbols. To Jung, the archetypes
were *real*.

Jung eventually came to believe that "archetypes were independent, autonomous entities with a will of their own; probably existent for all time. . . . In
effect, they are a symbolic representation that emerges to accomplish a purpose."[8] However, it's important to understand that there "is a decidedly nonpsychological aspect of them. Specifically, there is a reality of archetypes that
exists apart from the mind of man."[9] When archetypes are encountered, they
cannot be ignored as they inundate the conscious mind and are *experienced*
by the witness. The witnesses of an archetypal manifestation place a meaning
or interpretation on what they see, and that process is called "projection" in
psychology. That is, we mentally project a meaning onto things we observe. As
a simple example, people have always seen anomalous, hard to identify lights
in the sky. Some will immediately interpret them as alien craft, and others
will assume they are something else. The interpretation or meaning attributed
to the unidentified light is what is projected from the mind of the observer
onto the object. It is our beliefs and preconceptions that give a meaning to the
unknown. Today, many people attribute a technological meaning to such visible anomalies. But in the ancient past, they interpreted these events in a far
different way.

To Jung, archetypes always have a spiritual nature.[10] However, Jung cryp-
tically asserted that *archetypes could sometimes appear in physical, objective
reality*. He wrote, "The archetype as such is a psychoid factor that belongs,
as it were, to the invisible, ultraviolet end of the psychic spectrum."[11] That's
actually an amazing assertion few people have understood and the term
psychoid explains what Jung meant. "*Psychoid* is a Jungian term that means a
process that is able to bridge the gap between psychological reality and objective reality. Archetypes, as pure nature, are pure energy, remaining primarily invisible but occasionally manifest themselves. That is, *they occasionally
become a physical reality in an objective sense*."[12] One of Jung's closest friends
and associates, Marie-Louise von Frantz, often mentioned that Jung believed
in a nonpsychological reality of archetypes. By invoking the phrase "ultraviolet end of the psychic spectrum," Jung was relating that the psychoid nature
of archetypes was similar to and related to the electromagnetic energy spectrum (see fig. 3.1).

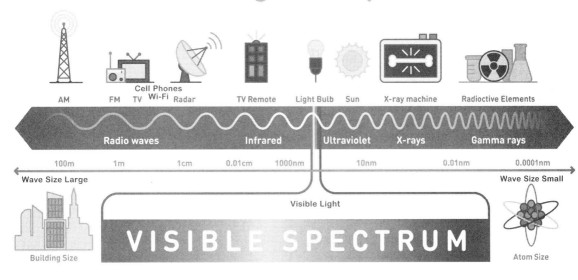

Fig. 3.1. Schematic of the electromagnetic energy spectrum. Visible light is in the center of the schematic, with infrared on the lower end (left side) and ultraviolet on the higher end (right side). Cell phone and Wi-Fi frequencies are located between TV and radar frequencies. Solid or physical matter is also vibrating energy that can be perceived through our senses. As Einstein stated, energy and mass are simply different manifestations of the same fundamental thing, something that's difficult to grasp.

The simplest definition of electromagnetic energy is that it is a form of energy reflected from and emitted from objects. The energy is composed of electrical and magnetic waves that travel through space. The electromagnetic energy spectrum ranges from very-low-frequency radio waves on one end to gamma rays and cosmic rays on the highest frequency end. Visible light is a narrow band in the middle range of the spectrum, with infrared light and ultraviolet light on the two edges of visible light. Visible light composes less than 5 percent of the spectrum. What Jung was asserting is that under some circumstances, the archetypes can move from the invisible ends of the electromagnetic energy spectrum to visible light frequencies, where they appear to manifest in physical reality. This is a process that was referred to as *transmutation* or *transmogrification* in occult literature.[13] It is truly an incredible assertion.

THE TRICKSTER

Jung was especially keen on Native American tales of the trickster and the connection to the paranormal. He related that "all mythical figures correspond to inner psychic experiences . . . it is not surprising to find certain phenomena in the field of parapsychology which remind us of the trickster."[14] According to Jung, the trickster played malicious tricks on humans, had the ability to change shapes, and often took the form of animals. Most importantly, Jung asserted that interactions with the trickster played a central role in all paranormal phenomena. Interacting purposively with the trickster also was, according to Jung, the primary activity underlying the practice of shamanism.[15] To Native Americans, the trickster was a spiritual entity that could impart deep knowledge or create chaos.[16] Shamans had to carefully navigate between the two distinctively different possible outcomes when dealing with tricksters.

In a psychological sense, Jung believed that the trickster was a way for humans to explain the chaos observed in the natural world as well as serving as a compensatory mechanism by which we could excuse ourselves after making blunders or errors in judgment. That was his explanation of the psychological function of the trickster, but it is very clear that to Jung the archetypal trickster was very real.

Tricksters as Animals, Fairies, and Little People

The trickster has been seen in many guises throughout history including the Muslim jinns, fairies and gnomes in European lore, poltergeists, the little people in Native American myths, and a variety of clever shape-shifting animals. Native Americans viewed the trickster in a multitude of animal forms: coyotes, wolves, ravens, and spiders, among others.[17] One aspect that is important to understand is that not all such animals were tricksters. Sometimes a coyote or spider was just that—a coyote or spider. The trickster took whatever form was most appropriate in the situation, and the form always related to the cultural expectations and beliefs of its witnesses. Even the so-called little people, a common theme mentioned in a wide range of Native American mythology, were often seen as tricksters, albeit very powerful forms of this spiritual manifestation.

The trickster is a temporary entity that can create fear, distrust, and confusion. In brief, the trickster seems to be one thing, but it is actually another: It seems to relate truth, but it often leads to deceit. It makes you think you are right when you are actually wrong. It is a creator of chaos and instigates entropy—the breakdown of order. However, as it fulfills that role, it also facilitates creation and can lead to a deeper understanding of life's many mysteries. If you can move beyond the deceptions of the trickster, you can come to see reality more clearly and gain power from the interaction. Encountering a trickster is always a test.[18]

The Native American conceptualization of the trickster is multifaceted and complex. Trickster stories were often told to children to explain many things, and virtually all of the stories boiled down to tales about morality—right and wrong. But it is clear that on a deeper level, the trickster can be seen as a way to truth and understanding.

It is important to keep in mind that the trickster is an *actual being* in Native American mythology, manifesting itself physically, if only for brief periods. As I wrote in *People of the Web,* "It was very real. . . . The trickster was not only a powerful figure from the spirit world who emerged to delude and toy with man, but he served as a test that initiates had to pass before they could gain access to higher spirit forms. . . . Long ago the ancient shaman realized that the trickster emerges in the real world along with other spirits whether they wanted them to or not. But they also found that by performing certain ritualistic behaviors at prescribed times in prescribed places, they could enlist the benign aid of the trickster and commune with deeper forces of nature. Ancient societies chose to harmonize themselves with those forces."[19]

JOHN KEEL AND THE TRICKSTER ELEMENT

In the late 1960s, the famed ufologist and paranormalist John Keel was deeply involved in the investigation of numerous bizarre accounts coming from Point Pleasant, West Virginia. Just about everyone is aware of *The Mothman Prophecies,* Keel's book about the events that ended with the tragic collapse of the Silver Bridge on December 15, 1967, and the deaths of some forty-six people.[20] Keel and many others saw strange lights in the sky during this 13-month-long affair, but the most impressive accounts were from literally a few hundred people who lived in the immediate area around Point Pleasant. They told of seeing a bizarre, 7-foot-tall, winged being with glowing red eyes that eventually became known as "Mothman" because its wings were featherless (see fig. 3.2, p. 26). Keel came to believe that it was a "trickster element" at work.[21]

Fig. 3.2. Statue of the Mothman in Point Pleasant, West Virginia.

In letters to UFO researcher Brent Raynes, Keel related that nothing stemming from the trickster could be trusted and that "it's a very mischievous force."[22] Keel eventually explained such events as originating from an intelligence he called "ultraterrestrial," meaning it came from some other part of our normal spectrum of senses and reality. Keel repeatedly mentioned the electromagnetic energy spectrum as their source. In his 1975 book *The Eighth Tower,* Keel summarized the idea by asserting that the ultraterrestrials were the ultimate source of power underlying UFOs, paranormal events, and religious and occult phenomena.[23] They can communicate to us mentally through electromagnetic waves or appear in a physical, visible form by altering their vibrational frequency into the narrow band of visible light.

We are, in Keel's view, biological antennas that exist within and physically move through an electromagnetic energy spectrum that produces a myriad of effects on us. In this perspective, we are like living radios tuned to pick up certain frequencies from the electromagnetic spectrum. The ultraterrestrials are intelligent electromagnetic spectrum entities existing outside the visible light frequencies that broadcast messages of all sorts. As biological antennas humans pick up these messages. In addition, the intelligence existing within this spectrum is able to temporarily manifest itself into what appear to be a host of physical forms. That is, it can temporarily appear to be physical. In essence, Keel and Jung were saying the same thing. In later chapters, we'll revisit these ideas.

4

THE LITTLE PEOPLE

It was in 1988 that Lou White Eagle, an arrow priest of the Cheyenne and grandson of the famed Cheyenne high priest Edward Red Hat, came to Memphis and stayed with my wife and me for 30 days. It transpired during a protest carried out by several tribal organizations against a proposed archaeological dig in downtown Memphis at a mound site many believe was where Hernando de Soto first viewed the Mississippi River in 1541. White Eagle and his family accepted our invitation to stay at our home. During those 30 days, we had the opportunity to hold some of the sacred arrows as well as engage in some deep conversations about shamanism and spiritual beliefs. It is a detailed story that I related in *People of the Web* and in many interviews since then.

At that time, I was working for the county government as a drug treatment program director in the local prison and was also engaged in a small private practice with a psychologist and psychiatrist. On a Sunday, I took White Eagle to my private practice office, where I had to complete some insurance paperwork. I invited him to try out an experimental device we had in the office, which was then known as the *Graham Potentializer*. It was essentially a comfortable "bed" about the size of a large couch that produced a field of electromagnetic energy that engulfed the individual reclining on it. The "bubble" of electromagnetic energy mimics the Earth's ambient field—the fundamental Schumann resonance. The device also does a gentle, cyclical, rotational up-and-down movement every seven seconds that is tuned to the average cycle of ocean waves. All of us who used the device had strange experiences, but White Eagle's one experience with it was the most vivid any of us reported. He declined subsequent invitations to use it because it produced what he interpreted as a powerful trickster experience.

When White Eagle reclined on the device, I turned it on, excused myself, and went to another office. About 15 minutes later, he came into my office visibly shaken. "Little blue people," he said. "What?" I replied. He said, "Little blue people are in the room."

He explained that after lying on the bed for a few minutes, he became aware of some sort of presence observing him. He opened his eyes and looked around the room, which had three large windows to the outside. He said that there were several small, blue beings peering into the room. He added that suddenly he couldn't move, and he said that the creatures then "passed through the windows and walls" and they gathered around his body. They were physical beings, about three feet tall and covered in some sort of blue, skintight fabric. They began poking at his body, which caused him major distress that appeared to break the spell of paralysis. He immediately sat up, got off the device, and came to my office.[1]

He wouldn't go back into the room after that, but I did, of course. I saw nothing out of the ordinary, but the machine was still moving. Later that day, I showed him some pictures of the traditional greys associated with UFO abductions. White Eagle related that they were similar looking, but not exactly the same. He wouldn't say much else about them at the time. He eventually said that they were the "little people" of Native American trickster lore and were physically real when they appeared to him. However, it's necessary to add that not all trickster or other encounters with the little people have been reported as negative. While interactions with the little people as tricksters were fraught with danger, great knowledge and power could be derived from the interactions with them if they were treated with care and respect.[2]

White Eagle sadly died in 2018. He was a Vietnam veteran, a Cheyenne Tsistsistas arrow priest, a bowstring headsman, and was well respected in the indigenous community. I learned a great deal about the ceremonial rituals involved with the Tsistsistas ceremony from White Eagle and about their beliefs about humans' purpose and role in the world, and we'll explore those in the next chapter. It was also the first time that I discovered that one of their most sacred beliefs was that the human soul went to the stars after death. But I also learned a lot about what I see as the archaeological community's disrespect for Native culture during those 30 days. Over that time period, I became privy to the archaeologists' discussions while the controversy took place. I had attempted to resolve the situation between the archaeologists and the Native American groups and became a mediator who talked privately with each group over a few days. Hearing what I interpreted as very demeaning attitudes held by both the students and the professors toward the Native Americans was very disheartening and left an indelible stain on me that remains to this day. I came to understand that Native Americans were seen by many as a hindrance to "real" archaeology and that their beliefs were seen as stupid, superstitious, and unscientific. Some of that has changed a bit since then, but not really all that much. I think those demeaning attitudes are just better concealed today. I'll add that the dig into the mound was canceled 30 days later when the Memphis City Council passed a resolution banning any excavations there. That was a battle the Native Americans won.

THE STORY OF THE CROW CHIEF RED PLUME AND THE LITTLE PEOPLE

Most books date the time of one of the most incredible and well-documented spiritual experiences ever reported by Native Americans to have taken place in the 1780s. But it was probably around 1762 or 1763 when a famous young Native American first ascended Medicine Mountain to the Big Horn Medicine Wheel (see plate 2).[3]

The young man, then about the age of twelve, was on his first vision quest. He was called Fool Boy because of his brash boasting about his destiny as a great warrior and leader. Like all the Crow tribal youth of his village, at the age of twelve, he ascended the mountain to the site of the Wheel, as it was then known. No one was sure who built the Wheel or when, but it was one of the most holy of places. The Wheel is a rock-formed circular formation with numerous lines of stone coming from its center like spokes. There is a large cairn (a large rock pile with a depressed center) located in the center. (The site is described in more detail in the next chapter.) He hiked about 10,000 feet (3,048 meters) up the mountain, well above the timberline, to a flat, granite plain where astounding views were seen to the distant horizon.

The adolescent vision quest was a very personal journey into adulthood, a venture to find personal medicine (or power), to affiliate with a spirit animal, and to find one's destiny. In brief, it was a formal process of discovering one's identity. It required the person to be alone for an extended period and make it through what psychologists might call a "dark night of the soul." It demonstrated the ability to sustain oneself in real darkness, to connect with the primeval forces of nature, to endure weakness and sorrow, and to do so alone. It was the final preparation step to adulthood.

The young man made offerings to the four sacred directions and then walked to the rock cairn located in the center of the wheel. After smoothing the surface, he placed a buffalo robe on the ground and reclined. For four days and three long nights, he endured great suffering. He had only the buffalo robe, no food nor water, and nothing else to give him comfort. As the third and final night began unfolding, he was in despair because all he had experienced was pain and torment, but he continued to pray and sing. As the long night unfolded, he became aware of sounds of something approaching him. Looking up, he could see the shapes of four small people coming toward him, beings who looked as small as children. They were three men and a woman. Instantly, he realized they were the little people, the most powerful spiritual beings encountered by only a very few privileged people. He knew the little people could be helpful guides or cause disaster. After a few words were spoken, the four little people moved close to the central cairn and disappeared. The young man stood up, shaking from exhaustion, a dark hole opened beneath him, and he suddenly found himself in the shaft of a cave leading to a tunnel complex.

Almost nothing is known about what transpired in the cave. But the young seeker supposedly remained there for three more days and nights. During this time, he went through a series of tests and was instructed in both warfare and leadership.

Here is what the historical records tell us about the encounter's outcome: In the end, he saw a vision of a soaring eagle, and he was handed a tail feather from a red eagle. It was to become his symbol and his spirit power. He was told to always wear the red feather and to never cut his hair again. His new name— his adult leadership name—was to be Red Plume.

As the known story goes, nearly four years later, he formed a small raiding party of young warriors and ventured off to the southeast, to the lands of the Lakota—then the sworn enemies of his Crow tribe. There they attacked a village and took many horses and scalps. Soon they repeated the same carnage on another Lakota village and returned to the Crow lands, where they were hailed as great warriors. He then became known as Red Plume. He supposedly never cut his hair again after descending the mountain as a youth. Whites came to know him as Long Hair when his hair reached 10 feet in length. He made many more successful raids and eventually became a highly respected chief of the Crow. In 1820 (around the age of 70), he survived a "miraculous" battle, and he later was a signer of the 1825 Friendship Treaty. He died at the age of 86 and allegedly had hair some 25 feet in length. A piece of his hair is kept in the Chief Plenty Coups State Park at Pryor, Montana. On his deathbed, he related that his spirit would reside at the Wheel and visitors could commune with him there.[4]

There are many Native American legends from virtually all tribes about the little people.[5] The 1993 book *Native Healer* flatly states that the little people, also known as the *wogey,* are exactly what modern people call "outer space beings."[6] The Choctaw, Cherokee, and Chickasaw all had myths that the little people would abduct people at night.[7] However, appearances of the little people and other spirits were often associated with unusual lights in the sky. For example, E. S. Curtis related the story of a vision quest where the seeker encountered a red-eyed, winged creature that appeared after a "star" came to the ground and flashes of light on the ground constantly appeared.[8] From other sources, we are told that Ojibwe shamans could conjure spirits that would cause small lights to fly around inside tents. A modern description of the process involved with the appearance of the lights related that ritualistic chanting creates "a psychic resonance needed to activate the archetypal energies" and revealed that the chant was "Open the sky from the center."[9]

Can we believe such stories, or are they all hallucinations or utter fabrications? I am certain that what Lou White Eagle related about the little blue people was sincere. I also know that the story of Red Plume is accepted as genuine. Native American mythology is generally ignored or derided by skeptics, and it is certain that some of their tales are embellished or simply not true, but should we just reject them all? The reality is that some incredible Native American practices and events have been studied scientifically and that the scientists involved are convinced there is something else—some other force— that intrudes. The incredible Massaum ceremony of the Cheyenne is one very important example.

5

THE CHEYENNE (TSISTSISTAS) MASSAUM CEREMONY

Lou White Eagle's grandfather, Edward Red Hat (1898–1982), was the Keeper of the Arrows for the Southern Cheyenne tribe until his death. Red Hat was the key source of information for Karl Schlesier's classic 1985 book *The Wolves of Heaven,* which to this day remains the most detailed description and explanation of the most sacred ceremony of the plains tribes. Schlesier began working with Red Hat in 1971.

The Massaum ceremony was more than a set of rituals; it was based on a deep belief system with a prescribed set of rites that evoked the physical appearance of spiritual entities. The Massaum ceremony is derived from the Tsistsistas cultural belief system, with Tsistsistas referring to the Cheyenne people who engage in that tradition.[1] The name Cheyenne is actually the Sioux term for "people of an alien speech."[2] The Cheyenne speak an Algonquin dialect related to the language of the Ojibwe, and many modern tribes in Canada and the northwestern United States share the same genetic lineage and customs. It is generally believed that all of the Algonquin groups, even their distant cousins, the Navajos, came to the Americas from Siberia long ago via the Beringia land bridge that formed at the end of the last ice age.

IDEAS FROM SIBERIAN SHAMANS

Schlesier traced the earliest conducting of the Massaum ceremony in North America to circa 500 BCE, when large numbers of the tribe migrated from the "east" to the plains region centering in the Black Hills area.[3] He repeatedly asserted that the Massaum had its ultimate origin from northern Siberian shamans who engaged in similar practices as long ago as 12,000 years.[4] To confirm this, Schlesier evaluated 134 different practices and elements of the Massaum ceremony and then compared them to a similar ceremony of the northern Siberian shamanistic societies. He found that 86 percent of the practices were a direct match and concluded that they were essentially the same set of rituals with the same underlying beliefs.[5] Wherever the origin of the Cheyenne is, the ceremony of the Massaum and the beliefs attached to it stem far back into time.

In addition to the knowledge Schlesier gathered from Edward Red Hat, he provided a detailed background on what was recorded during the few times the Massaum was conducted and witnessed by earlier ethnographers. The ceremony dissipated over time and gradually evolved into different practices because of warfare, epidemics, and governmental restraints on Native American religious practices. Now, Schlesier related, the practices "have perished," but there are still a few remnants of the ceremony.[6] Both the well-known sun dance and even the sacred arrow practices are far more recent spiritual ceremonies that developed out of the beliefs underlying the Massaum. We'll not go into details on the sun dance and the sacred arrows here, but we want to focus on the beliefs and rituals involved with the Massaum ceremony.

SECRET SOCIETIES AND THE PURPOSE OF THE MASSAUM

Secret societies are typically described as "exclusive, voluntary organizations that claim access to hidden bodies of knowledge and special skills."[7] Archaeologists are coming to recognize that these societies were far more important in the ancient world than they previously realized and were used as a mechanism for social control. The creation of mound complexes and earthworks and sites such as Stonehenge were likely the result of ritual practices by secret societies, and evidence of their existence goes back to at least 40,000 years ago.[8] Schlesier related that there were several secret societies involved in the Massaum ritual and that all of them had a special language that was privy only to the members initiated into that particular group. Most of the membership lines in the societies were hereditary, although there were occasional exceptions. There were two major divisions among the secret societies. There were the shamans and another grouping of secret societies that were tasked with "working for the sacred" in specific ritualistic roles dictated by the shamans and the other elites. One major purpose of the Massaum was to symbolically reenact the initial moment of creation.

According to Tsistsistas cosmology, all that existed before creation was a "singularity" of energy—with the word *energy* meaning "spirit."[9] Schlesier used the term *singularity* three times in his book for what he was told existed before creation. When the singularity split, it created the universe into three parts. The Massaum ceremony was a formal process to connect with the three created worlds: the upper world, the lower world, and the Earth (the middle world).[10] The Massaum allowed communion with the spiritual powers of all three worlds and maintained a balance and harmony among the powers of all three. It was a way to allow spiritual powers to interact with humans so that balance and harmony could be maintained.

The idea of *communing* with the powers of the spiritual world was taken literally by the tribe. That means that the spiritual powers could manifest visibly and physically to the tribal members. This was accomplished through a long set of intricate rituals performed by members of the secret societies who acted in specific roles after going through a spiritual cleansing. The playing of roles activated the spiritual forces of all three worlds and allowed them to manifest under what could be described as controlled circumstances. The ceremony was complicated and took a lot of time, but it allowed the forces of the spiritual powers of the three worlds to gather together and harmonize their activities and purposes.

It was a mandatory obligation to conduct the ceremony or the harmony of the universe would suffer and the tribe would experience calamity. The fate of the tribe was held in the balance, and the successful performance of the Massaum ceremony ensured the tribe's fate as a good one.

UNDERLYING BELIEFS

The Tsistsistas tradition recognized that humans gain most of their knowledge from interacting with the earth spirits that are routinely encountered during day-to-day life. Earth spirits are linked to our physical world, and they are the forces that the vast majority of the populace form connections with in the guise of spirit animals, birds, certain plants, landforms, weather phenomena, or waterways. However, the most powerful of the earth spirits were the *maiyun,* spirit entities that could be encountered in caves or when the seeker was grounded in deep earth. For example, one of the practices of the Massaum ceremony involved the construction of a circular ceremonial structure, which was prepared by removing all of the sod from the ground so that participants would be directly touching the deep earth with their bare feet.[11] Shamans and medicine people would perform hypnotic-like rituals within this sacred, grounded space, leading to a variety of experiences. Schlesier wrote, "Phenomena defined by modern parapsychology as out of body experiences and psychokinesis were integral parts of these séances."[12] Another related component of the Massaum ceremony was to orient the circular site toward Bear Butte, located in western South Dakota, which was the most sacred place where the maiyun could be encountered.[13]

Legends relate that it was at Bear Butte where the prophet Sweet Medicine was famously given knowledge by the maiyun. There is archaeological evidence that the site had been used for over 10,000 years. Two incredible cave systems are located about 85 miles south of Bear Butte. Both are considered to be places where the maiyun could be encountered. One is known as Jewel Cave. As of today, the site has over "208 miles of mapped and surveyed passages" and is the third longest-known cave system in the world.[14] The other cave system is Wind Cave. This cave was unknown to Whites until 1880, when three men stumbled on it, verifying several Native legends of rushing air from a hole.[15] Today it is a national park and is described by the Park Service as "one of the largest and most complex caves in the world."[16]

The circular ceremonial space and temporary village area had a single opening toward Bear Butte. That opening both invited and allowed the maiyun from Bear Butte to enter and manifest within the circular space. Before we move on, it is important to understand that in Native American beliefs, specific types of landforms held different types of spiritual power and attracted spiritual entities. The shape, material, and type of landform, both natural and man-made, were all important. Caves, which went into the deep earth, were believed to be a way to commune with both the maiyun and other spiritual forces of the underworld. Mountaintops were seen as a way to access the spiritual forces of the upper world.

All of the myriad of ceremonies and rituals of the Massaum had restricted levels of participation based on an individuals' membership in various societies. The masses participated in reenactments of certain events, such as a sacred hunt, where members of one secret society dressed as animals, but only some elite members engaged in the deepest rituals invoking and ultimately evoking some of the most sacred and powerful forces in the universe. The reenactment of the creation of the universe from a *singularity,* for example, was witnessed by only a select few. It is significant that the *physical appearance* of certain spiritual powers during the ceremony is often described.[17]

THE MASSAUM STARTED AND ENDED WITH SIGNALS FROM THE SKY

The Massaum ceremony was held in the middle of summer. As mentioned previously, it served as a renewal of a covenant between the Creator (called Maheo) and the created—humans—to ensure harmony. A signal from the sky, made by Maheo, served to notify the shamans of the timing to start the ceremony.

From the Cheyenne accounts, the signal to begin the Massaum ceremony was received at the Big Horn Medicine Wheel, a site mentioned in chapter 4, in the story of Red Plume (see plate 2).[18] The Medicine Wheel is an 80-foot-diameter (24.3 meters) circular formation made from carefully arranged rocks. The formation lies above the timberline in the Big Horn Mountains of Wyoming and allows a stunning view of the horizon on all sides. A total of twenty-eight rock-formed spokes radiate from the center of the formation, creating a wheel-like appearance. There are several cairns located in the wheel, including the large one in the center. In 1974, astronomer John Eddy calculated that the wheel had alignments to the summer solstice sunrise and sunset and the midsummer rising of the stars Aldebaran, Rigel, and Sirius. A year later, he found similar alignments at some twenty other medicine wheels in the United States and Canada. Eddy calculated that the formation's astronomical alignments were accurate from about 200 to 700 years ago.[19] In essence, if you lie down in a cairn, you can look down a spoke of the wheel and see the sun or a particular star as it rises or sets on the horizon on specific days and times.

The Massaum's preparations, combined with the ceremony, lasted 56 days. Preparations for the ceremony were started when shamans, watching from the Medicine Wheel late at night, observed the "red star" (Aldebaran) to rise on the northeastern horizon just before the sunrise around June 22. During the next four weeks, the tribes were gathered together and tasked with making a new, temporary living space, creating the circular ceremonial space, and making other preparations. The preparations ended exactly 28 days later, when the "blue star" (Rigel) was seen to rise on the eastern horizon just before sunrise. That was the signal for a sacred hunt to begin, along with a sequence of other complex rituals. Schlesier provided many details of the rituals involved in the long and complex ceremony, and we'll not go into them here. The ceremony ended 28 days later, when the "white star" (Sirius) rose on the southeastern horizon just before sunrise. It was a signal that the covenant between the Creator, Maheo, and the people was renewed.[20]

Both Schlesier and Lou White Eagle were quite clear about one aspect of the rituals. Spiritual forces or entities made physical appearances at certain times during the rituals.[21] These forces are activated by the ceremonies and rituals, and for their own reasons, the spiritual entities will occasionally appear in physical form to humans in many different guises. At least, that is what we are told. I vividly recall Lou White Eagle being hesitant to speak of such things, saying, "This is sacred knowledge." Before he would discuss such things, he went outside and gathered dirt. He then purified himself by tossing dirt over himself and occasionally on me. I'm pretty sure I needed purifying.

There are so many similar tales about various rituals from the oral histories of Native American tribes—found all over both North and South America— that it seems foolish to just dismiss them all. Are modern UFO abduction accounts any more or less valid than what Native tribes relate? Are modern paranormal events more believable because they are modern? The truth is that there are hundreds of accounts from Native sources telling about paranormal encounters. And they were far from savages living in superstition. The main fact that has to be kept in mind is that they lived in the natural world. They clearly evaluated everything in their natural world. And their medicine men and women were far from charlatans.

ZUÑI AND MOUND BUILDER ETHNOBIOLOGY

If you read ethnography books from the 1700s to the mid-1900s, you'll generally see the medical practices and shamanistic beliefs of Native Americans ridiculed and called superstitious. An 1896 book written by a professor of

American archaeology at the University of Pennsylvania related, "Nature, to the heathen, is no harmonious whole swayed by eternal principles, but a chaos of causeless effects, the meaningless play of capricious ghosts. . . . All events to him are miracles."[22] Native Americans are referred to as a "savage race" at least eighteen different times in the text. Such conclusions come from the biases of the observer, not from those who were observed. To some extent, it comes from the haughtiness of those who see themselves as "scientists" who believe they hold truth. But the attitude describing Native knowledge and beliefs as "heathen" and "savage" is simply wrong. These ancient people practiced science in their own way.

Just one example of what can really be seen as a Native American scientific practice is their effective use of the plants available to them for medical purposes. The first European visitors who observed Native American medical practitioners usually described them as being primitive and employing trickery. They were described as "conjurers"[23] with "superficial" knowledge.[24] It is clear that the historic-period European witnesses confused medical practices with shamanistic and spiritual practices. The deepest knowledge of the medicine people was a carefully guarded secret, something the early Europeans didn't realize. To put this into a cultural perspective, remember for a moment that bloodletting was a common practice in Western medicine until the early 1900s. The 1923 edition of the text *The Principles and Practice of Medicine* still recommended bloodletting for many disorders, although the procedure had been discredited and had all but ceased by then.[25] In brief, what purports itself to be science isn't necessarily factual and can essentially be superstition, savagery, and quackery itself.

In 1879, the Smithsonian Institution's Bureau of American Ethnology sent James Stevenson and his wife, Matilda, to the Zuñi tribe in New Mexico to investigate the Zuñi's knowledge of plants. In their report, the researchers noted, "While it was generally observed by early travelers among the Indians that they employed plants for medicinal purposes, it was long believed, even by scientific students, that the practices of Indian doctors were purely shamanistic."[26] However, the Stevensons quickly found that there were many effective and "legitimate" medicinal substances used by the Zuñi, including narcotics. After being accepted into the inner circles of the Zuñi shamanistic societies, they began an evaluation of the plant substances used by the shamans and medicine people. They eventually discovered sixty-three different plant substances that, surprisingly, were effectively used for a host of medical conditions. The Stevensons sent samples of each plant to the Smithsonian for chemical analysis. Some of these substances were eventually adapted into medicines used in the Western medicine, but you won't see that mentioned very often in mainstream literature. The Stevensons concluded that over the millennia, trial and error had led to the Zuñi's knowledge of the various plants, but the Zuñi related that the knowledge was given to their medicine people from the realm of spirits.[27]

The work of the Stevensons was all but forgotten and largely ignored, and once again, America's mainstream archaeological community relegated most of Native American medical practices to the realm of superstition and quackery. But in 1978 and 1979, two pharmacologists worked with twenty-seven different Zuñi medicine men and elders and managed to collect and evaluate 138 plant substances used by their healers. The vast majority of the plants were successfully used for a wide range of medicinal purposes.[28] They discovered there were thirty-one additional medical plants that the Stevensons were not informed of back in the 1800s, implying that many of their most effective remedies were kept secret from them.

The mound-building cultures of the eastern half of North America also developed extensive knowledge of plants. According to academic archaeologists, these ancient cultures "used 275 species of plants for medicine, 130 species for food, 31 species for magical purposes, 27 species for smoking, 25 species as dyes, 18 species for beverages and as flavoring, and 52 species for various other purposes."[29]

While it should be clear that there was a society of true medicine people within ancient Native American culture, the overriding belief of the culture was that a spiritual reality existed. Humans and everything in the physical world (plants, animals, and physical objects) and the powers and entities in the upper and lower worlds were all manifestations of this spiritual reality. People trying to understand what Native Americans really believe are biased by their own conceptions of shamans, medicine people, and spirituality.

THE SOURCE OF SUPERNATURAL BEINGS

In his 1914 book *Myths of the North American Indians*, Lewis Spence related that Native Americans had two different conceptions of the supernatural. That's misleading, but there is a useful bit of information within Spence's assertion. Spence states that they had a "Country of the Ghosts" and a "Land of the Supernatural People."[30] The country of ghosts was supposedly the "destination of human beings after death," while the land of the supernatural people was "the dwelling place of a supernatural race some degrees higher than mankind."[31] The concepts of ghosts and the destination of the dead are very complicated, and there are a few drastic differences between tribes that were separated in origin and heredity. The true beliefs about the fate of the dead were only revealed and widely known in anthropological circles in the late 1990s to mid-2000s.[32] It is clear that the deepest Native American beliefs about death were concealed from Spence and others. The "supernatural people," however, came from three very different but interconnected places. Supernatural powers and entities were attached to the upper, lower, and middle worlds. They were all created at the beginning of time, at the moment of creation. The earth spirit forces (those attached to the physical Earth space) interact with us on Earth, and the powers of the upper and lower worlds occasionally impinge on our physical reality, essentially fulfilling their roles.

The idea of a "role" being fulfilled by various spiritual entities can be understood by comparing it to the idea of an angel. Traditionally, an angel has a very specific role to perform. It is a *messenger.* Sometimes the message requires an action to be performed, and at other times, it requires an appearance to a particular person to whom the message is delivered. In the same manner, all spiritual entities in Native American lore have a role. They are all actors fulfilling their roles, and you never get to see what is really behind the mask they wear. That is one reason some tribes performed sacred ceremonies wearing masks (sometimes called *clowns,* but not in the common meaning) or dressed as animals or had painted faces and bodies. Revealing that which was behind the mask was forbidden.

The trickster also plays a role and is like an actor in a play. The little people also have a function; they fulfill a role. But they were all real entities. Iroquois tribes, for example, saw the little people as a race of spiritual "Pigmies" who are associated with certain landforms.[33] The Cherokee, distant cousins of the Iroquois, also viewed the little people as physically manifested beings who could be either helpful or malignant.[34] Shamans and medicine men and women had the ability to interact with all three spiritual realms. In fact, it was required that these holy people interact with the spiritual realm. But all of these ideas go far, far deeper. Ultimately, they are about the meaning of life.

6

ANCIENT ANSWERS TO
ETERNAL QUESTIONS

In the second part of this book, Andrew Collins will discuss other regions and cultures of the ancient world. However, there are good reasons for the focus here in the first part on what Native Americans believed about nature and the paranormal. Perhaps the most important reason is that it is widely thought that Native American beliefs are the closest we can ever get to how the ancients truly conceptualized reality. In *Indian Medicine Power,* Brad Steiger writes, "It may be seen that due to their hundreds of years of isolation from both East and West, the American Indians may have preserved the essentials of the ancient mysteries in their purest form."[1] But it is inappropriate to describe the beliefs and cultural traditions of ancient Native Americans as if they were all the same. *The Historical Atlas of Native Americans* lists forty-six "Algonkian" [sic] tribes as being present in North America from 1580 to 1880, along with 310 other tribes.[2] The U.S. Federal Register today recognizes nearly 600 different tribes within the United States, but many of them are localized political groups in a specific geographic area. There are likely around thirty somewhat different tribal cultures, but even among them, there are many smaller tribal groups that split off from the larger group of their ancestors, yet they retained the basic beliefs of their group of origin.[3] In reality, there are probably only three to five somewhat different cultural belief systems. However, they all share some major commonalities. In this chapter, we will look at the commonalities.

In chapter 5, an 1896 quote about Native Americans was cited: "Nature, to the heathen, is no harmonious whole swayed by eternal principles, but a chaos of causeless effects, the meaningless play of capricious ghosts."[4] Nothing could be further from the truth. In reality, the underlying beliefs of Native Americans were and still are the exact opposite of that statement. Over time, archaeologists and anthropologists began to better understand how these ancient people viewed the world.

In his classic book *The Southeastern Indians,* archaeologist Charles Hudson related, "If there is a single word which epitomizes the Southeastern Indian belief system, it is 'order.'"[5] The same word—*order*—accurately describes the key belief of the Algonquin-speaking tribes of the Northeast and the Great Plains as well as the southwestern tribes. Order, balance, and harmony in nature are the keys to understanding how they viewed the universe and their place in it. Events were not causeless or capricious in this belief system. Supernatural events, the appearance of strange beings, and lights in the sky were all part of the natural order. These ancient people developed their own theory of natural science that was expressed in ways that ethnographers and anthropologists described as "religious or magical."[6] In sum, the mound builders and the people of other Native American cultures developed a deep belief system that attempted to answer the eternal questions our evolutionary ancestors have probably been asking for at least the past million years: Who am I? Why am I here? Where did I come from? Where am I going? The most closely guarded shamanic secrets answered all of them.

COMMONPLACE MYTHS AND SACRED KNOWLEDGE

Mythologist George Lankford has written that many of the myths and tales we read in most books on Native American legends were composed for children. Lankford refers to such stories as *commonplace myths,* and they don't reveal the deeper core of the Native Americans' beliefs. On the other hand, there was a second category of beliefs Lankford referred to as *sacred knowledge.*[7] This chapter focuses on the sacred knowledge, which gave the deeper answers.

The sacred knowledge and the spiritual truths were held as closely guarded secrets by a select group of men and women who were directly tasked with controlling the life and death cycles of the tribe through periodic rituals.[8] The same can be said for their knowledge of medicinal plants and healing procedures. The transmission of this sacred knowledge from one generation to the next was done primarily through hereditary lines. The information was passed along verbally, with elders giving explanations of sacred objects, symbols, and rituals. The concealing of sacred knowledge was also a way the elite could maintain their power.[9] It may sound cryptic, but it isn't. We do the same today in medicine, science, politics, and religion. Each area has its own terminology, codes, symbols, and secrets, and its practitioners guard its information from outsiders. Today, we have "paywalls" and membership requirements to many scientific organizations that restrict scientific research information from the masses. And virtually all of our most effective medications require a prescription from one of our societal elites.

THE SHAMANIC CREATION STORY

In chapter 5, the Cheyenne Massaum ceremony was briefly described. It's important to remember that the beliefs underlying the Massaum were ultimately derived from Siberian shamanistic practices that were at least 12,000 years old. But it is now known that the shamanistic practices and beliefs go much further back in time, as Andrew Collins shall show in part 2. An understanding of the ancient Native Americans' beliefs and ideas about the paranormal, the purpose of life, and nature begins with their conception of the act of creation. In essence, the shamanic creation story reveals the origin of the gods as these ancient cultures conceptualized it.

Schlesier related that the Tsistsistas creation story began with a *singularity*.[10] The singularity that existed before creation was, according to this account, *a single point of pure spiritual energy.* Virtually all tribes simply refer to it as *spirit,* using the particular word in their language that gives that underlying idea. Many historic and modern tribes commonly refer to it as the Great Spirit. It was a pure energy that always existed. It had a type of primordial consciousness that defies our understanding. In modern physics, it is also referred to as a singularity, the only "thing" that existed before the supposed big bang. This science-based singularity also defies our understanding. Even the Zuñi, considered to be the most ancient of the Puebloan people, had a similar concept. Their creation story tells of a single "Container of All" that existed before creation that "thought outward in space," thereby bringing the physical world into existence.[11]

For its own purposes, which are incomprehensible to us, the singularity began churning within itself. It instantly evolved into two opposite and equal parts. This "two-part singularity" can be symbolized by the traditional yin-yang symbol. It is, of course, a contradiction in terms, and its occurrence led to the act of creation. In brief, the moment that the two opposing portions of energy formed, the singularity was no longer that. That imbalance caused the instantaneous creation of everything. This big bang, as modern physics calls it, or the act of creation by the Great Spirit, occurred as a way to maintain harmony while allowing the two opposing spiritual energies to exist.

THE THREE-PART UNIVERSE

When the swirling singularity instantly separated itself (the big bang), it created a three-part universe that was divided into an upper world, a lower world, and a middle world. The middle world is the physical world. To explain the created universe to the masses, Native American iconography depicted a three-part sphere, with the physical Earth suspended in the middle (see fig. 6.1, p. 46). Above the Earth was the upper world and below was the lower world. The upper world contained one of the two forces that had divided the singularity, and the lower world contained the other. Thus, the physical world was positioned *between* these two great spiritual forces.[12] There are a host of children's myths that mention how the three worlds were created and connected together in a way the masses could comprehend. As Lankford related, these were children's stories and the sacred knowledge was concealed.[13]

Here is one of the deepest secrets in this cosmology: When the spiritual singularity was split into two spiritual portions, the middle world appeared between them as a three-dimensional double reflection. *The middle world represents a three-dimensional mirror on which the two opposing spiritual forces can interact and play out their intended purposes.* The physical world is the interaction space for an ongoing spiritual cycle. In a literal sense, Earth was seen as a physical field allowing the interplay between the spiritual forces of the upper and lower worlds. The physical world was created as a place where the two opposing forces could each exist, express their spiritual essence, and remain in balance.

Fig. 6.1. The three-part Native American cosmos.

THE TWO OPPOSING FORCES:
CREATION AND ENTROPY

Native Americans observed the daily rhythms, cycles, and frequent chaos of nature. They came to understand the cycles of life and death, aging, the growing seasons, weather, the movements of the sun, moon, and stars, and the many conflicts encountered in life. All of these cycles and events were explained by invoking the interplay between the two spiritual forces: *order* and *disorder*.[14] These were the spirit of *creation* (order) from the upper world and the spirit of *entropy* (disorder) from the lower world. Creation always produces order by taking substances and linking them together into an organized whole. Creation also seemingly makes predictable cycles such as the movements of the sun, moon, and stars. They all appear to be in harmony. On the other hand, entropy produces disorder by methodically disturbing that which has been created. Unpredictable weather, an untimely illness, plague, a sudden death, or an invasion by unfriendly people are all part of the spirit of entropy or disorder. Note that I have chosen to use the term *entropy* rather than *chaos* because it better describes how disorder or chaos occurs.[15]

The process of entropy is a universal truth in physics. Everything gradually falls apart; everything eventually breaks down and degrades back into its most primordial state. Social systems and all relationships gradually fall apart because of entropy. In short, all things change. But entropy allows for a new creation. It is part of the great cycle.

THE FORCES OF NATURE
AS SPIRITUAL MANIFESTATIONS

One way to understand the myriad of paranormal experiences reported in Native American mythology is that on Earth there is a constant interplay between the spiritual forces of the upper and lower worlds. It is like Jung's opposing archetypes, where one force is seeking to create order and the other disorder. These two opposing archetypes can assume different guises and shapes. According to this idea, it is the interplay of these spiritual forces that creates the wide range of paranormal phenomena.

In this ideology, the creatures of the sky—eagles, hawks, swans, and such—represented real spiritual powers from the upper world. Creatures that lived underground or underwater represented powers from the lower world. Creatures that lived on the Earth were powers linked to the middle world.[16] But everything was imbued with spiritual energy, an energy that was in a never-ending cycle between the two great forces of creation and entropy. In this view, the entire universe was placed in a sort of balanced opposition between those two great forces.[17] The upper world also had major spiritual powers that appeared in predictable cycles: the sun and the moon. It is usually assumed that the sun is a male deity and the moon is female, but that isn't the case. Some tribes saw the sun and moon as male or female, depending on their commonplace myths.[18] However, the sun and moon were not worshipped in the sense usually attributed to the beliefs. It was the spiritual power behind them that was honored.[19] The lower world also had a major spiritual being. It was a giant snake that would hover along the horizon at night during certain times of the year. When it flew to the sky, it took wings and was the constellation of Scorpius.

Everything in the universe, everything in the physical world, was composed of the same primordial spiritual energy from the singularity that existed at the beginning. Modern physics tells us the same thing using different terminology: "We are all made from stars."* Thus, this primordial spirit exists in all physical objects and in all living things.[20] Spirit is the underlying composition of everything. Rocks were seen as solidified spirit. Water was flowing spiritual energy. Fire was the release of spiritual energy and was related to the sun. Crystals were viewed as a purified and dense form of spiritual energy. Dirt was the most primordial form of spirit in the physical world. All of these physical forms of spirit were used by shamans and medicine people to commune with the spiritual realm and even manipulate it. Landforms, rock formations, caves, earthworks, mounds, and water could all be arranged in ways that allowed for an interaction with the spiritual powers from both the upper and lower worlds. Carefully shaped landforms were created as sacred enclosures for the earth spirits to emerge. Crystals were used for making contact with the spiritual forces, and various plants were used in the rituals performed to achieve harmony and balance.[21] All of these spiritual objects could become physical points of contact where humans were able to directly interact with specific spiritual forces if the earth, rocks, and water were arranged in specific ways that shamans and medicine people dictated.

---

*Carl Sagan is cited as the first person to say this in his thirteen-part series titled *Cosmos,* which aired in the 1980s.

In addition, certain locations were known to be special points where the three worlds interconnected in a unique way. Many people today might refer to these points as *portal* or *window* areas. Portals and windows are places where spiritual forces emerge routinely. Such locations are epicenters for the interactions between the two primary spiritual forces (creation and entropy), where humans can be both witnesses and participants. It is the manifestation and interaction of spiritual energy that created the entire myriad of events that we today refer to as paranormal phenomena: lights in the sky, translucent beings, strange creatures, voices from nowhere, visitors from the sky, apparitional manifestations, and so much more.

Embedded within the ultimate spiritual reality of *everything* was an innate drive to manifest the particular essence of its underlying nature. That is, whatever form a spiritual force took reflected its underlying nature. Upper world powers reflected creation and lower world powers reflected entropy. The middle world forces were the earth spirits that both helped and hindered or tricked humans; that is, they could manifest both creation and disorder. The powers of all three worlds emerged on the physical Earth routinely in this sort of dance of opposites, because they had to do so. Thus, spiritual manifestations appeared everywhere in nature in the guise of paranormal phenomena and appearances of the little people, tricksters, and a vast myriad of other beings, including various animals. These spiritual forces were depicted symbolically in many ways on sacred artifacts, and rituals and celebrations were developed to commune with them. Everything in the universe was a manifestation of spiritual energy.

This belief in the spiritual nature of all that existed was interpreted by early ethnographers and European priests as *animism,* the idea that everything is alive. But in the Native American belief system, the spirit that inhabited every bit of matter was a sacred and holy part of the whole. It has a far deeper meaning than animism. Native Americans believe that there is purpose and meaning for all things. In the Native American beliefs, *everything is connected* because it is part of the whole.

One very large difference between Native American cultural beliefs and European beliefs relates to this idea. The Europeans essentially viewed nature as something to be exploited and used as humans saw fit: animals, trees, minerals, water, and land were here for humans to use as resources. Native Americans, however, saw nature as something to harmonize with, preserve, share, and nurture. In Native American beliefs, if nature was mistreated, it would "strike back."[22]

The two spiritual forces of creation and entropy explained the great cycle of life and death as well as virtually all other events observed in the natural world. The creation of the physical universe was a means for the primordial spirit to allow the two forces of creation and entropy to exist but to also remain in balance. Sent to the middle of this interplay between these two great forces were humans.

THE ROLE OF HUMANS

There are many indigenous children's stories explaining the entry of humans into the physical world, but most of them don't specifically relate the role of humans and their purpose. These tales vary considerably among tribal mythology. As mentioned previously, children's stories were ultimately about teaching skills, morals, and right and wrong.

The deeper purpose of why humans were created and sent to this world was to maintain balance. *Humans were tasked with maintaining harmony between the two major spiritual forces.* This is true in the Algonquin tribes, the Navajo, and virtually all of the southeastern tribes.[23] It is also true of the Hopi and Zuñi. There is acceptance in the mainstream archaeological community that the ancient mound-building cultures centered their spirituality on this idea of maintaining a balance between these two opposing forces.[24] In general, it can be said that nearly all Native American rituals and healing methods related to maintaining or regaining harmony.

Humans were special in that they could appreciate and comprehend the two primary spiritual forces—and humans were given freedom of choice. The Massaum ceremony and many other seasonal celebrations were about maintaining a balance in nature and harmonizing with the spiritual forces interacting with us. Embedded within the Native American belief system was that land could not be owned. Land could be used and lived on. It could be altered for spiritual or other purposes that supported maintaining balance and harmony. But it couldn't truly be owned by individuals; it was simply inhabited. All of nature had to be respected. Nothing could be killed without good reason. Everything had to be honored. The underlying reason was simple. Everything is connected and composed of the same primordial spirit. Disturbing one part of the interconnected web of life disturbed it all.

7

THE TWO SOULS AND
THE DEATH JOURNEY

Almost all ancient Native Americans conceptualized two different souls being present in human beings.[1] One soul was derived from the physical matter that composed our body, and the other was an entity of pure spiritual energy. The physical soul was called the *Life Soul,* and the spiritual soul was the *Free Soul.*

The Life Soul animated the body. It returned to its primordial state after burial or cremation. However, the Life Soul would wander as a dangerous ghost if it wasn't handled properly.[2] Thus, the "ghosts" of wandering souls were sometimes seen as the source of some paranormal manifestations.

The Free Soul originates from a spiritual realm that is beyond the upper world at a vaguely defined place sometimes referred to as the *Other World.*[3] The Free Soul, which is made from pure spiritual energy, enters a physical body once it begins to develop in the womb or at birth. It retains an individual's personality, memories, and deeds, and it has consciousness and freedom of choice. The Free Soul, having both consciousness and pure spiritual energy, can, under some circumstances, leave the body and travel to other realms. This was a process used by shamans and has often been described as an out-of-body experience.

After death, the Free Soul separates from the physical body. In some cases, the Free Soul can also linger on Earth and wander as a ghost. However, almost all Free Souls were tasked with making a journey to the stars in the upper sky world. Once in the upper world, they traveled on the Path of Souls across the sky to a final exit point that led to the Other World, the place of origin. There were three key locations in the sky related to the journey the Free Soul took, and here, we'll use their modern names: the Orion constellation, the Milky Way, and the Cygnus constellation. However, the fate of the Free Soul was also determined by the deeds of the individual in life. Some Free Souls could reincarnate or, depending on their actions in life, be cast into the lower world. All the other souls took the death journey to the stars.

THE PATH OF SOULS: THE JOURNEY TO THE STARS

The death journey of the soul will be described only briefly as we have extensively described it in several earlier books.[4] This summary comes from those prior publications and focuses on the ancient mound builder beliefs that have now been accepted as valid by academics in the mainstream archaeological community.

Following death, the Free Soul was believed to remain near the body for a brief time. There was a long process involved in preparing the body while an extended period of mourning was held. A stunning ritual was then held to release the soul to the stars. The underlying meaning of these rituals relates to the idea that the fate of the dead was partially controlled by how the physical remains of the dead were handled and the correct performance of the rituals. Knowledge of the mortuary practices was confined to secret societies and members of the elite. However, it is known that among the mound builder cultures it was important to hold the ceremony to release the Free Soul around the time of the winter solstice (December 21). Many Native American mound sites and earthworks were built to allow precise sight lines that were created by placing mounds, certain circular and square earthworks, and openings in geometric earthen embankments that were oriented toward important stars. These sight lines could be seen across the tops of two mounds or through openings in earthworks, and it is thought that most of the sacred enclosures created for this purpose were also used for other seasonal ceremonies. We have identified numerous mound complexes where these alignments have been verified, and they date in the time frame of roughly 500 BCE to CE 1400.[5]

That the Native American mound complexes contained stellar alignments is one of the more recent important discoveries in archaeology that has validated the Path of Souls concept. The key alignments were to the winter solstice sunrise and sunset, the setting of the Orion Nebula, and the setting of the star Deneb in Cygnus. Rituals involved with the death journey included displaying all of the astronomical observations to the populace along with cremation bonfires and the use of artifacts. Music, dancing, and the use of sacred objects with hallucinogenic liquids were conducted in a sequential fashion, with members of the priestly class controlling each step. The rituals were begun with the setting sun and continued throughout the night until dawn. The final ceremony was the release of the Free Soul, which made a leap to the Orion Nebula (Messier-42) just before Orion sank beneath the western horizon shortly before sunrise. The Orion Nebula was an *ogee*, a portal that allowed the soul to make safe passage through the underworld until the next night, when the constellation appeared again in the eastern sky. The importance of Orion to Native Americans has long been recognized, and archaeological evidence indicates that this goes back to at least 1000 BCE.[6]

The next night, the soul moved from the ogee to the Milky Way and began traveling to the north. The Milky Way is seen as a "trail for the spirits of the dead quite widely in the world."[7] It is known by many names, but almost universally, all the cultures of the ancient world saw it as a path for the souls.

As the soul moved north, it went through a series of trials and adventures. The specific trials varied somewhat among different tribes, and the creatures encountered along the trail slightly differ among different tribal cultures. Eventually, the soul reached a split in the Milky Way where it encountered a judge. Among the mound builders, the judge was usually depicted symbolically as a large raptor bird, typically an eagle. In 2004, both Andrew Collins and George Lankford published materials identifying this celestial judge as the Cygnus constellation.[8] Cygnus, also known as the Northern Cross, was seen as a swan in Greek mythology, and Lankford and other archaeologists have asserted that while Cygnus is traditionally viewed as a swan in Western cultures, visualizing the constellation as an eagle is just as logical since eagles were the dominant bird in North America. Since 2004, many in the archaeological community have accepted the identification of Cygnus as the "judge" in the path of souls journey. The star Deneb, the brightest star of Cygnus, was likely the final portal out of the sky world to the Other World.

The relatively recent discovery of the importance of the stars in the Path of Souls journey is far more important than most people realize, but not necessarily for the reasons that might immediately come to mind. Andrew Collins's 2006 book, *The Cygnus Mystery,* proposed that the ancient veneration of swans was a key to understanding the mindset of ancient religious beliefs.[9] Rather quickly, both Collins and I came to realize that the connection between Orion and Cygnus was sacred knowledge shared in both ancient Egypt and the Americas. The beliefs about the soul's journey to the stars were information that was never meant to become known to the masses. Thus, this information was concealed and made extremely difficult to understand because of what I believe was a trickster element built into it.[10]

THE IMPORTANCE OF THE NORTH

Cygnus (particularly the star Deneb) served as the celestial North Pole star roughly 15,000 to 18,000 years ago.[11] This, of course, was due to the phenomenon of precession, the wobble of the Earth as it spins on its axis across a cycle of approximately 26,000 years. At the times Cygnus served as the celestial North Pole star, *Orion was seen on the extreme southern horizon.*[12] Thus, Cygnus and Orion formed a north-south axis for a nearly 3,000-year period. This timetable aligns nicely with the idea that the belief system incorporating a journey in the sky from the south to the north developed at least 14,000 years ago or much earlier.[13] In addition, due to precession, Cygnus also served as the celestial North Pole star roughly 41,000 to 44,000 years ago, when, once again, Orion was seen on the southernmost horizon at the same time. In essence, it is very possible that the beliefs about the death journey formed over 40,000 years ago or even before.[14]

The importance of the North Star in ancient cultures cannot be overemphasized. It not only gave a reliable directional point, but it also was seen almost universally in the ancient world as the entry and exit point of the sky world (see fig. 7.1).[15] In essence, everything pointed toward the north, toward the "imperishable stars," the stars that never set. Of course, the northern stars' relative positions did gradually shift because of precession, but the movement of the pole stars spanned many, many generations, leading to the idea that they were in a permanent, fixed position. To those ancient astronomers, the stars at the north celestial pole were always seen in the same spot, night after night, while the remaining stars in the sky world rose and set during the night.

Fig. 7.1. This time-lapse photo of the northern sky at night clearly shows why the North Pole star was seen as a portal.

It is very likely that both Orion and Cygnus became focal points in the death journey because of their respective positions in the south and north long ago, and as their positions gradually changed because of precession, their significance was retained in the mythology that was handed down from one generation to the next. Over eons, the mythology related to the death journey adapted as the stars' positions changed because of precession. Various tribes based their legends and beliefs about the death journey on the different animals encountered in their location and other factors. While most Native American tribes saw Cygnus as a huge raptor bird, other cultures around the world saw it as a swan. The depiction and veneration of Cygnus as a swan was widespread in the ancient world,[16] and the absolute origins of its symbolism and use in shamanic traditions will become increasingly important in the last half of this book.

8

THE POLE HOLDING EVERYTHING TOGETHER

A Psychoid Reality

To the general population, the ancient Native American storytellers described the relationships among the three worlds (upper, middle, and lower) in a simplistic way. It was explained that the upper, middle, and lower worlds were physically connected. In this children's myth, the Earth was suspended between the upper and lower worlds by four ropes corresponding to the cardinal directions. The Navajo related that a swan was located at each connecting point.[1] The four directions, symbolized by different colors depending on the tribe, were important components of many rituals, but the elite retained secret knowledge about the connecting points of the three worlds. It is this deeper reality that is most relevant here.

In many ancient cultures, the connection of the three worlds was symbolically depicted as a tree. It was a simple visualization easily grasped by children and the masses. The roots of a tree came from the lower world and the tree's trunk emerged from the middle world, with its branches extending into the upper world (see fig. 8.1). In visual depictions of this symbol, various spiritual forces were shown in all three realms. Soaring eagles, hawks, and other birds were depicted in the upper world, humans and animals were shown on the middle world, and fish and underground animals such as snakes were displayed in the lower world. It is an elegant symbol that almost everyone easily grasps: in this

56

Fig. 8.1. Depiction of the World Tree in Norse mythology.
Almost every ancient culture embraced the same concept
(*Yggdrasil, the Mundane Tree*, Oluf Olufsen Bagge, 1847).

depiction, the three worlds are firmly held together and spiritual beings obviously exist in all three. It is the *World Tree*, commonly used by many other ancient cultures. Of course, it had a much deeper meaning held as a secret by shamans.

THE PSYCHOID POLE

At the deepest level of Native American cosmology, there is a "spiritual" pole that connected the three worlds together. The pole extended all the way through the Earth, reaching down into the lower world. The pole also reached high into the sky, pointing at the north celestial pole.[2] Symbolically, the pole was always depicted as striped like a candy cane (see fig. 6.1, p. 46). It was a cosmic axis connecting rod, the *axis mundi*. The stripes symbolize it as a revolving axis point, and it represents a spinning vortex of energy holding the cosmos together. All of the swirling energy associated with this magnificent symbol moved from the south to the north. Significantly, this was also the direction of the Orion-to-Cygnus Path of Souls concept. The underlying secret of the pole is this: under the right circumstances, this vortex of energy could manifest itself visually and physically; thus, it was a *psychoid* manifestation.

Recall from chapter 3 that the idea of a psychoid manifestation comes from Carl Jung. The pole remains unseen because it is in a portion of the electromagnetic energy spectrum outside of the visible light frequencies. Under the right circumstances, it can be brought into a physical, visual manifestation. Rituals employed to manifest the pole manipulated its vibration. It was this pole that allowed shamans to move through the different spiritual realms to commune with spiritual forces. This was accomplished in two different ways. The medicine people could attune themselves to the vibration of the pole through specific rituals to allow the shamans to consciously merge with it. Under that condition, shamans could mentally move through the spiritual worlds. Second, the pole could be vibrated through rituals that made it physically manifest. That allowed spiritual forces to temporarily physically manifest as well.

As part of the process of preparing for some rituals, a sacred space (made of rock or carefully piled earth) was first constructed, either in a circular or square shape, depending on the intention of the ritual. The sacred space was made with the purpose of confining the spiritual forces that were being called on. Then a carefully made wooden pole was pounded into the earth and tilted toward the celestial North Pole.[3] This pole was vibrated both physically and psychically through rituals involving repetitive sound and movement— vibration through drumming, chanting, singing, blowing whistles, dancing, and other movements. These vibrations were employed to change the frequencies of the vast interconnecting web. Both the sacred space and the individuals participating in the rituals were affected. The physical actions and sound vibrations produced a rapport between the participants and the spiritual forces and opened a physical, intersecting portal. Remember, everything in the natural and spiritual worlds was believed to be vibrating through an unseen spiritual energy force that permeated the universe. This, of course, is something modern physics asserts in different terminology.

As mentioned, in some rituals, the pole was physically shaken to create a resonance that allowed spiritual forces to physically manifest. This is similar to the occult idea of *transmutation,* the process of energy transforming into physical substance or vice versa. Shamans seeking to temporarily enter the upper or lower world to gain spiritual knowledge, insight, or power could use this vibrating axis like a mental elevator, moving their consciousness up and down the various spiritual levels. However, there were specific times of the year when various rituals were performed because of complex influences from the sun, the moon, and certain stars.

In sum, shamanic and native cosmology is based on something they believe is very real, but something that is not completely understood. In truth, understanding wasn't a necessary component of the rituals. But accepting the reality of the spiritual world was. Shamans and the medicine people retained their knowledge as sacred and secret information, but what has been presented here is a valid summary of their core ideas. I'm sure that the electromagnetic energy forces that surround us are related to how Native Americans came to understand the world. The Native American cosmology proposes a complex interaction between the myriad of physical objects and forces of nature, with normally invisible spiritual forces that affect everything. Their cosmology was their physics.

Mainstream academics have typically explained native concepts as irrational beliefs about the natural world that formed over time in an attempt to explain things they didn't truly understand. The esteemed George Lankford described Native American cosmology as their effort to survive in a complex, sometime chaotic world. Their belief system was a way "to reduce that complexity," and their ideas eventually became crystallized into a belief system.[4] Maybe so. But that somewhat demeaning idea disregards the fact that science does the exact same thing. As just one example, we don't truly understand gravity, which NASA today describes as "an invisible force that pulls objects toward each other."[5]

In our quest to understand the origin of the gods and the paranormal, it is not necessary to describe the specific rituals involved in the native worldview. In ancient Native American cosmology, the gods are components of the spiritual world that were created at the beginning of everything. The gods are spiritual entities that interact with us in accordance with their underlying nature and purpose. They are always present, they can become physically real, they can take on virtually any form, and they interact with humans as they fulfill their roles. By using certain ritualistic processes with the right mental intention, performed at specific times and conducted in special places, it was possible for humans to temporarily enter the realm of this spiritual world *or* have the spiritual realm manifest in our reality. It was communion with the spiritual world. Many Native American tribes, and their ancient ancestors, saw this as a necessity—a spiritual requirement. The purpose of humans was to maintain balance and harmony between the two great spiritual forces: creation and entropy. However, the spiritual entities and forces routinely manifested on their own to fulfill their purpose and express their true nature. But when they manifested on their own, they often took the form of the trickster.

While the preceding material barely summarizes a truly ancient and deep belief system—the Native American "theory of everything"—there are a few other ideas that have to be discussed about their concepts of the paranormal. Some tribes had legends that we came from the stars, most tribes asserted we would return to the stars after death, and there are many legends relating that other beings came here from the stars. And a lot of their legends are identical to historic and modern tales of the paranormal and UFOs.

9

WHAT CAME
FROM THE STARS?

There are dozens of Native American legends of visitors from the stars, trips into the sky world, and the journey of the souls to the upper world. However, it has only been in relatively recent years that many Native Americans have openly discussed it. Back in the 1960s, author Brad Steiger (1936–2018) began collecting claims of extraterrestrial contact from indigenous peoples while he was studying their medicine practices. He later recalled the difficulty he had during the endeavor. In an interview Steiger said, "When I first brought that up, when I was interviewing people for *Medicine Power* . . . so few Native Americans wanted to talk about it. . . . I found some Cherokee who did not hesitate because they said, 'We came from the stars,' but the others were really reluctant."[1] In his 2004 book *Visitors From Hidden Realms,* longtime ufologist Brent Raynes also mentions a discussion he had with mythologist William Henry. Their discussion involved a visionary experience of a female Cherokee shaman. Henry mentioned that a well-known Cherokee myth "tells how the first Cherokee came from the star system known as the Pleiades," then mentioned that "the first beings to emerge . . . were 'thought beings.'"[2] One implication of the term *thought beings* is that the beings are nonphysical entities coming to Earth, perhaps a way of describing the energy of a soul entering a physical body. But there are some Native accounts of physical visitors coming from the stars. Most of these tales about star visitors are long and involved and several could be interpreted as contact with ethereal entities. Here we'll only briefly describe a few them. It is important to note that these stories have a remarkable similarity to modern UFO and alien contact cases.

An ancient Yuchi legend tells of an "unknown and mysterious being" that descended to Earth.[3] This entity taught the Yuchi skills and religious ideas as well as explaining to them that the sun was their mother. From the Iroquois comes the story of a lone hunter who heard a voice asking him to "follow it." The hunter began to rise from the ground and soon found himself gazing down at the forest. He rose still higher into the clouds and then realized he was surrounded by a group of beings that had "the appearance of men."[4] Another Iroquois myth tells of a hunter who killed a bear after a long struggle with the beast. As he was preparing his kill, he began to hear muffled voices behind him. Turning around, he saw three "beings in the shape of men, clothed in strange, diaphanous [translucent] garments."[5] They explained that they were entrusted with the job of maintaining harmony between humans and nature. Another tale describes a Flathead tribal man whose wife had recently died. He was so grief-stricken that he went into the mountains to sit until his death. Early one morning, before dawn, a bright light from the eastern sky came toward him. The light instantly moved overhead, and a being enshrouded in light suddenly materialized before him. He was instructed to go down the mountain, where he would meet another being who would deliver a message to him. After meeting the being, he was told to return to his tribe.[6] A similar story comes from the Kalispel tribe. A chief was grief-stricken over the death of his son. He retreated to a mountain ridge and built a circle of rocks. While sitting in the circle, two beings suddenly appeared in front of him, instructing him to return to his tribe.[7]

Several episodes of *Ancient Aliens* have featured modern Native Americans citing legends from tribal lore relating that there have been visitations from various star systems in the galaxy. The places of origin that are mentioned include the Pleiades, Orion, Cygnus, and a few others. Of course, that idea is one major focus of *Ancient Aliens*. The theme of the long-running series is that the gods of the ancient world were actually visitors from other worlds who had technology so far advanced from the humans that they were seen as gods. Despite skeptics who routinely deride the idea as bunk, it is actually a very fascinating, if not compelling, idea. One of the famed science fiction author Arthur C. Clarke's three laws was, "Any sufficiently advanced technology is indistinguishable from magic."[8] So it's not a stretch to imagine what primitive people around tens or even hundreds of thousands of years ago might have thought if technologically advanced extraterrestrials did visit the planet. They would, as the astronomer Carl Sagan once noted, be seen as gods.[9] So here are a few possibilities for the ancient beliefs that developed about the "gods," the spiritual forces and entities they described, and the ideas about humans and other mysterious beings coming from the stars. First, it's possible that ancient astronauts did, in fact, come to Earth in ancient times. That is, contacts with technologically advanced aliens in ancient times resulted in the emergence of the cultural mythologies of powerful gods as the source of human development. Second, it's possible that the spiritual world—as described by ancient Native belief systems—actually exists and that it is not yet understood in scientific terms. This spiritual world is asserted to be the source of paranormal events, the appearances of entities and "star beings," and many odd light formations that have been reported for all recorded history. Third, perhaps it's all simply bunk and mental trickery at work, as most skeptics argue. Or, fourth, maybe all three of the above possibilities have some validity.

SKEPTICISM OF SHAMANIC PRACTICES

In 2002, Stanley Krippner, a well-known psychologist, published an analysis of skeptical Western interpretations of shamans and their practices.[10] Included in the skeptical explanations are a *demonic model,* that the shamans are *charlatans,* that they are afflicted with *schizophrenia* or other mental disorders, that they use *soul flight* trance techniques, and that they use what he calls *crude technology.*

The "demonic model" was attributed to shamanistic practices by the early European clergy, who viewed all of the shamans' practices as devil worship, witchcraft, and sorcery. While that idea has waned somewhat, it remains the prime belief of some people, and it laid the foundation for later ideas developed by the skeptical community. The "charlatan model" assumes that shamans and practitioners of "medicine" are imposters who use trickery to convince others that they have supernatural powers. It is likely that this remains the primary view of many skeptics, and it was the explanation I recall being given back in the 1980s when I interacted with the archaeologists who were attempting to excavate the Memphis mound site (see chapter 4).

The "schizophrenia model" asserts that shamans are mentally deranged and afflicted with psychosis or other mental illness. That is, their mental state has deluded them into believing things that are untrue and led them to engage in superstitious behaviors that have no genuine effect. The "soul flight model" implies that some shamans employ self-induced trance states to create ecstatic out-of-body experiences. That model is cited to explain various experiences shamans relate about their journeys into the spiritual world, but once again, these are hallucinatory or dream experiences that are not tied to reality. The soul flight model is the usual explanation that is given for the mental experiences that often follow exhaustive periods of rhythmic drumming, whistle blowing, chanting, dancing, and other repetitive rituals. Finally, there is the "crude technology model." It refers to the use of hallucinogenic substances to create mystical experiences. While psychedelic experiences do give an explanation of some shamanic and medicine practices, this model also implies that the experiences are not tied to reality and are merely chemically induced.

Western interpretations of shamanic customs and knowledge, at least those proposed by skeptics and academics, don't leave any room for the possibility that there may be an underlying truth to what the medicine people and shamans espouse as reality. So, in essence, skeptics tell us that the constructions of sacred spaces and mound and earthwork complexes, the building of stone circles, and the rituals and ceremonies conducted by indigenous people all around the ancient world were essentially superstitious practices. Skeptics assert that all these rituals are based on false beliefs. In addition, in the skeptical view, there are no underlying spiritual or energy forces being tapped into and interacted with. Thus, shamanism and all of its customs stem from either mental derangement or a primitive belief system that came to inaccurate conclusions about nature. It can be added here that the same ideas are often used by skeptics to explain all of the ancient reports of beings coming from the sky, sudden appearances of glowing or translucent beings, and journeys to the sky. Skeptics use the same explanations to dismiss virtually all modern religious beliefs and rituals, modern apparitional phenomena, paranormal events, UFO reports, and abduction reports. To skeptics, it's all mental derangement, trickery, or an inability to distinguish reality. Many skeptics apply the same explanations to the idea of ancient aliens, but here, they encounter a glaring weak spot in their arguments, one named Carl Sagan.

CARL SAGAN: THE FATHER OF THE ANCIENT ASTRONAUT HYPOTHESIS?

Back in 2014, I reviewed an archaeology book by skeptic Ken Feder.[11] In his 2010 textbook, which is 285 pages long and retails for $85.00, Feder claimed that the true origin of the "ancient astronaut hypothesis" came from a 1963 article by Carl Sagan. The only other person mentioned in that section of his text is Erich von Däniken.[12] However, it is well-known that many others proposed ancient visits by aliens long before Sagan or von Däniken. For example, even Sagan's article mentioned that in 1959 the highly regarded Soviet mathematician and physicist Matest Agrest claimed that the site of Baalbek was a spaceport for ancient astronauts and that the story of Sodom and Gomorrah was created by atomic detonations by extraterrestrials.[13]

Sagan began his 1963 article by noting that the idea of civilizations existing on other planetary solar systems in the galaxy was quite old. He mentioned that there had been a huge resurgence in the idea, presumably from all of the UFO reports from the 1940s to the 1960s and the release of dozens of books and hundreds of articles touting the idea of ancient astronauts. Sagan conducted a statistical analysis on the probability of intelligent and technologically advanced life existing in our galaxy and the odds that Earth had been visited by extraterrestrials. One of his conclusions was that "other civilizations, aeons more advanced than ours, must today be plying the spaces between the stars."[14] Sagan asserted that starting a couple million years ago, Earth would have been visited and monitored "about once every ten thousand years," but when the last ice age waned, contact would have increased dramatically because of the aliens' interest in human development.[15] His final statistical analysis contained this astonishing sentence: "The statistics presented earlier in this paper suggest that the Earth has been visited by various galactic civilizations many times (possibly ~ 10^4) during geological time."[16] That is 10,000 visits! He suggested that the visitors might have been seen as gods and that ancient Babylonian stories might be a genuine clue to their presence.[17]

Paradoxically, while Sagan believed that there were certainly many technologically advanced civilizations in other solar systems throughout the galaxy and that they had likely visited Earth in the past, he did not believe that the modern UFO phenomenon was extraterrestrial in nature.[18] There were a couple major reasons cited for this seemingly contradictory belief. Just one reason was that there were thousands of UFO reports being made in the 1960s and 1970s, and Sagan thought it beyond the realm of possibility that so many extraterrestrial craft were visiting Earth at the same time. In essence, Sagan believed that there was something real in the modern UFO phenomenon but that it was not a manifestation of extraterrestrial craft.[19]

Taking a cue from the amazing mind of Carl Sagan, what we are left with is this: There probably are many advanced civilizations out there in the cosmos, an idea that even skeptics usually accept. Aliens may well have visited here in the remote past, and it's certainly possible that these older and more technologically advanced civilizations still check up on us from time to time using remote drones with artificial intelligence. Of course, Sagan didn't think the modern UFO reports were alien in nature, but he certainly believed that *something* was at work in creating all the UFO sightings. There is *something more* than hoax, trickery, or delusion to some paranormal events as well as to the UFO phenomenon. Even Jung acknowledged that UFOs had an underlying reality and that whatever it was, it appeared to be related to paranormal phenomena.[20] While Jung did call the recent UFO phenomenon a "modern myth," he was cautious to add in his writings that "all myths have a basis in reality."[21] Another of Jung's simplest and deepest statements about UFOs and paranormal phenomena provides an elegant foundation for his basic assertion about UFOs: "Something is seen, one doesn't know what."[22] What this means is that when we are presented with an unknown reality, an unexplained event, or strange phenomena, the automatic human tendency is to project an explanation on that unknown. The interpretation or explanation is *projected* from our mind on whatever is observed. It is as if we have a movie projector in our mind, and when something unusual is seen, the projector flips on so that what we then see are contents of our own mind (our beliefs) being projected onto the unknown object. The unknown object we observe serves as a screen for our own beliefs. The specific explanation we project on it is generated from our prior learning, culture, expectations, language, and certain unconscious forces. For example, skeptics already believe that nothing in the paranormal realm is real, thus they immediately project an interpretation on inexplicable events as being hoaxes, delusions, mental derangement, or misinterpretations. On the other hand, when an unexplained sighting is made by someone who believes in the extraterrestrial hypothesis, that explanation is projected on the event. One conclusion that can be made here is pretty simple. A person's interpretation of unexplained phenomena or inexplicable events is influenced by their preexisting belief system. Our beliefs are psychologically designed and maintained in ways to have us ignore contrary facts while seeking out whatever observations will support the preexisting belief. This psychological process is very powerful and nearly always remains out of our conscious awareness.

SOMETHING IS SEEN, ONE DOESN'T KNOW WHAT

The ancient beliefs of Native American cultures, as well as all ancient cultures, came from their observations and interactions in the world. Imagine how early proto-humans millions of years ago might have explained weather phenomena, the animal kingdom, other elements of the natural world, and deeply important events like death. It's easy for skeptics and academics to explain it all away as superstitious belief systems. But that doesn't explain the underlying motivations for the building of things like the megalithic structures found all over the world. That doesn't explain the mound-building cultures that constructed incredible geometric earthworks as sacred ritual spaces. Nor does it explain all the paranormal events these ancient people recorded in their own way. In essence, they saw and interacted with "something else" that existed alongside the natural world. Their spiritual beliefs and rituals were a response to this "something else." The ancients explained it using their terminology and mindset. That is partly what Jung's statement that "something is seen, one doesn't know what" really means. There is something there. We are not sure what it is, but it is interpreted in accordance with personal and cultural expectations. Ancient cultures have long recorded contact with that "alien" force. The important questions are what is it, and is it still exerting an influence in modern times?

So now we move to more recent and more modern phenomena. But understand that the events we are about to explore aren't all that different from the legends of Native Americans. And we'll return to the ancient world eventually.

10

CONTACT WITH ALIENS

The ancient astronaut hypothesis has been around a long time. It is true that the idea stems from the long-held idea that there are other inhabited planets in our solar system as well as other solar systems full of life. For example, the Italian scholar Giordano Bruno was burned alive in 1600 for openly asserting that life existed on other planets.[1] Bruno was an Italian philosopher and Dominican friar who wrote that the stars were actually "suns" and that these distant suns had planets. His trial began in 1593, and after a six-year imprisonment, the Inquisition found him guilty of heresy. Not long afterward, many others wrote fictional works about life on other planets and the moon, but none of these early philosophers wrote about extraterrestrial beings coming to Earth and influencing human development.

The last portion of the preceding sentence is the key thing to understand. The idea behind the ancient astronaut hypothesis is that *ancient aliens visited Earth and somehow influenced the affairs on Earth.* Ron Story's *Encyclopedia of Extraterrestrial Encounters* relates that the ancient astronaut hypothesis "is a theory of ancient contactees."[2] Of course, we are often told that stories of biblical angels, the gods of ancient Sumer, Egypt, and India, and other similar legends are evidence of ancient aliens. But in those ancient legends and tales, the "visitors" aren't specifically identified as interplanetary aliens. That's a modern interpretation. Many people today *assume* that these angelic beings were astronauts from other inhabited worlds, but the idea of a contactee implies something more. It implies that the being identifies itself as coming from another planet—not from Earth. Most importantly, the ancient astronaut hypothesis implies that these extraterrestrial beings have not only visited Earth but also have influenced its history and events. You have to go back in history quite a ways to find what is *probably* the very first such reported encounter. The real start of the historic contactee movement and the ancient astronaut hypothesis can be traced to a very famous scientist.[3]

THE FIRST CONTACTEE

He was 55 years old when his contacts with alien visitors began. He was an energetic and well-respected scientist and nobleman who had worked for universities and his national government for decades. He traveled alone frequently in his official position and had just begun a leave of absence from his appointed government position. In the past few years, he had become obsessed with dreams about death, the meaning of life, and personal and ethical dilemmas that nagged him. The ethical and moral questionings about how he had led his life swirled in his mind continuously, and they needed some sort of recognition and closure, neither of which were desirable choices for the scientist. He had tried to forget strange events from his past by immersing himself in a quest to understand the natural world. So he wrote books in many areas of science and conducted research in an attempt to keep his mind occupied and his thoughts away from his own life and behavior. The strategy had worked—until now.

In his youth, he had often seen inexplicable lights darting around in the sky, experienced brilliant flashes of light that intruded into his room, and had visions of many kinds. He coped with these experiences by focusing on science. Few people knew about his early experiences with the paranormal. Even fewer people today recognize this aspect of his early life, but it has been well documented and even ignored by some who have studied the man.

At age 55, he was a highly regarded mathematician, a widely read natural scientist, and a sought-after engineer. His many books and projects made him famous throughout all of Europe and elsewhere. He had turned down the position of chairman of mathematics at the most prestigious university in his country, preferring to write books on science and take on appointed governmental tasks. He also disliked giving lectures because of a speech impediment, so a professorship was out of the question. He traveled quietly without fanfare, having contact mainly with close friends and a few ladies whose company he enjoyed. But he was filled with a secret sense of self-loathing and an irresistible impulse to make some sort of moral sense of his life.

He was staying in London when his encounters with aliens began. He was eating alone in a small side room of a local tavern. Suddenly, the room darkened. Then a man inexplicably appeared in front of him, sitting in a corner of the room—staring intently at him. Then the strange man said, "Don't eat too much." It was an inauspicious beginning to this remarkable story.

The unexpected materialization and demeanor of the strange man frightened the scientist so much that he immediately left without saying a word. He ran back to his hotel and was suddenly exhausted. He soon fell asleep and had disturbing dreams. There are numerous written accounts of this night, and in one of these written records, a physician was called to his room by the hotel management after some sort of disturbance occurred. The physician sedated the scientist, and a policeman was assigned to stay with the man through the rest of the night because he was an official representative of his government. Some accounts relate that the man from the tavern appeared in his disturbing dreams, but other accounts are different, and the scientist's own journal is silent on what happened that first night.

According to the scientist's written journal, it was on the *next* night that the "man" from the tavern again physically appeared to him. It happened in his hotel room. The odd man manifested into a physical form, sat in a chair, and stared at the scientist. He was described as an ordinary human without any real distinguishing characteristics, but he was wearing purple robes and basking in glowing light. The man explained that he was going to open the scientist's mind to the spiritual world. Open his mind it did, and his contactee experience began.

For the next 28 years, the scientist was frequently visited by a series of physical beings that claimed that they lived on other planets. The scientist also claimed he was taken to almost every planet in the solar system. Saturn was the outermost planet he claimed to have visited.

The visitors revealed that the moon was inhabited by living beings—as were virtually all of the planets and several other moons in our solar system. The scientist was told, "There are far distant earths, planets inhabited by beings similar to us." The universe, they said, was filled with countless suns and inhabited planets. Many of these beings were called "angels" in the past, but they were not exactly the type of spiritual angels depicted in the Bible.

They were physical humans who had not only played roles in the day-to-day life of humans on Earth, but *they also had helped shape history by visiting Earth from time to time in the ancient past.* In one of his most famous books, he wrote, "The ancients on our earth frequently spoke with them."[4]

And here is where the ancient astronaut hypothesis likely had its birth, with the first person who can be accurately described as a contactee. He was Emanuel Swedenborg (1688–1772), the famous Swedish scientist and mystic. The initial encounter in London occurred in 1743.

Like nearly all of the contactees who emerged into the flying saucer atmosphere of the 1950s, Swedenborg wrote of his interactions with the aliens and the cosmic information they bestowed on him. Thousands of pages were produced and published by him based on his visitations. *Heaven and Its Wonders and Hell* (1890) and *Earths in the Universe* (1758) were just two of his classic books describing his extraterrestrial contacts and the information he was given.

Today, some skeptics and many who follow and study Swedenborg ardently interpret what Swedenborg wrote about his interactions with the beings on other worlds as the result of "spiritual" and "visionary" (hallucinatory) experiences and contend that he was not describing physical beings. But if you read what Swedenborg wrote, it's clear: when his encounters began, he was describing physical beings and physical craft. They were people. People who were identical to humans on Earth.

In *Earths in the Universe,* Swedenborg wrote, "There are earths, inhabited by men, not only in this solar system, but also out of it in the starry heaven, to an immense number."[5] He also wrote, "On such occasions there appear chariots and bright horses of fire, by which they are carried away like Elijah."[6] In *Heaven and Its Wonders and Hell,* he wrote, "I have seen a thousand times that angels are human forms, or men; for I have conversed with them as man with man, sometimes with one alone, sometimes with many in company; nor did I discover in their form any thing different from the form of man; and I have repeatedly wondered that they were such. And lest it should be said that it was a fallacy, or a visionary fancy, I have been permitted to see them in a state of full wakefulness, when I was in the exercise of every bodily sense, and in a state of clear perception."[7] These descriptions are clear and vivid, and they are definitely not describing a typical psychic or visionary contact.

Swedenborg has been portrayed in many different ways, but in his later years, Swedenborg was, as William White called it, in a "chase for the soul."[8] It was a chase for meaning, a search for ultimate truth, and an attempt to understand Christianity and a host of key religious beliefs. Swedenborg himself eventually came to interpret many of his "alien" visitations as "spiritual" in nature. He gradually saw soul energies or entities as existing on all the planets, but he also stated clearly that "people" were also there.

Like many of the modern contactees and the more recent "abductees," Swedenborg felt compelled to write about his experiences and gradually cast them in a spiritual light. Contactees often form a religious or study group around the revelations received from the aliens. Likewise, nearly all of the later contactees combined interplanetary travel with life on other planets, cosmic knowledge, and a benevolence for the human race by the aliens. The "aliens" were, to them, truly "Space Brothers," kindred spirits with an interest in the human soul and its ultimate significance.

However, like the later contactees, we know now that a lot of the information given to Swedenborg by his visiting entities was simply untruthful—trickster-like. In *Earths in the Universe,* he mentioned that humans—like us—lived on the moon, Mars, Venus, and Mercury, and on the moons of Jupiter and Saturn. He even described their clothing. Today, we know rather conclusively that planets such as Mercury, Venus, Mars, and the outer planets likely don't have "people" on them—at least not people like us. But Swedenborg's writings were widely noticed and likely became the inspiration for many others who followed.

OAHSPE, 1882

When I was writing *The Archetype Experience* in the early 1980s, the most curious book I encountered was the *Oahspe.* The *Oahspe* is intimately related to the rise of Ray Palmer's once highly successful magazine *Fate.* When Palmer discovered the *Oahspe,* he found that the American publisher of the book, Wing Anderson, had died. Palmer bought the mailing list of people who had bought copies of the *Oahspe* from Anderson's family (some 40,000 people) and used the list to launch *Fate* with Curtis Fuller.[9] Palmer then started a publishing company, which reissued the *Oahspe.*

The *Oahspe,* containing over 900 pages in a large, oversized volume, was first published in 1882. A New York dentist, John Ballou Newbrough (1828–1891), supposedly wrote the book through "automatic writing" in

1881. To be more accurate, the term *automatic writing* here refers to "automatic typewriting," as Newbrough used the newly invented typewriter to produce the manuscript. (In my early career in psychology, I encountered one individual who had produced a manuscript through automatic typewriting. He was a clinical psychologist who related that images and sentences just appeared in his mind and that his fingers simply typed words as if some other force was in control of them.)

According to the explanation given in the *Oahspe*'s addendum, Newbrough became interested in the spiritualist movement in the mid-1800s, and he held disappointing séances until 1870. One night in 1870, he was awakened by a large number of glowing "angels" who had manifested in his bedroom. Newbrough was told to "purify himself for 10 years by doing charity work and by becoming a vegetarian. When he had completed the task, the angels promised to return."[10] He did as they asked, and when they returned as promised, he was told to sit at a typewriter each day at dawn and they would control his hands. He began on January 1, 1881, and finished on December 15 of that year.

The *Oahspe* was touted as a history of the past 24,000 years and gradually became widely read. It developed a cult following in spiritualist circles. It appears to be a source for story ideas used by several horror and science fiction writers in the 1800s and 1900s. The book is advertised as the "secret history of Earth," and it describes in detail the many extraterrestrial powers that have influenced the development of humanity. The book calls the extraterrestrials "angels" but makes it clear that they are physical beings performing the work of their leaders (called "gods"). It also makes it clear that all angels begin as physical beings: "Who are the angels of heaven? People who lived on earth or other corporeal [physical] worlds."[11]

The *Oahspe* tells of legions of flying ships coming to Earth from other worlds to teach mankind in ancient times. At least a hundred references in the book mention "fire-ships" that travel between planets and star systems—and their many inhabitants. Many descriptions in the book relate that there are "hundreds of millions" of these extraterrestrials and that they travel through "etherea," the vast space between stars and planets: "I send down from etherea ships."[12] "I send my angels with heavenly ships."[13] "The angels shall descend to the earth."[14] "Behold my otevan, my fire-ship, goeth that way on her cruise of ten thousand years."[15] "Provide an arrow ship of great velocity . . ."[16] "Four hundred million miles a day, sped the airvagna through the etherean worlds; like a flash of light shot forth the ship."[17] "The Gods were received by hundreds of millions called the receiving hosts, in fire-ships of great size and brilliancy."[18]

The *Oahspe* reveals that just as humans build physical ships to cross oceans, the angels built physical ships to cross the vast space between planets: "As mortals sail corporeal ships across the corporeal ocean, so sailed the ship of God in the atmospherean ocean."[19] According to the *Oahspe,* it was the fire-ships of the gods that inspired early humans to build ships to cross the seas: "As ye travel from heaven to heaven in this atmospherea, even shall ye inspire mortals to build corporeal ships, and sail across the oceans, that the inhabitants of different divisions of the earth may become known to one another."[20]

The book also gives descriptions of the "fire-ships" that are similar to many modern UFO reports: "A great light, like a sun, was seen descending from the firmament above." The section continues, "The light above us descended fast toward us, like a ship of fire it came nearer and nearer. . . . But the lights from the columns of fire, brilliant in all colors and shades and tints, baffled many of them from seeing plainly."[21]

In a way similar to modern UFOs, the fire-ships sometimes seem to vanish from sight, and the *Oahspe* explains why: "When the ship of the hosts of God came to the city of Ul'oo, mortals saw it high up in the air, and they feared and ran hastily to consult the prophet of the Lord. . . . And God caused the ship to be made unseen, that fear might subside on earth."[22]

In essence, the *Oahspe* presented the entirety of the ancient astronaut hypothesis: "The gods and their legions of angels are flying around the universe in circular, disk-like ships. They are called fire-ships, star-ships, and various other names. There are many inhabited worlds throughout the universe but the fire-ships are the vehicles of gods (the leaders) and angels (physical beings). The *Oahspe* reveals that just as we need ships to cross our oceans that the gods and their angels need ships to cross the atmospherean oceans between planets. The ships sometimes remain invisible because humans would fear them if they were able to see them."[23]

According to the *Oahspe,* "Early in man's development the angels descended from the heavens in their fire-ships to teach man. They first raised man upright and then taught him to dwell together in cities and nations."[24] This seems to be the earliest mention of genetic manipulation of humans by extraterrestrials (raising man upright).

That's all interesting, but the underlying foundation of the *Oahspe*'s emergence was based on a hoax. I'm not asserting that Newbrough hoaxed it, but the crucial event that led Newbrough to become involved in spiritualism was a hoax. That is, there was a trickster element involved, just as a trickster influence was present in Swedenborg's experiences. In Palmer's addendum of the *Oahspe,* added to his company's exact reprint of the original book, it is explained that the sensational claims made by the New York–based Fox sisters in 1848 led Newbrough into the spiritualist realm. The Fox sisters' experience is cited as the beginning of a new form of contact with the spiritual world.[25]

THE FOX SISTERS AND THE START OF AMERICAN SPIRITUALISM

It was in March 1848 that two young girls in Hydesville, New York, 14-year-old Margaretta Fox and her 11-year-old sister Kate, began reporting raps on the walls, furniture, and floor in their bedroom. This garnered a lot of attention and was the start of the heyday of America's spiritualist movement. The girls became a sensation as reporters, celebrities, skeptics, and other interested parties were given demonstrations of the phenomenon. Almost everyone came away from the displays convinced of their genuineness. In the demonstrations, a method was devised to speak to the spirits and have them answer questions through the numbers of knocking sounds. The Fox sisters eventually conducted tours to give "shows" to large audiences. Interest in Swedenborg also began to surge, and a variety of mediums, spiritualists, and early hypnotists began to attract their own followers around the world.

While earlier claims of a hoax had emerged, the Fox sisters' scheme completely collapsed on October 21, 1888, when Margaretta gave an interview with the *New York World* wherein she called it a "horrible deception." She not only gave a complete explanation, she also demonstrated the methods they used to deceive their audiences. Both of the girls were able to crack their knuckles, toes, and other joints rather loudly, and they also cleverly dropped an apple tied to a string on the floor at will to create floor knocking sounds. As in many such cases, one year later, Margaretta recanted her confession.[26]

MODERN CONTACTEES

We'll not discuss the modern contactees in any depth as there are a host of well-researched books on the phenomenon. These contactees are modern people who claim to have had face-to-face contact with extraterrestrials who identify themselves as such. Contactees are sometimes given rides on flying saucers and taken to other planets, just as Swedenborg was given. Ron Story related, "Shortly after the influx of UFO sightings in the late 1940s came a new phase of saucerism. . . . Suddenly, it seemed, the space people who piloted the heretofore unidentified craft were now introducing themselves to a select group of individuals, chosen, or self-appointed, to spread the wisdom of the 'Space Brothers' to all mankind."[27] In Coral and Jim Lorenzen's 1976 book *Encounters and UFO Occupants,* they relate, "We are faced with a growing spiritual hunger . . . it should not surprise us to find certain prophets profiting from it. . . . There seems to be, however, a considerable number of 'contactees' who are not charlatans —who conversely, give accounts of experiences which were, to them very real."[28]

That the contactees should emerge at a time shortly after the atomic bomb had been used and when the Cold War was at its start is not at all surprising. That was noted by Jung. Recall from chapter 3 that Jung thought that the fear generated by nuclear weapons created a desire for redemption from some supernatural source. Jung's essential idea was that something very unusual and unknown was being seen in the skies and that the desire for redemption was "projected" on the unknown phenomenon being observed. The fact that the fear of nuclear catastrophe occurred at the same time UFOs and flying saucers were being seen was a meaningful coincidence. Jung called that type of coincidence *synchronicity.* As I wrote back in 1984, synchronicity is more than just coincidence; it also is a type of enhanced awareness.[29]

Few academics have studied the contactee movement, and it seems that the few who do so simply don't look too deeply into it. Christopher Bader's 1995 article "The UFO Contact Movement from the 1950s to the Present" relates that George Adamski was "the first contactee" and also "the first person to claim extended interaction with aliens."[30] There is no mention of Swedenborg or the many others who preceded Adamski. Adamski claimed to have taken photographs of UFOs in 1947, but it was in 1952 when he first claimed to have met with the aliens from the saucers. But Adamski was surely the star and key personality who ignited the movement.

Perhaps the seminal book on contactees is by Nick Redfern.[31] Redfern discusses many contactees, some of whom seem to have credibility, others not so much. Jung took great interest in Orfeo Angelucci, a contactee who had his experiences with aliens begin in 1952. In Angelucci's book *The Secret of the Saucers,* the aliens explained that the saucers are "non-material, they are controlled in such a way that they can almost instantaneously attract substance to take on any degree of material density necessary."[32] For Angelucci, his aliens were "spiritual" in nature, and his book is filled with symbolic imagery. That's why Jung took so much interest in his account. As to who was truly the first contactee, it was probably Swedenborg, meaning he was the first person we know who claimed visitations by beings from other planets. As to the first modern contactee, it's debatable. Adamski was definitely the star of the act.

The Space Brothers said that they came from the moon, Venus, Mars, Jupiter, Saturn, Neptune, a hidden planet called Clarion, and even from hidden places on the Earth. Other contactees claimed that their visitors were related to Atlantis or Mu. The contactees often said that they had established telepathic communication with their visitors, but nearly all of them first encountered balls of light that appeared in close proximity.[33] Their interaction with the glowing lights is perhaps the key to understanding the genuine part of their claims. Recall that Swedenborg experienced unusual flashes of brilliant light in his childhood, and even John Ballou Newbrough's experience began with the appearance of "angels" bathed in light. So too did many ancient accounts of sky beings begin with flashes of light, as we have seen in previous chapters.

While some readers may disagree, there is strong evidence that humans and advanced civilizations probably do not exist on other planets in our solar system. It's possible that in the very remote past some intelligent life existed on some other planets in our solar system, but certainly not in the time of the contactees. I can't really comment on the possibility that these civilizations are hidden or perhaps underground, because scientifically, you can't prove something does *not* exist. You can say that that there is no evidence for it, but that's about it. The point being made here isn't that all the contactees lied and made up their tales for profit or notoriety. Nor do I believe that Swedenborg and the *Oahspe* were deliberate lies or deceptions. However, all of these tales bear great resemblance to Native American trickster accounts. Recall that tricksters always mislead; that's their function. One has to pass the tests a trickster presents before you can reach a genuine level of understanding.

In his 1980 *Encyclopedia of UFOs,* Story defined the ancient astronaut theory by relating that it "proposes that intelligent humanoid beings from outer space came to Earth in the distant past, created man in their own image, and then went on to develop human civilization."[34] Story asserted that the idea seemed to have its roots in the "Atlantis myth," and he cited twelve individuals who proposed the idea in articles and books prior to Sagan's 1963 article.[35] But as we have seen, it's probably a very, very old idea with obvious relationships to biblical, Vedic, and Babylonian tales.

So, what are we to make of the story told by Swedenborg and similar tales echoed by the much later contactee movement? Were they all lying, making up a tale to sell books or gain publicity? Were they all delusional, pathological liars, or psychotic? Probably not. At least not all of them. There is good reason to believe that Swedenborg related what happened to him as he perceived it to happen and that he interpreted it within his own mental state at that time. But a trickster element is lurking in the background of all of it.

John Keel made many comments in his books about the deceptive nature of the UFO field and the paranormal. In his biography of Keel, Brent Raynes related, "He [Keel] was of the opinion that an unknown cosmic trickster was behind everything and was capable—and determined—to keep us constantly confused and chasing dead ends, so that we would never discover the real truth behind any of the phenomena."[36] In brief, it's likely that some aspects of the contactee movement resulted from trickster interactions, but as we shall see, not all modern "paranormal" accounts are so easily dismissed.

11

THREE MYSTICAL, SPIRITUAL, LIFE-CHANGING EVENTS

The scientific method can be defined rather simply as a systematic process performed to find truth. That is, the scientific process is a method to get to the truth about a specific observation, thing, event, or phenomenon. We won't go into depth on the scientific process, but it relies on observation, forming a hypothesis about the observation, testing the hypothesis through experimentation, and replicating the results through more research. When a particular hypothesis is repeatedly confirmed, it becomes a theory and often gets incorporated into scientific doctrine until someone comes along and disproves it or has a better explanation. The law of parsimony, or Occam's razor, is usually part of the evaluation process. Occam's razor implies that the simplest explanation that accounts for all the observations and results is often the best or the correct solution.

One major problem in evaluating events such as UFOs, abductions, contactee experiences, Native American cosmology/beliefs, and the experiences of people like Swedenborg is that the observations and events can't be replicated. They are spontaneous events, sometimes one of a kind. To a very large degree, that's why science casts a skeptical eye on all of them. The simplest explanations for paranormal events always boil down to a few possibilities: hoaxes, lies, misinterpretations, or mental derangement. I will add that there has been some real laboratory experimentation done that replicates, to some degree, UFO and mystical experiences, and some of that research will be described in chapters 15, 16, and 17. However, this general inability to replicate such experiences in a laboratory is a big, important issue lurking in the background that has to be considered.

Science generally evaluates repeatable phenomena. Most paranormal events simply don't repeat reliably or consistently. They can be random events or sometimes a unique experience that seems inexplicable. Even more importantly, experiences resulting from mental derangement or psychosis can be almost indistinguishable from a genuine mystical experience. Conversely, genuine mystical experiences can be almost indistinguishable from mental derangement or psychosis. It's easy for those who deny the possibility of an "unseen world" intruding on ours to just see it *all* as mental derangement or simply hoaxes.

History is filled with inexplicable events, and a few of these are very impressive. In this chapter, we'll look at just three such cases. What they point to are two primary possibilities. The first possibility is that some visionary experiences created by psychosis, delusions, or hallucinatory experiences are followed by a remarkable series of seemingly impossible coincidences that confirm the "delusions" given in the visions. The second possibility is that there is some other external force that intrudes into our reality—with the results changing history.

JOAN OF ARC

Virtually everyone is familiar with the name Joan of Arc. Most people know the story from movies, which only give the briefest, often inaccurate, and somewhat sensationalized account of the Maid of Orléans, the heroine of France. During Joan's trial in 1431, extensive transcripts were made that revealed considerable details of her visions and actions. These transcripts told of how she first had her visions and how they continued. A fascinating and highly detailed book published in 1936 provided a rather deep view into her experiences by including extensive information from the many others who had interacted with her during her brief time.[1]

Jeanne d'Arc (1412–1431, fig. 11.1) was considered to be a very ordinary, pious peasant girl. At age thirteen, while she was tending sheep, she saw a lumi-

Fig. 11.1. Joan of Arc depicted on horseback in a 1504 manuscript.

nous, bright cloud descend to the ground, and a calm male voice emanated from it. Joan told her mother about the event, but not her father. Her mother was supportive but also decided not to tell her husband. Initially, the voice was gentle and encouraged her to remain pious and kind. Joan was frightened by it, but she returned to the same spot and the light started to appear more frequently. Gradually, the beings behind the light manifested physically. She was told by the voice that Saint Catherine and Saint Margaret would appear to her. Then she was told that she had been chosen to restore the kingdom of France from English rule. She was to wear men's clothing and become the head of the French army, which was then unsuccessfully fighting the English. She found the instructions to be beyond the realm of possibility.[2] It took three years for her to get the courage to do what the voice instructed. In her trial, she related that all of her actions were taken in accordance with the instructions given to her.

In 1428, she began the quest, but was thwarted in her initial effort to visit the dauphin (Charles VII, the heir to the French throne). The voice then told her to visit an uncle for help, whom she saw in 1429. Her uncle provided her with a horse, a sword, and men's clothing. By this time, Joan had become widely known throughout France because her predictions and intentions had spread quickly among a populace desperately looking for hope. It is known that the dauphin and other French royalty were quite aware of the young peasant girl who claimed that God had told her to restore the French crown and fulfill an old prophecy. Joan's notoriety among the people is the most likely reason the dauphin finally agreed to meet her. Joan made many predictions during this time, one of them being that she would be wounded in the first battle. She was also told by the voice that when she finally met the dauphin, she'd have one year to achieve her quest.[3] Both of those predictions turned out to be true.

Joan finally met the dauphin in 1429. In a private meeting with Charles, she asked him to give her armor and supplies and to make her the head of the army. Inexplicably, Charles granted her request, and she soon left for the French city of Orléans, which had been besieged by the English army for five months. It is generally thought that the Dauphin was convinced that Joan was telling the truth, that she had actually come under instructions from God. In just 8 days, Joan and her followers drove the English from Orléans and its surrounding outposts, but she was wounded by an arrow, as she had predicted. She then led the French army in a series of other battles that were quickly won, and Joan's forces managed to push the English armies closer to the coast. The famous sword that Joan found has been depicted in various movies as being recovered in a field; however, it was actually found where it had been hidden in a church. It had lain undisturbed since being deposited there by its owner, the celebrated Frankish military leader and statesman Charles Martel (688–741 CE), who had successfully saved France from Moorish invasion 600 years earlier. The sword was found in 1430 precisely where Joan said it would be.

In March 1430, England and France signed a truce, but the English soon laid siege to the city of Compiégne. Joan hurried to the city but was betrayed and captured by the English in May 1430. She was imprisoned in the French city of Rouen and tried for heresy and cross-dressing as a man. She was burned alive on May 30, 1431. In 1456, another court declared her innocent, and in 1920, she was canonized by the Catholic Church.[4]

It is an intriguing but sad story filled with symbolism and paranormal phenomena. It is not feasible to give the story a full telling here, since it is almost beyond the realm of possibility. Modern skeptical accounts relate that her experiences with the voice were hallucinatory, the result of mental disorders, epilepsy, or hoaxing. However, the visionary experiences detailed in her trial are extremely detailed and highly similar to UFO accounts, the reports of contactees, and the experiences reported by Swedenborg. Joan's visions *were always accompanied by a brilliant light,* which would appear first. She reported that she learned that the male voice she first heard was that of Saint Michael. She also saw Saint Catherine and Saint Margaret. She testified that all three of them appeared to her at once several times. They appeared in the light and they were physically real, and she related that on some occasions, she *physically hugged* them. She also saw the angel Gabriel with hundreds of other angels standing behind him. In brief, she stated that they always appeared in light. She saw them, touched them, and often felt their physical warmth.[5] There is also one report of a witness (Gui de Cailly) who watched Joan speaking to the light. He saw the same vision as Joan (the light and the beings in the light) on the night before Joan first entered Orléans in 1429.[6]

In her summary statements about Joan of Arc, the writer V. Sackville-West asked, "Is the visible world the only world we have to consider? Is it possible for mortal man to get into touch with beings of another world? I believe deeply . . . in some mysterious central originating force . . . in what we conveniently call the supernatural."[7]

There is no doubt that Joan changed the course of history, that many of her predictions came to pass, and that she was not hoaxing. That is, she believed that she had been in contact with supernatural forces. Of course, as stated previously, skeptics usually cite schizophrenia or other mental disorders as the source of her visions. I will mention that I know of no other cases of schizophrenic hallucinations that led to such a remarkable set of coincidences between the content of the hallucinations and the corresponding events that followed. In sum, either something truly remarkable intruded into the world of Joan or her hallucinations produced influential and prophetic coincidences. For skeptics, it won't matter how much evidence is given; their point of view is that it had to be hallucinatory.

EDGAR CAYCE

There are several excellent biographies accurately describing Edgar Cayce's life (1877–1945), so it seems pointless to recount the entire story.[8] But skeptics rarely address some of the more incredible events that are well documented from his life, so a brief description of Cayce's background is necessary, especially in explaining how such topics as ancient extraterrestrial visitations to Earth emerged in his psychic readings. However, it should be noted that this is only a brief chronology that leaves out many important and significant events.

Cayce's Early Life

Cayce was born on a farm 8 miles south of Hopkinsville, Kentucky, in 1877 into a deeply religious Christian family. (I have always found it an interesting coincidence that the Cayce farm was just 16 miles from the site of the famous 1955 Kelly-Hopkinsville "goblins" case, which occurred 8 miles north of Hopkinsville.)

During his early years, Cayce often conversed with dead relatives, groups of "little folk," and fairy-like beings.[9] After he witnessed the death of his grandfather (Cayce was 4 years old when it happened), he was found conversing with his deceased (invisible to others) grandfather several times.[10] As he grew older, Cayce continued to see more and more "little people," entities that played and conversed with him. By the age of twelve, Cayce was teased and was known to get into fights with other school children, apparently because the rumor was that he talked to ghosts.

Around the same age, Cayce was failing in school and struggling with spelling. When his father found that Cayce couldn't spell the word *cabin,* he punished the young man. During the episode, Cayce asked his father if he could take a brief nap, and he subsequently slept on the spelling book. After his nap, his father reported that Cayce knew every word in the book, word-for-word. He could tell his father what words were on each page and their exact place on the page. He related that he could visualize every page.

After this event, Cayce allegedly had the ability to sleep on any book and memorize it, word-for-word, page-for-page. My belief is that Cayce leafed through the books prior to falling asleep on them. There is a phenomenon commonly referred to as a *photographic memory,* also known as *eidetic memory.* It is somewhat controversial in psychology and thought to occur mostly in childhood. It is the ability to look at an object or a page of a book and then be able to visualize and recall the image perfectly. Sleeping immediately following study is known as an aid to memory consolidation, and those people with eidetic memory may well find that sleeping after viewing book pages enhances their memory. Cayce himself stated that he mentally "saw pictures of the pages."[11] I will certainly concede that sleeping on a book (without ever opening it) and having a photographic memory of its contents is virtually unheard of in the scientific literature; that's the reason I believe he may have flipped through the books before sleeping on them.

Cayce became somewhat of a local celebrity at a young age because of this ability to memorize vast amounts of material. When Cayce was fourteen, a former U.S. congressman named Jim McKenzie, who had just been appointed to be the ambassador to Peru by President Cleveland, put his memory to the test by making a $10 wager with Cayce's father. Cayce was to memorize, word-for-word, a 110-page speech that the congressman had presented while in Congress. The manuscript was not allowed to touch the young man's hands, and the speech was read aloud to Cayce on two consecutive nights by his father. After each reading was completed, Cayce fell asleep. The next day, Cayce stood in his schoolhouse in front of McKenzie and recited the entire speech verbatim. Over fifty other people witnessed the event, including teachers, a reporter, and local businessmen. The feat was reported in a newspaper article in the *Kentucky New Era.*[12]

But Cayce's abilities didn't end there. As with Joan of Arc, at the age of thirteen, Cayce experienced a visitation from what is described as an angel. He related that the event took place in his bedroom after spending the day in the woods, reading the Bible. While he was praying, the room filled with a bright light. Cayce felt himself rise, and then he saw a glowing angel in front of him. After a brief exchange, the angel told Cayce to "help the sick, the afflicted." Reportedly, it took him three years to get the courage to tell his mother about the encounter.[13] A year after telling his mother about the visitation, Cayce had another encounter with the angel. It was this visitation that led him to move from the farm to Hopkinsville in 1894.[14]

Cayce Becomes the Sleeping Prophet

In March 1900, Cayce became an apprentice in a photography shop in Hopkinsville, but he suddenly developed paralysis of his vocal cords and lost the ability to speak above a whisper. The local doctors were at a complete loss on how to treat him. This led to his psychic readings.

Early the next year, a traveling hypnotist visited Hopkinsville, and at the urging of many locals attending the event, the hypnotist brought Cayce to the stage. As he was a local celebrity, the audience was interested in what would happen to him. Surprisingly, under hypnosis Cayce was able to speak normally, but after the trance was lifted, his voice went back to a whisper. A different hypnotist, visiting Hopkinsville from New York, then hypnotized Cayce with the same results. Cayce then conferred with a local osteopath and hypnotist named Al Layne. On March 31, 1901, Cayce performed his first psychic reading—on himself—at the suggestion of Layne and another doctor who was present. Under a trance state, Cayce diagnosed his own problem and suggested that the subject (himself) increase circulation to his throat area. His throat grew bright red, he spit out some blood, and when he was awakened, he spoke perfectly.[15] (See a photo of Cayce in fig. 11.2.)

The first "patient" after Cayce was the osteopath Layne himself. Layne had tried everything medical to treat a gastrointestinal problem, to no avail, and he figured since the "sleeping" Cayce could heal himself, maybe he could do the same for him. The hypnotized Cayce diagnosed Layne's problem and recommended a remedy—which worked. Layne was both elated and surprised.[16]

Word spread in the community, and health readings were soon done for other locals. It is estimated that about eighty health readings were done during this very early time. In a newspaper article in 1922, Cayce related that he had helped 8,056 people through readings he gave from 1901 until 1922, but only 400 of these readings were "documented," meaning the entire transcript is retained by the A.R.E. (the Association for Research and Enlightenment, the official Cayce organization). Unfortunately, most of the transcripts of these early readings were given to the individual requesting them and they were never returned.[17] From 1922 until his death in 1945, he gave about 14,000 readings, all of which were fully documented. Today, 14,306 readings are available for view at the A.R.E Library in Virginia Beach and are online in a searchable database for members of the organization. The typewritten volumes of the readings contain over 150,000 pages. It should be noted that when he awakened after a reading, Cayce was totally unaware of what had transpired. That is one major reason the readings were written down.

Not long after the first readings, it was found that the patient did not have to be physically present for a health reading. When Cayce went into his self-induced hypnotic trance, he was able to telepathically zero in on the individual, and the words "Yes, we have the body here" were often the first ones uttered by the sleeping Cayce. He would scan the body, note various ailments and their causes, and then usually recommend actions. Then he would usually say, "Ready for questions," and answer them. When he was through with the reading, he usually stated, "We are through for the present." Cayce has sometimes been referred to as a "psychic diagnostician."

In 1903, Cayce married Gertrude Evans, and they moved to Bowling Green, Kentucky. In 1906, many local Bowling Green doctors began studying Cayce's ability, but several disastrous fires left Cayce in financial ruin. He remained in Bowling Green until 1909, when he had paid off all of his debts, and the Cayces moved back to Hopkinsville and then to Alabama. However, while in Hopkinsville, Dr. Wesley Ketchum visited Cayce and witnessed several readings. Ketchum and various other physicians were deeply impressed and

Fig. 11.2. Edgar Cayce in 1906, just 5 years after his first psychic reading.

at a complete loss as to how Cayce was able to diagnose patients so accurately and how his recommended remedies usually worked.

After evaluating Cayce's health readings, in 1910, Ketchum presented a paper on Cayce at a medical conference held at Cal Tech in Pasadena, California. Ketchum then allowed another physician to present the paper at a medical conference at Harvard to over 500 physicians. All of this was unknown to Cayce at the time.[18] When it was presented at Harvard, the paper caught the attention of the press, which initiated inquiries in Hopkinsville and other places where Cayce had lived. Reporters interviewed several physicians and people who had readings from Cayce. On October 9, 1910, the *New York Times* began publishing a series of articles on him. Soon other newspapers around the country published articles about him, and he was inundated with requests for health readings. The newspapers dubbed him the Sleeping Prophet, a man who became a doctor when sleeping, but he was also described as illiterate. That, of course, wasn't true, and it disturbed him when he first read the articles. His fame came suddenly and unexpectedly, as did the title of the Sleeping Prophet. But his fame led to huge amounts of mail requesting readings, and he continued to give readings as part of various agreements he made with others.

Past Life Readings Emerge

The year 1923 was the start of other types of readings—the readings that have received the most media attention. A wealthy Dayton, Ohio, businessman, Arthur Lammers, brought the Cayce family to Dayton and began a series of readings on topics Lammers had an interest in, and it was the first time anyone asked Cayce many questions outside the health area. Reincarnation emerged in an October 11, 1923, reading when Cayce was describing the life of the person requesting the reading: "Third appearance on this plane. He was once a monk."[19] This began what became known as "life readings," the story of an individual's influences from past lives.

The Cayce family was initially shocked and dismayed at the mention of reincarnation. They were a deeply religious Christian family, and Cayce was a popular and sought-after Sunday school teacher everywhere he lived. But the Cayce family knew that many people had been helped by the health readings, and they made a decision. They would continue with the psychic readings unless anyone was hurt. That never occurred. Between 1925 and 1945, about

2,500 life readings were conducted. In addition, specific readings were held so that the "source" of Cayce's information could address topics such as Atlantis,* creation, spirituality, and similar things. The life readings mentioned an astonishingly wide range of topics, which emerged as events in the past lives of individuals were described.

The source of the information Cayce was able to access during his trance states explained itself in many readings by relating that all events, thoughts, and actions are recorded in the "skein between space and time," which Cayce often referred to as the Akashic Record.[20] A way to visualize this is that all actions create vibrations, and these vibrations remain fixed in space like the grooves on a vinyl record. A search of the database of the Cayce readings reveals that nearly 1,500 Cayce readings used the term *vibration*. Many of these revealed that health was often related to vibrational forces. For example, in a 1943 reading, Cayce recommended the use of high vibrational lights. In the reading, he related, "Electricity or vibration is that same energy, same power, ye call God. Not that God is an electric light or an electric machine, but that vibration that is creative is of that same energy as life itself."[21]

From 1923 until Cayce's death in 1945, readings were held that fell into six general areas: (1) health readings, (2) personal life readings, (3) spirituality, philosophy, and religion, (4) ancient history, Earth changes, and prophecy, (5) business-related readings, and (6) readings that focused on specific mysteries. An example of the last type is represented in Cayce's readings for George Putnam regarding the disappearance of Amelia Earhart in 1937.

In recent years, the Cayce organization has released the names of some of the famous people who had readings from Cayce, corresponded with him, or met with him privately. Many of these can be found in Sidney Kirkpatrick's two books.[22] Notable people include President Woodrow Wilson (during his last years as president), Thomas Edison (in one instance, their discussion regarded a machine to record voices of the dead), Irving Berlin and George Gershwin, Nelson Rockefeller, George Meaney, Gloria Swanson, Ernest Hemingway's

---

*Cayce made his first mention of Atlantis during the 1923 Dayton reading series with Lammers. This was a horoscope, or life reading, essentially giving the details of a soul's influences and past lives: "In the one [life] before this we find in that fair country of Alta, or Poseidia proper, when this entity was in that force that brought the highest civilization and knowledge that has been known to the earth's plane" (Edgar Cayce reading 288-1). Probably the most media attention in modern times has been given to Cayce's readings mentioning Atlantis.

mother, David Sarnoff (founder of NBC), the founder of Goodyear Tires, the major film makers of Universal Studios and Paramount Pictures, and various others. Cayce was mentioned by many of these people as being helpful in several ways. For example, the inventor of FM radio, Mitchell Hastings, credited Cayce as helping him develop his radio.

As related at the beginning of this section, only the briefest background of Cayce has been given here. However, it is probably appropriate to summarize this information by repeating that Cayce's readings on health formed the foundation for the holistic health movement and that Cayce is widely acknowledged as its father.[23] In addition, Cayce's readings about the ancient world have proven to be an incredible inspiration for many researchers and writers. Skeptics will believe and assert the type of things about Cayce that define them as skeptics, but undeniably, Edgar Cayce stands as the greatest psychic who ever lived in America.

Cayce on Life in the Universe and Elsewhere

One important thing that should be stressed about Cayce's statements regarding life in the universe is that he made it clear in many readings that human life is composed of souls that pushed themselves into physical matter. These souls, composed of vibrational energy created at the beginning of time, had a mission. They essentially moved from planet to planet within star systems (solar systems) on what Cayce called *sojourns*. The purpose of the sojourns is to allow the individual soul to experience various things and develop and evolve a consciousness that would allow it to eventually rejoin with its creator. Souls were given free will by the creator, and when Cayce was asked why God would create souls and give them free will, he related that it was "God's desire for companionship and expression."[24] Another reading explained, "All souls were created in the beginning, and are finding their way back to whence they came."[25] It is as if the creation of souls was a consequence of creation.

The sojourns of souls to planets and stars were not done in physical bodies, but instead they were spiritual journeys during which the energy of a particular soul would spend time at various places where it would be immersed in "influences" emanating from the planet. According to Cayce, in our solar system, physical manifestation of souls in human form only took place on Earth. This is one aspect of Cayce that is unlike all the others who asserted that life existed on the moon, Venus, Mars, and the other planets of the solar system. However, it has a remarkable similarity to the Native American death journey ideas.

Several Cayce readings spoke of life elsewhere in the universe and the fact that other planetary systems not only existed but were also inhabited. A 1934 reading related, "As in the earth we find the elements are peopled, as the earth has its own moon or satellites enjoined in its environ, so is it with the other planets. The earth with its three-fourths water, with its elements, is peopled; yes. So are the various activities in other solar systems."[26] Several other readings mentioned other worlds in the universe: "For the earth is only an atom in the universe of worlds,"[27] and "There are "worlds without end."[28]

One of the most significant differences between Cayce's statements about life in the universe and the assertions made by Spiritualists, Swedenborg, the contactees, and some who touted the ancient astronaut hypothesis relates to life on the planets in our solar system. It was universally claimed by all of these "others" that Venus, Mars, the moon, and several other planets in the solar system were inhabited by humans. Swedenborg, Helena Blavatsky (the founder of Theosophy), the contactees, and many 1800s science-fiction writers all asserted that people similar to humans existed on these other planets. Cayce gave a completely different answer. He was specifically asked about this in two readings, but unfortunately no one ever asked him any follow-up questions.

In 1923, Cayce was giving one of the Dayton, Ohio, readings, which collectively covered a vast range of topics. During the reading, he was unexpectedly asked, "Are any of the planets, other than the earth, inhabited by human beings or animal life of any kind?" Without any hesitation, he answered, "No."[29] Oddly, and frustratingly I'll add, Cayce was not asked a follow-up question.

Some 13 years later, a life reading was held in Virginia Beach when the same essential question was posed. He was asked, "Upon what planets other than the earth does human life exist?" Cayce's reply was, "None as human life in the earth."[30] But once again, not a relevant follow-up question was asked.

In his 2007 book *Edgar Cayce and the Cosmos,* astronomer James Mullaney makes it clear that the Cayce readings that relate that no "human or animal life" exists on any other planets refer specifically to planets in our solar system.[31] Cayce himself made it very plain that life existed elsewhere in the universe and that there were "worlds without end" and other "people of the universe."

With our current exploration of Mars and the moons of other planets, it will be quite interesting to see if Cayce's statements prove correct. Mars, perhaps, may have once been inhabited by humans or other intelligent beings, but according to Cayce it isn't now, and that does appear to be the case. But it is becoming increasingly likely that the explorations of Mars and the moons of Jupiter will reveal some form of life (most likely microbial) and perhaps evidence of intelligent life that existed there in the remote past. In any case, Cayce stands alone in the crowd of people who asserted that "people" exist on our other solar system planets. He is the only one who stated strongly that neither human nor animal life is present in the solar system—except on Earth.

Cayce and Ancient Astronauts

As related earlier, the idea of ancient astronauts visiting Earth and influencing its development is far from modern. It is a theme that runs deep in many other psychics and spiritualistic belief systems, but it wasn't a topic of much interest in the Cayce readings. There are only two very obvious references to ancient astronaut visitations in the Cayce readings, but enough information was given in the readings to know the time frame and the basic location of both.

In a 1938 life reading, Cayce was describing the past lives of an inquirer when he stated, "Before this we find the entity was in the land now known as the Mexican and Yucatan land . . . and there were the beginnings of the unfoldments of the understanding that there were other portions of the same land, or those that were visiting from other worlds or planets."[32] The time frame of this reading indicated that the visitation took place around the time of Christ.

The second reading detailing visitations from other worlds is slightly less obvious, and it could be interpreted in at least two different ways. In 1938, Cayce was giving a life reading, and after going through astrological influences on the individual, he went through the person's past lives. When he reached the person's earliest lifetime, this is what emerged: "Before that we find the entity was in the Atlantean land. There we find the entity was very close to those in authority; being that one who was the keeper of the portals as well as the messages that were received from the visitation of those from the outer spheres, in the latter part of the entity's experience there."[33]

In this 1938 reading, the man who received the messages from these visitations was told of a coming destruction of Atlantis and the need to make a record of their history. This individual then became involved in the creation of a "Hall of Records" in three locations: in Egypt (under the Sphinx), in the Yucatan (probably at Piedras Negras, Guatemala), and in a now-sunken temple near the island of Bimini in the Bahamas.[34]

Cayce's use of the terms *portals* and *messages* might imply that the information about the coming destruction of Atlantis came from some sort of tele-pathic or electronic "portal." In fact, Cayce's story of Atlantis details a crystal that was used by the Atlantean priests and priestesses for telepathic contact with other realms. The crystal was called the *Tuoai Stone*. However, in the same reading, Cayce used the phrase "visitation . . . from the outer spheres." That implies actual physical visits.

Like Joan of Arc, Cayce had a visitation from an angel at age thirteen that changed history. While skeptics deny anything paranormal about Cayce and deride the accuracy of his readings, the truth is that something rather profound lies at the core of Cayce's story. It is clear evidence of the existence of a para-normal world. It is another large piece to the puzzle of how our ideas about the gods formed and how the forces underlying paranormal manifestations operate.

WHAT IS EXTRAORDINARY EVIDENCE?

Carl Sagan is credited with the phrase, "Extraordinary claims require extraor-dinary evidence." It is a variation of the French scholar Pierre-Simon Laplace's famous line, "The weight of evidence for an extraordinary claim must be propor-tioned to its strangeness."[35] We often hear that idea bantered around as if it is true, but the reality is that for most claims in ufology, Native American mythology, and the cases of individuals such as Joan of Arc and Cayce, there is no amount of evidence that is acceptable to skeptics. In truth, it is probably accurate to simply state that claims of any type simply require *proof*. By requiring "extraordinary evi-dence" as the bar of acceptance, it implies that no amount of evidence will ever be acceptable. There is, however, one other event we'll discuss here that leads us to the inescapable conclusion that something paranormal is out there—something that manifests, is seen by thousands of people, and is inexplicable.

APPARITIONS IN ZEITOUN, EGYPT

Of all the so-called Marian apparitions, the apparitions at the Church of Saint Mary in Zeitoun, Egypt (see plate 3), from 1968 to 1970 stand out as the most spectacular case and also the one with the most documented evidence. Ironically, it also may be one of the least known. The idea that it has the most documented evidence comes from the testimony recorded by countless thousands of witnesses, hundreds of actual photographs of the apparitions, and even some scientific study.

Zeitoun is a small suburb in northern Cairo, and legends associated with this particular Coptic church relate that it was a specific location visited by Mary and Joseph during their trip into Egypt. According to church records, the church was built in 1924 after "the Virgin Mary appeared to the late Khalil Pasha Ibrahim [and] requested him to build a church after Her name in this place."[36] It is also stated in the historical record that she promised to reappear at the church some 50 years in the future.

The events at Zeitoun took place at a time of heightened tension between Israel and several Arab countries including Egypt, thus the event was only scantly reported outside of Egypt. It began less than a year after the Six-Day War between Israel and the combined forces of Egypt, Jordan, and Syria. By the time a cease-fire treaty was made, Israel had taken the Gaza Strip, the Golan Heights, the Sinai, and the West Bank of the Jordan River, including parts of Jerusalem. In the years that followed, many Arabs were under Israeli rule, and conflicts raged near the Sinai. The tensions and the uncertainty in the region have been cited by many as the primary cause of the apparitions in Zeitoun.

No one knows for certain how many people saw and photographed the apparitions, but it is estimated to be in the hundreds of thousands to several million. It began on April 2, 1968. That night, two Moslem mechanics were working in a garage across the street. One of them spotted a woman dressed in white, standing on the large dome located at the center of the church's rooftop. They initially thought that a nun was about to commit suicide, and one of the witnesses went into the church to get the priest while the other left to get an ambulance. By the time they returned, the figure was gone. The priest was mystified but came to think that they might have seen some sort of apparition.[37] Word of the apparitions spread quickly, and people started watching the church every night from that time on. They were not disappointed, and immediately it was believed that the Virgin Mary was appearing. On May 5, 1968, the *Egyptian Gazette* ran a front-page headline: "Virgin Mary Appeared at Zeitoun." The *New York Times* reported on the apparitions that same day, relating that the apparitions "had been witnessed by 'thousands of Egyptians and foreigners.'" According to the *Egyptian Gazette* of April 11, 1969, on the night of April 2, 1969, over a quarter million people assembled outside the church to mark the first anniversary of the apparitions.

Starting on April 3, 1968, thousands of people began attending the nightly watches, and the apparitions continued until mid-1970, when the appearances became infrequent. Until late 1969, the apparitions were viewed almost every night. The alarmed Egyptian government made several official reports on the phenomenon, as did the Coptic Christian Church. The appearances always started with brilliant flashes of light appearing on the church's domes, and the lights were often so bright that the witnesses were unable to distinguish details or features of the apparitions. The blinding flashes typically lasted for about 15 minutes until more solid forms materialized near the central dome. Two distinct figures were nearly always seen when the apparitions materialized inside the light. The first apparition was a veiled female draped with a flowing white robe. She was often seen holding what appeared to be an infant, and a starry crown floated above her head. At times, she seemed to offer an olive branch to the witnesses. Occasionally, she appeared in a solid, easily recognizable form and moved around the rooftop. The second apparition consisted of what were interpreted as luminescent, glowing dove-like forms circling overhead. The doves typically appeared after a shower of sparkling lights rained down over the crowd, and they were usually present the entire time of the joint apparition. On June 8, 1968, the apparition was viewed continually from 9 p.m. until 4:30 a.m.[38] There are hundreds of black-and-white photos made of the apparitions, with several photos deliberately placed into the public domain (see figs. 11.3–11.7). Many photos show the doves, the figure of the woman, and amorphous blobs of light around the church domes.

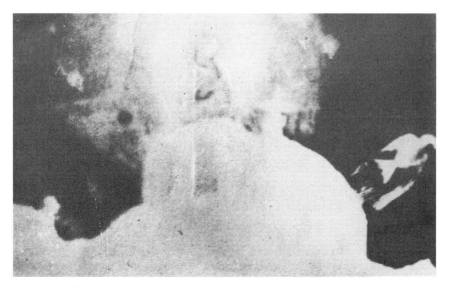

Fig. 11.3. Zeitoun photo showing the central dome with what appears to be
a seated figure holding an infant with a crown above the head.
The large form on the right-hand side is one of the doves (from Pilichis 1975).

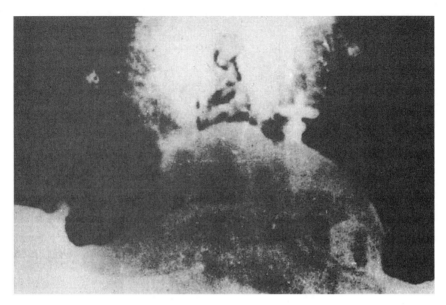

Fig. 11.4. Different Zeitoun photo of the central dome with what appears to be a seated figure holding an infant with a crown above the head. Dove forms are manifesting on both sides of the apparition (from Pilichis 1975).

Fig 11.5. One of the best photos of the Zeitoun apparition, showing the figure standing near the central dome of the church. Note the illumination on the heads of the witnesses at the bottom of the photo (from Pilichis 1975).

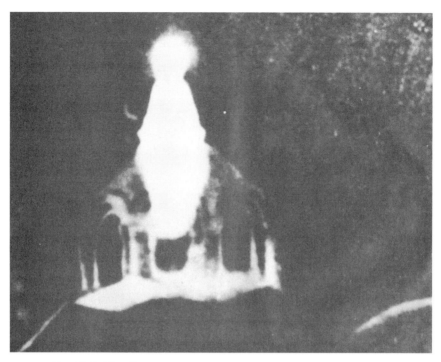

Fig. 11.6. The Zeitoun apparition sometimes materialized from
a blob of amorphous light around the central dome
(from Pilichis 1975).

Fig. 11.7. When the apparition at Zeitoun made its initial appearance,
it often formed from an amorphous plasma-like discharge and into the air
before taking the shape of a person (from Gayed 1985).

In 1996, my wife and I visited the church, and we were able to obtain copies of the original Egyptian newspaper accounts as well as interview several of the witnesses, including a couple who were there at the very beginning. The witnesses had all become devout believers in the phenomenon and were clearly very sincere. All of them were more than willing to share their stories. A newspaper account from April 11, 1969, reported that the pope of Alexandria, Kyrillos VI, commissioned a committee to evaluate the events starting the moment they began. The committee members themselves witnessed the events, relating, "It looked like an illuminated, dazzling white cloud, 100 cms by 60 cms in size. It formed the sad shape of the virgin after the crucifixion of Christ. The apparition was preceded by a shining, quick moving white cloud forming the shape of a dove. On one occasion I saw the vision in a full-size human form surrounded by a glorious halo of shining light."[39]

Bishop Athanasius, one of the committee members, stated, "The crowd was tremendous. It was too difficult to move among the people. But I tried and worked my way to the front of the figure. There she was, five or six meters above the dome, high in the sky, full figure, like a phosphorous statue, but not so stiff as a statue. There was movement of the body and the clothing. It was very difficult for me to stand all the time before the figure, as human waves pushed me in from all sides. One would estimate the crowd at 100,000. In an hour or so I think I stood before the figure eight or nine times. . . . It never disappeared. Our Lady looked to the north; she waved her hand; she blessed the people. . . . Her garments swayed in the wind."[40]

Another witness was Wadie T. Shunbo, a Protestant and a Mobil Oil employee. He related, "About 9:50 we saw lightning appear over the church. . . . Within seconds it formed into the shape of the Virgin. . . . I could distinguish only a difference in color between the skin in the face and the hands in the veil. It was evident when St. Mary walked back and forth. When she disappeared from our side of the church, the people from the other side shouted they were seeing her. Then she returned to our side for five minutes."[41]

Science on Zeitoun

In 1989, the late Canadian neuropsychologist Michael Persinger and the geologist John Derr analyzed the Zeitoun apparitions from the idea that they may have resulted from plasmas or piezoelectric discharges emanating from the church domes. They statistically calculated the relationship between the dates of the appearances and regional seismic disturbances (earthquakes) for a time period of just over a year during which most of the sightings were reported. They found that the resulting correlation was able to correctly predict 80 percent of the actual nightly appearances as well as 92 percent of the nights when there were no reported sightings. However, they found that the earthquake activity centered some 400 kilometers away, leading them to conclude that "some fundamental variable has not been accommodated."[42] Persinger and Derr speculated that the church's rooftop domes had become the focal point of plasmas discharging from the Earth as a result of underground tectonic strain located some 400 kilometers away. As for the impression that the emerging forms of the apparition took on the shape of a female, they asserted that individuals' underlying beliefs, hopes, and imaginations did that through psychological processes.

A recent psychological analysis of the Zeitoun phenomenon relied heavily on Jung's speculations in his book *Flying Saucers*.[43] According to the underlying idea, Egypt in 1968 was a place of great turmoil, and the populace was looking for an outside intervention and salvation. In brief, the event supposedly occurred because the male-dominated culture in Egypt was being counterbalanced by the feminine side, appearing symbolically in spectacular form for all to see. This idea was somewhat echoing a 1973 study that related, "The Apparition of Zeitoun expresses the yearning for salvation from suffering, the hope of a millennial dream. . . . And it seems to me that the appearance of the Virgin symbolizes the disillusionment with secular political explanations and a turning toward the religious—to a deeper level of existence in terms of which it all makes sense."[44]

Despite the idea that the populace witnessing the event was motivated by turmoil and was seeking salvation from unbearable conditions, we are left with this: The apparitional forms were often seen as solid and distinguishable objects. They moved, were seen to sway in the wind; they interacted with the witnesses and were documented by hundreds of photographs.

SUMMARY

How can we link together three such seemingly different tales? How do we connect Joan of Arc, Cayce, and the Zeitoun apparitions? First, all of them began with brilliant flashes of light. Within the lights, solid forms took shape, forms that were recognizable to the witness or witnesses. All three events had a rather profound effect on history and individuals' lives—extending far beyond the lives of the people directly involved. Both Cayce and Joan of Arc attest to some otherworldly force intruding into our reality. Zeitoun also shows us that there is clearly something else that exists. Whatever it is, it does, indeed, intrude into our reality and interact with us in profound ways. And it is clearly the same force that ancient Native Americans spoke of and communed with. It may also be the same force that interacted with some of the contactees, individuals like Swedenborg, and perhaps even with the biblical prophets and ancient Babylonians. With respect to the skeptical phrase, "Extraordinary claims require extraordinary evidence," it should be clear that all three of the "events" cited in this chapter are extraordinary. All three certainly have evidence. But even the "proof" of the Zeitoun apparitions is insufficient for skeptics. Zeitoun had hundreds of thousands—to millions—of witnesses, hundreds to thousands of photographs, and investigations by both the government and officials of the church have confirmed the event. That's extraordinary evidence. But it all comes from Egypt. So it is easy for skeptics to ignore or discount it. Whatever force or phenomenon is behind such events, it is clearly something *paranormal,* something beyond the reach of current scientific understanding. What is the origin of this force, what is its nature, and what is its purpose or intention? As we continue on this quest, we now move to more recent events. Events that also have millions of witnesses.

12

SCIENTISTS LOOK
AT THE
UFO PHENOMENON

A 2019 poll revealed that more than half of Americans believe that life exists elsewhere in the universe and that nearly 30 percent believe that aliens are currently visiting Earth.[1] A 2018 poll by Chapman University tells us that nearly 57 percent of Americans believe that advanced, ancient civilizations like Atlantis once existed and more than a quarter of Americans believe in telekinesis.[2] Perhaps more importantly, a 2019 Gallup Poll found that 16 percent of American adults admit that they have personally seen a UFO.[3] Today, there are about 209 million adults in America, and 16 percent of them would represent an astonishing 33 million individuals who claim to have had a UFO sighting. As is commonly known in ufology, somewhere around 95 percent of UFO sightings are something misidentified: weather phenomena, experimental aircraft, perceptual errors, and a number of other possibilities, including hoaxes.[4] But excluding that 95 percent from the total still leaves us with more than 1.6 million unexplained reports. And that's just in America. Polling data from the United Kingdom and Germany show similar findings among their populations.[5] As we begin to explore modern phenomena, it might be useful to first examine the psychological state of people who claim contact and interaction with alien beings.

ARE ABDUCTEES AND CONTACTEES ABNORMAL?

Skeptics have often asserted that many people who reported close contacts with UFOs had mental disorders, were temporarily impaired, or were hoaxing. However, in the early 1990s, several psychiatrists and psychologists began studying the phenomenon. One of the first studies related, "Biographical analyses of 152 subjects who reported temporary abductions [and] persistent contacts with UFO occupants show that these subjects are remarkably devoid of a history of mental illness."[6] The authors cited "fantasy proneness" as a possible, alternative explanation to the absence of mental illness. The tests for fantasy proneness include *having a belief in psychic or paranormal phenomena*. However, experiencing a UFO contact leads many people to believe in the paranormal. In short, fantasy proneness may well be the *result* of paranormal experiences rather than being the *cause* of them.

In July 1990, ufologist Brent Raynes conducted a survey of forty-six people who reported UFO contacts, finding that the vast majority of his sample had a host of other paranormal experiences.[7] Included were psychic experiences, telepathy, multiple UFO experiences, out-of-body experiences, and precognition. The rates of mental illness and other disorders found in his sample were in the normal range. Raynes, who has been active in the UFO field since the late 1960s, has concluded that the entire phenomenon is intimately linked to psychic and paranormal phenomena.[8] In an encyclopedia commentary on psychiatrist John Mack's well-known research into abductees, skeptic Joe Nickell concluded that fantasy proneness is clearly linked to the phenomenon, implying that this personality characteristic likely *causes* people to have imaginary experiences.[9] However, as mentioned above, fantasy proneness may well be the *result* of experiencing paranormal phenomena rather than their cause. Such experiences are proof to that person that psychic and paranormal phenomena do, indeed, exist. The vast majority of fantasy proneness assessments done on abductees and people who reported contact experiences ask if they believe in such phenomena *after* they report paranormal experiences.

More recently, the Edgar Mitchell Foundation for Research into Extraterrestrial and Extraordinary Experiences (FREE) published the results of an impressive study that was begun in 2013.[10] In their Experiencer Research Study, FREE performed an extensive evaluation of 3,256 individuals who had reported contact experiences. A contact experience involves close contact with a UFO and/or interaction with the occupants of the UFO. The average age of the subjects was 49.5 years, with 57 percent of the subjects being female and 71 percent White. Most of the subjects (70 percent) saw themselves as being *contacted* rather than being *abducted*. The vast majority of the subjects related that the "objects" they saw, called unidentified aerial phenomena (UAPs) in the report, appeared to be under intelligent control. Half of the subjects interacted with a "being" from the objects or, in some cases, with multiple beings. With respect to the UAP objects, nearly all were described as brilliant lights or large, glowing, translucent orbs. Perhaps most interesting was the typical description of the beings associated with the contacts. More than half of the subjects described the entities as "energy beings" with human characteristics, and nearly all of the contacts involved some type of communication between the beings and the humans. Significantly, almost all of the individuals in the study reported that after their experience, they had a greatly heightened interest in spirituality. In its conclusion, the FREE report related that the UAP experience is primarily a "paranormal" phenomenon with both physical and psychic aspects.[11] Interestingly, all of these findings match Nick Redfern's conclusions about the contactees from the 1950s and 1960s. Redfern related, "A common factor among many of the Contactee encounters is that they involved direct interaction with unidentified aerial balls of light . . . balls of light that seemed to exhibit a degree of intelligence, and that then transformed into either gleaming flying saucers, or benevolent extraterrestrials."[12]

It is generally accepted in ufology that most UFO reports are of unknown lights in the sky. As the brightly lit, often translucent balls of light get closer, they often transform into different shapes and the witnesses become mentally changed. There have been several field studies of this phenomenon made by scientific teams. These studies are usually ignored or dismissed as irrelevant by many in the UFO field because they don't fit their idea of what a UFO should be. But the core of the UFO phenomenon, as well as that of the beings associated with the phenomenon, is likely revealed within this research.

PROJECT IDENTIFICATION AND THE MISSOURI UFOS

In 1973, a seven-year UFO field study, dubbed Project Identification, began at Southeast Missouri State University (SEMO) in Cape Girardeau, Missouri.[13] The study traced its inception to scattered reports that emerged in 1967 of strange lights and disc-shaped objects hovering and moving over the Mississippi River in southeastern Missouri. The area where the most reports were made ran from New Madrid, Missouri, extending 70 miles north to Cape Girardeau and some 75 miles or so to the west to the Piedmont area of Missouri. Local and state newspapers published numerous articles about the 1967 events, but the national media and UFO investigators initially took little notice. By early 1973, UFO activity in the western part of this area had increased to such an extent that virtually all the state's newspapers and TV stations were issuing stories every day. This flood of reports caught the attention of several UFO researchers.

In the Piedmont region, literally hundreds of people were reporting odd, multicolored lights darting around in the sky. The lights were popping on and off, changing colors and shape, and instantly changing directions. Many witnesses also reported that, when closely viewed, the lights looked like saucer-shaped craft.

In 1973, a team of researchers from the International UFO Bureau in Oklahoma City went to the Piedmont region and interviewed 200 witnesses over 11 days. It was eventually reported that at least 500 different people had witnessed the UFOs in the Piedmont area alone. Hayden Hewes, the author of several UFO books, was the lead investigator. Hewes had some interactions with the university officials who were also organizing their field study at that time. He published a two-part article in 1976 in the now defunct magazine *TRUE Flying Saucers and UFOs Quarterly.*[14]

The most common reports described small balls of glowing and pulsating lights that moved over towns, farms, roads, police stations, and even TV and radio stations. The lights were of multiple colors: white, orange, green, and red being the most common. The lights often changed colors as they were viewed. Transmitter towers were knocked off-line by many of these events, including at least one police radio tower. Numerous reports of scrambled reception of radio and television signals were made by the population. Several newspaper reporters witnessed and photographed some of the events leading to a brief visit in March 1973 by the famed ufologist and former head of the U.S. Air Force's Project Blue Book, J. Allen Hynek, who visited the area at the behest of a Missouri state representative and the local police chief. Hynek saw nothing in the sky in his brief one-day stay, but he interviewed a couple of "excited people," leading him to conclude that the "power of suggestion" was at work and that the cases were "uninteresting stuff."[15] Hynek inspected a few photographs taken by witnesses and immediately dismissed one as a lens flare. Then he left. His disinterest and dismissal of the ongoing flap was a curious twist to the affair. In brief, Hynek left almost as soon as he arrived—just before the most impressive reports and photos were made. Hynek never investigated the oddest reports, he did not interview the various policemen who made reports, and he never went to the area where the current activity was taking place. Hynek did mention that one report, made by Coach Reggie Bone and five players on his high school basketball team, was inexplicable.[16]

The Coach Bone Reports

According to Hayden Hewes's *TRUE* articles and the book *Project Identification* by Harley Rutledge, the chair of SEMO's Department of Physics, in 1973, Reggie Bone was touted as "the best-known and most popular person in the area."[17] He was the highly successful basketball coach of Clearwater High School and was idolized in the entire region. On February 21, 1973, Bone and some members of his team were returning to Clearwater after playing in a tournament in Dexter. It was a dark night with the moon below the horizon. As they drove by flat, agricultural fields, they spotted a light hovering above the tree line across a field. The light was rotating rapidly and alternating colors from red to green to amber and to white, after which it repeated the same cycle. They also saw an intense light shining down on the ground from the hovering and rotating form. Bone recalled that they first suspected the object was some sort of aircraft but concluded that they didn't know what it was.

About a half hour later, the group again encountered what they thought to be the same object. The light was now floating over an open field next to the road. Bone stopped the vehicle, and everyone got out of the car. The object was less than 200 yards (183 meters) away, hovering silently about 50 feet (15 meters) above the field. It was rotating and showing the same varying light pattern as they had previously observed. After watching the object for 10 minutes, the group saw it rise, and in complete silence, it quickly flew over a nearby tree line and out of sight. Bone asked the players to keep the event secret, but the media was tipped off the next day. Bone reluctantly verified the details after reporters contacted him. All of the players and Bone gave essentially the same descriptions and details about the event. (As a footnote, Bone tragically died from a rare disease in 1977 at the age of forty-eight, but his story never wavered.)

Other witnesses to UFO events during this massive flap included police officers, engineers, college students, and reporters.[18] Piedmont Police Chief Gene Bearden stated that in early 1973, his office had received "over 500 reports during the first month of sightings." Bearden stated, "There's no doubt there's something up there, we just don't know what it is." On March 22, a student took eight infrared photos of the objects while accompanied by radio station KPWB news reporter Dennis Kenny. Kenny reported, "It looked like a big orange light, glowing from white to orange." An odd report on the same day came from 80 miles away. The operating engineer and another employee at the Grand Tower power plant witnessed an object hovering over a transmission tower. The engineer reported, "There it was, hovering about 1500 feet [450 meters] in the air and about 200 yards [180 meters] away. It was a round-shaped object, about 25 to 30 feet [7.5–9 meters] in diameter. It looked like a high-intensity red light, with lots of light coming out of what seemed to be portholes. The lights were flashing and causing a spinning effect. . . . I looked at it for two or three minutes until it darted behind the power plant, almost like a blur."[19]

In April 1973, Bone and five others witnessed two more objects. One of the witnesses was KPWB's manager, Dennis Hovis. Two glowing orange lights were watched as they floated silently over a nearby tree line. Another curious report came from a nearby housewife at the same time. She was driving home in the daytime and was slowed by another car she couldn't pass. Looking off to the side, she was stunned to see an object hovering over trees. "It was round, with the exception of three domes on the top, one on top of the other. It appeared to have a dull band or something going around the center. . . . The craft emitted no sound, and looked like aluminum . . . and was at least 40 feet [12 meters] across."[20]

HARLEY RUTLEDGE AND PROJECT IDENTIFICATION

At the same time that Bone's first encounter was reported in newspapers, two physics students at SEMO went to Rutledge, the chairman of the Department of Physics,* and told him they had observed a large silvery disk in the sky during

---

*Rutledge had received his Ph.D. in physics in 1966 from the University of Missouri but was promoted to the SEMO department Chair in 1964 after teaching there for a few years with his master's.

the daytime. Rutledge, then in his tenth year at the university, was well aware of all of the UFO reports in the region. He was acquainted with Bone and the students, and he found their reports credible.[21] Rutledge did not believe in UFOs, nor did he disbelieve. He simply decided to see if he could observe, measure, and identify what the people were reporting.

Rutledge started by convincing SEMO astronomer Milton Ueleke to accompany him to the Piedmont area to take a cursory look at the events and talk to a few local officials who had been involved. Rutledge informed the university president (Mark F. Scully) of his plans and added another physicist, Sidney Hodges, and two senior students to his initial team. On April 6, 1973, the project began. Gradually, the scientific team was enlarged. The full details of the study were published in Rutledge's 1981 book, *Project Identification: The First Scientific Field Study of the UFO Phenomena.*

The Missouri UFO field research took place over a seven-year span and eventually included over thirty-five physical scientists, several engineers, some university students, and many others serving on observation teams. A total of 158 different viewing stations were employed in the study, with 620 total observers. During the seven-year study, there were 157 documented sightings of 178 different UFOs (typically described as anomalous "lights"). In many of the reports, the "lights" were observed close-up and were revealed to be more than simple balls of light. Equipment that was used included binoculars, telescopes, cameras and light-sensing devices, a magnetometer, sound recorders, Geiger counters, a spectrum analyzer, field meters, and radios.

Project Identification Findings

The number of UFOs observed by the team was the greatest in 1973, when 106 different cases were recorded. In 1974, there were 26 cases. The years of 1975 to 1979 (inclusive) totaled only 25 cases. It was clear that the phenomenon they were observing dropped precipitously around 1976. This region is in the heart of the highly active New Madrid Seismic Zone, and several moderate earthquakes occurred just before the frequency of the lights dropped off. In March 1976, a 5.0 earthquake struck the New Madrid Seismic Zone.[22] After that earthquake, the UFO flap all but ceased.

In the 157 sightings the project team recorded, they counted 178 different UFOs, meaning that some cases had multiple objects. For example, one case recorded ten different objects observed at once. A typical observation was of a light that blinked on far in the distance above the horizon. The light would usually be an orange or amber ball that would eventually move rapidly in one direction and then make a sudden 90-degree turn. The light would often move rapidly up and down, take off suddenly for some distance, and then change directions. In some cases, the objects rapidly flew directly over the observers. Some sightings included rectangular objects with four lights, which were observed close-up with telescopes. The observers reported that the lights had what appeared to be "windows" on them, with light shining through the windows from the inside. Triangulation and timing equipment were used to measure the speed, distance, and size of the objects. Many of these calculations showed that the objects accelerated instantly to thousands of miles an hour and made sudden, seemingly impossible turns. The group also recorded numerous instances of disk-shaped objects both at night and in the daytime, although they were never able to get a single photo of these where the saucer-shaped objects were visible on the processed film.

A military presence was noted in several of the most spectacular cases. Numerous fighter jets and helicopters occasionally flew in areas where the phenomenon was actively being observed and photographed. Rutledge tried to determine if the military presence was *causing* the phenomenon or *investigating* it, and his contacts with the military revealed that no experimental craft was being tested. The project team concluded that the military was also trying to discover the origin of the light phenomenon. In the late 1990s, I was told that the Missouri Air National Guard was, in fact, responding to the reports and making attempts to discover their source. I was also able to interview a handful of witnesses.

Rutledge, who lived in Cape Girardeau, eventually began seeing UFOs frequently in the city, and he organized an observation team in his own yard on several occasions. In one quite peculiar case that occurred on June 19, 1973, Rutledge watched a 210-foot-long (64 meter) "bullet-shaped" object silently fly over the Mississippi River. Rutledge wrote, "It was not like anything I had seen before. I looked at the craft. It had no wings. I did a double-take: It had no tail structure either. . . . A slight feeling of nausea overcame me. Any lingering doubt I had about the existence of UFOs had vanished with the object."[23] In the 1990s, I managed to interview another witness to this event, who confirmed the details.

While he was generally noncommittal on the nature of the UFOs, Rutledge determined that some of the discs and lights observed in the daylight by the teams were perhaps plasmas with some sort of guiding intelligence. In his summary he wrote, "The plasma balls seen in daylight certainly suggest remote control."[24] He also suggested that "radiation in the form of microwaves" was perhaps the way the light-forms moved.[25]

An unexpected finding of Project Identification was that everyone on the team became convinced that the objects responded to being observed. The project cited thirty-two different cases where the UFOs directly responded to the ground station observers.[26] Rutledge and his team concluded that the objects were aware of their presence and would interact with them, sometimes seemingly toying with them. As he became more and more enmeshed with the research, he became haunted by the light-forms. It was as if the phenomena he was studying became interested in him.[27]

As the project began to wind down, Rutledge noted in later interviews that some balls of plasma, 2 to 6 inches (5–15 centimeters) in diameter, would actually follow him around and even appear inside buildings on the university campus. He found, as do many people who become intrigued by the UFO phenomenon, that when you get deeper into it, strange things begin happening. An observation once made by John Keel seems appropriate. Keel mentioned that if you notice and become interested in the phenomenon, it can notice you and become interested in you.[28] That is essentially what Rutledge concluded.

Rutledge retired from SEMO in 1992 and died at the age of eighty in 2006. Even though he gave a presentation at a MUFON (Mutual UFO Network) conference and his work was occasionally noted in MUFON publications, his statements about plasmas and his overall findings are essentially dismissed or ignored by ufology, which prefers to believe in something else entirely.

At least one other scientist independently investigated the Piedmont UFOs. John Mullen, a research chemist working for the McDonnell Douglas Research Laboratories visited Piedmont several times. Mullen, who specialized in plasma gas research, reported that what was being seen were plasma formations, which he added, were poorly understood.[29] Indeed, in the 1970s, plasmas were known to be the fourth state of matter and were then simply defined as ionized balls of gas. Plasma research at that time was truly in its infancy. In 1968, Philip Klass, the ultraskeptic regarding UFOs, called plasmas a family of freak atmospheric electrical phenomena related to ball lightning—a collection of highly electrified air that glows intensely in a wide spectrum of colors.[30] The ideas that plasma might have some form of intelligence, be able to interact with those witnessing it, have the ability to change shapes, and have some intrinsic purpose was unimaginable back then. But when Klass issued his highly skeptical books on UFOs, attributing them to the brief appearance of plasma, *plasma* became a dirty word in the entire field.[31]

THE YAKAMA TRIBE RESERVATION STUDIES

Washington State has certainly had its share of UFO reports, and virtually everyone interested in the phenomenon is aware that the whole flying saucer craze was started by Kenneth Arnold's 1947 encounter, which took place only 71 miles (114 kilometers) from Yakima. A series of "UFO-like" sightings, in many ways similar to the Piedmont UFO reports, began in the late 1950s on the Yakama Reservation, not far from the city of Yakima in south-central Washington State. (The tribal name and city name are different by one letter.) While the number of these reports peaked from 1972 to 1974, the phenomenon in this region continues to this day. The activity today centers around Mount Adams and occurs frequently. Also notable is the fact that highly scientific research on the Yakima phenomenon began during the peak years of its manifestation.

Although there were fewer scientists involved in the Yakima studies, in some ways the research is more important than that at Piedmont. The Yakama tribe has legends and an oral history that takes the UFO-like activity on their reservation well back into time. For example, they have stories of "little people" known as "stick Indians" and legends of light-forms that interacted with observers. However, the earliest documented UFO report that I can find from Yakama comes from 1957.[32] That report was gathered by ufologist Greg Long in an interview with Larry George, who was then stationed at a no-longer-existing fire lookout on Simcoe Butte on the southern extreme of the 1.3-million-acre reservation. George was scanning the forests for fires when he saw a light in the sky, about the size of Venus, suddenly dip into a canyon. During the next few years, George had more sightings, but the vast majority of reports came in the early 1970s. Another article by Long, published in the July/August 1994 *International UFO Reporter* journal, related that fire lookout Dorothea Strum was reporting the strange lights as early as 1960.[33] The reports of the lights were remarkably similar to those in Missouri. Globes of multicolored light were seen to hover, dart between the mountain peaks and valleys, and make impossibly rapid movements. There were many cases where the lights interacted with the observers. There were reports of discs, fluorescent, metallic craft, and brilliant lights hovering over automobiles that heated the cars' interiors.[34]

Many of the most credible Yakama reports were made by trained fire lookouts stationed at three key locations on the reservation. One particular ridge on the reservation, called Toppenish Ridge, was a focal point of the sightings (see fig. 12.1, p. 112). In general, most of the fire observers' reports described glowing orbs of light, often orange in color, that floated up and down over one hundred geological fault lines that cover Toppenish Ridge. Other reports involved red, white, green, blue, and yellow balls of light. From 1972 to 1978, engineer Bill Vogel collected ninety-two sighting reports, and in a 1978 article in the *Tri-City Herald,* Vogel stated that in 1975 and 1976, there were two or three reports made each night.[35] In another article published by the *Yakima Herald-Republic* in 1978, Vogel said that virtually all of the people engaged in fire lookout posts had seen the anomalous lights.[36] On the few occasions where the lights were in close proximity to them, the observers had odd physical sensations and curious mental experiences. Most of the strangest reports came from ranchers living near the base of Toppenish Ridge. In one report, two men who were plowing a field at night reported that the alternator on their tractor became highly active when a glowing object hovered overhead. About twenty reports made from this location involved very close interactions with the globes of light that included radio interference. Some observers described paralysis, hearing footsteps outside, hearing whistle sounds, and smelling fumes. A mother and daughter reported encountering a huge, 7-foot tall creature on the road beneath Toppenish, one of some twenty-five Bigfoot-like reports made during the flap.[37]

One book on the Yakima research, *Examining the Earthlight Theory: The Yakima UFO Microcosm,* written by Greg Long was published by the Center for UFO Studies in 1990.[38] In the book, Long relates that in 1972, Vogel contacted J. Allen Hynek, who met with Vogel in April at Toppenish Ridge. Hynek then made a request to the tribe for permission to study the phenomenon. The Tribal Council granted the request, and engineer David Akers from Seattle was asked to organize and conduct the research. Akers set up a variety of instruments and finished a two-week study for Hynek's organization. However, Akers continued research into the anomalous lights at Yakima until about 2002, when the Tribal Council decided that it was time to discontinue the study. Akers maintained a research website on Yakima and is associated with a worldwide scientific group devoted to studying anomalous lights.[39]

The results of the research led Akers to have a disdain for using the term UFO to describe the Yakima phenomenon, because to most people it immediately implies something extraterrestrial.[40] But the anomalous lights are certainly unidentified and very real, at least in the sense that they can be seen, photographed, and measured in various ways. In some cases, the lights appeared to follow fault lines on Toppenish Ridge, but the vast research that was done shows that the lights were seen nearly everywhere in that region. Akers also found that unusual magnetic phenomena are associated with the lights.

A 2001 study conducted by Akers reported on the results of a 12-hour magnetometer recording made from the Satus Fire Lookout on the Yakama Reservation.[41] The study found numerous inexplicable magnetic pulses lasting from 30 milliseconds to 15 seconds. The pulses showed a "patterned symmetry," with characteristics of some sort of an unknown "mechanical origin." Akers related that no anomalous lights were observed during the study but that there were similarities between the collected data and data recorded during anomalous light displays elsewhere. A total of "845 pulse events of unknown origin" were recorded.

Fig. 12.1. Toppenish Ridge on the Yakama Reservation. It was the location of the most UFO reports as well as the area with the many strange reports.

Long's 1990 book on Yakima concluded that the phenomenon greatly diminished after Mount Saint Helens erupted in 1980 and that plasma and related tectonic strain theories probably have some relationship to the Yakima reports. The region did see less earthquake activity after Mount Saint Helens erupted, but activity has increased in recent years. Akers informed me that in 1980, the phenomenon did appear to lessen somewhat, but it has continued to the present.[42] In essence, what the Yakima research certainly demonstrates is that something very real does manifest into UFO-like light and that it can create bizarre experiences when witnesses are close.

In the mid-1990s, I spent many weeks in Washington State doing consulting work for the state, including three weeks at Yakima, where I had several nightly vigils watching the focal point of the activity: Toppenish Ridge. Several government officials of Washington State accompanied me on these visits. I also gathered as many newspaper articles and reports as possible, and I talked to a lot of people. I saw nothing whatsoever unusual there at night. However, what I did find came as a surprise, the type of surprise that occurred before digital cameras were invented, when we still had to have film developed. One of the things that I did was take about a dozen 35 mm photos of Toppenish Ridge during the daytime. Appearing in many of those photos, and significantly on none of the other photos on the same roll of film, were opaque blobs of amorphous white light and what look like smoke rings in the sky. The blobs were not at all similar to modern "orbs" but were oddly defined shapes. According to the university photo lab I was using, they were not film-developing defects but were just curious anomalies that they couldn't explain. It was intriguing, but at the time I was diligently working on other professional matters. I also interpreted it as a trickster effect, something to divert my attention.

SPACE CRITTERS

One of the most unpopular UFO theories of all time was actually proposed by Kenneth Arnold[43] and can also be found in the 1949 government *Project Sign* UFO report.[44] Naturalist Ivan T. Sanderson and mysteries writer Vincent Gaddis were both proponents of this idea. But the major author associated with this seemingly bizarre idea is Trevor James Constable. It goes by several different names, but it is best known as the "space animal" or "space critter" theory.[45] Arnold wrote that UFOs are "groups and masses of living organisms that are as much a part of our atmosphere and space as the life we find in the oceans." Sanderson wrote that this was "the most probable explanation" of UFOs. Constable, however, gave the most detailed explanation, writing that they "are amoebalike life-forms existing in the plasma state. They are not solid, liquid, or gas. Rather, they exist in the fourth state of matter—plasma—as living heat-substance." He went on to relate that they are in the infrared portion of the electromagnetic energy spectrum and are thus typically invisible.[46]

As a section in Ron Story's *Encyclopedia of Extraterrestrial Encounters* relates, "The space animal theory has never captured the public imagination, and it has not been seriously considered by most UFO researchers."[47] Indeed. Rutledge's research has also been largely ignored because there isn't much in it that pointed to an extraterrestrial presence. There were no crashed saucers. Yakima remains only a curiosity to UFO researchers because it also doesn't point to something extraterrestrial. No crashed saucers or obvious aliens there, either. In mainstream ufology, Yakima and the Piedmont investigations are used as evidence that scientific research has proven the existence of UFOs. But this statement is then used as a springboard to ideas that do capture the imagination of the public.

So, what conclusions can we make here? First, the vast majority of UFO witnesses do not have mental disorders and, after experiencing an unknown, seemingly paranormal event, they tend to embrace spirituality. We can also conclude that the vast majority of UFO reports are associated with, and often begin with, glowing balls of light that appear to interact with witnesses. When the light forms are close to the witnesses, the percipients' mental state changes and the light can take on humanoid or alien forms. Even the scientific analyses of some of the most important UFO flaps reached the same conclusions. Many of the scientists involved concluded that they were dealing with a plasma-based phenomenon that was poorly understood at the time. In essence, paranormal and UFO phenomena appear to form a massive, interconnected puzzle with so many pieces that it is incomprehensible to those who focus on just one aspect.

13

THE JIGSAW PUZZLE OF
THE PARANORMAL

August "Augie" C. Roberts (1920–1994) was one of the first ufologists. While Roberts was interested in the modern UFO phenomenon from its inception, it was his own UFO sighting in 1952 that led him to collect some of the most intriguing UFO photographs in existence. Roberts was one of the first to obtain photos of the enigmatic "foo fighters," balls of light observed by pilots and crews during World War II. Roberts changed his views about the UFO phenomenon at various times and eventually came to see it as a huge, multifaceted puzzle formed from many interconnected pieces. Back in 1984, Roberts wrote a book review of *The Archetype Experience* in an issue of the defunct magazine *Would You Believe?* In it, Roberts described ufology as a gigantic jigsaw puzzle of an incomprehensible size. Ufology is clearly split into so many factions, belief systems, and different interest sectors that it defies normal understanding. That is one reason skeptics just dismiss the entire UFO field. For skeptics, it's simpler to just deny it all than try to look at the pieces. In 1994, I paraphrased Roberts's idea:

> Imagine a gigantic jig-saw puzzle spread out over the land. The puzzle extends as far as you can see in each direction and you have no idea how far it goes. Its pieces are scattered over miles and miles. No matter where you walk on the puzzle you can't see all of it.

You observe people working on the puzzle in different places, and, as you walk to where someone is busily fitting some pieces together, they tell you they have "solved" the entire puzzle. Others working on the puzzle in a different area come to a completely different conclusion. . . . As you continue to walk around the puzzle you notice that each person has completely focused his or her attention on one tiny area. Their "solutions" to the mysterious puzzle only take into account the small area where they are working. They conveniently ignore all the other areas of the magnificent, enigmatic puzzle. Not surprisingly, no one's "solution" explains the entire puzzle—only they don't know it.[1]

Robert's idea is probably an apt description of the UFO field. Contained in the vast range of phenomena are sightings of strange lights, various creatures and occupants associated with the objects, materializations of luminescent beings, bizarre sexual encounters, conspiracy allegations, psychic abilities, contactees, abductions, ancient reports of phenomena, religious/spiritual/angelic events, and many other strange things such as electrical and radiation effects. Everything mentioned in this book somehow fits into it. But most people working on this huge puzzle focus on just one area of it. That is, they confine their study to reports that only confirm their beliefs.

For example, in 1985, Walt Andrus came to Memphis to make a presentation to a local UFO group. Andrus was then the international director of MUFON, and his certainty that UFOs were nuts-and-bolts craft piloted by extraterrestrial beings was apparent during his lecture.

In Story's *Encyclopedia of UFOs,* Andrus wrote, "My initial conclusion is that our Earth is being visited by entities from an advanced intelligence in their spacecraft conducting a surveillance of life on this planet," adding, "I cannot lose sight of the probability that they could constitute some unknown physical or psychological manifestation that cannot be explained by present-day science."[2]

Despite that added caution about other possible psychological explanations, at his Memphis talk, Andrus was clearly irritated when the extraterrestrial hypothesis was mildly challenged by me. "We already know what they [the extraterrestrial craft] are," he shot back when I questioned him, adding, "We need to find out what their propulsion system is and where they come from." I vividly recall asking him about a couple psychological explanations, but they were completely brushed off. "They [the UFOs] are definitely physical extra-terrestrial craft," was his reply.[3]

I also asked Andrus about John Keel's ideas about the relationship between UFOs and the paranormal. "They [paranormal events] aren't part of the UFO phenomenon," was his reply. In my professional career in criminal psychology, I have written many times about the psychology of beliefs. Once a belief gets accepted, it becomes self-perpetuating because of two well-known psychological processes. These are *perceptual bias* and *confirmation bias.* In their simplest explanation, these processes mean that we have a strong tendency to only perceive and accept things that confirm what we already believe. In short, we interpret events by what we already believe about reality.[4] Those biases are the greatest impediments to finding the truth about the paranormal, as well as countless social issues.

The type of accounts from Keel that Andrus immediately dismissed are the "high strangeness" experiences many people have reported. These include some of the bizarre abductions, apparent paranormal events, odd glowing entities, and the like. They are typically witness accounts of events that are so bizarre and absurd that, at face value, they are usually thought to simply be impossible. Examples of high strangeness reports are the Mothman episode that took place in the area of Point Pleasant, West Virginia, in 1966 and 1967, the Kelly-Hopkinsville, Kentucky, "goblins" case in 1955, the Zeitoun apparitions, various abduction reports, Swedenborg's visitations, and many others. We won't discuss them more here, but what is important to understand is that nuts-and-bolts ufologists don't like them and typically dismiss or simply ignore them. The main reason is that these reports don't fit the preconceived idea of what an extraterrestrial craft "should" be. Nor do they conform to beliefs about what alien visitors "should" do while visiting or observing Earth.

LOOKING FOR A NEEDLE IN A HAYSTACK OF NEEDLES

It's clear to the present authors that ufology is essentially a portion of the larger field of paranormal phenomena. The paranormal and the UFO phenomena have been welded together into a nearly impenetrable conglomerate of strangeness. Ufology has often been said to be like looking for a needle in an ever-growing haystack. A lot of people choose to focus on only one aspect of it all.

It is also clear that imagination, misperception, hoaxes, and psychological disturbance have influenced ufology. But those who have truly studied the field of ufology know that *something* extraordinary is going on and that cases like those of Swedenborg, Joan of Arc, and Cayce are related to it all.

Perhaps dismissing it all is the right approach for those who have a need to deny the reality of a genuine phenomenon outside of human control or understanding. Saying "nothing is there" can create a feeling of safety in a world where so much happens so fast and most things are viewed as out of one's control. So be it for the skeptics. If the belief that "it's all about nothing" gives people comfort, then that's fine for them. The same can be said for any other belief about the phenomena. The extraterrestrial hypothesis may give some people comfort and hope for some sort of redemption, as Jung suggested. People tend to believe what they choose to believe and do so for reasons they seldom understand. But many of us know that something that defies our understanding is at the heart of the paranormal and UFO fields. The oddities, the high strangeness events, appear to be at the core of it all—as Keel and a few others have asserted. But the truth is concealed by the constantly increasing mass of strange reports, misidentifications, and hoaxes that interact with preconceived beliefs. That is, an endless number of new reports are continually being piled onto the conglomerate of ufology. In 1984, I related that it was like "looking for a needle in a haystack of needles."[5]

In brief, the core of the paranormal, the source of all the high strangeness events as well as the mythology of the ancient gods, may well be related to human interactions with exotic, Earth-generated energy. Many of the greatest thinkers who have investigated UFOs have come to that conclusion. For example, in 1988, Jacques Vallee wrote "We are dealing with an unyet recognized level of consciousness, independent of man but closely linked to the earth."[6] Indeed, plasma, with powerful EMFs interacting with witnesses, is clearly involved.

14

INTELLIGENT LIVING PLASMAS

In the 1960s, plasma only was known to be "a collection of highly electrified air."[1] Back then, over 50 years ago, that explanation was about it, but a lot of physicists were very interested in it. Plasma is the fourth state of matter, with solids, liquids, and gases being the others. The modern, overly simplistic definition of plasma is that it is a *highly charged* ball of gas, but that's misleading. A plasma is an *ionized* mixture of excited atoms that has a positive charge. Plasma is so exotic that it represents a completely different state of matter. "Normal gas" is composed of atoms and molecules that have a neutral charge. In a plasma, electrons are ripped from atoms, creating a soup of positively charged ions and swirling electrons that produces powerful electrostatic interactions within a confined space. In essence, it is a swirling mix of superheated gas and electrons. Plasma takes on a fluid-like, changable shape and often become magnetic, and an EMF forms around it like a containment field. Plasma can conduct electricity, and its electromagnetic waves can exert influence at a great distance. Plasmas are influenced by both natural and artificial magnetic fields.[2] Close human interaction with plasmas has been shown to produce a multitude of mystical experiences.[3] Research has shown that the strange experiences humans have when near powerful plasmas are due to the effects of the EMFs on neural processes.

THE CONDIGN REPORT

In 2006, in response to a freedom of information request, the United Kingdom's Ministry of Defense declassified and released a 460-page study called *The Condign Report*,[4] which evaluated the UFO activity over the United Kingdom from the late 1980s to the end of 2000. In the report, secretly issued first in 2000, UFOs are referred to as UAPs, or *unidentified aerial phenomena*. The report attributed the source of genuine UAPs as "exotic plasmas."[5] The term *exotic* implies that the plasmas display characteristics that science cannot yet explain. In some cases, the plasmas rotate and flatten out into a disc shape, beam out different colored lights, and take on a myriad of other forms. In the report, it was conceded that plasmas were not yet fully understood. "Dusty plasmas" and "buoyant plasmas" were two types given close scrutiny in the report. They can be dense and seemingly fly. The report mentioned that plasmas were picked up on radar, moved quickly and in seemingly impossible angles, and were visible in various configurations. Sometimes they change shape quickly and dramatically. *The Condign Report* also hinted that research was ongoing into possible military applications of the phenomena.

In a 1996 interview, I mentioned that over 3,000 studies had already been conducted on the effects of plasma and electromagnetic frequencies on humans and that the U.S. government was sponsoring ongoing research for military applications. I also mentioned that "the most important findings would never see the light of day."[6] Some of that research has been published in military and technical journals contained in government repository libraries. I accidently stumbled onto the research after accessing the government repository library at the University of Memphis in the early 1990s. But the studies often referenced other reports not available publically. Specifically, many grant-funded reports are referenced in these published studies but are not publically disseminated.

MILITARY PLASMA RESEARCH

Today, the military has developed various technologies from the plasma research, and a lot of it has become known. My guess is that the public release of the military applications is not accidental. A 2018 article in *Popular Mechanics* summarized some of it.[7] In the late 1990s, a pulsed impulsive kill laser was developed. It was designed to focus a large plasma burst, but it required too much energy to be practical. In 2000, a pulsed energy projectile was developed that created a small fireball on a distant focal point. It was tested on animals and caused neurological impairment. In 2013, a plasma acoustic shield system was perfected. It produced a sustained plasma in the air that could be moved around and split into smaller plasmas. Also in 2013, they developed the laser induced plasma effect (LIPE). The frequencies of the induced plasma *could produce a spoken message* at its focal point. (My hunch is that the LIPE was created from the earlier research of Michael Persinger, who in 1997 was able to manipulate choices made by human subjects by using small EMFs that created spoken words heard by the subjects mentally. This is like beaming voices or thoughts into a person's head.)[8] In 2018, the military created a scalable compact ultra-short pulse laser system. It produces flash bangs of plasma of any size or duration and causes skin pain and burning. It can also transmit verbal messages a mile in distance. In 2020, *Popular Mechanics* issued a follow-up report on the U.S. Navy's "new" plasma-based missile fooling technology.[9] A laser device was described that created three-dimensional plasma "objects" in the air that rotated, moved as directed, and could be picked up by radar. The plasmas can be tuned to any electromagnetic frequency signature desired and can create a ghost image that is real but temporary. This was first reported by *Forbes* when they discovered that the U.S. Navy had filed a patent on the technology. All of this research was foreshadowed in *The Condign Report*.

THE GULF BREEZE LIGHT

Back on May 24, 1992, my wife and I were in Shoreline Park in Gulf Breeze, Florida, with eighty-five other people.[10] We were there to see the Gulf Breeze UFO, a frequently appearing aerial light the locals called "Bubba." It had appeared in the same spot eight nights in a row. At 9:30 p.m., several people asserted that it would appear shortly and would last for 90 seconds. At 9:40 p.m., the light appeared several miles away to the southeast. It was very bright and intense and remained completely stationary. It was several times larger than Venus would appear in the sky. For the first 80 seconds, it pulsed slowly between the colors of red and white, and in the last 10 seconds, it expanded to ten times its size, turning bright white, and then disappeared instantly when a ring of sparkles appeared uniformly around its perimeter. It did not fade out. It was as if a light switch had turned it off. There was no discernable noise. The light ceased its appearances shortly thereafter. I wrote that I suspected that it was an Office of Naval Research (ONR) study and that they were probably studying the responses of the observers by planting researchers in the crowd.[11] I reached that conclusion because both the Naval Aerospace Medical Research Laboratory, which is an arm of the ONR, and Eglin Air Force Base are located in that general area.

Back in 1972 and 1973, I was in graduate school in psychology at Memphis State University working as a research assistant. I was assigned by the department to work on a research grant study for the Pensacola ONR station. Another graduate student and I spent many weeks at seven different naval air stations conducting tests on Navy pilots. I visited the Pensacola ONR lab only once. As a young, lowly research assistant back then, I was only able to talk to some of the "lower" Navy research staff members at the ONR, who were my age. I described a lot of the drug research I had conducted from 1970 to 1972, evaluating some of the newer hallucinogenic drugs that the DEA had sent to the university's psychopharmacology labs for study. In response, the young ONR staff members told me of their "I wonder what will happen if" experiments. I was told that they routinely did studies just out of curiosity, just as we did. These are initial studies that are conducted when you have no idea what the outcome will be. For example, when confronted with something new with unknown effects, an informal study might be done quickly to answer the question, "I wonder what will happen if we do this?" My hunch is that Bubba was an early research project into plasma-created decoys and weapon systems.

Oddly, as this chapter was being written I was led by a colleague to a 1999 article in the *New Scientist Newsletter*.[12] In the article it was claimed that in the late 1980s a military research base in New Mexico had been experimenting with high-power lasers. By crossing the laser beams they were able to create multiple glowing plasmas in the sky that could be moved around instantly in the sky. The objects could change shape and color and appeared to be solid objects when viewed from the ground or sky. One possible conclusion here might be obvious to people who have become enthralled by the recent U.S. Navy pilot videos and reports of encounters with unknown objects. As related in the prior chapter, the whole UFO phenomenon can be seen as a gigantic puzzle, and military decoy research may be one piece to the puzzle.

LIVING, SENTIENT PLASMAS

Plasma research has come a long way since the 1960s, but we are still scratching the surface in many ways. It is likely that there are more than a few different types of plasma. Some of them, as the British *Condign Report* stated, are "exotic." It is recognized that there is an interaction between plasmas and human observers and that this neurological interaction is under study. But no one expected *physicists* to assert that plasmas may be a form of intelligent life.

In August 2007, six physicists published an article in the *New Journal of Physics,* a peer-reviewed publication, asserting that plasmas exhibit the characteristics of a type of *living, intelligent,* inorganic matter.[13] It has been known that dusty plasmas, a type of exotic plasma formed from cosmic or other forms of "dust," develop internal crystalline structures. However, the physicists found that the crystalline structures displayed the characteristics of living organisms. They formed an internal double helix DNA-like formation, showed "autonomous behavior," and had both reproductive and evolutionary properties. The crystals that formed within the plasmas often started as a corkscrew shape and then evolved into the recognizable shape of DNA—the double helix. It was a "self-organizing," autonomous process similar to how DNA forms in organic life. The idea of "reproduction" comes from the observation that the double helixes were seen to split and create duplicates of themselves, which is identical to cellular reproduction in organic life. The duplicates, in turn, continued to replicate in the same manner. The idea of "evolution" emerged when the physicists observed weaker crystalline structures to disintegrate, leaving behind the stronger and more stable structures. These processes continued as long as energy supporting the plasma was sustained. In brief, plasmas exhibit all the fundamental characteristics of being alive. A followup article citing this research ended with, "The question is then raised: given their fragility and slow pace of development, can they become intelligent or sentient?"[14] That, of course, was not the first time such ideas have been proposed.[15]

In 1989, Paul Devereux related an encounter with ball lightning reported by two professors at the University of Illinois at Chicago. Ball lightning is a long-recognized plasma form that remains enigmatic to this day. The professors watched a basketball-sized bubble of light squeeze through a one-inch window crack into a cabin. The exterior of the bubble was a yellow-white light, while the interior of the object was dark orange. As the object floated through the room, the two saw what looked like "writhing worms" in the interior of the plasma. The object moved to the other side of the room and simply shrank down and disappeared into the floor.[16] From this description, it would appear that what these two professors saw were the crystalline structures forming into a corkscrew-shape double helix inside the plasma.

Few ufologists, especially the extraterrestrial proponents, seriously consider plasma a key to understanding UFOs, and the same can probably be said for those whose main interest is paranormal phenomena. It is also likely that many people will scoff at the idea of plasmas having an intelligence. Of course plasmas are primarily a type of natural phenomena, and we know through research that they interact with human percipients. This interaction occurs through electromagnetic influences on brain chemistry. It is not really a new idea and would probably have been asserted by both Carl Jung and the great ufologist John Keel had they known more about plasma at that time. But both Keel and Jung cited electromagnetism as the key to it all.

15

JOHN KEEL'S ULTRATERRESTRIALS

John Keel (1930–2009) was certainly one of the most influential writers in the UFO field. He began his career in writing about the paranormal in the 1950s and probably reached his peak in the 1970s and 1980s. He started out supporting the extraterrestrial hypothesis but completely abandoned it in 1967 when he realized that the UFO phenomenon was part of the bigger picture of the paranormal and psychic realm.[1] He asserted that the small core of *genuine* paranormal and UFO cases were related to quantum physics ideas about the space-time continuum.

In his 1971 book *Our Haunted Planet,* Keel related that an intelligent electromagnetic energy source created "parahumans," mimics of humans, that appeared in the same places, century after century. Such locations are often described as "window areas," "portals," or "gateways." They are "weak spots in the Earth's etheric envelope through which beings from other space-time continuums seep into our reality."[2] He mentioned that the gods of the ancient world had warned humans to not look directly at them because the manifestations were "composed of pure electromagnetic energy" radiating large amounts of x-rays, ultraviolet light, and gamma rays. Exposure to such energy causes conjunctivitis and skin burns, something many close-contact witnesses experienced.[3] It was the transmogrification of electromagnetic energy that caused changes in color and light intensity in the objects and the light beings that were created by this force. The entities gathered electrical energy to assume a temporary physical, visible form, and he called them "ultraterrestrials."[4] Keel made two basic assumptions about the manifestations. First, the entities *are real* and not purely a psychological phenomenon, but they do affect human consciousness. Second, *they have a purpose or need* to communicate with humans.[5]

In 1970, Keel mentioned that the vast majority of genuine UFO reports were of luminous, transparent, or translucent "light," forming visual objects that changed shape and color. We know today that assertion is true. To Keel, they were "paraphysical" manifestations, not composed of "solid matter" as we conceptualize it.[6] When a human witness gets close to the manifestation, reality is distorted by forces that alter the normal space-time continuum. At the time Keel was writing, quantum physics was in its infancy.

Keel related that the underlying force was composed entirely of electromagnetic energy that could change its frequency at will. It remained invisible most of the time because it was outside the visible electromagnetic frequencies, but it could become visible by manipulating its own electromagnetic frequency. An intelligence of some kind was behind the force, but it never appeared in its true form. That is, it adjusted its appearance to the situation. It had a purpose behind its actions, but Keel related that the purpose was beyond our understanding. He also asserted that the entities involved in UFO contact experiences are the same entities involved in religious and spiritual manifestations.[7] People such as Joan of Arc, Cayce, and Swedenborg would be included in this list, along with the many Native American shamans who had experiences during rituals. The entities, which are typically described as angels, aliens, or earth spirits, start out as an energy mass and then alter their electromagnetic frequency into the visible light frequencies. At that point, an entity "organizes itself into atoms and can produce any desired form."[8] Its visible form adjusts to the unconscious expectations of its percipients and the general cultural beliefs dominating at that particular time. That assertion certainly fits the manifestations that occurred at Zeitoun.

ELECTROMAGNETIC ENERGY

While we have mentioned the electromagnetic energy spectrum many times, it's necessary to review some aspects of it again. The electromagnetic spectrum is a vast range that extends from extremely long radio waves to extremely short gamma rays. (See fig. 3.1 on page 23.) Near the middle of the electromagnetic spectrum is visible light, which makes up less than 5 percent of the entire spectrum. Our eyes contain rods and cones that function as tiny, biological radio frequency antennas that are tuned to receive only a small portion of the electromagnetic spectrum. If we were able to see *all* of the electromagnetic waves, we would be completely blinded by the myriad of waves around us that are continually generated by both natural and human-created electromagnetic fields.[9]

AEROFORMS AND BIOLOGICAL ANTENNAE

One of Keel's inspirations came from a 1957 book by Meade Layne (1882–1961).[10] Layne called UFOs "aeroforms" and said that they emerged into visible light frequencies from a plane of existence different from ours. Layne described the process as a "conversion of energy and a change of vibratory rate." The materializing object or entity appears to be solid substance until the energy and frequency are reconverted back to their starting rate.[11] Keel related that "the source has to be a form of intelligent energy" that can create and then disintegrate matter by manipulating its frequencies. It was also timeless because it existed in a different realm not confined to our normal realm.[12] It has existed from the beginning of time. However, it needs a source of energy to materialize, and back when Keel was writing, little was known about earth-generated plasmas.

Earlier, it was mentioned that the rods and cones in our eyes function as biological antennae that are tuned to receive only visible light frequencies. In his 1975 book *The Eighth Tower,* Keel proposed that the entire human body functions as an antenna receiving messages: "You and I are biochemical robots controlled by the powerful radiations being broadcast" over the electromagnetic spectrum.[13] Neuropsychologist Michael Persinger spent his entire career publishing dozens of research studies showing how human consciousness and other biological functions were affected by electromagnetic frequencies. Over the course of his decades-long research, Persinger was able to beam thoughts and words into the minds of subjects through small EMFs using varying frequencies.[14] Persinger's research was able to open the minds of subjects to experience UFO abductions, to meet what were interpreted as angels and gods, and to experience spiritual rapture, all through the use of small EMFs—while the subjects were enclosed in a copper-shielded laboratory setting.[15] The copper shielding blocked out all intrusive electromagnetic waves, allowing the subjects to only experience the specific EMF under study.

One of the consistent findings from Persinger's field research was that most odd and unusual paranormal experiences in the natural world tended to take place during times of relatively unstable geomagnetic activity that was produced by *building* tectonic strain. The tectonic strain that is *building* appears to be a clue to the continual and sustained release of the energy necessary for a manifestation to occur.[16] In short, the electromagnetic energy emerges when seismic pressure gradually builds, but the complete release of the strain leads to the energy being depleted. That is, when a large earthquake occurs, the tectonic pressure is reduced, leading to a cessation of paranormal activity. Persinger suspected that piezoelectricity, the release of electrons by certain rock and crystal formations when under pressure, was one probable source of the released energy. When rock with an internal crystalline structure (such as granite) is put under pressure, electrical charges form on the surface of the rock. The more pure the crystals involved and the larger the size, the greater the charge is. It has been found that tectonic strain can generate huge electrical charges and that the charges follow fault lines or travel to a specific spot where they are discharged to the air, thus creating plasmas. Devereux reported that such charges could reach "10,000 to 100,000 volts per square metre."[17]

While it might seem incredible that the needle in the UFO haystack is the idea that sentient plasmas emitting powerful electromagnetic waves produce paranormal events, that is not necessarily the entire story. But it is very likely that Keel was correct. The UFO phenomenon, spiritual experiences, and paranormal manifestations are all related, and they most likely stem from electromagnetic energy intrusions produced by natural Earth energies that are well-recognized by geology but not yet fully understood. Close contacts and interactions with intelligent plasmas have created mystical and spiritual experiences involving angels, glowing beings, and the gods of ancient cultures. At the same time, long-range observations of these plasmas have created typical UFO sightings of glowing orbs and flattened disks. When we are close to these emerging plasmas, we are the antennae that receive their messages. It is also very likely that "intelligent," or sentient plasmas, held together by self-generated magnetic fields, are the source of many ancient beliefs, a matter Andrew Collins reiterates and expands on in part two of this book.

When the plasma forms, it creates an electromagnetic shell or bubble around itself. When one of these forms appears near a human, the electromagnetic bubble surrounds both the plasma and its percipient. The electromagnetic field creates an energy wall, forming a consciousness interaction field, meaning that the beliefs and mental state of the human inside the bubble interact with the purposes of the plasma. Science completely breaks down at this point. My hunch is that quantum physics and nonlinear causality are directly related to how human consciousness and plasmas interact. However, the purpose and intelligence of the plasma are likely linked to dark energy, dark matter, and string theory. It is human interaction with these forces that has been the primary source of the gods. These interactions have occurred for all time. Of course, there remains the strong probability that ancient astronauts did make visits to Earth and interact with humans. As Sagan pointed out, it is a near certainty. But it was likely not as prevalent as many people hope for or suspect. The fact that the many interactions reported with aliens in modern times involve what is a trickster element clearly points to the involvement of plasma-based manifestations. It's the critical needle in the haystack of needles.

16

ARCHETYPES AND
SYNCHRONICITY

Carl Jung's ideas about UFOs closely paralleled his ideas about the paranormal. Both UFOs and paranormal phenomena, Jung believed, were related to *synchronicity*. The simplest definition of synchronicity is "meaningful coincidence." It is when at least two events occur in simultaneous space and time that seem to have a *meaningful* connection, but they apparently have no *causal* connection. A really simple example is when you think about a person, and then the phone rings and it is that person. Jung would call that a meaningful coincidence: synchronicity. Jung proposed the theory in a 1952 monograph after conversations with Albert Einstein.[1] Synchronicity events always involve archetypes. Synchronicity is, in fact, an *archetype experience.*[2]

As related in chapter 3, Jung viewed the UFO phenomenon as a synchronicity between the mandalas (UFOs) being seen in the sky at the same time humanity was fearful of nuclear annihilation. The witnesses to the UFO appearances were psychologically looking for salvation and redemption from the increasing conflicts and thus interpreted the disklike objects as salvation from space. Of course, that's the same essential message many of the Space Brothers gave the contactees and the same explanation skeptics attributed to Zeitoun. However, we know that many UFO-like events occurred in ancient times and have certainly continued unabated in recent times. The phenomenon appears to have always been with us. One could also speculate that humans are *always* in a time of conflict, always seeking redemption.

Also mentioned in earlier chapters, there are numerous archetypes. Except for the mandala, they come in opposite pairs such as hero/villain, angel/demon, helper/trickster, and so on. Jung saw all archetypes as having a *psychoid* quality, meaning that they bridged the gap between psychological reality and physical reality. At times, archetypes could temporarily manifest into physical reality. According to Jung, they emerged from the ultraviolet end of the psychic spectrum.

Back in 1984, I theorized that all of the archetypes that Jung conceptualized as opposites came into being at the time of creation. The resulting archetypal opposites were *splinters* from the whole—the mandala, the symbol of the whole.[3] After I learned much more about the Native American beliefs, it became clear that *Jung's concept is the same fundamental idea presented in the Cheyenne and mound builder's creation story.* In that Native American story, the big bang occurred when the unity of the universal singularity began to swirl into two opposing forces: the dueling forces of creation and entropy. What emerged was a three-part universe with the physical Earth as a space where the spiritual representatives of creation and entropy could act out their respective roles. Animals and various elements of the physical world represented aspects of this spiritual world, and all of them fit somewhere in the duality of creation versus entropy. Humans were placed on the physical Earth to harmonize with these forces and maintain a balance between the opposites. Shamans sought to harmonize with these forces and thereby become aware of the connections that exist among everything.

One way of looking at shamanistic practices is that their techniques are secret methods to produce synchronicity through conscious awareness. "The secret is that synchronistic events are not created. . . . What synchronicity really is then, is a fleeting glimpse at the overall network of interrelated events that is present (but nondiscernable) at all times. *Synchronicity is a special condition of awareness that results from energization of the mandala archetype.* It is a sudden conscious awareness of the meaningful connections that exist between seemingly unrelated and noncausal events"[4] (italics in original). Synchronicity is becoming aware that all things are connected. It was this awareness that many shamans and Native American ceremonies sought to achieve and even manipulate. Touching, vibrating, or interacting with any part of the whole affected everything. That's really an awesome responsibility if you think about it. It implies that every action you take, every thought you have, somehow produces effects everywhere else. Many of the ancient cultures took that responsibility very seriously. It was seen as an obligation. Clearly, that idea is now lost.

Of course, there is a bit more to this idea. The particular form that an emerging archetype takes on always relates to whatever cultural expectations the witnesses to it have. This is an interaction between the underlying essence of the archetype and the mental state of the observer. It is as if the observer's beliefs are projected *into* the archetype, which then acts in accordance with the projections. To the legitimate contactees, the archetypes they saw were interpreted as spaceships and beings from space because in that era such images and ideas became popular in the culture. In ancient times, they were the gods, sometimes residing on mountains or descending in fiery chariots. To the spiritualists, they were angels or ghosts. To Native Americans, they were the maiyun, powerful earth spirits, or tricksters. They have always been with us and always will be. However, let's be very clear here. Their experiences were not imaginary. To the percipient, they were real.

When the Cheyenne arrow priest Lou White Eagle experienced the little people while resting within a bubble of electromagnetic energy in my office many years ago, what he experienced was an updated form of the little people. Their appearance was one that fits more modern ideas of what these entities might look like. Their form of manifestation changes and alters to the expectations of their observer, but you never see their true identity or true form. The reason is simple. *They have no true underlying form.* They are pure energy that configure themselves into whatever the circumstance requires. *The energy involved is exotic plasma.* But as the plasma forms and interacts with humans through the powerful EMF it produces, something else happens because of the observation. The plasma begins to crystallize internally and create what appears to be a living, sentient being. The plasma's purpose, if it can even be called that, is to express creation or entropy in varying ways.

In theory, this leads us to the conclusion that this force is located everywhere, virtually waiting for whatever synchronistic circumstance that may arise. Remember that synchronicity is an awareness of the interconnectedness of everything, so there is a mental aspect in the observer who interacts with the materializing plasma form. Thus, the intentions and mental state of the observers play a very large role in such events. Think for a moment about Swedenborg, Joan of Arc, and Cayce. All three of them saw unusual lights. All three had experiences with angels. All three were deeply religious. Their intentions probably had a similar root, but Swedenborg was in mental turmoil and crisis. Thus, Swedenborg never made it past the trickster aspect of his experience.

At Zeitoun, the emerging plasmas formed into symbolic, religious figures as the witnesses to the manifestations were living in a highly secular society in crisis, but the population was, in fact, deeply religious. The apparitions interacted with the observers' unconscious expectations and hopes for salvation, and what resulted was a powerful manifestation clearly symbolizing those hopes. By contrast, the scientists involved in the UFO studies at both Yakima and the Piedmont area in Missouri saw what they interpreted as natural plasmas: plasmas that inexplicably interacted with them and even played with them. But they didn't reveal anything else to the scientists, whose expectations were that what they would find was a natural phenomenon. By contrast, many other witnesses in Missouri and Yakima had quite different experiences than did the scientists. They encountered entities as the objects drew near, they saw definite structures, and they experienced powerful psychological effects. What all of this means is that the expectations and intentions of witnesses play a huge role in what manifests. The plasma forms adjust to the observers.

Had Jung been around long enough to witness modern plasma research and advances in physics, I am certain that he would have incorporated those concepts into his ideas about archetypes. I also think his idea about the psychoid nature of archetypes would have been explained by intelligent plasmas. But there is another element that's necessary to mention. It has been stressed that these entities and forces clearly interact with us and respond to that interaction. That is, *they can appear when we seek them, but they will come even if we don't seek them out.* The energies involved are everywhere, but they manifest in certain places frequently. We can call these locations haunted places, window areas, or portals. Ancient cultures created spaces specifically intended for contact with the energies. When done correctly, we can, given the right circumstances and mental framework, somewhat control the interactions. We can achieve a type of harmony and balance when this is done properly, with the right intentions. But when we ignore the energies, their appearances bring disorder. And they do appear, probably far more frequently than we realize. With our modern environment swirling with man-made EMFs almost everywhere, chaos may well be the result.

In essence, what we are left with is that the legends of ancient gods may have come from multiple sources. Ancient astronauts may have really visited

Earth, and their influence may still be seen today. It's also possible that many of the reliable, modern UFO reports may well be stimulated by military research and natural plasma phenomena. But we know that for all recorded history shamans and medicine people have deliberately sought out contact with spiritual energies. And their interactions proved, at least to them, that whatever is behind these energies has an intelligence and purpose. Becoming in tune with the spiritual energies involved synchronicity.

17

ALL THINGS
ARE CONNECTED

Carl Jung's concept of synchronicity, much like the ancient Native American idea of an interconnected web linking all things to the whole, can be compared to the modern internet. Imagine, for a moment, if in the year 1900 Jung was in need of both writing paper and pens and, at that exact time, someone came to his door selling pens and paper. Jung would call it synchronicity. If you get notifications on your smartphone, it's likely that you get ads or notices of nearby restaurants and services as you travel to different places. If you search the internet for a particular product or service, you'll likely see ads immediately show up that try to steer you to a similar product. Jung might see that as synchronicity. But it's how the web works. It's all connected. It all interacts. Everything you do on the internet is recorded and entered into an electronic file that sorts it all, creates your preferences, predicts your cultural expectations, formulates your likes and dislikes, and more. There is a largely unseen energy grid working behind the scenes and making lots of connections. Information derived from you goes into this swirling electronic soup, and you, in turn, are presented with continual interactions derived from it.

The internet, of course, is designed to sell you stuff, to sway your beliefs and opinions, to provide some education or entertainment, and to just allow communication. In a similar way, we have connections with the underlying reality of the paranormal web. This web functions through interactions between living beings (us) and the electromagnetic-geomagnetic web created by naturally occurring earth energies. The most important needle in the hay-stack of needles is a sentient energy contained in the electromagnetic spectrum. Plasma manifestations are at least one important way, if not the primary way, that this force appears to us and interacts with us. There is purpose in that interaction, but the purpose may be, as both Keel and Jung related, beyond our understanding. I simply view it as creation versus entropy. Plasma manifestations and paranormal events produce the same possible effects in that they can be helpful or destructive. They can create something new or cause entropy. *But it's all part of the natural world.* A mechanism to allow creation and entropy was set into motion at the time of creation. But we don't truly understand the exotic energies involved, so it all seems to be supernatural.

In many ways, we are far less knowledgeable of our relationship with this geomagnetic web than were our ancestors. They lived in it every day. They had to have a relationship with it. The ancient ones connected with it every day, just as most of the people reading this connect to the modern web. However, most of us today avoid the natural earth forces as much as possible. We avoid touching the earth, and despite many people probably disagreeing with this, we also avoid nature. Today, we live in a swirling mass of human-generated electromagnetic frequencies, pollution, and noise, and we keep ourselves insulated in concrete, brick, and steel. We are usually out of touch with the natural web.

TIIME: TEMPORAL INTRUSIONS OF INTELLIGENT MANIFESTING ENERGY

For decades, I have struggled to find a simple descriptive term that adequately encompassed the crucial attributes of this force. The terms *plasmas, earth lights, ghost lights, light-forms, unexplained aerial phenomena, ball lightning,* and even *UFOs* all fail to cover what it is. All of these terms fall short, and all of them place limits on our understanding. Even when we mention plasmas as the form of manifestation the ancients saw as gods, a set of preconceived beliefs is stimulated by the terms *plasmas* and *gods*. However, this paranormal energy phenomenon does have a set of consistent characteristics.

It is *temporal,* meaning that its appearance is always transient. It is a localized *intrusion,* meaning that it suddenly manifests within a confined physical space, sometimes not even discernable to others within rather close proximity. It has *intelligence* and is able to interact and respond to its percipients. It is a *manifestation* of *energy* that is often plasma-based, if not always plasma-based. This energy moves between different electromagnetic spectrum wavelengths. It is a fluid-like manifestation that forms on the edges of what we think of as physical reality versus pure energy. For lack of a better term, I now simply refer to it as TIIME: *temporal intrusions of intelligent manifesting energy.* It has been on Earth since the beginning. It is the force that generated the angelic appearances seen by the ancient prophets and the beings of light that visited Swedenborg, Joan of Arc, and Cayce and the manifestations at Zeitoun. It was the force behind many contactee reports and abduction stories and countless other tales thought by skeptics to be so bizarre that the stories simply could not be true. But it is a genuine force that the ancients came to see as an important source of knowledge, especially if one could get beyond the initial trickster-like aspects that usually occurred. The ancients willingly sought out connecting with these TIIME forces and did so when human-created EMF pollution was not present.

NATIVE AMERICAN CONNECTIONS

One crucial reason that so much emphasis was placed on ancient Native American beliefs in the first chapters of this book is very simple. That is, we know a great deal about their beliefs and practices. Native Americans and their ancient practices continue to exist to this day. We have access to a rich mythology from Native Americans that tells us of their beliefs about creation and the spiritual powers that inhabit our universe. In addition, we have modern shamans who can explain it and attest to its reality. The same cannot be said for many other ancient cultures around the world. In addition, the Native American cultures recognized that this force was everywhere and in everything. They saw it as a powerful spiritual manifestation of energy that would appear on its own in certain special places again and again. These places were used by shamans and by the masses for lonely vision quests. Natural spaces such as mountaintops, rock formations, intersections of waterways, and caves were used by shamans as spots where they could consistently gain contact. These were places where the connection could be more easily established and where the spiritual forces seemed to emerge on their own. Today, we know that all of these types of places have magnetic anomalies, nearby tectonic fault lines, and radioactive energy sources.[1]

In ancient times, when electromagnetic pollution was not prevalent, there were certain individuals who were especially sensitive to the subtle differences found at such natural spaces. I have long suspected that the mineral magnetite, which was first identified in the human brain in 1992, may well be the sensory mechanism used by ancient shamans.[2] Magnetite in the human brain may also turn out to be the cause of *electromagnetic sensitivity*, a condition mentioned in the first chapter. However, we do know that magnetite in the human brain allows us to sense magnetic fields.[3] This ability was experimentally demonstrated right at the edge of the Earth's fundamental Schumann resonance: 8 Hz. Recall that the fundamental Schumann resonance is 7.83 Hz. Human theta waves cover the range from 4 to 8 Hz, while alpha waves start at 8 Hz and extend to 12 Hz. It is likely that humans are most susceptible to paranormal experiences at the transition point (8 Hz), when a relaxed state similar to meditation occurs. Thus, specific natural locations such as caves or mountaintops where an individual could attune to the Earth's fundamental Schumann resonance would be ideal places for interactions between human consciousness and TIIME forces.

The elite of ancient cultures used natural landforms to connect with the TIIME forces, but it became known by shamans that landforms could be shaped to allow the masses to commune with these spiritual forces. Many of the most incredible sites, such the circle and octagon earthworks in Newark, Ohio, were made in a way to evoke, contain, and control spiritual manifestations. Earth, as the most primordial spiritual substance, was carefully piled in specific formations as a barrier. Circular enclosures without an opening were made to confine the manifesting spiritual entities. Lines of parallel earthen walls were used to move both the spiritual forces and participants from one sacred location to another. Rituals that vibrated the electromagnetic web were used to connect with the TIIME force. This knowledge was, and still is, known by the shamans and medicine people who are entrusted to maintain the connection. Medicine people and shamans understood that there were specific angles of earth and rocks that enhanced the effects of rituals and attuned the participants in such rituals to the TIIME forces. A detailed description of how these elements—the rituals and the landforms—were conducted and interacted with is beyond our scope. However, recall from earlier chapters that all rituals were designed to vibrate the sacred, ritual space and the participants to resonate with the desired spiritual force.

HOVENWEEP

As mentioned in chapter 5, many ancient cultures believed that the universe was composed of three worlds. Some cultures subdivided these three worlds into multiple layers, each with its own forces and entities inhabiting it. Many ancient cultures, especially Native Americans, believed that humans were tasked with a special role. In that role, humans interacted with spiritual entities, or *gods,* as they were called in Old World belief systems, as an obligation. If this obligation wasn't fulfilled, it meant chaos and entropy would ensue. The obligation was to harmonize with the spiritual world.

The people of these cultures recognized that there were certain places on Earth where the interactions with this spiritual world were intensified. Shamans and medicine people sought these places out and even erected special buildings where the forces would be encouraged to emerge. This was a common practice throughout the ancient world. In the Southwest of the United States, the ancient Puebloan people—the Hopi, the Zuni, and the Navajo—constructed circular structures in the ground as sacred spaces. Mound-building cultures constructed earth lodges as sacred, communal spaces. They all literally grounded themselves by placing their bare feet on the soil. In that process, they harmonized themselves with the Schumann resonances and the Earth's ambient frequency. As discussed in chapter 1, Hovenweep was one of these places. There, a special tower was erected at the bottom of a high canyon (see plate 1). The tower was entered from the top via a ladder and had a few small windows to view certain stars. It was an immensely quiet place, had a good view of the sky, and was "grounded" into the deep earth. From the depth of the canyon, it reached into the sky, connecting the earth spirits to the spirits of the sky. But it was accessible only by a privileged few.

TURNING TO THE OLD WORLD

As we transition to the second part of this book, Andrew Collins will show that humankind's attempts to access the TIIME forces are far older than anyone has previously expected. Until fairly recent times, it was thought that human civilization (as we commonly think of it) began with the invention of writing and permanent building construction, sometime around 5,000 years ago. The areas of Mesopotamia, the Indus valley, and Egypt were long thought to be the oldest civilizations. However, Malta, the United Kingdom, and other sites in what we call the Old World have massive and impressive stone constructions dating to that same time period and even earlier. Göbekli Tepe, in Turkey, dates to over 12,000 years ago. Mounds were being constructed in South America some 10,400 years ago. It appears that all of the underlying belief systems driving the construction of such sites had a common purpose. They all were used to conduct rituals to contact and harmonize with the spiritual world.

All of these ancient cultures revered certain animals because the animals were representations of aspects of the three-part universe. Some of the most important spiritual symbols were from the upper world: large birds that flew in the sky world, landed on the Earth (the middle world), and also were at home in water, the surface of the lower world. These large birds were the manifestation of creation, the sky world, the keepers of the soul. They were revered and held in the highest esteem by the ancients. The ancients performed rituals with birds' body parts, and the elite often dressed themselves in bird garb. The Algonquin tribes revered swans, and the Navajo saw four swans located at the four corners of the world. Other tribes had powerful swan clans. It appears that the gods have always been with us, and it is likely that humans have always interacted with them. Humans have always sought contact with them and engaged in rituals to commune with them, and some have tried to control them. And it is all a *lot* older than anyone has suspected.

PART TWO

Contact with the Outside

Andrew Collins

Some of us have always been able to manipulate the energies of our reality through thought. Some of us have always stood on the threshold of the door that joins our reality to scores of others, and a few of us have been able to shuffle back and forth through that doorway, wandering among dimensions, exchanging greetings with entities made of an energy different from our own.

JOHN KEEL, 1975

18

THE FIRST SHAMAN

Qesem, a Hebrew word written קסם (QSM), is found twenty-six times in the Old Testament. Primarily, it means "divination"; that is, foreknowledge conveyed to an individual or group by a god or spirit.[1] It can additionally imply a divine pronouncement or sentence, the telling of fortunes, and even a "diviner," that is, a practitioner of divination.[2] The best example of a character in the Hebrew Bible who expresses the concept of qesem is Balaam, a priest and sorcerer of the god Baal who appears in the book of Numbers. Through him, the god Yahweh is able to deliver prophecies regarding the future destiny of the Israelites as they are about to cross the River Jordan into the Promised Land of Canaan after 40 years in the wilderness of Sinai.[3]

Beyond its connection with divination and prophecy, *qesem* (also spelled *kesim* or *qasim* and pronounced "kez-zem") today has a quite different connotation. For Qesem is the name of an important cave site located approximately 6 miles (10 kilometers) east of the modern city of Tel Aviv in current-day Israel (see fig. 18.1). Situated close to the start of the Samarian Hills, near the Arab-Israeli city of Kafr Qasim (hence the name), the Qesem Cave was discovered at the beginning of the twenty-first century. Since then, it has produced highly compelling evidence of the extraordinary human innovation of its inhabitants, who thrived toward the end of the Lower Paleolithic age, circa 420,000 to 200,000 years ago.

The wave of revelations coming out of Israel concerning the technical achievements of the Qesem people (see chapter 20) had been on my radar since 2010. It was, however, an article posted on September 23, 2019, by the Israeli

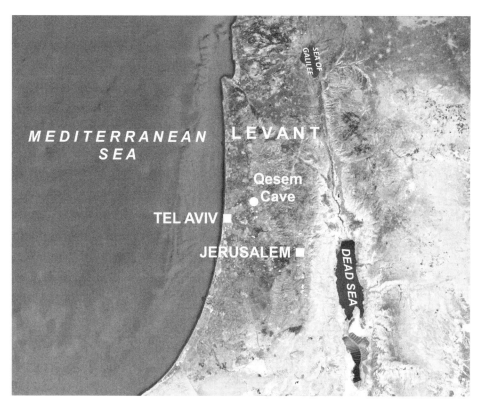

Fig. 18.1. Map showing the site of the Qesem Cave near Tel Aviv
in modern-day Israel.

newspaper *Haaretz* that piqued my interest in the cave site and caused me to
drop everything to determine the full facts about what might have been going
on there as much as 400,000 years ago.[4]

THE FIRST SHAMAN

The article stated that a swan wing bone found in the Qesem Cave was being
hailed as evidence of an extremely early form of shamanism, with deep ontological and cosmological implications for our understanding of the peoples of the
Lower Paleolithic age (which ran from approximately 2.7 million years ago to
approximately 200,000 years ago; see fig. 18.2, p. 144). The bone in question—
a proximal carpometacarpus shaft of an adult swan—bore cut marks consistent with the use of a sharp tool to remove the bird's long white feathers (see
fig. 18.3, p. 145 and plate 4).

Geological Epochs	Years Before Present	
Pleistocene		
Early	2.6 million–781,000	
Middle	781,000–126,000	
Late	126,000–11,600	
Holocene	11,600–present	
Cultural Periods		**Examples mentioned in this book**
Paleolithic		
Lower	2.7 million–200,000	Ubeidiya; Gesher Benot Ya'akov; Jaljulia; Qesem Cave; Yabrud Cave; Sede Ilan
Middle	200,000–45,000	Es Skhul; Qafzeh Cave; Denisovan Cave; Baishiya Karst Cave
Upper	45,000–11,600	Mal'ta; Hilazon Tachtit
Mesolithic/Neolithic	11,600–7,500	Göbekli Tepe; Tell Idris; Çatal Höyük
Ceramic Neolithic/Copper Age	7,500–5,300	Harran
Early Bronze Age	5,300–4,000	Tell Balata (Shechem)
Middle Bronze Age	4,000–3,550	
Late Bronze Age	3,550–3,200	

Fig. 18.2. Timeline of geological epochs alongside the archaeological cultural periods of the *Homo* species.

Since there is no meat to be had on a swan wing bone, the removal of its feathers was clearly done with a specific purpose in mind. Perhaps they were to be used for personal adornment. Maybe the bird's feathers formed part of a headdress or garment or, arguably, they were used to decorate something, most obviously a weapon such as a wooden spear.

Even though the feathers could well have been used for decorative purposes, it was more likely their removal had a more symbolic (that is, nonutilitarian) function. What is more, to date, the example in question is the only swan bone to have been found at the site; this being despite the fact that every occupational layer of the cave, from 420,000 years ago through to around 200,000 years ago, is littered with countless thousands of bone fragments belonging to a wide

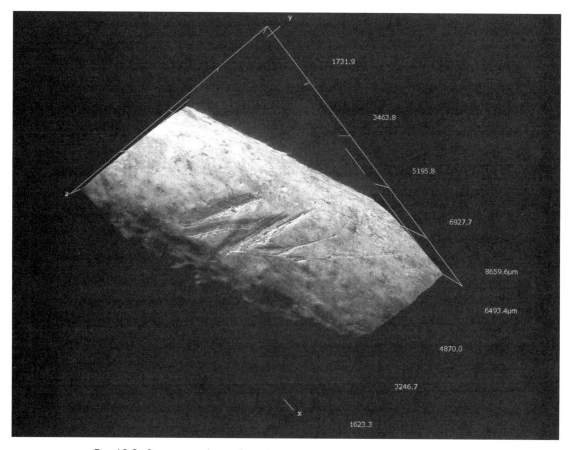

Fig. 18.3. Swan wing bone found in the Qesem Cave and thought to be between 300,000 and 330,000 years old.

variety of animals. Among these are a number of bird species, including the brown-necked raven, Eurasian scops owl, gadfly petrel, common quail, and at least two species of pigeon.[5] Yet all of their bones, with the possible exception of any corvids or owls, were likely either the product of food consumption by humans or, in the case of bones from smaller birds, regurgitated owl pellets.

Thus the presence of the swan wing bone was seemingly representative of something else—some kind of ritual activity taking place in the cave, the opinion certainly of the lead archaeologists working at the site.[6] Adding still further to the mystery is that the bone was recovered from beneath a rock overhang inside the cave that had been formed by the erosion of softer sedimentary material lying beneath a much harder rock member. This has come to be known as the Shelf.

SPHEROIDS AND POLYHEDRONS

Around the time the swan bone was deposited, as much as 330,000 to 300,000 years ago, this particular area of the cave would appear to have been reserved for special activities, very much as if it acted in the same capacity as a holy of holies or religious shrine in a church or temple.[7] This seems likely from the discovery very close to the swan bone, although within a different occupational layer, of a multifaceted, fist-sized polyhedron (see plate 5).[8] Many other spheroids and polyhedrons, some of extraordinarily symmetrical design, have been recovered from other parts of the cave, most of them perhaps deposited as purposeful caches.[9] All these other examples are made of a hard limestone. Only one is fashioned from flint, and this was the example found close to the swan wing bone.[10]

A microscopic analysis of some of the spheroids and polyhedrons found at the Qesem Cave, which seem deliberately fashioned to be handheld, has revealed damage to their sharp edges consistent with them being used to smash open animal bones to expose their nutritious marrow.[11] However, what also seems clear is that this was not their primary function. All those found so far display a heavy patina, or surface coating, that long predates their use as objects to break open bones.[12] Moreover, the type of limestone used to manufacture the spheroids and polyhedrons is not local to the Qesem site. Indeed, the source of the limestone remains a mystery.[13] What is more, no debitage (wasted flakes produced during the toolmaking process) consistent with the manufacture of these strange objects has so far been recovered from the cave's occupational levels. This suggests that some and perhaps even all of them were made elsewhere and brought to the cave in a finished state.[14] Thus they were probably heirlooms from a much earlier epoch and could therefore be hundreds of thousands of years older than the earliest occupation of the Qesem Cave.[15]

The fact also that many of the limestone spheroids and polyhedrons were found in caches suggests they must have played a symbolic function in the lives of the Qesem inhabitants. This seems emphasized by the fact that these caches were *all* found in the same area of the cave—its southwest corner (see fig. 18.4). Thus the deposition of the single *flint* polyhedron immediately beneath the cave's rock shelf was perhaps significant. The fact that it is the *only* flint polyhedron found so far could imply that it bore some kind of special status beyond that of the many limestone variants and may even have been seen as the only example important enough to be deposited in the cave's holy of holies.

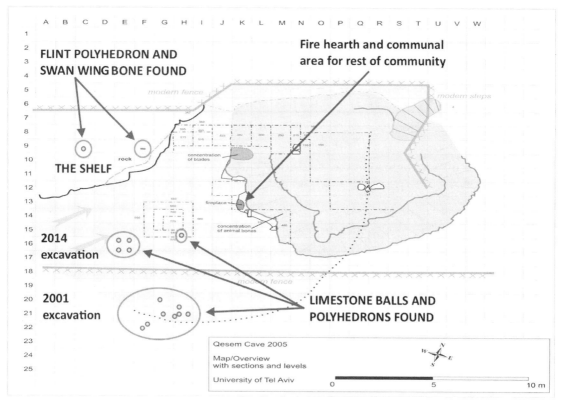

Fig. 18.4. Plan of the Qesem Cave showing the locations of the fire hearth and communal area, along with the spots where the swan wing bone, flint polyhedron, and caches of spheroids and polyhedrons were found. Measurements in meters.

SHAMANIC STATES OF CONSCIOUSNESS

The knowledge, therefore, that the only swan wing bone found in the cave was placed in the same vicinity as the flint polyhedron tells us that this, too, was the product of some kind of symbolic activity. The fact that nearly all the bird's primary feathers would have been attached to this single bone only increases its meaning and significance. Indeed, it leads toward the conclusion that animism, the act of accrediting inanimate and animate objects with spirit, and shamanism, where altered states of consciousness are used to connect with perceived unseen worlds where spirits dwell, were both important to the inhabitants of the Qesem Cave.

Israeli archaeologist Ran Barkai of Tel Aviv University's Department of Archaeology and Ancient Near Eastern Cultures is also convinced that the swan wing bone found in the Qesem Cave, as well as the purposeful defeathering of the bird, is indicative of otherworldly practices involving the employment of shamanic states of consciousness. He told *Haaretz* that, in his opinion, "using swan feathers could have transformed them [that is, the Qesem people] into swans."[16]

Someone like Barkai, a respected paleoarchaeologist and lead spokesman for the Qesem excavations, will not have made such statements lightly. Indeed, in one of the most comprehensive papers ever written on the relationship between birds, shamanic flight, and the modification of avian bones, Barkai, along with his colleagues Ruth Blasco,[17] Jordi Rosell,[18] Antonio Sanchez-Marco,[19] and Avi Gopher,[20] provides compelling evidence that the swan wing bone from the Qesem Cave was seen as an object of great symbolic value to the Qesem people. They link it with the fact that humans "have ever since [the disappearance of elephants from the Levant toward the end of the Lower Paleolithic some 450,000 years ago; see chapter 21] viewed birds as elements connecting between the earth and the sky, the lower world and the upper world, and thus as granted with potency and supernatural abilities."[21]

A SHAMAN'S WORK

Such ideas form part of the belief patterns adhered to by shamans, priests, and initiates worldwide since the Paleolithic age, with the principal purpose being to communicate with otherworldly denizens. This would have been for a number of reasons, such as healing members of the community, soul retrieval, the accompanying of souls to and from the next world, the dismantling of curses, battles with rival priests and shamans, the appeasement of supernatural creatures seen as responsible for both benevolent and malevolent activities in the physical world, and finally, the attainment of otherworldly knowledge.

In the case of the Qesem Cave, its inhabitants would appear to have recognized an importance in the avian attributes of the swan, a powerful symbol in much later times of the soul's journey to and from an afterlife located somewhere in the vicinity of the stars of Cygnus, the celestial swan or bird of transformation.[22] All this might be so, but can such practices be attributed to archaic peoples thriving in the Levant as much as 400,000 years ago? Did their achievements really extend to shamanic activities and communication with perceived otherworldly intelligences?

19

FLY LIKE A BIRD

Outside of the Qesem Cave, the earliest possible understanding of shamanism comes from Neanderthals (*Homo neanderthalensis*), the hominin species that thrived across the Eurasian continent between around 40,000 and 250,000 years ago. They deliberately sought out the claws and feathers of large birds, such as eagles, vultures, and ravens. These were used for personal adornment, most obviously to create necklaces and garments (see fig. 19.1).[1] This much seems certain, but there is tantalizing evidence that they might also have used bird paraphernalia for ritualistic and perhaps even shamanistic practices.

One person who has championed the symbiotic relationship between Neanderthals and large birds is Gibraltarian zoologist, paleoanthropologist and paleontologist Clive Finlayson, currently the incumbent director of the Gibraltar Museum. In a series of papers and in a recent book, he has highlighted the coexistence between Neanderthals and vultures in particular.[2]

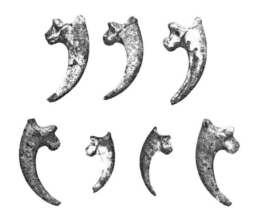

Fig. 19.1. Bird talons found between 1899 and 1901 during excavations in the Krapina Cave, a 130,000-year-old Neanderthal site in northwestern Croatia (after Lambrecht 1933).

VULTURE SHAMANS

As a comparison of this relationship between shamanic practices and vultures, Finlayson cites the discovery during the 1950s by American archaeologists Rose and Ralph Solecki of a large cache of goat skulls and bird wings deliberately deposited close to the exterior wall of a stone building at a site in the Zagros Mountains of northwestern Iraq named Zawi Chemi. This is located close to the Shanidar Cave, a famous Neanderthal site overlooking the Upper Zab River, a tributary of the Tigris River. The bird wings, which are around 12,000 years old, come almost exclusively from species of eagle and vulture. Many were still articulated when unearthed, meaning that the wings had been buried still with their feathers attached. This was made clear by cut marks on various of the bones, showing that the wings had been deliberately detached from the bodies of the birds postmortem.

Further evidence of the significance of the vulture, and birds in general, within shamanic activities is found in wall frescoes seen at the 9,000-year-old Ceramic Neolithic urban complex of Çatal Höyük in southern-central Anatolia. Vultures are shown engaged in strange pursuits revolving around the practice of sky burial (the deliberate defleshing and consumption of human bodies by vultures) and human-bird hybrids (probably bird shamans).[3] Even older still are carved reliefs of vultures on T-shaped pillars at the 11,500-year-old Pre-Pottery Neolithic site of Göbekli Tepe in southeastern Anatolia. There they are seen in association with human heads, an abstract symbol of the human soul.[4]

Symbolism of this sort implies a relationship going back to the Paleolithic age between the journey of the soul—whether this be of a deceased person in death or a shaman in a death-like trance—and the vulture in its role as *psychopomp*. This is an ancient Greek word meaning "soul carrier" or "soul accompanier," used in association with the concept of guiding the human spirit from its earthly existence to a perceived realm of the afterlife, or indeed, vice versa.

ON THE WINGS OF A SWAN

Does the discovery of a single swan wing bone at the Qesem Cave provide convincing evidence that shamanism was indeed being practiced hundreds and thousands of years *prior* to Neanderthals adopting the use of vulture and corvid paraphernalia to seemingly engage in ritualistic activity? If the bone had come from anywhere other than the bird's wing, the answer would probably be *no*. However, the fact that the bone is a carpometacarpus upon which the largest of the bird's feathers would have been attached tells a different story.

In ancient shamanic tradition the wing bones of birds were deemed essential in achieving shamanic flight. As evidence of this powerful psychological process, we have not only the articulated wings found at Zawi Chemi but also a considerable number of avian wing bones found in the Mesolithic cemetery of Yuzhniy Oleniy Ostrov on Southern Reindeer Island, situated in Lake Onega. This is Europe's second largest lake, located in the Russian republic of Karelia near the border with Finland.

There, circa 7000 to 6000 BCE, as many as 170 human interments were made.[5] Individual graves were found to contain substantial quantities of bird bones, many coming from the shoulders, legs, and wings (radii and ulna).[6] The only instances of single wing bones being found alongside individual burials were those of whooper swans (*Cygnus cygnus*).[7] This led Kristiina Mannermaa and her colleagues from the University of Helsinki, in a detailed study of the bird remains found in the cemetery, to write that the wings of whooper swans "carried some special symbolic significance."[8] Mannermaa and her colleagues stated further that "such graves where bird wings or parts of wings have been deposited near the hands strongly suggest that these birds may have played a role as carriers between different places or states of being"[9] and that "wing bones have perhaps symbolized complete wings or a living bird."[10] Thus the deposition of single wing bones most likely substituted for the use of whole birds or, more logically, their entire wings.

The important role played by swans in rock art found on the shores of Lake Onega has led to the conclusion that some of the burials in the Yuzhniy Oleniy Ostrov cemetery, particularly those where individuals were found interred in a standing position, belong to shamans.[11] Moreover, swan-human hybrids seen among the rock petroglyphs of Lake Onega probably depict shamans adopting the guise of a swan to enter the next world (see fig. 19.2, p. 152). In some instances, small figures, perhaps signifying the souls either of a deceased person or that of a shaman, are depicted walking up and down elongated and quite linear, swan necks, suggesting that they represent the journey from this world to the next with the swan acting as psychopomp.[12]

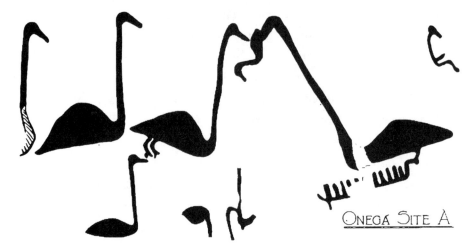

Fig. 19.2. Examples of long-necked swans found among the rock art on the shores of Lake Onega, Karelia, northwestern Russia (after Burkitt 1921).

SWAN BURIAL AND THE AFTERLIFE JOURNEY

From the same epoch is the curious swan wing burial found at Vedbæk in Denmark (Grave 8), which dates to approximately 5000 BCE. A fragmented proximal part of the right carpometacarpus of a whooper swan was placed next to a newborn baby buried alongside its mother.[13] Some scholars see this act simply as a sign of the harmonious coexistence that prevailed between humans and swans at this time.[14] More likely, however, is that this deliberate deposition in a grave of a swan's wing was an attempt to ensure the child's transition from the land of the living to the realm of the dead. It was this same bone, a swan's carpometacarpus, that was found deposited in the Qesem Cave.

The connection, however, between swans and the soul's journey to the afterlife would appear to be infinitely older than the Mesolithic age. For instance, at the Upper Paleolithic site of Mal'ta on the Belaya River, a branch of the Angara River, west of Lake Baikal in southern-central Siberia, no less than fourteen mammoth ivory bird pendants of straight-necked swans were found during excavations in the 1920s, some with eyeholes indicating they were used as pendants. All are approximately 24,000 years old and depict swans in flight (see fig. 19.3).

When uncovered, at least four of the swan pendants were found to be oriented north-south, something noted by German Medvedev of the Irkutsk State

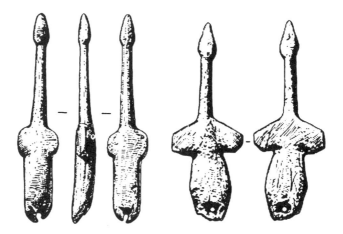

Fig. 19.3. Swan pendants from the 24,000-year-old
Upper Paleolithic settlement of Mal'ta, near Lake Baikal,
southern-central Siberia.

University, Irkutsk, Siberia, one of the foremost experts on the Mal'ta site.[15] He wrote that the pendants' deliberate directionality, along with the special attention paid to them by the Mal'ta community (one was found alongside a child burial), showed a connection with both the migration of birds and the universal idea that in death the human soul takes the form of a bird to reach the afterlife.[16] What is more, Medvedev saw the manufacture of the swan pendants as perhaps a "significant first appearance of animism" in Siberia.[17] The pendants therefore constitute what could be the oldest evidence yet for the relationship between swans, animism, and the soul being seen as a bird in flight.

All this helps us to better understand why the Qesem people might have singled out the wing bone of a swan as in some manner special to their symbolic activities. Even though there are no other precedents of this type of ritual activity dating back to the Lower Paleolithic age, there *is* evidence of an early relationship between bird wing bones and shamanism much closer to the Qesem Cave.

A SHAMAN'S GRAVE

In 2008, it was announced that a woman found in a 12,000-year-old Natufian grave during excavations at Hilazon Tachtit, a cave west of the Sea of Galilee in current-day Israel, had probably been a shaman. The excavation team, led by archaeologist Leore Grosman of the Hebrew University of Jerusalem and the Israel Antiquities Authority, determined that the woman, who was probably around 45-years-old at death, had a pelvis and spine that were very obviously deformed. She had also been deliberately interred away from all other burials found at the site, while inside the grave was a collection of strange artifacts of probable ritual significance, among which were two wing bones belonging to a golden eagle (*Aquila chrysaetos*). These were a carpometacarpus and a first phalanx of digit II from the bird's wing tip, which supports the eagle's large and very colorful primary feathers.[18] Indeed, the feathers might even have been attached to the bones when deposited next to the woman's right arm.

"The goods accompanying the burial are," Grosman and her colleagues have stated, "typical of shaman burials."[19] This led them to the overwhelming conclusion that the "petite, elderly, and disabled woman" interred at Hilazon Tachtit was almost certainly a shaman.[20]

Thus the eagle wing bones deposited in this unusual grave almost certainly signified the power of flight, the eagle having long been seen as an important soul bird in shamanic tradition. For instance, certain Siberian and Mongolian tribes speak not only of the first shaman being born of an eagle, but also of the shamanic arts having been taught by an eagle.[21]

THE ACTIONS OF SHAMANS

As modern scholars have amassed a wealth of evidence from archaeology, ethnology, and folk tradition showing the close relationship between bird wing bones and soul flight, there seems every reason to conclude that the activities taking place as much as 330,000 years ago at the Qesem Cave, just 90 kilometers away from Hilazon Tachtit, could constitute the actions of the earliest known shamans. If so, then how were the inhabitants of the Qesem Cave able to make the transition from what we can only assume was a primitive form of animism to a more complex belief system involving the existence of otherworldly realms that, according to shamanistic tradition, are navigable by adopting the mantle of a bird or animal?

Did they see these otherworldly realms as the place of destination of the soul in death, classifying it as an abode of the ancestors? And last, how might any of this have impacted on the series of advancements in innovation accredited to the Qesem people? To even begin to answer these questions, I knew that my next step was to make contact with the key archaeologists responsible for the extraordinary discoveries being made right now at the Qesem Cave, and through them to find out whether it might be possible to visit the site. Within just a few days, I was in communication with Ran Barkai and his colleague Avi Gopher, two of Israel's top archaeologists, and shortly afterward, I was on a flight bound for Tel Aviv, an important exploration ahead of me.

20

QESEM AND THE GENESIS
OF INNOVATION

My scheduled meeting with Ran Barkai and Avi Gopher, two of Israel's most well-known archaeologists, was to take place in a modest room located somewhere within the maze of corridors making up Tel Aviv University's Department of Archaeology and Ancient Near Eastern Cultures. Inside it were shelves stacked high with cardboard boxes clearly full of objects found during excavations, while taking up the room's central area was a large "finds table" covered in trays filled with stone tools of every shape and size.

Two of the department's undergraduates rose from workstations to introduce themselves, with my first question to them being, Where did all these stone tools come from? The answer was the Qesem Cave, and having gained permission to pick a few of them up, I took hold of a perfectly symmetrical prismatic blade; that is, a blade tool with a triangular profile. It was made of blue-grey flint and reminded me of very similar blade tools I had seen at the Pre-Pottery Neolithic site of Göbekli Tepe in southeastern Anatolia, which thrived circa 9600 to 8000 BCE. Put them side by side and you would hardly know the difference (see plates 6 and 7), something that confirmed the immense skill of the Qesem people, who lived toward the end of the Lower Paleolithic age.

I was still admiring these beautiful stone tools when Ran Barkai entered the room. He immediately pointed out that not all the blades from the Qesem Cave were quite like these. Many were of a quite different nature and included what are known as naturally backed blades (that is, a long slim tool with the flint's original light-colored cortex forming its blunted rear edge; see plate 6), an example of which was immediately handed to me. Curiously, this, too, matched similar tools I had seen at Göbekli Tepe (see plate 7).

THE STORY OF THE QESEM CAVE

Almost immediately, we were joined by Barkai's colleague Avi Gopher, one of the world's leading authorities on the Paleolithic and Neolithic cultures of the Levant. For many years, I had been referencing his work in my books, and here he was curious to meet this science and history writer from the United Kingdom who had flown all the way to Israel to see the Qesem Cave. With both Barkai and Gopher now in attendance, I pressed "record" on a voice recorder and asked them to tell me the story of the Qesem Cave.

The Qesem Cave

It was found, they said, in the year 2000 during the construction of the Trans-Samaria Highway that now links Tel Aviv and Israel's Mediterranean coast with the Palestinian West Bank. Apparently, the construction company responsible for this immense project had found its way barred by a large rocky outcrop just beneath the Arab-Israeli city of Kafr Qasim. Controlled explosions shattered the rock into manageable pieces, which laid bare the entrance to a cave covered with a carpet of stone tools and animal bones, most of them held tight in a thick cement-like matrix.

Thereafter work on the Trans-Samaria Highway ceased to enable a suitable archaeological team to begin investigating the site. This is something required under Israeli law. Indeed, any construction company uncovering what is quite clearly a major archaeological discovery is legally bound to supply the necessary funds for a proper survey of the site, along with any "rescue work" necessary before construction work can continue. Archaeological institutions are encouraged to bid for the opportunity to carry out this work, with the one submitting the *lowest* quotation winning the contract.

The successful bidder for the contract to explore the Qesem Cave was the Tel Aviv University team put together by Barkai and Gopher. They inspected the collapsed cave entrance and instantly recognized its immense importance.

EXPLORATION BEGINS

Two rescue digs took place, one in October 2000 and a second in 2001, to evaluate the full extent and potential of the Qesem Cave. So important were the team's findings that the construction company was persuaded to move the intended path of the highway some 6.5 feet (2 meters) south of its original course, allowing a little more of the cave site to be preserved.

Having been enclosed behind a fenced metal cage with a corrugated roof, excavations recommenced at the Qesem Cave in 2004. They continued until 2016, with each year's results eclipsing those of the previous one. What the excavations have confirmed is that occupation of the cave began around 420,000 years ago and continued until around 200,000 years ago.[1] Thereafter the site was abandoned, its entrance and interior—which currently measures around 30 meters in width, 20 meters in depth, and 15 meters in height—gradually being lost beneath many tons of rock-hard sediment.

From then on until its rediscovery in 2000, the cave's precious contents were preserved relatively intact, presenting the Israeli archaeologists with an unimaginable time capsule of early human activity. But who exactly were the inhabitants of the Qesem Cave? What exactly were their achievements, and why should we be taking such an interest in them?

BLADE TOOL TECHNOLOGY

We talked next about the finds themselves, starting with those beautiful stone tools seen on the table in front of us. Although blade tools had previously been noted among much older Lower Paleolithic cultures in Africa,* what was so special about those being manufactured in the Qesem Cave, Barkai and Gopher explained, was the sheer quantity and systematic regularity in their production.[2]

---

*For instance, blade production formed part of the Fauresmith stone tool industry of South Africa, which appears also in Kenya in East Africa and as far north as Gondar, Ethiopia (see, for example, Herries 2011 and Wilkins and Chazan 2012). The Fauresmith technocomplex is considered a transitional phase between the Acheulean of the Old Stone Age and the Mousterian industries of the Middle Stone Age. It dates to circa 435,000 to 511,000 years ago (Herries 2011), and was thus established prior to the emergence of the Acheulean-Yabrudian cultural complex (AYCC) in the Levant.

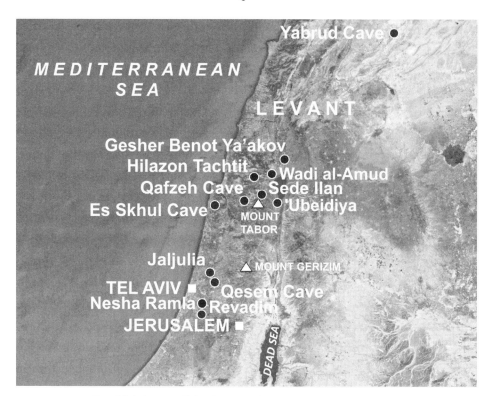

Fig. 20.1. Lower Paleolithic and Middle Paleolithic sites in
the Levant featured in this book.

Blade tools of the Lower Paleolithic age had previously been recorded at
other cave sites in the Levant.[3] Indeed, their presence had led to them being
assigned their own cultural horizon, or technocomplex, as it is known. This was
the Amudian,[4] after Wadi al-Amud, their initial place of discovery in the Upper
Galilee area of northern Israel.[5] German prehistorian and archaeologist Alfred
Rust (1900–1983) had come across a number of these blade tools during excavations at the Yabrud Cave in Syria between 1930 and 1933 (see fig. 20.1, showing Lower Paleolithic sites in the Levant). He compared them to similar blade
technologies found across Eurasia during the Upper Paleolithic age, circa 45,000
to 11,600 years ago.[6] Indeed, this same style of blade tool technology continued
in use through until the age of Göbekli Tepe, the reason why tools found there
resemble those manufactured in the Qesem Cave as much as 400,000 years ago.

The initial culture responsible for the manufacture of blade tools during
the Upper Paleolithic age was that of the Aurignacian, which takes its name
from Aurignac in the Haute-Garonne region of southwestern France. Its

distinct style of culture was first identified in the nineteenth century. For this reason, Rust decided to classify the much older Lower Paleolithic blade tools being found in the Levant as *Pre-Aurignacian*. It is a term that, although misleading in many respects (since those of the Qesem age were made using a completely different knapping technique), has persisted to this day.[7]

In an attempt to condense down all the different terms being used for the blade-manufacturing peoples who suddenly appeared in the Levant, as if out of nowhere, toward the end of the Lower Paleolithic age, archaeologists settled on the name Acheulo-Yabrudian cultural complex, or AYCC for short. (The term Acheulean refers to a highly specialized toolmaking process that thrived between approximately 1.76 million years ago and 200,000 years ago; see chapter 21.)

SCHOOL OF ROCK

How then did the Qesem people come to create these highly sophisticated stone tools? The answer probably lies in the fact that their community was unique and their minds ripe for new innovations, both in material culture and in spatial dimensionality. There is compelling evidence, for instance, that different areas of the cave were used for different functions, including the manufacture of specific types of tool and the deposition of certain objects, like the spheroids and polyhedrons found in its southwestern section.[8] This implies a spatial organization in production methods among its occupants, which apparently included allocating areas of the cave for what can only be described as a teacher-pupil relationship dubbed a "school of rock" in the popular press.[9]

In addition to this, there is evidence that the raw materials used to manufacture the many thousands of tools found in the Qesem Cave came not only from surface and subsurface sources but also from underground locations.[10] This hints at the possibility that Qesem's inhabitants were digging deep for suitable materials with which to make stone tools.[11] What is more, the people of the Qesem community were arguably the first to recycle stone and bone objects, taking discarded or unusable items and refashioning them into new tools with specific functions.[12]

FIRE FOR A REASON

Other areas of the cave were reserved for different functions, including a centrally located fire hearth.[13] Like the making of stone tools, the persistent creation of fire is thought to be one of the achievements defining humanity's uniqueness as an intelligent thinking species, and to date the earliest evidence for the use of fire among early hominins, that is, members of the genus *Homo,* comes from South Africa's Wonderwerk Cave. This is a huge cavern located near the edge of the Kalahari Desert. There early hominins, arguably members of the *Homo erectus* population, were creating fires as much as 1.7 million years ago.[14] The first appearance in Africa of *Homo erectus* is thought to have occurred some 250,000 years earlier, around 1.95 million years ago. (The African form of *Homo erectus* is known as *Homo ergaster* or *Homo erectus ergaster;* see fig. 22.1 on page 176 for the phylogenetic tree of the *Homo* species.)

Fire also was being used by *Homo erectus* groups around 780,000 years ago at Gesher Benot Ya'akov, an archaeological site in Israel, located north of the Sea of Galilee.[15] The importance, however, of fire in the Qesem Cave is that its hearth would appear to have been a permanent fixture from around 350,000 years ago through until the site's abandonment some 200,000 years ago, the evidence coming from thick layers of in situ ash deposits, along with the discovery of stone tools and animal bones displaying clear signs of burning.[16] The cave's inhabitants would also appear to have used fire from the hearth to split rocks to obtain the raw materials needed to make stone tools, the first hominin group anywhere in the world to do so.[17]

Among the culinary delights on offer at the Qesem Cave was roasted tortoise, the creature's discarded shells having been found there in some quantity.[18]

PREHISTORIC FOOD PRESERVATION

There is also compelling evidence that the inhabitants of the Qesem Cave were the first to invent what has been described as "canned food."[19] Let me explain. Throughout human history, our ancestors have split open animal bones to extract the nutritious marrow contained within their hollow interiors. For instance, some 500,000 years ago, *Homo erectus* at a site named Revadim in Israel were butchering elephants and breaking the animals' long bones to extract bone marrow.[20] At the Qesem Cave, they went one further by realizing that if you severed the metapodial (the bone that connects the hoof to the leg) of a fallow deer and then wrapped it immediately in skin, its marrow could be preserved as an ample source of food for at least nine weeks.[21] What's more, since these "canned" bones were mobile, it meant they could easily be carried.

In addition to this, it has now been determined that the Qesem people invented the first freezers! Not the style we might be familiar with today, of course. They discovered they could "freeze-dry" food as well as animal hides by immediately storing them in wood ash from the central fire. This enabled the food to be preserved across an extended period of time, arguably even several months.[22]

WHO WERE THE QESEM PEOPLE?

Something quite special was clearly going on inside the Qesem Cave, not just at the start of its occupation some 420,000 years ago, but thereafter for around 220,000 years until the cave's final abandonment some 200,000 years ago. So who exactly were the Qesem people who were able to achieve so many firsts in the name of human progress, including, as we have seen, the earliest known evidence of shamanism?

As Barkai, Gopher, and their colleagues make clear, the answer does not lie with the region's *Homo erectus* population. Whereas they had been behind many of the cultural achievements of the Lower Paleolithic age beginning as early as 1.95 million years ago, something else was going on in the Qesem Cave and elsewhere in the Levant from around 450,000 years ago onward. Compelling evidence now suggests that the cave's inhabitants could have been "proto-" versions of ourselves; in other words, *Homo sapiens,* anatomically modern humans.

We know this from the fact that dental fossil remains, in the form of thirteen teeth, recovered from various layers of occupation inside the Qesem Cave, all bear a striking resemblance to those of modern humans. Some do display certain traits characteristic of Neanderthals, who were themselves inhabitants of the Levant by around 200,000 years ago.[23] However, these traits could have come from the fact that both the Qesem people and the Neanderthals shared a common ancestor in their distant pasts, or it might have been the result of introgression, the two hominin groups having interbred at some point. We simply do not know (although see chapter 22 regarding the more recent discovery of a 130,000-year-old human skull at an Israeli site named Nesher Ramla located at the base of the Judean Hills southeast of Tel Aviv, which throws more light on this subject).

Previous evidence of what are considered pre-dispersal, early modern humans who after departing Africa reached no farther than the Levant has long been available. Several skull fragments as well as complete craniums came to light during excavations at two sites in northern Israel—the Es Skhul Cave in the Mount Carmel range and the Qafzeh Cave overlooking the Jezreel valley not far from the town of Nazareth. These individuals, known today as the Skhul-Qafzeh hominins,[24] are thought to have lived between 90,000 and 120,000 years ago.[25] They are classified as early modern humans even though they displayed some so-called robust or archaic features characteristic of the Levant's Neanderthal population.[26]

OUT OF AFRICA?

If the Qesem people really were a precursor to anatomically modern humans who in their final form departed Africa around 65,000 years ago and went on to colonize not only the Eurasian continent but also Australia as well, then we have a major problem. The oldest known proto–*Homo sapiens* remains are much *younger* than the initial occupation of the Qesem Cave. For instance, human fossils found at Jebel Irhoud in Morocco, including two humanlike skulls, are only around 300,000 years old,[27] while a similar skull found in 1932 at Florisbad, South Africa, is approximately 260,000 years old.[28]

The next oldest human remains were those found between 1967 and 1974 at Omo Kibish, near the Omo River in southernwestern Ethiopia. They are approximately 196,000 years old and for a long while were considered the oldest known remains of *Homo sapiens*.[29]

So claims that an even earlier form of *Homo sapiens* might have thrived in Israel some 100,000 years *before* our ancestors' earliest appearance in Africa was always going to lead to the rather premature, and somewhat misleading, claim that Israel and not Africa was the true cradle of humanity.[30]

The showcase site responsible for this unparalleled evidence of our ancestors' greater antiquity is, of course, the Qesem Cave, where its inhabitants would seem to have undergone extraordinary advances in human progress as much as 400,000 years ago. Why, exactly? How did they become so advanced so quickly? Was it connected in any way with the fact that the Qesem people would appear to have invented the earliest known form of shamanism to presumably make contact with denizens of unseen realms? This was something I put to Barkai following the departure of Gopher, who had to return to other duties. It was then that I learned more of the true ontological and cosmological background behind the apparent emergence of shamanism in the Qesem Cave.

21

COMETH THE HANDAXE

Ontology is an area of metaphysics in which the nature of being is considered, while cosmology examines the question of how both as individuals and as a group we fit into the greater scheme of things, in other words how we relate to the cosmos as a whole. Philosophers and sages throughout the ages have pondered the greater meaning of humanity's material and spiritual existence, their opinions often being preserved for posterity. Yet can we assume that proto–*Homo sapiens* living in the Levant as much as 420,000 years ago were beginning to ask questions about the nature of life and our place in the universe?

Ran Barkai suspects we can, and he is not simply basing his thoughts on the very real possibility that the Qesem community had a predilection for swan shamanism. To explain where he was going with this line of thinking, he wanted to show me some of the so-called Acheulean handaxes found in the cave, the importance of which will need some explanation.

THE ACHEULEAN HANDAXE

The foremost signature of human progress during the Lower Paleolithic age was the Acheulean handaxe (see fig. 21.1 and plate 34). This was a large, multifaceted, generally almond-shaped, bifacial (that is, shaped on both sides) stone tool, the purpose of which was manifold. It was the Swiss Army knife of its day—used for butchering, chopping, digging, cutting, and flaying, among a host of other things. In size, they can be anything between 15 and 30 centimeters in length.

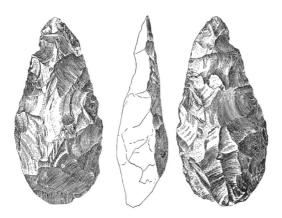

Fig. 21.1. Acheulean handaxe
from San Isidro, Madrid, Spain
(after Obermaier 1925).

The earliest known example of an Acheulean handaxe is 1.76 millions
years old and comes from an important archaeological site near Lake Turkana
in northwestern Kenya.[1] From then on, handaxes were manufactured with very
little change for almost 1.5 million years, through until around 200,000 years
ago. In fact, the consistency in the style and manufacture of Acheulean
handaxes throughout the Lower Paleolithic age is remarkable, bringing to
mind the old adage of "if it ain't broke, don't fix it"; in other words, if it works
satisfactorily, then there's no point in changing it.

Over the past 250 years, Acheulean handaxes have been found in the
countless thousands across both the African and Eurasian continents. Indeed,
they were the first artifacts ever proposed to be the work of Stone Age human
beings. In the late eighteenth century, English antiquarian and collector John
Frere (1740–1807) wrote, "The situation in which these weapons were found
may tempt us to refer them to a very remote period indeed; even beyond that
of the present world."[2]

Frere's suspicion that Acheulean handaxes were human made, based on
examples being found in his hometown of Hoxne in Suffolk, was not taken
seriously by the scientific community. To them, these asymmetrical stone
objects were works of nature, "generated in the air" and called "ceraunia, or
thunder stones."[3] Indeed, it would not be until 1846, when the famous French
anthropologist and antiquarian Boucher de Perthes (1788–1868) once again
presented evidence that these handaxes were of artificial manufacture, that
their true place in human prehistory would finally be recognized among academics.[4] Today, Acheulean handaxes—named after Saint-Acheul near Amiens
in northern France, where they were found in large quantities during the

nineteenth century—are seen as the handiwork of *Homo erectus*. This hominin species is considered the direct precursors of early modern humans, as well as the populations of so-called archaic humans such as Neanderthals and Denisovans, who would all come to inhabit many parts of the ancient world. (See fig. 22.1 on page 176 for the phylogenetic tree of the *Homo* species.)

Even though as many as seventeen Acheulean handaxes have been found in the Qesem Cave, they are not considered the handiwork of its Acheulo-Yabrudian inhabitants, whose principal stone tool industry was, as we have seen, quite different from that of their *Homo erectus* forebears.[5] Indeed, according to Barkai, there is every chance that *all* the Acheulean handaxes unearthed at the site are simply heirlooms, collector's pieces brought to the cave by its inhabitants long after their manufacture.[6]

From one of the large cardboard boxes stacked on the shelves, Barkai removed some superb examples of Acheulean handaxes from the Qesem Cave, which, one by one, he handed to me for study. "You can see this from the thick patinas, and none of them show signs of modification after being taken into the cave," he made clear, holding up an example himself (see fig. 21.2). "They were

Fig. 21.2. Paleoarchaeologist Ran Barkai with an Acheulean handaxe found in the Qesem Cave.

not brought back as raw material to make new tools. They served a function on their own."

Did he believe these heirlooms might have held some special meaning to the Qesem community?

"Absolutely," he said, matter-of-factly. "It is our understanding they were being seen as a connection with the Acheulean toolmakers, *Homo erectus*."

So these toolmakers, they would have been a completely different population from the Qesem people?

"Yes, exactly," Barkai confirmed. "The AYCC wanted to reconnect with their forebears by introducing handaxes like these into the cave."

Why would they have wanted to reconnect with *Homo erectus,* the inhabitants of the Levant *prior* to the emergence of the Qesem people around 420,000 years ago?

Barkai's answer was at first difficult to understand: "It relates to the disappearance from the Levant sometime around 450,000 years ago *of the elephant,*" he revealed. "It was an event that coincided with the disappearance of *Homo erectus* and the appearance in this same region of the AYCC."

So what was it that linked all these seemingly quite disparate events, and what does it tell us about what was going on in the Levant at this time? More pressingly, why might the Qesem people have been so affected by the disappearance of the elephant, something that occurred before their own emergence on the scene? It was these questions I put to Barkai next. What he said makes a lot of sense.

EPOCH OF THE ELEPHANT

The elephant was the principal large game of the Levant during the Middle Pleistocene (see fig. 18.2 on page 144 for a breakdown of the Earth's geological epochs and how they correspond date-wise with the archaeological periods of the *Homo* species). It not only satisfied the dietary needs of the *Homo erectus* Acheulean culture, but it also exemplified the symbolic ties that existed between them and the animal world as a whole. This is demonstrated, Barkai explained, by the fact that in the aftermath of a kill, *Homo erectus* would use bones from the slaughtered animal to fashion Acheulean-style handaxes, which being relatively soft had no obvious utilitarian function.

These elephant bone handaxes would thus seem to have been created for no reason other than to convey the deep respect *Homo erectus* possessed not just for elephants as a whole but also for the individual animal to which the bones belonged. Indeed, Barkai considers it quite probable that the elephant bone handaxes acted as symbolic points of contact with the animistic form of the animal in question and, by virtue of that, with the world in which they were thought to exist, *even in death.*[7]

THE INVISIBLE REALM

With this realization came several others. The concept of panpsychism—the idea that material objects, whether dead or alive, can display individual consciousness—among the Levant's *Homo erectus* population must by its nature have had to incorporate a belief in the existence of a world in which the spirits of the animals were thought to dwell. As such, the animal spirits would perhaps have been considered able to communicate with human beings sympathetic to their continued existence in this nonmaterial realm.

Where exactly this imagined spirit realm of *Homo erectus* might have been thought to exist is something worth thinking about. Aside from being seen to overlap with the world of the living, it would perhaps have become accessible to these people through nocturnal dreams, daydreams, spontaneous visions, and other types of transformative experiences. It must also be assumed that they experienced shifted states of consciousness.

VISIONS IN SMOKE

Whether altered states of consciousness among early members of the genus *Homo* were induced deliberately or accidentally remains to be seen. However, one of the earliest and easiest ways that natural hallucinogens might have been introduced to bodily systems is through the inhalation of smoke from psychoactive plants. This was the conclusion of Daoist scholar and ethnobotanical writer Frederick R. Dannaway in an important study on the early use of psychoactive substances.[8] He writes that psychoactive plants burned on bonfires lit in confined spaces like caves and rock shelters could very easily have introduced our earliest ancestors to the hallucinogenic effects of such substances.

It would not have been very long before early hominins realized that by burning a particular type of plant they could achieve communion with coexisting realms and through such connections attain otherworldly knowledge and information. The alleged external reality of such communications need not detain us here. Greg Little has discussed this topic in the first half of the book, and we shall return to it in due course. What is more important right now is to establish whether transformative experiences of this type had any lasting impact on the minds of early hominins and whether these communications might have led to genuine inspiration and innovation as well as the birth of shamanism (something that Graham Hancock speculates did indeed occur among our earliest forebears).[9]

When any of this might have begun is open to debate, although the chances are it was soon after the earliest sustained use of fire, which, as previously noted, is likely to have occurred in South Africa as much as 1.7 million years ago. Fire was thereafter introduced to the Levant by *Homo erectus* many hundreds of thousands of years prior to the emergence of the Qesem Cave's Acheulo-Yabrudian community around 420,000 years ago.

CONTACT WITH THE ANCESTORS

We have no idea how the *Homo erectus* population of the Levant might have perceived spirit presences existing in some otherworldly realm that coexisted with our own. Most likely, the spirits would have taken the form of animals, birds, or aspects of nature normally encountered in the physical world. Communion would, it seems, have been possible with these spirit animals, including elephants killed during the hunt.

One can almost imagine this unseen realm, arguably one of the earliest belief systems involving the concept of an afterlife, to be something like the imaginary world of animals created by British writer Rudyard Kipling (1865–1936) in his classic work *The Jungle Book* (1894).[10] Here, the animals are able to communicate not only between themselves and other animal species but also with human individuals who enter their world. Something similar could have been taking place in the minds of the *Homo erectus* inhabitants of Africa as much as 1.7 million years ago and in the Levant at important Acheulean sites such as 'Ubeidiya, south of Lake Tiberias in the Jordan rift valley of Israel, as much as 1.5 million years ago.[11]

THE LONG DISASSOCIATION

The sudden disappearance from the Levant around 450,000 years ago of first the elephant and immediately afterward the Acheulean-handaxe-producing *Homo erectus* population prompted the region's Acheulo-Yabrudian inhabitants at places like the Qesem Cave to adopt a slightly different lifestyle, Barkai now explained. Fallow deer, aurochs, and wild pigs became the main game of the hunt, and to catch them a completely different strategy was required. This in turn led to the invention of a completely new tool kit that included the various forms of blade tool seen at sites like the Qesem Cave.[12] But then something strange happened, for instead of ignoring those who came before them, the Qesem people would appear to have adopted the Levant's *Homo erectus* population as their revered ancestors. However, with this came something completely unexpected, as Barkai now made clear.

"The AYCC inhabitants at Qesem saw the epoch of the Acheulean handaxe makers as representative of their own direct ancestors," Barkai explained, "but with the disappearance both of the elephant and of *Homo erectus,* there now existed a kind of void that was seen in terms of a complete severance with the realm of the animals."

This, Barkai said, caused them to explore new and unique ways to try and resume contact with this invisible world of the animals, where both the former elephant herds *and* the Levant's now vanished *Homo erectus* population existed in their own form of afterlife. This necessitated the use of Acheulean handaxes, which were brought into the cave and used as portable points of contact with their makers. Since their size and shape allowed them to sit snugly in one hand, they became perfect objects of focus, allowing both contemplation and the chance of direct communication with the invisible world of the animals. That Acheulean handaxes were used in this way is supported also by the discovery in the Qesem Cave of the spheroids and polyhedrons. As we have seen, these were also most likely heirlooms from the age of *Homo erectus.*

It was at this point that Barkai went across to further storage boxes placed on shelves in his office and from one pulled out a selection of multifaceted polyhedrons found in the Qesem Cave (see fig. 21.3). Some were quite rough—the reason why they are sometimes referred to by paleoarchaeologists as bolas or throwing stones. However, some were not only perfectly spherical but they also

Fig. 21.3. Andrew Collins holds one of the limestone polyhedrons found during excavations at the Qesem Cave.

Fig. 21.4. Drawing of one of the multifaceted polyhedrons found in the Qesem Cave.

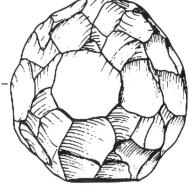

bore multiple facets, making it feel like you are holding a kind of Stone Age Swarovski crystal (see fig. 21.4). What is more, there seems little question that they were manufactured, like the Acheulean handaxes, to sit comfortably in one hand.

So in the knowledge that the most enigmatic of these polyhedrons, the single flint example, would seem to have been deliberately deposited beneath the cave feature known as the Shelf, where the swan wing bone was also recovered, what then was the true function of these extraordinary objects? Could they have been used, like the handaxes, as points of contact between the Qesem shamans and the realm of the ancestors, the realm also of the lost elephant herds?

"Absolutely," Barkai agreed. "They were part of the attempt by the AYCC to reconnect with this lost world."

This was an extraordinary realization, allowing me to push the matter one step further. If the spheroids and polyhedrons really *were,* like the Acheulean handaxes, being used as handheld points of contact with the realm of the ancestors, then in many ways they constituted the first ever "crystal balls" in human history.

Barkai accepted that the only possible answer to this question was a cautious, "Yes, indeed."

When I got over the idea that I might be holding one of the oldest crystal balls in the world, I pondered over what exactly this might mean.

AN ACT OF QESEM

According to the *Cambridge Dictionary,* a crystal ball is "a transparent ball of crystal or glass that produces images of future events by magic."[13] Maybe so, but surely this is not entirely right. Yes, they are thought to produce "images of future events," and certainly "magic" might be involved, but the principal use of a crystal ball is to make a valid connection with the perceived world of spirit to gain answers to questions posed. In this manner, the medium or psychic can advise the sitter of ongoing or upcoming situations they are unable to know about or address under any normal circumstances. Strangely, in ancient Israel, this would have constituted an act of *qesem*—divination through the intervention of a spirit or god. Thus to find that some of the oldest known crystal balls in the world come from a cave called Qesem is a very curious fact indeed. With these thoughts in mind I felt that I had questioned Barkai enough for one day. We had arranged to go to the Qesem Cave the following morning where our extraordinary conversations would surely continue.

22

PATH OF THE SWAN

Decomber 19, 2019. The brief drive out to the Qesem Cave that morning was not without incident. One of the tire's on Ran Barkai's car sprang a leak on a busy highway coming out of Tel Aviv. Following some tricky maneuvers to reach a nearby filling station, I found myself unexpectedly sitting on an old plastic chair outside an empty café as the tire was changed in an on-site workshop.

I guess the question on my mind at that moment, following my in-depth conversations with Barkai the previous day, was just how important were the Qesem people to the emergence of human civilization? Very likely they helped accelerate the growth of human progress in the Levant, while at the same time codifying ideas in the existence of an afterlife and elevating the swan as an important totemic symbol in their shamanic-based beliefs and practices.

So what then was the final fate of the Qesem people? Were they simply absorbed by the emerging Neanderthal population of the Levant, leaving as their sole descendants the Skhul-Qafzeh hominins who thrived there around 100,000 years ago? Or did some part of their population leave the Levant and continue its existence elsewhere in the ancient world?

Ran knew I had recently written an article proposing that the archaic *Homo sapiens* of the Qesem Cave could be related to the mysterious lineage of the genus *Homo* known as Denisovans.[1] Just like the Qesem people, the Denisovans are thought to have been incredibly sophisticated in a number of different ways.

THE DENISOVAN LEGACY

The existence of the Denisovans was only realized in 2010 following the sequencing by the Max Planck Institute for Evolutionary Anthropology in Leipzig, Germany, of an approximately 70,000-year-old bone from a little finger (a phalange) found during excavations at the famous Denisova Cave in the Altai Mountains of Siberia (see plate 8).[2] This showed it belonged to a previously unknown type of archaic human that had broken away from a common ancestor it shared with the Neanderthals somewhere between 380,000 and 470,000 years ago.[3]

Even earlier, somewhere between 550,000 to 770,000 years ago, this forerunner of both the Denisovans and the Neanderthals had itself diverged from a common ancestor it shared with the forerunners of anatomically modern humans. (See fig. 22.1, p. 176 for a simplified phylogenetic tree of the *Homo* species.)[4] The Altai Denisovan genome also revealed that several modern human populations—most notably in southern, eastern, and southeastern Asia as well as in Melanesia, Oceania, and Australia—have genes displaying anything between 2 and 5 percent Denisovan ancestry, with the highest level recorded to date being found among a Philippine Negrito ethnic group called the Ayta Magbukon. These indigenous peoples of the Philippines have up to 30 to 40 percent more than the Australopapuans of New Guinea, who were previously thought to have the greatest amount of DNA derived from Denisovan ancestry.[5] This knowledge tells us that our earliest ancestors interbred with Denisovan populations as they moved gradually eastward toward the extreme limits of the Euroasian continent (see fig. 22.2, p. 177).

It should be pointed out that there were in fact two main strains of the Denisovan population, both of which would appear to have displayed different levels of genetic evolution. One branch, determined from the genome sequenced from the finger bone found at the Denisova Cave, after leaving Africa passed through the Levant and went on to inhabit the more northern regions of the Eurasian continent including Siberia, Mongolia, the Tibetan Plateau, and northern China. They existed through until around 45,000 years ago and are known today as Altaic or Siberian Denisovans. The second branch, after leaving Africa journeyed eastward, perhaps passing through the Arabian Peninsula, until they eventually reached mainland Southeast Asia and what is today Island Southeast Asia.

SUNDA DENISOVANS

Anthropologists and geneticists refer to the more southerly branch of the Denisovans as Sunda Denisovans—after Sunda, the name given to the former Indonesian landmass, one of the places they are thought to have inhabited before their final disappearance anything down to around 30,000 years ago. Another area where they are now thought to have thrived is the Wallacea island group, which lies between Sunda in the west and Sahul, the name given to the former much larger Australian landmass, in the east. This new information comes from knowledge that the skeleton of a young female hunter-gatherer thought to be 7,200 years old was unearthed recently at Leang Panninge in South Sulawesi. Her genome has revealed that she possessed Denisovan ancestry.[6] The girl in question was found buried alongside stone tools that indicate that she belonged to the local Toalean culture, which occupied the island around 8,000 to 3,500 years ago.

The individual's genome was sequenced from a petrous bone and found to contain around 2.2 percent Denisovan ancestry. The rest of her genome indicated that she was closely related to the indigenous Andamanese peoples of the Andaman Islands, which are located in the Bay of Bengal in southern Asia. The Andaman Islanders, however, display no such Denisovan ancestry, so if their ancestors did migrate eastward into Sunda and also Wallacea then it becomes possible that introgression between the two populations must have occurred there and not during any overland migration through mainland Southeast Asia. If so, this would confirm that Sunda and Wallacea were once Denisovan strongholds. When exactly the forerunners of the current Andaman Islanders made their migrational journey eastward is unclear, although it is worth noting that on Sulawesi is the oldest rock art in the world, with a minimum age of 43,900 years.[7] Whether this was done by Denisovans or *Homo sapiens* is unclear, although if by the latter then it means they must have reached the island by this time.

If the Denisovans really did reach Sunda and Wallacea before *Homo sapiens,* then it would mean that this hominin group must have had seafaring capabilities. I say this as between thse two island groups is a deep-sea trench marked today by the Lombok Straits, which has a minimum width of 12 miles (20 kilometers). This means that both the Denisovans and the modern humans that replaced them must have crossed this straight by boat. Under what

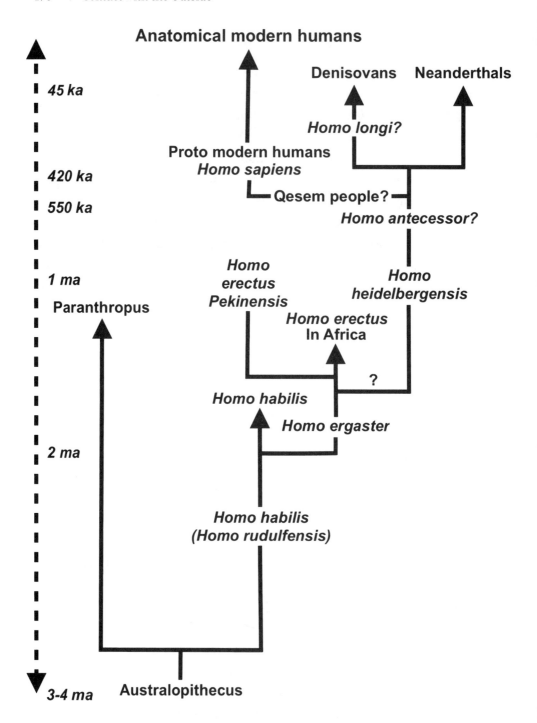

Fig. 22.1. A basic phylogenetic tree of the *Homo* species. Note that the timeline on the left-hand side is speculative and not necessarily to scale, while all origin points of archaic species remain tentative. Abbreviations: *ka* is "thousands of years" and *ma* is "millions of years."

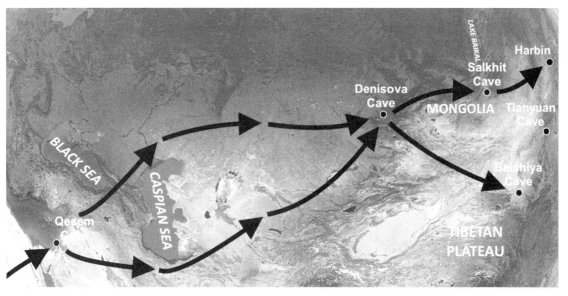

Fig. 22.2. Map showing the possible migration route of the Siberian Denisovans from Africa via the Levant to Siberia, Mongolia, China, and the Tibetan Plateau.

circumstances this occurred remains a mystery. What we *can* say is that the DNA of the Sunda Denisovans has a structure vastly different to that of their northern counterparts, the Siberian Denisovans, the two types having split and gone their own ways as many as 283,000 years ago. This knowledge comes from a detailed study of Sunda Denisovan DNA in modern human populations from Island Southeast Asia in particular.[8]

DENISOVAN TECHNOLOGIES

The reason for providing a full background to recent Denisovan discoveries is that from the same living floor of the Denisova Cave that produced the Denisovan little finger bone, as well as two extremely large molars also determined to belong to Denisovans, has come extraordinary evidence of this archaic population's advanced human behavior and apparent technical capabilities. This includes the manufacture of a 45,000-year-old bracelet made of a green mineral known as chloritolite that, in addition to being perfectly symmetrical and highly polished, has a hole bored through it displaying evidence of high-speed drilling (see fig. 22.3, p. 178).[9] From the same occupational layer (Layer 11) have come fragments of the earliest known musical instrument

Fig. 22.3. The extraordinary Denisovan bracelet found in Siberia's Denisova Cave and thought to be around 45,000 years old. Illustration by Nick Burton.

in the form of a whistle or flute, suggesting that the Denisovans had a basic knowledge of music and musical notes.[10] Found also in the same layer was a bone needle—the earliest example anywhere in the world—used most probably to create tailored clothing.[11]

In addition to these finds, archaeologists have recovered an exquisite example of Paleolithic art. It takes the form of a carving of a cave lion made from woolly mammoth ivory.[12] Incredibly, it has a series of incised markings in sequences suggesting a basic knowledge of the movement of the sun and moon (see the "Marking Time" section in chapter 23).[13] Then, in 2019, it was announced that the presence in the Denisova Cave of a highly developed blade tool industry, found also at other cave sites in the region, most likely developed first among the Denisovans before being passed on to the earliest human groups to establish settlements in Siberia and Mongolia as much as 45,000 years ago.[14]

This constitutes the first reappearance of blade tool technology since its disappearance in the Levant around 160,000 years ago, where, as we have seen, it dominated the tool kit of the Qesem inhabitants. Further evidence of the interaction between Denisovans and modern humans in Mongolia comes from the discovery by the Max Planck Institute for Evolutionary Anthropology that the genome of a 34,000-year-old human individual whose remains were found at the Salkhit Cave in eastern Mongolia contains evidence of Denisovan ancestry.[15] This, and the discovery of further Denisovan ancestry in the genome of a 40,000-year-old individual whose remains were found in the Tianyuan Cave outside Beijing, China, points to early contact between Siberian Denisovans and *Homo sapiens* occurring somewhere in the area of Mongolia.[16]

As Barkai and his colleagues have themselves noted, around the time of the establishment of the Qesem community some 420,000 years ago, the forebears of the Siberian Denisovans were very possibly passing through the Levant, their ancestors having previously thrived on the African continent.[17] Not only would these proto-Denisovans have come into contact with the Qesem people, but introgression between the two populations is also likely to have taken place. If so, this might have resulted in a Denisovan-archaic *Homo sapiens* hybrid lineage that thereafter continued its migrational course into the central part of the Eurasian continent, where this population evolved into the Siberian Denisovans who inhabited places like the Denisova Cave, as well as sites in Mongolia, and parts of China, including the Tibetan Plateau.

THE TIBETAN CONNECTION

Back in 1980, within the Baishiya Karst Cave on the northeastern edge of the Tibetan Plateau, near the town of Xiahe in China's Ganzu province, a Tibetan Buddhist monk found a large mandible of the *Homo* species that has now been determined to be that of a Denisovan who lived around 160,000 years ago. This was achieved through a comparison between protein found in one of the mandible's molars and Denisovan materials found in Siberia's Denisova Cave, which is around 2,400 kilometers northwest of the Baishiya Karst Cave.[18] Then in 2020, it was announced that Dongju Zhang, an archaeologist and associate professor at the College of Earth and Environmental Sciences of Lanzhou University, China, and her team, had discovered Denisovan mtDNA (that is, mitochondrial DNA) during examinations of sediment in the Baishiya Karst Cave, a popular place of pilgrimage for Tibetan Buddhists even today.[19] This is the first Denisovan DNA that has been discovered at a location outside of Siberia's Denisova Cave.

The new mtDNA evidence from the Baishiya Karst Cave shows that the Denisovans were on the Tibetan Plateau around 100,000, 60,000, and 45,000 years ago, with the even older Xiahe mandible suggesting they were present as much as 160,000 years ago. It also shows that Denisovan occupation of the cave stretched across an incredibly long period of time.[20]

Indigenous inhabitants of the Tibetan Plateau today have a specific gene (EPAS1) inherited from the Siberian Denisovan population, allowing them to exist in extreme high altitudes; the Baishiya Karst Cave itself being located at a height of 10,500 feet (3,200 meters) above sea level.[21] So the new discoveries make it clear that introgression between the Denisovans who survived in the harsh cold environments of the Tibetan Plateau and the first modern humans to reach the area probably occurred around 45,000 years ago, with their descendants still living today in the region.

GIANTS AND OGRES

Confirmation of the long-term habitation of Denisovans on the Tibetan Plateau begs the question of whether their presence has been recalled in the folklore and legends of indigenous peoples of the region. Ancient Tibetan texts speak of giants called *bdud* and ogres named *srin-po* that were encountered by the earliest humans to reach the plateau. It is even said they organized themselves into ruling dynasties, with the giants and ogres working together in some accounts.[22] Are these stories memories of encounters with either Denisovans or Denisovan–modern human hybrids, their presence remembered in somewhat naïve form across countless generations of human occupation of the plateau? This was something Greg Little and I predicted might well have been the case in the book *Denisovan Origins,* published in 2019. The discovery of Denisovan mtDNA in the Baishiya Karst Cave is now making this prediction even more likely to be correct.

NEW DISCOVERIES AT THE DENISOVA CAVE

The discovery in the Denisova Cave during excavations in 2020 of two new teeth and two further bone fragments only adds weight to the idea of contact between the Acheulo-Yabrudian inhabitants of the Levant and the forerunners of the Siberian Denisovans.[23] All were discovered in the cave's Layer 22, its oldest occupational floor, with one of the teeth (a milk tooth) being as much as 250,000 years old; the other tooth (a molar) and the two bones were found to be around 170,000 years old. What this tells us is that the Denisovans reached the Altai Mountains of Siberia during the same epoch that the Acheulo-Yabrudian population still thrived at places like the Qesem Cave. This means there is every chance that the two groups did indeed encounter each other. If so, then the result of this meeting was the earliest Denisovans carrying with them the technological, and perhaps even the shamanistic, legacy of the Qesem people, an exciting prospect indeed.

SWAN ANCESTRY

If all this is possible, it could explain why not only swan shamanism involving soul flight but also the concept of swan ancestry (tribes and clans claiming descent from a female progenitor in the form of a swan)[24] have long thrived among the indigenous peoples in former strongholds of the Siberian Denisovans including Siberia, Mongolia, and Tibet.[25] Did these traditions derive, at least in part, from hybrid descendants of the Denisovans who saw the swan as an important and very ancient symbol of soul flight and human transformation into a bird?

The discovery that Denisovans existed in the cold, harsh terrain of the Tibetan Plateau focuses these conclusions even further in the knowledge that the swan has been a powerful symbol among the indigenous peoples there since time immemorial. For example, it was on Lake Manasarovar, close to the base of Mount Kailish, Tibet's most sacred mountain, that the gods Brahma and Shiva[26] (or Shiva and Indra in some accounts)[27] are said to have arrived in this world as swans. In the Indian Vedas, Lake Manasarovar becomes the summer residence of swans that migrate southward to Indian lakes across the winter months. These swans are said to possess magic powers, while in Vedic mysticism the swan signifies moksha, the release of the soul from the cycle of samsara.[28]

It is intriguing to think that at least some of the ideas in the Hindu and Tibetan Buddhist traditions regarding the swan's role as a vehicle of soul flight might have had their origins as far away as the Qesem Cave in the Levant as much as 330,000 years ago. There we can imagine the first shaman picking up a swan wing bone and, through the attainment of a shifted state of consciousness, achieving soul flight in order to enter a perceived afterlife wherein dwelt both the forebears of the earliest proto–*Homo sapiens* as well as animals killed during the hunt.

THE BLACK DRAGON SKULL OF CHINA

Since the writing of this chapter some dramatic developments have occurred in our understanding of the Denisovans and their relationship to the Qesem people of Israel. The first of these was the announcement by a Chinese-led team of paleoanthropologists in July 2021 regarding the discovery of a quite remarkable skull belonging to what is being hailed as a previously unknown member of the *Homo* species. It was found as long ago as 1933 by a laborer during the construction of a bridge pier on the Songhua River in the city of Harbin in northeastern China.

Since the region was at the time under the control of an invading Japanese army who were in charge of the bridge construction project, the laborer hid the heavy cranium at the bottom of a well. On his deathbed the man revealed the whereabouts of the skull to his son, who went and retrieved it. It was finally donated in May 2018 to the Geoscience Museum at the Hebei GEO University in Shijiazhuang, China.[29]

An international team led by Qiang Ji of China's Hebei GEO University has made a detailed study of the Harbin cranium, the results of which were published in three separate papers in the one-year-old journal *The Innovation*.[30] Their findings are simply astounding. The skull is massive. Indeed, it is the largest cranium of the genus *Homo* ever studied by science (see fig. 22.4, p. 184).[31] What is more it is almost perfectly preserved, which is highly unusual. At approximately 9 inches (23 centimeters) in length and 6.5 inches (16.5 centimeters) in breadth it displays a cranial vault that is extremely long and very low.[32] Its estimated minimum age is 146,000 years,[33] and it is thought to have belonged to a male who was around fifty at the time of death. The individual's brain capacity is estimated to have been around 1,420 milliliters, which is in the same range as modern humans.

What's peculiar about the skull is that it bears physiological characteristics in common with both archaic humans, such as Neanderthals, *Homo erectus,* and *Homo heidelbergensis, and* early modern humans (*Homo sapiens*), including the two 300,000-year-old skulls found at Jebel Irhoud in Morocco (see chapter 20). Its archaic traits include a thick, heavy brow ridge, a large triangular nose cavity, deep set eye sockets, rectangular orbits, receding frontal region, and an extended cranium, while those characteristics of an early modern human include a low facial height, relatively flat face, and low cheek bones.

Although no jawbone was found with the heavy cranium, its shape, size, and single remaining molar, which is huge, make it a close match to the mandible found in the Baishiya Karst Cave near Xiahe at the northeastern edge of the Tibetan Plateau.[34] Similar to the Harbin skull, the Xiahe jawbone displays archaic features such as a complete lack of chin and extremely large molars.

The Chinese-led team studying the Harbin cranium applied a Bayesian-style method of statistical analysis on dozens of previously recorded archaic human skulls to determine the Harbin cranium's place in the *Homo* species' phylogenetic tree.[35] Quite amazingly they came to the conclusion that both the Harbin skull *and* the Xiahe jawbone belong to a previously unknown member of the *Homo* species—one they have called *Homo longi,* meaning "Dragon Man."[36] The name honors the Chinese province where the skull was found, which is Heilongjiang, meaning "Black Dragon River."

The Chinese-led team's announcement that the Harbin cranium belongs to a previously unknown member of the *Homo* species has baffled Western paleoanthropologists, especially since to date no DNA testing has taken place. Many are in agreement that the skull is in fact that of a Denisovan,[37] which if correct would be the first time we have ever gazed upon the face of a member of this long lost human population (see fig. 22.4). Everything about the Dragon Man skull matches what we know already about the Denisovans, including the huge teeth found in Siberia's Denisova Cave and the enormity of the Xiahe mandible. These, and other facts, have long indicated that at least some Denisovans were of great size and strength, comparable perhaps with the largest known WWE wrestlers of today.[38] The Harbin cranium, being so large, fits perfectly with this conclusion.

THE NESHER RAMLA INDIVIDUAL

The reason why this discovery is so important to this current work is that a separate skull found recently at a Middle Pleistocene site southeast of Tel Aviv in Israel and thought to be as many as 130,000 years old is not only being linked to the Qesem Cave population, but is also being seen as a close cousin of China's Dragon Man skull. The site in question, a former quarry belonging to a cement factory, is at Nesher Ramla in the foothills of the Judean Hills, just 14 miles (22.5 kilometers) south-southwest of the Qesem Cave. There, between 120,000 and 140,000 years ago, thrived a highly diverse human community producing both crude stone tools as well as much more advanced tools like those fashioned by the modern human groups who would afterward come to settle in the region.[39]

It was during extensive excavations conducted at the Nesher Ramla site in 2010 and 2011 by a team put together by the Hebrew University of Jesusalem and Tel Aviv University that large fragments of a human skull and a lower jaw with teeth were unearthed. When pieced together the Nesher Ramla individual was seen to have similarities with not only the Dragon Man skull from China but also the proto–*Homo sapiens* teeth found in the Qesem Cave.[40] Indeed, the Nesher Ramla and Dragon Man skulls are so similar that some Israeli paleoanthropologists now believe that the direct ancestors of the Nesher Ramla population migrated eastward into eastern Eurasia and are thus related to the human group now identified with China's Dragon Man skull.[41]

So if the Dragon Man skull *is* that of a Denisovan, and the Nesher Ramla human group is indeed a descendant of the Qesem community, then this backs up the hypothesis proposed in this book that proto-Denisovans on their migrational course out of Africa did indeed pass through the Levant where they encountered proto-*Homo sapiens* like those who inhabited the Qesem Cave

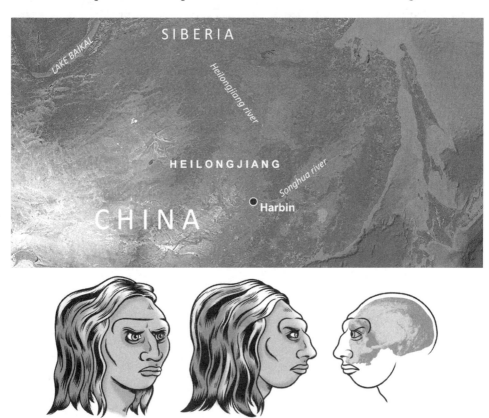

Fig. 22.4. Map of northern China showing the location of the city of Harbin where the Dragon Man skull was found in 1933; *lower left*, three-quarters view and side view impressions by artist Nick Burton of what *Homo longi* might have looked like (based on original sketches by George Hernandez); *right*, the Harbin skull with projected head outline.

between 420,000 and 200,000 years ago. The result of this introgression was a hybrid human population that on the one hand continued its migrational journey into eastern Eurasia to become the Denisovans of Siberia, Mongolia, China, and the Tibetan Plateau, and on the other remained in the Levant, eventually settling at occupational sites like Nesher Ramla. This explanation would ably explain the mix of archaic and modern human traits seen both in the Dragon Man skull as well as in the Nesher Ramla individual.

THE DRAGON PEOPLE

I cannot leave this subject without mentioning a curious fact about the location where the Dragon Man skull was found; this being amid the mud and gravel beneath Harbin's Dongjiang Bridge, which still spans the Songhua River today. The river flows into the much larger Heilongjiang River, which forms the northern boundary between China and Siberia, where the Russian name for the river is the Amur.

The indigenous Manchurian peoples of Heilongjiang province have a legend regarding how the river got its name.[42] A woman long ago gave birth to a black dragon, which her husband attempted to kill, chopping off its tail as it escaped through a window. The creature went down to the local river where it fought and defeated a rivaling white dragon. It was for this reason that the river was named after the Black Dragon. The curious thing is that in Chinese popular culture this tailless creature has been identified with a mythical primate with opposable thumbs.[43]

Is it possible that the Manchurian legend of the Black Dragon is an abstract memory of the former presence in the region of Denisovans (or the "Dragon people" as the Chinese media are calling *Homo longi*)[44] in the same manner that the Bdud and Srin-po giants and ogres of Tibetan tradition could likewise be age-old memories of the presence on the Tibetan Plateau of Denisovans? This must now become a very real possibility indeed.

23

MOON MAGIC

With the tire repair taking longer than expected at the car workshop on the outskirts of Tel Aviv, one of Ran Barkai's friends, a local filmmaker and writer, was drafted to take me out to the Qesem Cave; Barkai himself would join us there as soon as the vehicle was fixed. I used the opportunity to ask about the Arab-Israeli city of Kafr Qasim, which lies immediately beyond the now fully opened Trans-Samaria Highway. Although it is often considered that Kafr Qasim takes its name from the Arabic root *qasim,* meaning "owner of beauty,"[1] there is an equally strong case for it deriving from the Hebrew קסם (QSM), which, as I had established, alludes to prophecy and divination.

It was a matter I put to my driver, who said that the name means "magic" or the "occult," confirming the site's more ancient Hebrew roots. (Indeed, an article published following my return from Israel states that the root *qsm,* as in Kafr Qasim and the Qesem Cave, does indeed mean "magic").[2]

Before the journey had really even got under way, I saw the Qesem Cave coming up quickly on the left-hand side. Located at coordinates N 32°6'7.28", E 34°59'11.89", it is situated at the base of a fairly steep hill slope that comes right down to the hard shoulder of the road (see plate 9). To access the cave from the direction of Tel Aviv, you have to first overshoot it and then find a suitable exit off the highway, allowing you then to double back and approach the site from the east.

Before stopping, I asked my filmmaker friend if I might be permitted to climb one of the rocky escarpments overlooking the cave entrance. I needed photos and wanted also to examine the local terrain to get an idea of how it might have appeared to the inhabitants of the Qesem Cave as much as 420,000 years ago.

THE IMPORTANCE OF LOCATION

It had been my hunch that the occupation of the Qesem Cave had not come about in some random manner. I felt there was a good reason why its Acheulo-Yabrudian inhabitants had chosen to inhabit this cave as opposed to any other cave in the area. The previous day, Barkai had pointed out that another cave on the edge of Kafr Qasim, confusingly known as the Qasim Cave, had been completely ignored by the area's Lower Paleolithic inhabitants. No evidence of any early human activity has been found there.

Although it might seem an impossible task to get into the heads of proto–*Homo sapiens* who lived in the Levant as much as 400,000 years ago, some idea of their relationship to the local environment is, I believe, possible. If correct, then one of their primary concerns would have been the rising and setting of celestial bodies such as the sun and moon. To this end, I had asked British chartered engineer Rodney Hale, whom I have worked with on matters relating to archaeoastronomy (the study of ancient astronomies) for the past 25 years, to examine the local horizon to see whether any prominent ground-sky correlations might be discerned that could have been visible to the inhabitants of the Qesem Cave during their occupation of the site.

The cave entrance today is directed south, toward the high-rise tower blocks of Rosh HaAyin.* Yet so much of the cave's roof has either eroded away or been destroyed in more recent times that it is now impossible to know exactly what direction the entrance once faced. It could have been south, but equally, it could have looked out toward the southwest or southeast. No one really knows.

Since very few solar or lunar risings or settings occur in these directions, I considered the possibility that the use of the cave might well have reflected its accessibility to a nearby hill. This made sense, for the slope immediately behind the Qesem Cave rises up to an elevated ridge approximately 1,575 feet (480 meters) to the northwest (N 32°6'21.69", E 34°59'3.98"). If the cave's inhabitants were going anywhere to observe celestial events, it was to this

---

*Founded as recently as 1949, this modern city is known for its extensive oil field, one of the largest in Israel, as well as the fact that it was the childhood home of celebrated Israeli actress Gal Gadot of *Wonder Woman* fame.

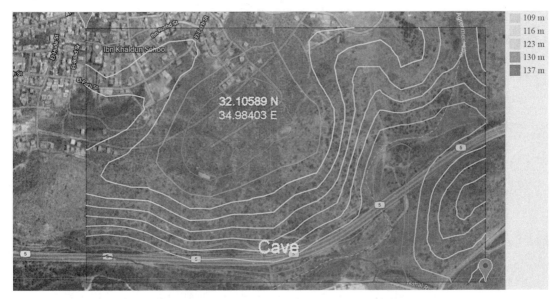

Fig. 23.1. Contour map of the area around the Qesem Cave showing the hill to its north on the edge of the modern city of Kafr Qasim.

location, which is today situated at the very edge of Kafr Qasim's urban sprawl (see fig. 23.1).

So from this spot Hale made his calculations, and although nothing specific was determined for the sun, he observed that during the month of October, the full moon would have been seen to rise in accordance with two distant peaks located some 18 miles (30 kilometers) east-northeast of Qafr Qasim. These were Mount Ebal and Mount Gerizim, which face each other across a valley containing the biblical city of Shechem, the modern Nablus, famous as the location of Jacob's Well and the tomb of the prophet Joseph.

Hale observed, "The full moon, on October 7, rises slightly to the left of Mount Ebal, but as Mount Ebal's peak is seen as about 1.5 degrees altitude from Qesem, the moon floats to the right as it rises and probably has a near miss of the peak. The next day, one day past full moon, it rises between the peaks [those of Mount Ebal and the more southerly Mount Gerizim]. Then on 15 October, the now last quarter moon again rises over the peaks."[3]

The year used for this exercise was 2006, since this was the last recorded most northerly rising and setting of the moon during its 18.61-year standstill cycle. Such an alignment seemed serendipitous if nothing else, but it might easily have been acknowledged by past inhabitants of the site. Moreover, interest in these twin peaks, as we shall see shortly, goes back at least as far as the Bronze Age, circa 3300 to 1200 BCE (see chapter 27).

SENSING THE CYCLES OF THE MOON

Why might the archaic *Homo sapiens* of the Qesem Cave have been interested in the first appearance of the full moon? Very clearly, this is a visual spectacle that human beings wonder at every time it occurs, especially when the moon is at its closest point to the Earth, creating a so-called supermoon. This said, almost all scientific studies on the possible effects of the full moon (and indeed that of the new moon) on human behavior have been unanimous in their conviction that no patterns can be found, overturning thousands of years of belief in the relationship between lunacy, mania, and the cycles of the moon.

This all might be so, although in the past our ancestors would have been much more sensitive to the effects of subtle changes within nature, especially in connection with the position and visibility of the moon. Moreover, an ancient connection between the female cycle and the moon's periodicity seems inescapable. Scientific studies have shown that the two can be artificially synchronized simply by sleeping with the light on during certain days of the month.[4] Artificial light can substitute for that of the moon, whose own cycle of 29.5 days might easily have been synchronized with that of a woman's optimal fertility cycle.[5] Indeed, it has been theorized that in the distant past women might have been able to menstruate at the time of the new moon and ovulate during the full moon, or vice versa.[6]

The age-old connection between the moon and the female cycle is further emphasized by the fact that the words *menstruation* and *menses* both come from the Latin *mensis,* meaning "month," while the Greek *mene,* from which the Latin *mensis* derives, means "moon."[7] All these might stem originally from the Proto–Indo-European *mēnes* and *mēn(n)s-,* meaning "moon" and "month," seemingly from the same root *mē-,* meaning "measure,"[8] implying that all three words—*moon, month,* and *measure*—are interrelated. If a link between the female menstrual cycle and the moon's periodicity can be confirmed, the chances are it has been important to human behavior since the very beginning.[9]

MARKING TIME

At some early stage in human development, lunar phases would have been observed and, finally, recorded, leading eventually to the prediction of eclipses. Prehistorian Alexander Marshack (1918–2004) wrote extensively on his discovery of meaningful notations on portable objects from the Upper Paleolithic and Mesolithic periods that seem to record aspects of the lunar cycle, such as a 28- or 29-day month, or parts thereof.[10] It was probably at this early age that the connection between the Proto–Indo-European words for *moon, month,* and *measure* had their inception, since all three were thought to derive from the same source, involving the measuring of time using the moon's periodicity.

The carved mammoth ivory figurine of a cave lion found in Siberia's Denisova Cave, attributable most probably to its Denisovan inhabitants, appears to display a basic understanding of the cycles of the sun and moon. It has eighteen sets of four incised parallel lines across its quite polished surface, making seventy-two in all (see fig. 23.2). These notches, which as an art piece represent the animal's body fur, perhaps signify the number of years in a lunar eclipse cycle or lunar standstill cycle, which in both cases is 18, along with the number of days in one-fifth of a 360-day year, in other words, 72 days. Seventy-two is also the number of years in a "century" found in an extremely archaic calendar cycle of 432 years (72 × 6), which is adhered to even to this day by the shamanic peoples of the Altai region of Siberia.[11]

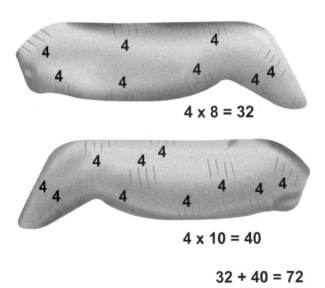

4 x 8 = 32

4 x 10 = 40

32 + 40 = 72

Fig. 23.2. Mammoth ivory carving of a cave lion found in the Denisova Cave and thought to be around 45,000 years old. As can be seen, it bears eighteen sets of notches in groups of four, making seventy-two notches in all. This seems purposeful, reflecting perhaps knowledge of the cycles of the sun and moon.

Although the aforementioned carving of a cave lion was manufactured as much as 155,000 years after the abandonment of the Qesem Cave, it is possible that the cycles and movement of the moon played some role in the lives of the Lower Paleolithic inhabitants of the Levant prior to this time.

SWANS AND MOONFLIGHT

A long-held association exists between swans and the moon. For example, both the Greek and Latin names for the swan, *kuknos* and *cygnus,* derive from the root *kuk,* linked perhaps with the Finno-Ugric word for the moon, which is *ku* or *kuu.*[12] This connection with the moon probably comes not just from the bird's white plumage but also because there exists a clear relationship between bird migration and the lunar cycle. In a recent study of bird migration led by Gabriel Norevik of the Department of Biology at Lund University, Sweden, it was determined that more migrations take place when the moon is visible since it is easier for birds to catch insects in the moonlight.[13] There could, of course, be additional reasons for moonflight, including the possibility that the presence of the moon might be used for navigational purposes.

Should any of this knowledge have been available to the inhabitants of the Qesem Cave, then it seems feasible they deliberately synchronized their rituals involving the use of swan bones to accord both with the lunar cycle and the nocturnal migration of swans. On this basis, it is easy to imagine their shamanic journeys to the supernatural realm of the animals being timed to coincide with the full moon. All of these ideas might have had their inception in places like the Levant as much as 400,000 years ago. What is more, if hybrid descendants of the Qesem people really did go on to become the Siberian Denisovans then this could help explain why this interest in swans and lunar cycles might have become so important to the inhabitants of central and northern Asia from very earliest times.

24

WITHIN THE CAVE

Having exited the Trans-Samaria Highway, our vehicle soon reached the pull-in area beyond the hard shoulder used by visitors to the Qesem Cave. From there, we walked on foot through thick, unforgiving undergrowth and across a small stream until finally we reached the archaeological site. This, as I had seen online, was caged within a tall perimeter fence and covered over with a metal corrugated roof (see plate 10).

As we approached the site, Ran Barkai was unlocking the gate into the enclosure, having arrived minutes earlier. There were good reasons, he explained, for this strict security. Immediately behind the cave is an old burned-out portable building, the last remains of the archaeological team's work station. Being so visible from the highway, it has twice been broken into, and when, on another occasion, looters found it to contain nothing but archaeological tools, they vented their frustration by setting fire to the place. That's why the cave has to be protected.

ROCK CONGLOMERATES AND THE FIRE HEARTH

The site itself was not quite what I'd imagined. Instead of entering the mouth of a cavern, there is simply a series of stepped layers at the base of a rocky slope, any remaining fragments of the roof having been carried away during the construction of the highway.

Scattered across the floor were rock-hard conglomerates of what looked like lumps of fossilized concrete. Each contained congealed masses of animal bone and stone tools. Seeing them told me just how difficult it has been for excavators to fully investigate the site. Clearly, much work was still to be done there.

Barkai now showed me the site's main feature—the hearth. It was marked out by a large dark layer of burned material left behind by bonfires kindled across a period of as long as 200,000 years (see plate 11). Learning that this fire pit was anything up to 350,000 years old and had been created by some of the earliest human beings to walk the Earth brought with it an eerie sensation. However, the greater implications of this early use of habitual fire went far beyond the knowledge that these proto–*Homo sapiens* were able to use it to cook meals, temper tools, and even use wood ash to freeze-dry food and animal hides. Analysis of the dental calculus, or tartar, present on the human teeth found at the site revealed the chemical absorption of "respiratory irritants" caused by the owner's long exposure to smoke from indoor fires.[1] Arguably, this is something that must have occurred across a considerable period of time, perhaps even an entire lifetime.

The habitual use of fire, as previously made clear, was almost certainly the manner in which both *Homo erectus* and later proto–*Homo sapiens* first came to learn of the effects of hallucinogens. The smoke from easily sourced psychoactive plants burned on fires in confined spaces like caves would have alerted these earliest humans to the potential effects and outcomes of entering into altered states of consciousness. This would have included the achievement of communion with perceived otherworldly realms as well as the entities or beings considered to inhabit them.

It is impossible to say at this time exactly what psychotropic (that is, psychoactive) plants might have been burned on fires during the occupation of the Qesem Cave. One species that does come to mind is Syrian Rue (*Pegamun harmala*), also known as African Rue, the smoke from which can induce altered states of consciousness. More obvious, however, would be the Acacia plant, which is known to contain psychoactive alkaloids such as Dimethyltryptamine (DMT). These alkaloids can be found either in their leaves or in their root bark.[2] Several species of Acacia are known to exist today both in northern Africa and in the Levant including *Acacia albida*. So there is every chance that at least some of these species were present in these same regions during the occupation of the Qesem Cave.

INSPIRED BY FIRE

Might the cave's inhabitants have been inspired by such otherworldly contacts with the ancestral realms into developing new technologies and new ideas in innovation on various levels? Was this knowledge thought to have originated from spirit presences encountered during altered states of consciousness? I believe the answer is *yes,* although the greater question then becomes, What is the true source of this otherworldly information? Was it simply entering the minds of these early human beings from deep subconscious levels of the brain, or is there a remote chance that the perceived intelligences thought to be present during altered states are in fact real?

HOLY OF HOLIES—THE SHELF

With Barkai's filmmaker friend having now departed the site due to a prior engagement, Barkai was eager for us to explore the cave's deeper recesses. This began with a descent down a metal ladder, bringing us level with the area known as the Shelf, the cave's holy of holies. This, he pointed out, was where both the swan wing bone and flint polyhedron had been found (see plate 12). He wanted to emphasize, however, that although they were placed near to each other spatially, they were not deposited at the same time. Many thousands of years divided these two important acts, a realization made all the more easier to understand when it is remembered that the cave was in use across a period of around 220,000 years.

That said, there seems no getting away from the fact that this area of the cavern was seen as special in some manner. The alcove itself is situated in the northern part of the cave, its interior facing toward the south. Yet whether any kind of directionality was intended by its usage remains unclear.

Continuing our descent into the deepest part of the cave, Barkai explained that we were now around 36 to 39 feet (11–12 meters) below the gated entrance to the cave.

What I saw before me now were walls of speleothems, secondary mineral deposits that form in caves through the presence of flowing, dripping, or seeping water (see plate 13). These seemed to be thick with animal bones and stone tools.

"As you can see, it is full of finds," Barkai confirmed, having stepped off the ladder and onto the lowest occupational floor explored to date. "You see, it is full of flints and bones, and everything here is AYCC, and we have not even reached the bottom yet."*

I joined him in the confined space, which seemed to open out slightly toward the north, the direction that digging had continued until the end of the last scheduled season of excavations back in 2016.

I suggested that it was going to take a very long time to get some final answers here, especially with people constantly trying to break into the portable building outside and big trucks careering past on the road outside, causing the whole place to shake on a fairly regular basis.

Ran agreed, adding, "Sometimes when a truck goes past, you have the feeling of fresh air coming from this area." He gestured toward the opening in the northern wall. "So it is clearly connected to some other chambers."

So the cave could go on and on, with no end yet in sight. There were clearly decades of exploration ahead.

"Yes, but there is a limit on how far you can go," he pointed out.

So why have there been no excavations at the site since 2016?

"For a different number of reasons," he replied. "In the last season, we went on mainly to find bedrock and to find whether there was something earlier underneath. But we were not able to do it, and there is a limit to how much you can do.

"We accumulated tons of material that needed to be understood and processed. We were working for 17 years in a row, and this is too much. This is why we stopped."

What does he feel he would find if they continued to excavate? What would be his holy grail if he could find it here?

Barkai's answer was immediate. "My holy grail would be to find an Acheulean layer with elephants," he revealed.

Why was this so important?

"This would be evidence of the mechanism behind the transition from the Acheulean to the AYCC following the disappearance of the elephants, which was crucial in this transition."

And obviously, the swan wing bone is extraordinary too, since it shows that

---

*All quotes from Ran Barkai in this chapter are accurate and in context. They have been edited slightly for publication.

shamanism, in whatever its form, was present here as much as 330,000 years ago, and arguably earlier still.

Barkai had his own thoughts on the matter. "Yes, but if I am right, and the scenario I'm suggesting took place, then these people must have felt severely disappointed by the universe, because what they depended upon, the elephants, were not available anymore.

"They were in a kind of crisis, and they had to renew their relationships with the cosmos. So I think this wing bone could be an indication of the origins of something new beginning to happen."

I had to agree. But the choice of the swan—it is beautiful, powerful, and migrates, and the links between swans and animism are currently thought to go back at least 24,000 years.

"Everything was done with a reason," Barkai responded. "They realized they had to change their relationship with the cosmos, and the swan maybe was one of the elements of this change. But it wasn't just the swan. Another example is the use of fallow deer bones to shape stone tools."

Barkai explained how the Qesem inhabitants hunted fallow deer, butchered them, ate them, and then broke the bones for the marrow they contained. They then picked up the bone fragments and used them to shape tools. These in turn were used to butcher more fallow deer. It was a symbiotic relationship between deer and human, "a kind of cosmological circle," as Barkai described it.

Thus with the disappearance of the elephant herds, the Qesem people were forced to create a new but much deeper and more meaningful relationship with the world of spirits in order to restore this lost connection with the cosmos.

"So when you put this together with the use of the swan bone and the stone balls or spheroids, you get a more fuller picture," he continued. "So not only was there a new mode of adaptation following the Acheulean, but also a new mode of relationship with the universe."

A NEW HUMAN LINEAGE

So the use of the spheroids and polyhedrons—was this part of this renewal process? Was it really to create a much stronger connection with the ancestors?

"Absolutely," Barkai affirmed. However, he admitted, "Most of my colleagues would say I'm crazy. But most of my colleagues are not asking the most basic question, which is *why?*"

The "why" in this instance was the emergence of the AYCC through the need for a renewal of connection with the cosmos following the disappearance of both the elephants and the *Homo erectus* population. And, of course, the added dimension to all this is the modern humanlike teeth found at the site. They suggest we are also dealing with a completely new . . .

"A new hominin lineage," Barkai cut in, finishing my sentence. "Yes, indeed."

Its unexpected appearance signaled a huge shift from the preexisting *Homo erectus* way of life to that of the earliest modern humans.

"If you can come across a paper that presents the question 'Why did *Homo sapiens* emerge?' please send it to me," he now teased, with a smile. "People are simply not dealing with these issues."

These matters become even more pertinent when you realize that the Qesem people represent a form of proto–modern human thriving in the Levant at least 100,000 years before the earliest known appearance of anatomically modern humans in Africa around 300,000 years ago.

"Absolutely, but we still can't be more precise about the colonization of the Levant," he admitted. "My daughters are angry because they keep saying to me 'How come you stopped excavating at the Qesem Cave before you found a human skull?' There must be more remains here. If we have teeth, there's got to be more. But we are not fossil hunters," he made clear. "We want to understand the whole picture. So another good reason to continue excavating is to answer the question 'Who are these people?'"

This was an extraordinary vision of the past and one I felt privileged to share with Barkai as we stood there in the deepest part of the Qesem Cave. Yet where did it all begin, and why did the Qesem people become among the most advanced human beings on the planet around 400,000 years ago? These are questions that will have at least some answers by the end of this book.

25

MOUNTAINS OF POWER

Prior to departing Tel Aviv University for our memorable visit to the Qesem Cave, Ran Barkai had spoken about the discovery of a new archaeological site—one of great importance to our understanding of the development of the Acheulo-Yabrudian culture responsible for the emergence of the Qesem Cave community some 420,000 years ago.

The site in question was uncovered at Jaljulia, a town located around 12 miles (20 kilometers) north-northeast of Tel Aviv and just under 4 miles (6 kilometers) northwest of the Qesem Cave (see figure 20.1 on page 159). There, in 2016, during the construction of a new road, the Yitzhak Rabin Highway (Highway 6), and the building of a nearby urban complex, workmen started to uncover scatterings of prehistoric tools. This led to a team headed jointly by Maayan Shemer of the Israel Antiquities Authority and Ran Barkai from the Department of Archaeology and Ancient Near Eastern Cultures at Tel Aviv University to begin investigating the site.

At a depth of around 16 to 19 feet (5–6 meters), excavators came across large quantities of Acheulean handaxes that were around half a million years old. They also found a large number of flint tools that adequately displayed the inhabitants' remarkable "technological innovation, development and creativity."[1]

Jaljulia, it was soon realized, had played host to an enormous open-air camp as much as 1 hectare in size, situated in a more-or-less paradisiacal setting on the banks of a long-vanished stream—an area rich in vegetation, herd animals, and suitable materials for making tools.

The bulk of the stone tools retrieved from the site, which today, unfortunately, lies beneath a modern housing development, were for the most part manufactured by *Homo erectus* sometime prior to 450,000 years ago. However, excavations have also revealed a quite separate set of tools that are somewhat similar in style to those found manufactured just about 4 miles (6 kilometers) away at the Qesem Cave. What this suggests is that Jaljulia represents a place of transition between the Acheulean industry of *Homo erectus* and the emerging Acheulo-Yabrudian culture, which we know to have been in full swing by around 420,000 years ago. The future examination of literally thousands of stone tools found during precious salvage operations at Jaljulia will now hopefully tell us more about this time of transition in tool manufacturing toward the end of the Lower Paleolithic period.

THE ENIGMA OF THE EOCENE FLINT

Yet for me the most important point about the Jaljulia site was the fact that whereas some of the tools found there came from local flint available even today in a local stream, some were manufactured from a quite distinctive type of flint identified as having come from the Samarian Hills well to the east. The significance of this finding is that similar tools made of the same flint have been found at the Qesem Cave.[2]

The type of flint in question has tentatively been identified as coming from Eocene beds around 34 to 56 million years old and present to this day on the slopes of Mount Gerizim, which overlooks the Palestinian city of Nablus in the West Bank. It lies approximately 18 miles (30 kilometers) east-northeast of the Qesem Cave and a similar distance away from Jaljulia (see fig. 25.1, p. 200). What this implies is that the inhabitants of both sites deliberately sought out pieces of Eocene flint that had accumulated in the drainage channels formed by water running off the slopes of the mountain. This revelation was highly significant indeed.

As previously indicated, Rodney Hale had noted that during the northernmost risings of the moon during its 18.61-year standstill cycle, the lunar orb can be seen to rise in accordance with the twin mountains of Mount Gerizim and Mount Ebal as viewed from the hill immediately above and behind the Qesem Cave. Even before my visit to Israel, this fact, and others we shall explore shortly, had alerted me to the potential importance of these twin mountains to the area's Acheulo-Yabrudian population.

Fig. 25.1. Map of the Levant showing the locations of Jaljulia, Qesem,
and the twin mountains of Gerizim and Ebal.

To now find that the terminal Acheulean and later Acheulo-Yabrudian peoples of Jaljulia and Qesem might have taken a direct interest in the Eocene flint available on the slopes of Mountain Gerizim was compelling indeed.

MOUNT TABOR

Supporting this hypothesis is another similar association between the Lower Paleolithic peoples of the Levant and an important mountain site, in this case Mount Tabor in the Lower Galilee region of northern Israel. As much as 400,000 years ago, Eocene flint was being quarried from a site named Sede Ilan, close by, which, as Ran Barkai and Avi Gopher have noted, is Mount Tabor, arguably one of the most prominent and iconic natural landmarks in the region.[3] Since quarries in many indigenous cultures—such as those in New Guinea, Australia, and Polynesia, for example—have always been seen as "highly important, dangerous and sacred places," there seems every reason to suspect that the collection of flint from a location so close to Mount Tabor had a special meaning, its flint perhaps being seen to have special properties.[4] If this scenario is correct, then it is possible that similar quarries existed during this same epoch in the foothills of Mount Gerizim, a landmark that, as we shall see, was also considered to have a special place in the local environment.

LIMINAL REALM

What then can we make of the Lower Paleolithic inhabitants of Jaljulia and the Qesem Cave potentially taking an interest in Mount Gerizim? Was it simply an iconic landmark in the local landscape, or might it have played a more symbolic role, the appearance of the full moon above the peaks of both Mount Gerizim and nearby Mount Ebal marking this territory out as some kind of liminal realm?

Crediting such beliefs to the proto–human beings of the Lower Paleolithic age might seem far-fetched. As we have seen, however, there is growing evidence that the Qesem people displayed advanced human behavior on an unprecedented scale and that they were among the most intelligent people on the planet at this time.

THE BLUESTONES OF STONEHENGE

That said, we would need to come forward hundreds of thousands of years before seeing similar patterns of ritual procurement of materials from sites deemed to have special powers. Although no real studies have been done into this subject, one might consider the obtainment of the "bluestone" megaliths of Stonehenge from their place of origin 140 miles (225 kilometers) away in the Preseli Hills of Pembrokeshire, West Wales, as a prime example of this type of human behavior. (In actuality, the term *bluestone* refers to several different types of similar-looking hard rock, including spotted dolerite and rhyolite.)

One of the sites where these bluestones were quarried some 5,000 years ago has recently been identified by a team led by Mike Parker Pearson of the Institute of Archaeology, University College London, as a rocky spur of rhyolite at the western end of Craig Rhos-y-felin.[5] Thus one has to question why the Neolithic peoples of West Wales would have wanted to take with them to the future site of Stonehenge, on what is today Salisbury Plain in southwestern England, large numbers of bluestones, which they then used to create circular megalithic monuments.

According to Colin Richards from the University of Manchester, who is a specialist in Neolithic quarries, Craig Rhos-y-felin probably possessed a "special significance for prehistoric people."[6] Parker Pearson and his colleagues go further, proposing that for the people of that time, the removal of the stones from Wales "probably related to their significance as symbols of identity" and that their identity was thus "ancestral, with stones representing the deceased ancestors, because the earliest contexts in which bluestones were placed . . . were monuments with ancestral and funerary associations."[7] In other words, the transfer of the bluestones from West Wales to Salisbury Plain brought with it a perceived liminal link with the ancestors of the Neolithic peoples who would eventually come to settle in the vicinity of Stonehenge. These individuals, Parker Pearson and his colleagues firmly suspect, not only came from West Wales but also presumably saw the Craig Rhos-y-felin quarry site as a symbol of sacral power.[8]

Other examples of the procurement of stone materials from locations deemed to have special qualities can be cited. They include Kanawha black flint from Mount Armstrong in West Virginia, which was used across North America from the Pre-Clovis age, circa 14,000 years ago, through to the Mississippian period of Native American history. The fact that stone tools and projectile points made of Kanawha black flint have been found alongside burials of supposed shamans tends to suggest not only that this material was considered to have some special significance but also that this power originated from Mount Armstrong.[9] In many ways, the attributes of Kanawha black flint can be likened to those of the black volcanic glass known as obsidian that was procured from the foothills of sacred mountains by many Mesoamerican cultures from circa 1500 BCE through until historical times. Obsidian was deemed to contain the power of the volcanoes that ejected it in the first place. The fact that in Aztec mythology obsidian was associated with the god Tezcatlipoca, meaning "Smoking Mirror," who was himself a personification of the mountain Popocatépetl near Mexico City, is a good example of this relationship.[10]

AN ANCIENT POWER

From these examples alone, we can begin to see the importance surrounding the removal of geological materials from sites deemed to have special properties associated with supernatural forces and ancestral spirits. If we are then to see something similar occurring in the Levant as far back as the Lower Paleolithic

age, then it is tempting to speculate just how these hominin populations, originally *Homo erectus* and later proto–*Homo sapiens,* might themselves have identified with prominent landmarks in the landscape. Is it possible that as early
as the Lower Paleolithic age, mountains such as Mount Gerizim and Mount
Tabor were seen as places of great power associated with otherworldly activities?

All of these mountains, and many more besides in the Levant, feature heavily both in the Hebrew Bible and also in the New Testament. Mount Tabor,
for instance, is said to be the location of the Transfiguration of Jesus following the Resurrection.[11] Mount Gerizim, on the other hand, plays an infinitely
more important role. As we shall see next, from the age of the great patriarchs
down to the entry into Canaan of the children of Israel under the leadership of
Joshua, the mountain features heavily in the establishment of Israelite religious
tradition. As far away as this might seem from the Lower Paleolithic world of
the Qesem Cave some 400,000 years ago, it is a story that simply has to be told.

26

CENTER OF THE WORLD

Mount Gerizim (Samaritan: Ar-garízim; Arabic: Jabal Jarizīm or Jebel el-Tor) is seen as a sacred spot in the minds of all those who live in the West Bank, although none more so than the Samaritans. Their ever-dwindling community (now down to just 250 members) continues to exist in a modern town situated on the southern slopes of the mountain. (A second, somewhat smaller Samaritan community exists today at Holon, a city just south of Tel Aviv.)

THE GREAT SCHISM

The Samaritans claim to be direct descendants of the original Israelites, in particular the house of the prophet Joseph, which combines two tribes, that of Ephraim and that of Manasseh, with Ephraim and Manasseh being the two sons of Joseph. The ancestors of the Samaritans are said to have remained in and around Mount Gerizim after two of the original twelve tribes, those of Judah and Benjamin, broke away to form a separate community at a place called Shiloh, a story told in chapter 38.

Thereafter the tribes of Judah and Benjamin, along with members of the Levite priestly caste, turned their attentions to the ancient city of Jerusalem, which until that time had been the homeland of a people known as the Jebusites. This took place, we are told, during the reign of King David, sometime during the eleventh century BCE.[1] It would not, however, be until the reign of King Solomon, David's son, that a magnificent temple would be built

204

in Jerusalem as the principal place of worship of an amalgam of the two tribes, which was thereafter known as the house of Judah.

THE DWELLING PLACE OF GOD

The establishment of Jerusalem as God's dwelling place (an important term that we will discuss as we go along) was quite obviously contested by Israel's other tribes, whose own center of worship was Shechem, the ancient name for the Palestinian city of Nablus, located at the base of Mount Gerizim in the northern part of the country. Not only did the other ten tribes see the sons of Judah and Benjamin as apostates who had turned their backs on the pure faith of Israel, but for them Mount Gerizim was the sole place where Yahweh had chosen to gift the land of Canaan to the Israelites. This was something done through the covenant made with Abraham, his son Isaac, and Isaac's son Jacob.

More significantly, Gerizim, and Gerizim alone, was seen by the northern tribes as God's sole dwelling place, as well as, in their opinion, the very center of the Earth.[2] This claim, made in Judges 9:37, speaks of the mountain as being *ṭab-būr hā-'ā-reṣ,* "the center of the land."[3] Moreover, Mount Gerizim, the Samaritans would go on to claim, had been Yahweh's chosen place of dwelling since before even the time of Adam. So it could never simply be discarded in favor of Jerusalem, somewhere not even mentioned in the Pentateuch. This is the name given to the first five books of the Old Testament, which were accredited to the hand of Moses himself. It should be pointed out that the Samaritans accept only the Pentateuch as their holy books. They reject the rest of the Hebrew Bible (or Old Testament as it is known in Christian tradition) as noncanonical.

MOUNT GERIZIM VERSUS JERUSALEM

In contrast, the Levites—the hereditary priesthood of Israel, who for the most part departed Shechem to join with the tribes of Judah and Benjamin—would go on to proclaim Jerusalem as God's *chosen* dwelling place, rejecting much older traditions regarding the supremacy of Mount Gerizim (see fig. 26.1, p. 206).

Even in the post-exilic period, following the northern tribes' captivity in Assyria toward the end of the eighth century BCE and the captivity of the house of Judah in Babylon some 140 years later, both the Samaritans and

Fig. 26.1. Mount Gerizim and Nablus (ancient Shechem) as seen from Mount Ebal. Drawn by W. L. Leitch from a sketch by L. F. Cassas and engraved by W. Forrest (from Davidson 1862).

Judaeans, initially under Persian control and later under the Hellenic Greeks, continued their bitter rivalry. Each built their own temples—the Second Temple in Jerusalem and a Samaritan temple on Mount Gerizim—to further establish their claims of superiority when it came to the blessings of Yahweh.

The weapon of choice in this fierce theological war was the pen of the priestly scribes, whose primary goal was to subtly alter the Hebrew Bible in favor of their own place of worship, whether this be Mount Gerizim in Samaria (the name given to Israel's northern kingdom) or Mount Zion, Jerusalem's easternmost hill. And there could be only one victor—Gerizim or Zion.

Because of the fierce rivalry between the Samaritan and Jerusalem priesthoods, it seems important to present the reader with all the relevant facts regarding their claims of divine superiority when it comes to holy mountains. Only then can we go on to better understand why Mount Gerizim might have been seen as special by the Lower Paleolithic inhabitants of the region. So please excuse this brief excursion into the lives of the earliest patriarchs of the Bible, which is something many of us will have left behind in school.

27

AGE OF THE PATRIARCHS

Our story begins with the arrival in Canaan, the land of the Canaanites, of Abraham, the great patriarch of the early Israelites. At the time, Canaan consisted of a series of city-states located in what is today Syria, Lebanon, Israel, and the Palestinian territories. Those who inhabited these city-states were mostly peoples of a West Semitic background, their main gods being El, his wife Anat, his son Baal, and his wife Ba'alah or Asherah. When exactly Abraham lived is open to debate, although according to biblical chronology, his entry into Canaan occurred probably around 2100 BCE (+/- 150 years), placing him within the late Early Bronze Age or early Middle Bronze Age periods of Near Eastern history.

UR OF THE CHALDEES

We are told that Abraham spent his early life in Ur of the Chaldees,[1] the city of the Chaldeans. The Chaldeans, or Sabians as they became known, were the celebrated astronomer-priests, astrologers, and worshippers of the stars and planets whose great center of learning was the ancient city of Harran in what is today southeastern Turkey. At some point, so Hebrew and Samaritan legends record, Abraham comes into conflict with a pagan tyrant named Nimrod, who in both Hebrew and Christian tradition was said to have been the builder of the Tower of Babel. According to Samaritan tradition Nimrod tries to put Abraham to death by fire,[2] but after he fails to do so, Abraham gets the call from Yahweh to go in search of what will become the Promised Land of God, the future home of his descendants, which turns out to be Canaan in the south.

Fig. 27.1. Illustration by German landscape artist Johann Wilhelm
Schirmer (1807–1863) showing the patriarch Abraham entering Shechem
after his arrival in the Promised Land of Canaan (from Sparrow 1905).

Where exactly Ur of the Chaldees was located has been a subject of fierce debate among academics and biblical scholars for the last 150 years. The British archaeologist Sir C. Leonard Woolley (1880–1960) put claim to its discovery following extensive excavations of a royal cemetery of Sumerian age in Lower Iraq between the years 1922 and 1934. However, this conclusion, widely accepted today, ignores extremely old Moslem, Kurdish, and Christian traditions identifying Ur of the Chaldees with the ancient city of Urfa, modern-day Şanlıurfa, in southeastern Turkey.[3] Urfa is just 28 miles (45 kilometers) north of the Sabian city of Harran (or Haran, as it is written in the Hebrew Bible), where Abraham tarries for a while before making his final departure for Canaan.

THE PROMISED LAND

Abraham's epic journey southward brings him eventually to the Canaanite city of Shechem, modern Nablus, located on the west side of the Jordan valley around 30 miles (50 kilometers) north of modern-day Jerusalem.[4] Towering over Shechem to the north is Mount Ebal (Arabic: Jabal ʿAybāl; Hebrew: Har ʿEval), which is 3,083 feet (940 meters) in height, while immediately to its south is Mount Gerizim at the slightly lower height of 2,890 feet (881 meters). Nablus itself is located in an east-west aligned valley basin situated exactly between the two mountains.

The book of Genesis—compiled in its present form around the time of the Babylonian captivity of the Jews (the term deriving from Judeans; that is, those belonging to the house of Judah)—makes it clear that Abraham's first stop upon his arrival in Canaan was Shechem (see fig. 27.1). It is almost as if he knew where he was heading, even though this is not specifically stated. What was going on in and around Shechem before Abraham and his entourage arrived there also is not stated, although clearly it was already a well established Canaanite city in its own right.

THE OAK OF MOREH

The book of Genesis tells us that after arriving in Shechem, Abraham rested by "the terebinth tree [*ʾê-lō-wn*] of Moreh,"[5] which is also often translated, perhaps correctly, as "the oak of Moreh."[6] The Hebrew word *moreh* (מוֹרֶה) is usually translated as meaning "teacher" or "learning" and is generally assumed to be the personal name of a Canaanite who owned the site of the tree.[7] However, *moreh* means far more than simply "teacher" in the conventional sense, for it can also mean "oracle giver"[8] or "that which speaks," suggesting that the tree was a shrine "where oracles could be obtained."[9] This suggests that Shechem was a place of oracular communication or divination (Hebrew *qesem*) long before Abraham's celebrated arrival in the city.

YAHWEH'S FIRST APPEARANCE

All this makes sense of what happens next, for as Abraham rests by the "terebinth tree" or "oak" of Moreh, Yahweh, the god of the Israelites, appears to him, saying "To your descendants I give [this] land."[10] So thereafter Abraham builds there "an altar to Yahweh who had appeared to him."[11] These passages are meant to establish Shechem not only as the first recorded place of manifestation of Yahweh in the Promised Land but also as the location where God first promises to deliver Canaan to the patriarch's descendants and the children of Israel as a whole.

Curiously, the ancient Canaanite/Israelite city found at the eastern edge of modern Nablus, at the place called Tell Balata, takes its name either from the Hebrew *balutt,* meaning "acorn,"[12] or from the Arabic *ballutt,* meaning "oak,"[13] both originally deriving from an Aramaic word meaning "oak tree."[14] The Samaritans know Tell Balata as the site of "the Holy Oak" and "Tree of Grace,"[15] an allusion once again to the original site of the "terebinth tree" or "oak" of Moreh first mentioned in Genesis 12:6. Almost certainly, Tell Balata was the site of ancient Shechem as well as the "terebinth tree" or "oak of Moreh."

THE 'AQEDAH OR BINDING OF ISAAC

Much later, so the book of Genesis tells us, Abraham's wife, Sarah, becomes pregnant, even though she is ninety years old. She gives birth to a son, Isaac, with whom Yahweh pledges to make his covenant after his father's death. However, Yahweh tells Abraham to go to the "land of Moriah and offer him there as a burnt offering on one of the mountains of which I will tell you."[16] There the patriarch builds an altar and binds his son in readiness for the sacrifice.[17] As he takes out his knife to slay the child, the angel of God prevents him from completing the act, his faith in Yahweh having been successfully tested.[18] Instead, a ram caught in brambles nearby is offered in Isaac's stead.[19]

Thereafter the angel of Yahweh calls out a second time, saying that since Abraham has done this, his son alone will receive the blessing of God, something that will be inherited by his descendants, who will prosper in this land.[20] This important incident in the book of Genesis is known in the Jewish faith as the 'Aqedah, or the Binding of Isaac, since it confirms Yahweh's wish to establish his kingdom on Earth with the descendants of Abraham. Identifying where this event took place became of paramount importance to the later Israelites.

WHERE IS MORIAH?

The book of Genesis gives no clear indication where the 'Aqedah might have occurred, saying only that it was a mountain at a place called "Moriah," a name found nowhere else in the Pentateuch. Yet the fact that Abraham goes straight there following the calling from God implies he knew full well where it was located. The Levitical priests of the house of Judah would come to identify Moriah with Jerusalem's Mount Zion. This, however, was long after the establishment of Jerusalem as the capital of Judea. So where exactly was Moriah?

The answer is simple, although it involves either innocent revision or, more likely, deliberate alteration of the original text of Genesis, for there is every indication that the *true* spelling of Moriah (מוֹרִיָּה) should be Moreh (מוֹרֶה), the simple addition of an extra "plene" *yod* (יְ) altering the name to Moriah.[21] This can be determined by the fact that the same line in the Samaritan Bible reads "Moreh" and not "Moriah."[22] So how did this happen? When was Moreh changed into Moriah?

The changing of Moreh to Moriah was almost certainly meant to disassociate the site of the 'Aqebah from the "oak" or "terebinth tree" of Moreh at Shechem, where Abraham set up the first altar after Yahweh had appeared to him. In creating a new location named Moriah, the Levitical priests of the house of Judah could now go on to identity it with Mount Zion, Jerusalem's own holy hill. This philological sleight of hand was completed by introducing a *separate* reference to Moriah elsewhere in the Hebrew Bible, in this instance, 2 Chronicles 3:1, which reads: "And Solomon beginneth to build the house of Jehovah, in Jerusalem, *in the mount of Moriah,* where He appeared to David his father, in the place that David had prepared, in the threshing-floor of Ornan the Jebusite.[23] (current author's emphasis)

Yet it can easily be shown that the words "*in the mount of Moriah*" constitute an interpolation, a later addition, into the existing text; this being done to tie in the entire passage with the *other* reference to "Moriah" in the book of Genesis, which can itself be shown to be false.[24] The purpose of this exercise was thus an attempt by the Levitical priests of Jerusalem to establish Mount Zion (under the invented name Moriah) not only as the site of the 'Aqedah, the Binding of Isaac, where Yahweh made his covenant with Isaac, but also as the deity's true Bethel, or chosen place of dwelling. This final claim concerning Jerusalem's Mount Zion being the true Bethel, or House of God, then becomes important in the next Genesis story we explore, which is Jacob's dream vision of angels seen moving up and down a ladder between heaven and earth.

BETWEEN HEAVEN AND EARTH—
THE STORY OF JACOB'S LADDER

On his way between Beer-sheba in the Negev region in southern Israel and a place called Padam-Aram in the north (almost certainly an Aramean kingdom in northern Syria associated with the ancient city of Harran), Isaac's son Jacob, we are told, rested for the night (see fig. 27.2).[25] There he took a stone and used it as a pillow,[26] and as he slept he dreamed of angels climbing a ladder that stretched between heaven and earth.[27] It is a familiar story we all probably remember from our youth. The actual words offered in Genesis 28:12 are: "And he dreamed and behold a ladder set up on the earth and its top reached to heaven; and there the angels of God were ascending and descending on it."[28] As this dream vision occurs, Yahweh stands beside Jacob and says, "I am the Lord, the God of Abraham your father and the God of Isaac; the land on which you lie I will give to you and to your offspring."[29] He adds that he will bring him "back to this land; for I will not leave you until I have done what I have promised you."[30] Jacob awakes from his dream believing the location is the "house of God" (Hebrew *bet-elohim*) as well as the "gate of heaven."[31]

In the morning, Jacob took up the stone on which his head had lain all night and "set it up for a pillar and poured oil on the top of it."[32] It is said that Jacob thereafter "called that place Bethel," that is the "house or dwelling of God," after which the narrative crucially adds that "the name of the city was Luz at the first."[33] In other words, before being given the name Bethel, the "city" in question was known under the name Luz. This we know was located

Fig. 27.2. Jacob falls asleep and sees angels climbing a ladder that stretches between heaven and earth (from Foster 1897).

somewhere in the vicinity of Shechem from the writings of the English traveler John de Mandeville, who made a pilgrimage through the Holy Land during the first half of the fourteenth century CE.

In his *The Travels of John Mandeville,* first circulated between 1357 and 1371, de Mandeville records that "a mile from Sichar [that is, Shechem] is the city of Luz; and in that city dwelt Abraham a certain time."[34] From the narrative's description of the northern foothills of Samaria, it is clear that the author, whether John himself or someone else, was privy to firsthand knowledge of the area around Shechem.

Since both Luz and Bethel can be identified with a location near Mount Gerizim, we can say with some certainty that both sites must have been in the vicinity of Tell Balata, ancient Shechem, where the "terebinth tree" or "oak of Moreh" was located. It is a conclusion emphasized still further by the fact that following his dream, Jacob goes on to say, "This stone which I have set as a pillar shall be [the] house of God [*bet-elohim*]. And of all that You give me I will surely a tenth to You [give]."[35]

The word here for "pillar" is *massebah* (plural *masseboth*), a Hebrew name for standing stones found throughout the Levant and used to mark places of special or cultic significance.[36] So Jacob's Pillow was most probably a massebah pillar erected somewhere in the vicinity of Mount Gerizim. This same standing stone is alluded to in Genesis 31, when Jacob receives a visit from a divine figure who states, "I [am] the God of Bethel, where you anointed a pillar and made a vow to me."[37] So here then is even further evidence that the dwelling place of Yahweh, as the God of Bethel, was (and, for the Samaritans, still is[38]) Mount Gerizim.

JACOB RETURNS TO BETHEL

Later on in Genesis, we find Jacob (whose name is changed by God to Israel, making him the eponymous ancestor of the Israelites[39]) returning to Bethel after 21 or more years away in Paran-Aram and Haran (Harran) in the north, where he was able to secure a suitable wife (actually two, Leah and Rachel). On his way back to Canaan, he encounters his brother Esau, whom he has already cheated out of his inheritance. It is a story we need not explore here, although suffice it to say that the events leading up to this uncomfortable meeting must have troubled Jacob greatly. It is at this point that Yahweh intercedes, telling

Jacob to go to Bethel and there build an altar.[40] Yes, another altar! The communication inspires Jacob to inform his household to turn out any "foreign gods"[41] or "gods of the strangers,"[42] that is, personal idols (so-called *teraphim*), and prepare themselves for the journey to Bethel, where he will build this new altar. So after going up to Bethel,[43] everyone hands over their idols as well as the rings from their ears (presumably because they were also seen as potentially idolatrous), which Jacob then hides "under the oak which [is] by Shechem."[44] This confirms once again that Bethel is Luz and that Luz was either Shechem or somewhere very close by.

The Hebrew word used in this passage for "oak" is *hā-'ê-lāh*, which is given as "terebinth [tree]" in some translations of the Old Testament.[45] Whatever the case, it is clear this is the same "oak" or "terebinth tree" of Moreh where Yahweh first appeared to Abraham upon his arrival in Shechem and where, afterward, Abraham sets up the first Israelite altar in Canaan. So not only is this story even further evidence that Bethel is either Shechem or that it lies somewhere nearby, but it also shows that Jacob, by going back to Bethel, is returning to the very tree where his grandfather had set up his own altar two generations earlier. Even further confirmation of this surmise is presented by the passage that immediately follows the one above, which reads, "So came Jacob to Luz which [is] in the land of Canaan that [is] in Bethel, he and all the people who [were] with him. And he built there an altar and called the place El Bethel [that is, "El the House of God"] because there appeared to him God [*hā-'ĕ-lō-hîm*] when he fled from the face of his brother."[46]

MOUNT EBAL—CURSES AND BLESSINGS

We move forward in time now to the entry into Canaan of the children of Israel following the 40 years they spent in the wilderness of Sinai. Just before this happens, the Israelites reach Mount Nebo on the eastern side of the Jordan valley. There, according to Deuteronomy 27:4, Moses and the Elders of Israel command the twelve tribes to cross the river into the Promised Land and there raise up great stones "in mount Ebal,"[47] which are to be whitewashed with lime, translated elsewhere as meaning "plaster" (see below). Thereafter they are to build there "an altar of stones"[48] to honor Yahweh with "burnt-offerings" and "sacrificed peace-offerings."[49] On the stones are to be written "the words of this law, well engraved," in other words, the Ten Commandments granted by

Yahweh to Moses and Israel on Mount Sinai. All of this is to be conducted on "Mount Ebal," Gerizim's northern counterpart, under the charge of Joshua, the son of Nun, who will become commander of the Israelite armies after Moses's death.

Before this happens, Moses, who is about to die, addresses the people, saying, "These [tribes] shall stand to bless the people on Mount Gerizim when you have crossed the Jordan: Simeon, and Levi, Judah, and Issachar, and Joseph, and Benjamin. And these [tribes] shall stand to curse on Mount Ebal: Reuben, Gad, and Asher, and Zebulun, Dan, and Naphtali."[50]

Following Moses's death, the Israelites cross the River Jordan and enter the Promised Land of Canaan. Upon their arrival at Shechem, Joshua climbs "Mount Ebal" and creates a monument of stones as well as an altar for burnt offerings and peace offerings to Yahweh, all just as Moses had instructed him to do. Thereafter the twelve tribes are split in two, with six commanded to ascend Mount Ebal to pronounce a series of curses against those who go against the Laws, while the other six ascend Mount Gerizim to pronounce blessings on those who adhere to the Laws.[51]

These passages from the book of Deuteronomy are crucial, since they make clear the fact that upon entering the Promised Land, the Israelites proclaim the Laws of Moses from the slopes of Mount Gerizim and Mount Ebal. Not only does this confirm the importance of these twin mountains to the Israelites, but it also tells us that reaching Shechem was a primary concern for the children of Israel upon entering the Promised Land of Canaan.

The incredible significance of Mount Gerizim in particular is echoed in the holy books of the Samaritans. These tell how Moses, after climbing Mount Nebo, gazes longingly out toward Mount Gerizim on the other side of the Jordan valley. Even though it is the true dwelling place of Yahweh and the mountain of the patriarchs, it is somewhere he knows he is fated never to reach.[52]

The Mountain of Offerings—Gerizim or Ebal?

There is something else of significance about this account of the curses and blessings being sounded out from the slopes of Mount Ebal and Mount Gerizim. Among the tribes that climbed Mount Gerizim to broadcast the blessings was the house of Joseph, to which Joshua belonged. He, as we shall recall, was commanded by Moses to set up a monument of stones as well as an altar for burnt offerings and peace offerings on Mount Ebal, this being the Mountain of Curses. If so, then why did Joshua then have to go across to Mount Gerizim, the Mountain of Blessings, to join not only the house of Joseph but also those of Benjamin and Judah, who would very soon abandon northern Israel in favor of Jerusalem? Why were these particular tribes on Mount Gerizim, the sole holy place of the northern tribes, and not on Mount Ebal, where Joshua had set up the first altar of the Israelites upon reaching the Promised Land?

The Deliberate Alteration of Deuteronomy 27:4

The answer is, once again, simple—a deliberate obfuscation of the facts by the Levitical scribes in Jerusalem. Let me explain. *Joshua was never on Mount Ebal.* He never set up Israel's first altar there at all. He was *always* on Gerizim, something known to the Levitical scribes, who deemed to take away the obvious importance of Gerizim in the establishment of the first altar by Joshua by substituting the word *Ebal* for *Gerizim* at some point during the rewriting of the Hebrew Bible in the post-exilic period.

The Samaritans have always maintained that the true site where Joshua set up the first altar of the Israelites was Mount Gerizim. It is for this reason that in the Samaritan Pentateuch, Deuteronomy 27:4 has "Gerizim" and not "Ebal."[53] The Samaritans' claims, however, regarding the superiority of Gerizim over Ebal are generally ignored by Hebrew and Christian scholars alike.

Various pieces of evidence do, however, appear to support the Samaritans' claims. For instance, in an Old Latin form of the Septuagint (OL Codex 100), the Greek rendering of the Old Testament, Gerizim appears instead of Ebal in Deuteronomy 27:4,[54] while Gerizim not Ebal appears also in the *Vetus Latina,* another old form of the Greek Septuagint.[55] Since both texts were almost certainly copied from quite separate Greek originals, which were themselves based on preexisting versions of the Hebrew Bible, they are unlikely to have been influenced by the Samaritan Pentateuch.

DEAD SEA SCROLLS DISCOVERY

More important is the recent surfacing of a previously unrecorded Dead Sea Scroll fragment containing the text of Deuteronomy 27:4. It was found, apparently, in Qumran Cave 4, where many of the main scrolls were unearthed in 1946 and 1947. Dating from circa 175 BCE, the tiny fragment has been carefully examined by James H. Charlesworth, the director of the Dead Sea Scrolls Project at the Princeton Theological Seminary.[56] He is satisfied that it is genuine,[57] as are other scholars in the Dead Sea Scrolls community.[58] Aside from various lacunas, most of the text of Deuteronomy 27:4 is preserved, including the all-important passage: "[When] you [have crossed] the Jo[r]dan, you shall set u[p] these stones, about, [which I charge you] today, on Mount Gerizim, and coat [them with plaster. And there, you shall build an altar to the LORD your God, an altar of st]ones."[59]

Although some scholars remain skeptical about the fragment's authenticity,[60] its existence strongly suggests that the Samaritans have been correct all along and that it was not "in Mount Ebal" that Joshua set up the first altar upon the Israelite's entry into the Holy Land, *but on Mount Gerizim,* Yahweh's *original* dwelling place.

It should be pointed out that I am not attempting to promote the religious doctrines of the Samaritans over and above those of the Jewish faith. What I *will* say, however, is that there is every reason to believe that the Samaritans preserve a very ancient form of the Israelite religious tradition, and one that very clearly shows Mount Gerizim and the area around Shechem as having been extremely important to both the Israelites and their forerunners, the patriarchs Abraham, Isaac, and Jacob.

So exactly what was it about Mount Gerizim that so inspired the earliest peoples to inhabit the Jordan valley? The biggest clue, as we see next, comes from Gerizim and Shechem's close association with pivotal dreams and waking visions attributed by both Jews and Samaritans alike to the presence of Yahweh, the god of Israel.

Plate 1. The Square Tower, located in the bottom of the canyon at Hovenweep. It was used by shamans and medicine people to harmonize with the spiritual forces of all three worlds.

Plate 2. The Big Horn Medicine Wheel. Three photos have been carefully put together to provide a wide-angle view of the stone formation. Lora Little is standing in the upper middle to give an idea of the size of the structure.

Plate 3. The Coptic Church of Saint Mary in Zeitoun, a suburb of Cairo, Egypt. The existence of bizarre nightly plasma light manifestations in the 1960s and 1970s challenges our understanding of the relationship between this very real phenomenon and the human mind.

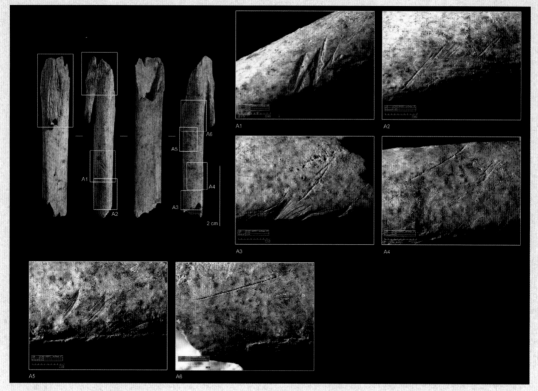

Plate 4. *Top left:* A proximal carpometacarpus shaft from an adult Swan found in Israel's Qesem Cave and thought be between 300,000 and 330,000 years old. The various boxes (*right and below*) show the deliberate cuts on the bone confirming it has been modified to remove the feathers for separate use. Does the existence of this swan wing bone constitute the earliest evidence of shamanism anywhere in the world? Units of measure in boxes are millimeters.

Plate 5. The polyhedron made of flint found in the Qesem Cave beneath the rock feature known as the Shelf. Is it the oldest crystal ball in the world? Units of measure in centimeters.

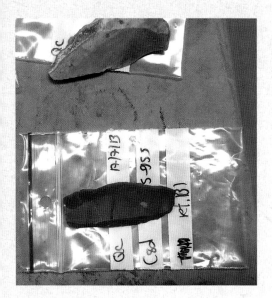

Plate 6. Flint tools from the Qesem Cave manufactured between 200,000 and 420,000 years ago. The upper example is a naturally backed blade; the lower example is a prismatic blade. Note their similarity to those manufactured by Göbekli Tepe's Pre-Pottery Neolithic culture as recently as 11,000 years ago (see plate 7).

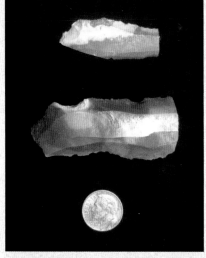

Plate 7. Two blade tools manufactured by Göbekli Tepe's Pre-Pottery Neolithic culture. The similarity to those made in the Qesem Cave at least 200,000 years earlier is unmistakable.

Plate 8. In the box on the left is a large molar found at the site (Denisova 4) identified as belonging to a Denisovan inhabitant. In the box on the right is (on the left) one of the ostrich shell beads found within the site's Denisovan layer (Layer 11) and (on the right) the Denisovan chloritolite bracelet also found in the same layer.

Plate 9. The exterior of the Qesem Cave looking out and across to the modern city of Rosh HaAyin.

Plate 10. Interior of the Qesem Cave enclosure showing archaeologist Ran Barkai and behind him the Trans-Samaria Highway.

Plate 11. The site of the Qesem Cave's approximately 300,000-year-old hearth, where fire was kindled across a period of around 100,000 years.

Plate 12. The view from beneath the rock feature in the Qesem Cave known as the Shelf, where both the swan wing bone and the flint polyhedron were found during excavations.

Plate 13. Andrew Collins looking up from the deepest level of Qesem Cave. Air coming from a deeper level suggests the cave might go on for some distance.

Plate 14. Painting by American-born artist Benjamin West (1738–1820) showing Joshua
and the Israelite tribes arriving in the Promised Land of Canaan having just crossed
the River Jordan. Note the pillar of light rising up from the Ark of the Covenant,
signifying the Shekinah, Yahweh's visible presence on Earth.

Plate 15. The Great Sand Dunes National Park and Reserve in Colorado. The movement of
the sand combined with the valley basin's unique geology makes it a perfect location for the
appearance of plasma light-forms and other strange phenomena.

Plate 16. General view of Taishan Mountain (Mount Tai) in China. The oldest sacred mountain in the country, it was seen as a gateway for souls wishing to enter the land of the dead.

Plate 17. Taishan Mountain is a place of pilgrimage for those of all three main faiths in China—Buddhism, Taoism, and Confucianism. Many visitors have reported the appearance of mysterious light phenomena.

Plate 18. Montage of eleven frames taken consecutively across a 69-second period between 21:18:09 and 21:19:18 on May 31, 2019, showing the peak of Taishan Mountain. Light anomalies appear clearly in two frames (#7507 and #7516).

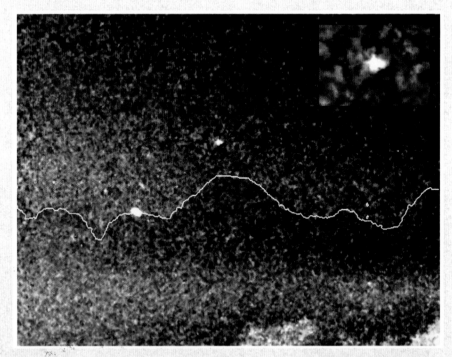

Plate 19. Two frames of Taishan Mountain taken on May 31, 2019, no more than a minute apart and superimposed and enhanced to show the positions of their respective light anomalies. As can be seen, one anomaly sits on the mountain, while the other light is clearly high above the mountain. Does this second anomaly show a plasma manifestation known as an earthquake light?

Plate 20. Jacob's Well in the Bir Ya'qub monastery, located close to Tell Balata on the eastern edge of the ancient city of Nablus, has been associated with the patriarch Jacob for at least 2,000 years (John 4:5–6). According to the Gospel of John, it is where Jesus sat down and talked to a Samaritan woman (John 4:7–29).

Plate 21. The ruins of Tell Balata, an urban center of the early to middle Bronze Age, located on the eastern edge of Nablus. It is thought to be the site of the Canaanite/Israelite city of Shechem. Note the base of the massebah pillar at its center, which might well be of Israelite origin.

Plate 22. Mount Gerizim as seen from Tell Balata. This is the view the Israelites under Joshua would have seen during the ceremony of the curses and blessings, during which the Ark of the Covenant rested in the vicinity of the massebah pillar seen in the picture.

Plate 23. Mount Ebal as seen from Tell Balata, this being on its northern side.

Plate 24. Mount Gerizim and the city of Nablus as seen from the heights of Mount Ebal.

Plate 25. Samaritan priests and elders gather on Mount Gerizim for the feast of the Passover.

Plate 26. The peak of Mount Athos in Greece. Monks and hermits of the Eastern Orthodox Church have long recognized the importance here of mysterious light phenomena identified with the Holy Spirit.

Plate 27. Painting from Mount Athos, Greece, showing the religious icon of the Virgin Mary known as the Virgin of the Gate. It appeared miraculously offshore around the year 800 CE and is said to have floated on the water for 70 years, during which time it produced columns of light that reached the sky, highlighting the repeated presence around Mount Athos of strange light phenomena.

Plate 28. Northern mesa at Skinwalker Ranch with Homestead #2 in the foreground. The geology of both the mesa and the ranch is conducive for the production of plasma light-forms and other strange phenomena.

Plate 29. Photo of Skinwalker Ranch taken by Andrew Collins in August 2019 showing the tree-enshrouded ruins of Homestead #2 with the northern mesa in the background. The strange creature seen above Homestead #2 is a complete mystery. Nothing was seen at the time.

Plate 30. Sign at Marfa, Texas, explaining the presence of the Marfa lights, a mostly plasma-based phenomenon that has appeared locally for at least 150 years.

MARFA MYSTERY LIGHTS

The Marfa Mystery Lights are visible on many clear nights between Marfa and Paisano Pass as one looks towards the Chinati Mountains. The lights may appear in various colors as they move about, split apart, melt together, disappear and reappear.

Robert Reed Ellison, a young cowboy, reported sighting the lights in 1883. He spotted them while tending a herd of cattle and wondered if they were Apache Indian campfires.

Apache Indians believed these eerie lights to be stars dropping to the earth.

Many viewers have theories ranging from scientific to science fiction as they describe their ideas of aliens in UFO's, ranch house lights, St. Elmo's fire, or headlights from vehicles on US 67, the Presidio highway. Some believe the lights are an electrostatic discharge, swamp gases, moonlight shining on veins of mica, of ghosts of Conquistadors searching for gold.

An explanation as to why the lights cannot be located is an unusual phenomenon similar to a miracle, where atmospheric conditions produced by the interaction of cold and warm layers of air bend light so that it can be seen from afar, but not up close.

The mystery of these lights still remains unsolved.

Plate 31. Gregory Little sets up a camera at the observation platform located at Marfa, Texas, to witness the regularly occurring Marfa lights. Despite skeptics' claims that the Marfa lights are simply the headlights of distant cars and trains, the lights continue to appear on a regular basis.

Plate 32. American journalist and paranormalist John Keel (1930–2009), left, with Andrew Collins in Salisbury, southern England, in 1992. Keel's vision of the intelligence behind the UFO phenomenon has greatly influenced the theories of this book's authors.

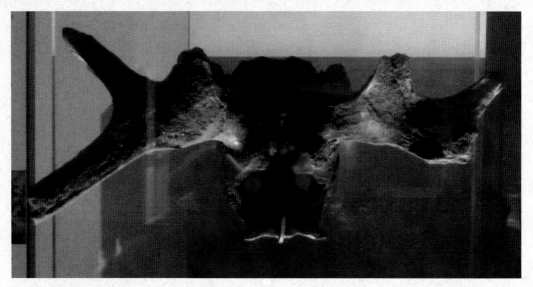

Plate 33. Modified red deer skull complete with antlers found at the Mesolithic ceremonial complex of Star Carr in Yorkshire. Shamanism involving both the red deer and wolf that took place there as much as 11,000 years ago might be responsible for the local appearances of lycaons (canine-headed anthropoids).

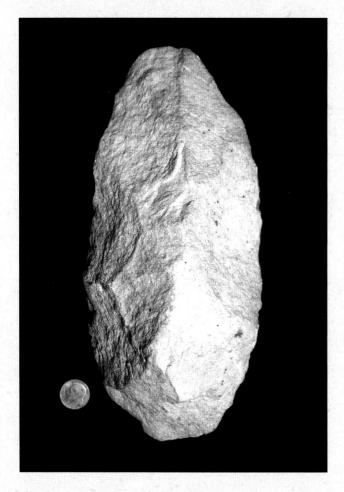

Plate 34. Acheulean handaxe retrieved from a dry riverbed in Simon's Town on the Cape Peninsula in South Africa. Made of hard quartz-bearing sandstone, it is around 1 million years old and was probably manufactured by a member of the African *Homo erectus* population.

Plate 35. The First Shaman—an artistic impression by Russell M. Hossain of a shaman at the Qesem Cave circa 300,000 to 330,000 years ago using swan paraphernalia, spheroids, and polyhedrons to contact the ancestors and using intoxicating smoke from the fire to enter a shifted state of consciousness.

28

REALM OF THE MOUNTAIN GOD

Prior to the Israelites' own entry into Canaan, Moses, his brother Aaron, and even other members of the Israelite tribes all saw and experienced the presence of Yahweh during their 40 years in the wilderness of Sinai. However, Yahweh's appearances there, initially on the mountain of Horeb[1] and afterward on the mountain of Sinai,[2] were outside the Promised Land of God. For this reason, these mountains, as important as they are to the establishment of Israelite religious tradition, were not seen as permanent dwelling places of God. They were simply used by Yahweh to communicate what he wanted to his chosen people.

In the case of Mount Sinai, these communications were so that Moses could receive the Requirements of the Covenant on behalf of Israel.[3] These came with detailed instructions on how to build the Ark of the Covenant, meant both to contain the Tablets of the Law and, via its so-called mercy seat on which were affixed two golden winged cherubim, to act as a portable place of dwelling for Yahweh prior to the permanent settlement of the children of Israel in Canaan. In this manner, the Ark of the Covenant assumed the role previously played by the mountain summits of Horeb and Sinai; in other words, it acted as a temporary point of contact between Yahweh and his chosen people.

The form of Yahweh venerated in the wilderness of Sinai would unquestionably have absorbed elements of local deities seen to inhabit the mountains in question, Mount Sinai in particular. So the fact that the Tablets of the Law were made from stone cut from the mountain[4] can be seen as a deliberate attempt to transfer some small part of its power into portable form so that communication was possible with Yahweh anywhere that the Israelites set up the Tabernacle or Tent of Meeting in which the Ark of the Covenant was housed at night. This connection between the power of mountains and the taking away of representational objects from such locations echoes the manner that the Lower Paleolithic peoples of the Levant sourced Eocene flint from both Mount Tabor and Mount Gerizim to make stone tools.

SINAI IN THE EDOM AND THE LAND OF SEIR

The Sinai of the Old Testament, where the Israelites dwelled during their 40 years in the wilderness, was not, it has to be stated, the region we identify today under the same name. For the most part, the Sinai of the Hebrew Bible was east of the River Jordan in the land of Seir or Edom, modern-day Jordan.[5] Indeed, and as I have adequately demonstrated elsewhere, there is every reason to suspect that the true Mount Sinai was located in the vicinity of the ancient Nabatean city of Petra. Most probably it can be identified with Jebel al-Madhbah, the sacred mountain that serves the ancient rock-cut citadel, or it is nearby Jebel Haroun, on which is the supposed tomb of Moses's brother Aaron.[6]

The far greater importance placed on Mount Gerizim by the Israelites, once they had crossed the River Jordan, confirms its role as the primary dwelling place of Yahweh *in Canaan, God's chosen homeland.* So we can totally understand why the Levitical priesthood serving the house of Judah needed to undermine Mount Gerizim's pivotal role in the establishment of Israel so that they could replace it with Jerusalem's own Mount Zion.

This all might be so, although the greater mystery here is how Mount Gerizim came to be seen as the dwelling place of Yahweh in the first place. Was it simply down to the visionary experiences of individuals like Abraham and Jacob, or had there been something significant known about the area beforehand—something that had caused the inhabitants of the region to be attracted to this mountain as far back as the Lower Paleolithic age?

These are matters we must address next, with the biggest clue being a term I have so far avoided using in connection with Mount Gerizim's role as the dwelling place of Yahweh. I speak here of the mountain's compelling connection with the so-called *Shekinah,* a shining radiance that in Jewish and Samaritan tradition constituted visual confirmation of God's presence on Earth.

29

THE DIVINE SHEKINAH

Mountains in the Levant were seen as geographical centers of supernatural activity and points of communication with local deities long before the arrival in Canaan of the biblical patriarchs. For example, Canaanite gods such as El and Baal, whose mythological traditions undoubtedly contributed to the emergence of the cult of Yahweh, were both thought to inhabit tents pitched on the summits of holy mountains.[1] Clearly, these tents were the precursors of the Tabernacle created by the Israelites to contain the Ark of the Covenant. So Mount Gerizim being God's chosen place of dwelling is nothing out of the ordinary when it comes to cosmological interpretations of a regional, geographical landscape. What *is* important, however, is something quite specific that was said about Mount Gerizim and Yahweh's presence there.

According to the holy books of the Samaritans, God is able to manifest on Mount Gerizim in his form as the Shekinah (Hebrew: שכינה, *šekīnah,* also written "Shekina").[2] This is an ancient Hebrew and Aramaic term meaning a "presence" associated with Yahweh's ability to appear in physical form as a shining radiance.[3] As James Alan Montgomery writes in *The Samaritans, the Earliest Jewish Sect,* "There is also reference [in the works of the fourth-century CE Samaritan theologian Marka] to the Shekina, or manifest Residing of God over Gerizim."[4]

Although the term Shekinah does not appear in the Hebrew Bible, it can be found frequently in the Targums, which are Aramaic renditions of the Pentateuch stories. They date generally from the first century CE, when

Hebrew was no longer in use as a spoken language. Often Shekinah is used alongside another key term for God's presence on Earth, which is *kavod,* interpreted as "honor" or "glory."[5] Both relate to the way Yahweh is able to make his presence known through divine manifestation, either directly or via the intercession of angels.

THE LIGHT OF GOD

The greater significance of the term Shekinah, however, is that it refers not just to God's presence at a particular location but also to the fact that this presence can take the form of an unearthly brilliance or illumination. As the medieval Sephardic Jewish philosopher Moses ben Maimon (1135/1138–1204), known also as Maimonides, makes clear, the Shekinah constitutes "a light created to be an intermediary between God and the world."[6] Again and again, there is an emphasis in Jewish Rabbinic literature to the Shekinah appearing as a "physical light,"[7] a conviction that in the Targum to Numbers 6:2 is expressed with the statement, "Yhwh [Yahweh] shall cause His Shekinah to shine for thee."[8]

Such shining radiances showing the presence of God occurred, for instance, when Moses encountered the burning bush on Mount Horeb,[9] and when Moses saw God as like a "consuming fire" on Mount Sinai as he receives the Tablets of the Law as well as the instructions on how to make the Ark of the Covenant.[10] After this time, God's Shekinah accompanies the Israelites through the wilderness as a cloud of glory by day and as a pillar of fire by night, this being caused by Yahweh's manifestation as a divine presence either between or above the two cherubim mounted on the Ark's Mercy Seat (see fig. 29.1).[11] The tent or Tabernacle constructed, like the Ark, using specific instructions given by God to Moses on Mount Sinai,[12] had the specific purpose of containing the holy vessel so that God's Shekinah "might dwell on earth."[13]

Thus Yahweh was able to follow the Israelites when they were in the wilderness, appearing to them in visible form, but once they settled in Jerusalem and built Solomon's Temple, the Shekinah, we are told, came to rest in its holy of holies. The temple was, of course, built specifically to contain the Ark.[14]

Fig. 29.1. Engraving showing the Ark of the Covenant with a
shining radiance above the mercy seat (circa 1883).

GLORY OF THE SHEKINAH

Countless references to the "glory" of the Shekinah are to be found in the
Targums, with one of the most compelling examples appearing in the Targum
on Exodus. It speaks of how the "Cloud of Glory overspread the tabernacle of
ordinance, and the glory of the Shekinah of the Lord filled the tabernacle,"
after which the text continues, "And Moseh [that is, Moses] was not able to
enter the tabernacle of ordinance, because the Cloud of Glory rested upon it,
and the glory of the Lord's Shekinah filled the tabernacle." The Targum thereafter states:

> At the time when the Cloud of Glory ascended from the tabernacle, the
> sons of Israel went forward in all their journeys; but if the Cloud of Glory
> went not up, they did not go forward until the day when it ascended. For
> the Cloud of the Glory of the Lord overspread the tabernacle by day, and
> (as) a column of fire it gave light in the night, that all the sons of Israel
> might see in all their journeys.[15]

THE ARK IN SHECHEM

If these accounts are to be taken as authentic, then very clearly something extraordinary was going on in the wilderness of Sinai following the Israelites' Exodus from Egypt. It is important to add here that after the death of Moses, the Israelites crossed the River Jordan and entered Canaan under the command of Joshua. They carried with them the Ark of the Covenant, which was instrumental, apparently, in parting the waters so that the children of Israel might safely cross the river.[16]

What seems significant here is that upon entering Canaan, the Ark of the Covenant was taken straight to Shechem, modern-day Tell Balata, on the eastern side of modern Nablus. According to Samaritan tradition, it was afterward carried to the top of Mount Gerizim, where it was interred inside the newly erected Tabernacle,[17] an act not only ensuring the continued presence of the Shekinah but also confirming the mountain's role as the rightful dwelling place of God.[18]

The Ark also featured center stage in the ceremony involving Mount Ebal and Mount Gerizim as, respectively, the Mount of Curses and the Mount of Blessings. The background to this ceremony is given in chapter 27, however, I was intrigued by an account of this important event given by Catholic writer and author Maria Teresa Petrozzi. In her book *Samaria,* she describes the setting in the following manner:

> The tribes arranged themselves on the slopes of the mountains: Simeon, Levi, Juda, Issachar, Joseph and Benjamin on Gerizim; Reuben, Gad, Aser, Zabu lon, Dan and Nephtali on Ebal. In the middle, in the valley, the priests and the Levites surrounded the ark over which hovered the "shekina," the presence of God.[19] (English translation of the original Italian text)

Biblical artists across the centuries have attempted to paint or draw the Ark of the Covenant with the Shekinah hovering over it in the form of a shining radiance or column of fire (see fig. 29.2 and plate 14). Many of these paintings or illustrations leave one in awe of what the Ark represented and how exactly it was able to emit a divine light that could act as a conduit through which God could speak to his chosen people.

Across the centuries, there have been many attempts at interpreting the

Fig. 29.2. Engraving by English illustrator Paul Hardy (1862–1942) showing the
Glory of God or Shekinah in the form of a pillar of fire above the
Ark of the Covenant (from Fell 1896).

true nature of the Cloud of Glory and Pillar of Fire that accompanied the Israelites through the wilderness of Sinai, with explanations ranging from distant volcanoes[20] to the appearance of alien spaceships,[21] so entering this debate based purely on the narrative of the Pentateuch and the later Targums can inevitably lead only to guesswork and gross assumptions. It is even possible that the biblical stories are either confabulations or parables that should not be seen as literal fact (although theologians would, of course, argue against this sentiment). Knowledge, however, that the Samaritans saw Mount Gerizim as imbued with God's presence in his form as the Shekinah provides a completely different perspective on the matter.

Samaritan texts speak of this divine radiance under such terms as the "holy light,"[22] the "divine fire,"[23] "gleaming lightning,"[24] and even the "devouring fire."[25] So what exactly was this light or radiance associated with the manifestation of God, and how might it have been connected with Mount Gerizim? Could it have something to do with why the mountain came to be seen not only as the dwelling place of the god Yahweh but also as the center of the world and Gate of Heaven? Clearly, Mount Gerizim must have had something very special going for it to have gained these powerful attributions.

For me, the answer has to lie in the fact that God's presence, his Shekinah, was said to dwell on the mountain. So what exactly was the Shekinah, this shining radiance that was said to represent God himself? Was it something that appeared on the slopes or summit of the mountain, and if it was, then was it present only during the age of the patriarchs, or might it have been there as far back as the Lower Paleolithic age, when the peoples of Jaljulia and Qesem would appear to have gone to Mount Gerizim to procure nodules of Eocene flint in order to make tools? More pressingly, is it still present on the mountain today? It is time to switch up the narrative and go in search of the divine light of God.

30

LET THERE BE LIGHT

In the opening lines of the book of Genesis, we are informed that God created the heaven and the earth, yet everything was without form and darkness was everywhere.[1] As this was going down, the "Spirit of god" is said to have moved across the face of the waters that existed in some kind of realm of eternal nothingness.[2] Then, and only then, does God utter the immortal words, "Let there be light."[3]

At this, light bursts forth out of the darkness like some immense cosmic spotlight, illuminating existence for the first time. Thereafter, "God saw the light, and it was good; and God divided the light from the darkness."[4] After this time, God goes on to create the world in just six days, allowing him to rest on the seventh day, following the completion of his monumental task.

No one has to believe this story. It is what it is—a simple creation myth explaining how the world and everything in it came into being. The main point of interest for me is that these words from the book of Genesis introduce God's ability to be able to produce light as if by magic. The appearance of this light becomes a visible sign of God's presence as well as that of his divine messengers, the angels.

If we accept that God and his angels really can make their presence known by the manifestation of a shining light or radiance, then it seems important to understand what this light is and how exactly it comes into being. Once this has been established, we can go on to ask whether or not light can in any way be described as representative of an omnipotent, monotheistic deity. Confusing the issue, however, is that there is more than one form of light: there is light created by fire and combustion, light emitted through bioluminescence, light created as a chemiluminescence, as well as light produced by more violent energetic actions within nature.

Light from a fire comes through the ignition and sustained combustion of inflammable materials, whether they be solids, liquids, or gases. Bioluminescence in creatures like glowworms and fireflies, as well as some jellyfish, plankton, and cephalopods, is produced by a chemical process using proteins called luciferases. Chemiluminescence is where light is created through a chemical reaction when two different substances are brought together, creating a high-energy excitation with light as the result. (Glow sticks are a good example of chemiluminescence.)

SPLITTING THE ATOM

Quite obviously, none of these forms of light can be described as a brilliant shining radiance. This can come only through the introduction of higher energetic activity that causes greater temperatures and the release from atoms of subatomic particles called electrons. (Atoms are made up of three types of subatomic particles: protons and neutrons make up an atom's nucleus, and electrons that are arranged in shells spin around the nucleus.) The separation of electrons from an atom results in an uneven number of protons and electrons, transforming the atom into what is known as a *positively charged ion,* while at the same time causing the free electrons to become *negatively charged ions.*

Electrons released from atoms are able to move about, colliding with other nearby atoms, causing them to release some of their own electrons. It becomes an ever-expanding process referred to in scientific terms as ionization.

When freed-up electrons collide with an atom or particle, it places both of them in an excited, energetic state in which they can both release and absorb packets of light called photons. The sudden appearance of whole seas of photons in a literal soup of positive and negative ions produces a burst of light. As simple as this process might seem, it is behind everything from the light of the sun to the light of stars, the light we see in lightning bolts, the light we see in the flames of fires when they reach extremely high temperatures, and the light that illuminates the screen of our smart TVs.

AND THEN THERE WAS PLASMA

As these displays of light are created, something profound takes place. The generation of whole systems of negatively charged free electrons and positively charged ions results in the coming into being of a *fourth state of matter*—one wholly different from the first three states of matter, which are solids, liquids, and gases. This new state of matter is called *plasma,* although scientists often refer to it somewhat more prosaically as ionized gas. However, this term implies that plasma is a form of gas, which it certainly is not. It is something quite unique that goes beyond a material existence.

Plasma is not simply something we know from experiencing lightning or gazing at the sun or watching TV. (You can actually create short-lived bursts of plasma in a microwave oven by placing inside it a single grape that has been severed lengthways and then turning on the device. I kid you not, look it up on YouTube). In reality, plasma is now thought by some scientists, including Dennis Gallagher, a plasma physicist at NASA's Marshall Space Flight Center, to make up as much as 99.9 percent of the material universe. "Very little material in space is made of rock like the Earth," he says.[5]

Plasma is the light of stars and galaxies, the glow of nebulae, the stuff of solar flares, and even the light of the biggest and brightest meteors streaming across our skies. All this is plasma. It is bright, it is radiant, and it is blinding just like the Shekinah, the visible presence of God on Earth according to Hebrew and Samaritan tradition. But can plasma be divine or intelligent? Is it really the answer to the burning bush seen by Moses on Mount Horeb or the consuming fire encountered by the lawgiver as he talked to God on Mount Sinai or the Glory of the Shekinah that manifested above the Ark of the Covenant as a cloud of glory by day and a pillar of fire by night? Is God himself light?

LIGHTS OF THE EARTH

To even begin to answer these questions, it is important to understand that the Earth has its own way of generating light. Moreover, it does so in a manner that has baffled scientists, theologians, and philosophers for thousands of years. I say this because there is today growing evidence that plasma might well be behind the reported manifestations of mysterious lights, be they electrically charged mists, columns of light, or luminous globes that have appeared all over the world for hundreds and arguably even many thousands of years. Such lights have especially been seen in association with extreme geological events such as volcanism and earthquakes. (They were, for instance, seen in abundance in the skies prior to the earthquake and subsequent tsunami that devastated Southeast Asia in 2004.)[6] How is this possible? How are glowing plasmas able to manifest—either in the local environment or up in the atmosphere?

ELECTRICITY IN ROCKS

The fact is that the release of electrons, and the manner in which they flow to produce what we call electricity, is something that is fairly easily generated in rocks, and this is important since it is their presence that helps create plasma. There are three basic mechanisms behind the production of electricity in rocks, with these being piezoelectricity, seismoelectricity, and triboelectricity.[7] Explaining their importance is crucial to understanding how plasma is created in the environment, so please bear with me as I explain all three.

Piezoelectricity

We start with the first and arguably the most important of these processes, which is piezoelectricity. This is where pressure put on certain types of rock, most obviously quartz and quartz-bearing rock such as quartzite, sandstones, and aggregates like granite, deforms their crystalline structure enough to cause the release and flow of electrons.[8] *Piezoelectricity* is a term derived from the Greek πιέζειν (*piezein*), meaning "to squeeze" or "to press," and *electron,* from the Greek word for amber, which is ἤλεκτρον (*elektron*). Amber was an ancient means of generating an electrical charge, hence the origin of the words *electron* and *electricity.*

The discoverers of the piezoelectric effect in rocks and minerals were the brothers Pierre Curie and Jacques Curie, French scientists at the Faculty of Sciences in Paris.[9] (Pierre Curie was married to Marie Skłodowska Curie, who conducted pioneering research into radioactivity and discovered the elements radium and polonium; she was also the first woman to win a Nobel Prize.) In 1880, the brothers found that by applying pressure to crystals such as quartz, tourmaline, and Rochelle salt, they could generate an electrical charge across the surface of these materials, caused by the flow of free electrons from a higher to a lower potential.

Piezoelectricity is employed industrially in a number of different ways.[10] This includes the ignition of gas lighters and gas ovens and the generation of electrical voltages used to power small devices. It is employed also in the production and detection of sound, in inkjet printing, in driving ultrasonic nozzles, and in the focusing of optical assemblies.

Seas of electrons freed up due to the piezoelectric effect create an electrical charge that passes through rocks. This will flow in line with the axes and symmetry of the crystalline rock structures in poly-crystalline aggregates, following also veins and seams within rocks.[11] Upon entering the local environment, free electrons are thought to be able to trigger rapid ionization, which in turn generates bright, glowing plasmas held together by self-generated electromagnetic fields (EMFs).

Seismoelectricity

Seismoelectricity is another mechanism that might be responsible for triggering ionization in the local environment. This is the name given to changes in the electrical potential found naturally in water-bearing, mostly sedimentary rocks (chalk in particular) that contain water moisture in large amounts, the result of either rain precipitation or the presence of underlying aquifers. Seismic waves passing through the rock will cause an increase in electrical currents, in other words, the free flow of electrons. Earthquakes and tremors can produce seismic waves, as can impacts created by explosives or the introduction of acoustic vibrations.[12] The bigger the seismic wave, the greater the change in potential, and the higher the porosity and water content of the rock, the greater the electrical field produced.[13] The salinity (that is salt content) of the subsurface water also increases the flow and release of electrons. Seismoelectricity is described as a resonant phenomenon of electrical kinetic origin,[14] and this too could well contribute to the production of plasma in the environment.

Triboelectricity

Triboelectricity is the third and final mechanism that could play a role in the manifestation of plasma lights. This is where an electrical charge is generated in rock through mechanical actions, such as friction; its strength being dependent on temperature, humidity, pressure, and the presence of static electricity in the air.[15] Not only can an electrical current result from friction within quartz-bearing rocks caused by tectonic activity, but it can also be produced by winds that create movement within silica-based sands.[16] Through the excitation and release of electrons into an already electrostatic environment, this can produce something known to geologists and physicists as crystalloluminescence or triboluminescence.[17] Not only does this result in the creation of plasma light, but at the same time there is also a significant increase in the electrification of the local environment, a process dependent on temperature, with higher temperatures causing increased emissions of electrons.[18]

Light displays created by buoyant plasmas held within self-created EMFs— plasmoids as they are known—can be sustained for anything from a few microseconds (where they would be seen simply as sudden, bright flashes) to a few minutes (and arguably even longer still). Indeed, plasma-based light-forms will exist as long as the ionization process continues.

GREAT SAND DUNES AND BLANCA PEAK, SAN LUIS VALLEY

The effects on the environment of crystalloluminescence brings to mind the Great Sand Dunes in southern Colorado's San Luis Valley, a place that has been the focus of strange lights and other mysterious phenomena since at least the 1960s. The presence there of an enormous area of sand dunes (see plate 15) that are underlain with extensive water aquifers and various fault lines immediately to the east combine through the collective processes of piezoelectricity, seismoelectricity, and triboelectricity to create a highly charged electrostatic and electromagnetic environment conducive to plasma manifestations.

Although the Great Sand Dunes National Park and Reserve has seen innumerable appearances of mysterious lights as well as other unusual activity, the main center for the appearance of plasma-based phenomena in the San Luis Valley is Blanca Peak. Lying around 12 miles (20 kilometers) to the southeast of Great Sand Dunes, it forms part of the Sangre de Cristo mountain range (an extension of the Rocky Mountains). This contains an entire north-south running faulting system,[19] the reason perhaps why large numbers of strange lights have been seen either above the peak or in the vicinity of the mountain. To the Navajo (or Dine) people of the region, Blanca Peak (known as Sisnaajiní in the Navajo language) constitutes one of their four sacred mountains, the suspected historical presence there of materializing plasmoids arguably playing some part in this ancient sanctity. All these matters have been adequately explored by key investigators of the San Luis Valley phenomenon such as Christopher O'Brien.[20]

So what exactly is the relationship between plasma manifestations and holy mountains like Blanca Peak? More pressingly, how might such phenomena be connected with the Shekinah, the divine radiance affirming Mount Gerizim's role as the true dwelling place of God?

31

MOUNTAINS OF LIGHT

Far to the west of Beijing, at the headwaters of the Qingshui River in China's Shanxi Province, is the mountain named Wutaishan, also known as Mount Wutai and Mount Qingliang. It is a very holy place to the Chinese as well as to Mongolian and Tibetan Buddhists. Each of Wutaishan's four main peaks is sacred to a different bodhisattva, who can be either a previous incarnation of the Buddha or someone who has achieved a state of enlightenment during their lifetime.

It was in 1937 that John Blofeld (1913–1987), a British writer on such matters as the history, philosophy, and beliefs of Taoism and Chinese Buddhism, came to be on Wutaishan Mountain. He and a group of companions visited a temple on the most southerly of Wutaishan's peaks, which had a tower on its highest part with a window overlooking what appeared to be empty sky. Blofeld was told that the window had been placed there specifically to watch the bodhisattva lights, something he was finally able to see when sometime after midnight he was awoken by monks, who asked him to climb the tower and look out the window.[1]

What Blofeld and his colleagues saw was truly amazing. Floating by were "innumerable balls of fire." He could not judge their size, "for nobody knew how far away they were, but they appeared like the fluffy woolen balls that babies play with seen close up. They seemed to be moving at the stately pace of a large, well-fed fish aimlessly cleaving its way through space, unhurried and majestic—truly a fitting manifestation of divinity!"[2] They watched the lights make their course before, finally, they disappeared in the west. Apparently, the lights only usually appeared between 12 a.m. and 2 a.m., the reason why the monks had known when to wake their Western guests.

CHINA'S TAISHAN MOUNTAIN

Wutaishan is not the only sacred mountain in China associated with what might be described as bodhisattva lights. The similarly named Taishan Mountain (also known as Mount Tai) is located north of the city of Tai'an, around 485 miles (785 kilometers) north-northwest of Shanghai in China's Shandong province. It also produces very similar light phenomena. Perhaps not unconnected is the fact that the mountain (see plates 16 and 17) has been a holy site and place of pilgrimage for the people of China for at least 3,000 years, with evidence of activity in the region going back to the Paleolithic age.[3] Geologically, it is "an uplifted northward-dipping monoclinal fault-block mountain . . . 95% composed of ultrabasic magmatised granite-gneiss with diorite intrusions (batholiths and sills)."[4] In other words, the mountain can be classed as highly active tectonically, with a very real chance of electrical activity caused by deformation of its quartz-bearing granitic and dioritic rock.

AN EVENTFUL PILGRIMAGE

Very little of this was known to me when I visited Taishan Mountain with a large group from the Chinese branch of the Edgar Cayce Foundation in May and June 2019. I would eventually climb the mountain once and climb down it on a separate occasion, the latter via a disused stone path that took nearly four hours to navigate. Some of the extraordinary adventures that occurred on the two occasions I reached the summit of the mountain are recorded elsewhere.[5] The principal reason for mentioning this visit is what occurred on May 31, the day *before* climbing Taishan for the first time.

Watching an open-air theater production of what is known as the Feng Shan ceremony, which celebrates the emperors who climbed the mountain during special pilgrimages when they would visit all five sacred mountains of China, I began to see small white lights appear on Taishan's highest peak. This lay less than 2 miles (about 3 kilometers) away and had been clearly visible above and behind the stage before the approach of darkness.

At first, I assumed the lights were the result of visitors to the mountain—flashlights, perhaps, in people's hands. I soon realized, however, that this was highly unlikely because some of the lights appeared to be *above* the mountain peak. I saw about ten lights in all across a period of around 30 minutes. They would just blink into existence, move either upward or sideways, and then blink out. They were not Chinese lanterns, which move very slowly, stay in the air for some time, and are generally orange-white in color.

I used an iPhone to take a series of photos in the hope of capturing the lights on camera. Just two frames managed to record their presence. These were analyzed by Rodney Hale, who was able to determine that in one of the photos the light source was clearly above the mountain peak; in the other, it was on the side of the mountain (see plates 18 and 19).

BUDDHA'S GRACE

The next day, I enquired locally to see whether the mountain was known for the manifestation of mysterious lights. It is, and sometimes they are encountered at close quarters. In one instance, a mysterious light-form appeared in front of a temple dedicated to the Taoist goddess Bixia Yuanjun, located close to the summit of the mountain. However, since the mountain is sacred to all three principal religions of China—Taoism, Buddhism, and Confucianism—the lights are usually interpreted as manifestations of divinities such as immortals or saints. One name given to the light manifestations of Taishan is, I was told, Buddha's grace, an expression normally used to describe a radiant light that shines through the boundless universe. Interestingly, the mysterious lights on Taishan Mountain are said to be more common when people visit there on holy days.

The bizarre and quite extraordinary epilogue to this story is that at 7:17 a.m. local time on June 11, 2019, just eleven days after the lights were seen above Taishan Mountain, Shangdong province was rocked by an earthquake. Registering 2.9 on the Richter scale, its seismic wave apparently reached a depth of 4.3 miles (7 kilometers) below the surface of the Earth. The epicenter of the quake was given as the city of Tai'an, which lies at the base of Taishan Mountain. This suggests that what I witnessed were in fact tectonically induced mountaintop discharges of what are known as earthquake lights. These often occur before, during, or immediately after earthquakes and tremors.[6]

✳ ✳ ✳

It would be wrong to say we understand everything about the manner in which plasma is able not only to manifest but also to sustain its presence at a particular location for extended periods of time. Science simply does not have all the answers right now. However, that buoyant plasmas or plasmoids exist and have been seen for hundreds if not thousands of years all across the globe simply cannot be denied. Yet did such phenomena ever occur on Mount Gerizim, as they would appear to have done on other holy mountains around the world? Incredibly, the answer to this question, as we see next, is a resounding *yes!*

32

SAMARIAN LIGHTS

Was it possible that Mount Gerizim's role as the dwelling place of God was inspired by the appearance on its slopes of mysterious light phenomena, like those interpreted as Buddha's grace on China's Taishan Mountain and as bodhisattva lights on Wutaishan Mountain elsewhere in the country? Was this why Mount Gerizim had drawn so much attention across the ages? With such thoughts in mind, I searched online, looking for any reports of strange lights or mysterious objects seen in the vicinity of modern-day Nablus. This led me to a highly significant incident recorded in the writings of an English cleric and traveler named Thomas Shaw (1694–1751).

THOMAS SHAW'S ENCOUNTER WITH IGNIS FATUUS

In his comprehensive work titled *Travels or Observations Relating to Several Parts of Barbary and the Levant,* published in 1738 and based on events that occurred between 1720 and 1732, Shaw speaks of encountering *ignis fatuus,* an old Latin term for mysterious light phenomena meaning "foolish fire," as he and his entourage were traveling by night through "the Valleys of Mount *Ephraim.*"[1] (original emphasis) This we can take to be somewhere in the vicinity of Shechem and Mount Gerizim (see below). The incident in question is said to have occurred at the beginning of April, when the weather was "thick and hazy; and the Dew, as we felt it upon our Bridles, was unusually clammy and unctuous."[2] According to Shaw's detailed account of the phenomena observed, it assumed a variety of forms.

For it was sometimes globular, or like the Flame of a Candle; immediately after it would spread itself, and involve our whole Company in it's pale inoffensive Light; then at once contract itself, and suddenly disappear. But in less than a Minute, it would again exert itself as at other Times, or else, running along from one Place to another, with a swift progressive Motion, would expand itself, at certain Intervals, over more than two or three Acres of the adjacent mountains.[3]

In the book of Joshua, chapter 20, verse 7, within a list of Canaanite cities appointed by God as places of asylum for Israelites, it speaks of "Shechem in mount Ephraim," which probably alludes to Mount Gerizim, due to its importance in ancient Israelite religious tradition.[4] Thus there seems every reason to conclude that Shaw and his party were traveling through the valley containing the city of Nablus when they encountered a form of plasma manifestation that was constantly shifting its shape and dimensions and almost appeared to be sentient in nature. It should be noted that this is the only time Shaw reports seeing ignis fatuus during the whole of his quite extensive travels through North Africa and the Levant, which makes this incident highly significant indeed.

NABLUS SIGHTING FROM 1954

Coming forward in time to 1954, we find an example of a strange aerial phenomenon seen at Nablus itself. It is recorded by Howard T. Wilkins, a popular writer of the 1950s, in his book *Flying Saucers Uncensored,* published in 1955. Clearly citing information from a more primary source he states, "An 'oblong saucer' startled Arab bedawin [*sic*] when it whizzed, with lights all around, through the skies over Nablus, Jordan."[5]

Although Wilkins's account of this mystery object implies it was some kind of spaceship, in line with the popularized vision of flying saucers and UFOs at the time, it seems more likely that what the Arab Bedouins encountered was something akin to the phenomenon witnessed by Shaw and his party in the same landscape over 200 years earlier. It should also be pointed out that from the center of Nablus, no matter which way you look, your eyes are greeted by the ominous presence of mountain peaks and ridges, whether forming part of Mount Ebal to the north or Mount Gerizim to the south. So any strange phenomena observed from this valley basin is always going to be seen in connection with these mountains.

Historical cases like these were beginning to confirm what I suspected about the Shekinah, the visible manifestation of Yahweh in luminous form, being some form of plasma phenomena seen in the vicinity of Mount Gerizim. What is more, a strange account found in a Samaritan holy book of medieval origin titled the *Kitāb al-Asāṭir* also seems to allude to a similar phenomenon that was thought to occur somewhere in the region of either Mount Gerizim or Mount Ebal. It comes from a reference to a tomb in the vicinity of Mount Ebal supposedly belonging to the prophet Enoch, which reads, "As {Enoch} Adam had said: 'this is the "place of worship (Shekem)" for the God of the world and above it is the Gate of Heaven. For the fire does not approach the vicinity of Mount Gerizim at two thousand cubits; this is called the Shelter for the Fugitive, the Rock of Salvation.'"[6]

What kind of "fire" is being alluded to here? Clearly, it was considered to appear locally, otherwise there would be no reason to infer that it could not come within "two thousand cubits," that is around 1 kilometer, of Enoch's tomb, or some part of the landscape around Mount Gerizim. Was it an allusion to some kind of fire-like manifestation similar to that encountered by Shaw in the eighteenth century? Even though some members of the local population might have interpreted these manifestations as evidence of the Shekinah, God's presence on Mount Gerizim, it is possible they were also considered ill omens and potentially dangerous by other inhabitants of ancient Shechem. If correct, then it is important to understand why this area might have become susceptible to such phenomena in the first place.

LOCAL FAULTING AT NABLUS

As previously indicated, locations where plasma phenomena repeatedly occur are often close to major faults (fractures in the rock along which tectonic movement can take place). Nablus itself is located in a valley attached to the north-south aligned Jordan valley, which is underlain along its entire length by the Jordan valley fault. This runs from the Gulf of Aqaba on the Red Sea along the course of the Dead Sea all the way up to the source of the River Jordan, located at the base of Mount Hermon. In actuality, the fault is an extension of the Great Rift Valley that cuts through the greater part of East Africa.

What we also know is that a series of northwest-southeast trending faults are to be found between Nablus and the Jordan valley, with additional faults at the western limits of Mount Gerizim and another aligned north-south at its easternmost extreme. A further northeast-southwest trending fault underlies Nablus, with another east-west aligned fault running through Mount Ebal.[7] Most of the bedrock making up the two mountains is a mixture of chalk, limestone, and flint laid down during the Eocene epoch of geological history, circa 23 to 56 million years ago. It is this Eocene flint that the Lower Paleolithic peoples of Jaljulia and the Qesem Cave would appear to have taken away to make their tools.

TRANSFORMATIVE EXPERIENCES

All this is a good indication that the area around Nablus is a suitable location for the production of plasma-based light phenomena. However, this in itself was not enough to validate the claim that transformative experiences triggered by the appearance of such mysterious lights might have been impactful on the Lower Paleolithic peoples of the region as much as 400,000 years ago. Nor was this evidence enough to say that the appearance of such lights locally influenced the development of early Israelite religious beliefs during the age of the patriarchs.

Sensing, however, that the evidence was indeed out there, I realized the only way I was going to get any real answers was to visit Mount Gerizim myself. Only by going there and speaking to members of its Samaritan community could I determine whether any ancient knowledge or anecdotal stories existed that could help me with my research. It was with such thoughts in mind that before my visit to Israel in December 2019, I had, with the help of Ran Barkai, secured a Palestinian driver and guide who had agreed to escort me into the West Bank after my visit to the Qesem Cave. Once there, he could hopefully introduce me to some of Mount Gerizim's Samaritan inhabitants. It was a journey, I have to admit, I looked toward with some trepidation.

33

IN THE LAND OF ANGELS

December 21, 2019: winter solstice. After meeting my driver and guide, Hasan Mitwalli, outside Tel Aviv University, I was quickly on my way to the disputed West Bank, an Arab Palestinian territory at the very heart of the Palestinian-Israeli conflict ever since the establishment of the Jewish State in 1948 (the history of which I cover in detail elsewhere).[1] The driver had to be Palestinian as it is virtually impossible for an Israeli citizen to cross from Israel into the West Bank without special written permission.

In some ways, I was a little apprehensive about entering what I saw as wholly unfamiliar territory, simply because I had no idea what to expect. I need not have worried, for I was cordially welcomed wherever I went and learned much about the life and culture of Palestinians living in the West Bank today.

So having left behind Israel, I soon found myself passing through the deep fertile valleys forming part of the Samaritan Hills that in biblical times had belonged to the tribe of Ephraim. I saw Palestinian villages located on low hills, as well as some extremely modern Orthodox Jewish West Bank settlements, before reaching the outskirts of Nablus. Even though it was only midmorning the city's busy streets were a hive of activity, with market traders selling their wares and crowds of local people going about their daily business.

JACOB'S WELL

First stop was Jacob's Well, an extremely ancient water source contained today within the crypt of a Byzantine-period church on the grounds of the Bir Ya'qub monastery (see plate 20). No one else was there, other than a single caretaker, who allowed me to turn the well's handle to wheel up a pail of water dangling on a very long rope. The water came from an aquifer located at least 325 feet (about 100 meters) below the surface. How old Jacob's Well might be is unclear. It is supposed to date back to the time of Jacob and Joseph, the latter of whom has a tomb nearby. What we do know is that, according to the Gospel of John, it was here that Jesus sat down to talk to a Samaritan woman about the riches of the kingdom of heaven on offer to those who embraced the word of God.[2] It was a very humbling moment, sitting down and contemplating this incident at the exact spot it is considered to have taken place.

TELL BALATA AND THE STONE OF JOSHUA

Thereafter we moved on to the nearby remains of the Canaanite/Israelite city of Tell Balata, the true site of ancient Shechem, which dates back at least 5,000 years to the Early Bronze Age. Once again, we were totally alone, with not even a local guardian to collect our entrance fee. There somewhere was the site of the "oak" of Moreh, where Abraham had erected an altar after encountering Yahweh on his arrival in Shechem and where also Jacob had buried the pagan idols (teraphim) belonging to family members upon his party's return to Shechem. No prominent tree is to be found there today, although there *is* the base of an enormous rectilinear standing stone or massebah (see plate 21). Being at least 4,000 years old, it could well be of early Israelite origin. It was discovered in 1926, along with a stone platform, thought to be an altar, approached by a ramp, during excavations by a German archaeological team under the leadership of Protestant theologian Ernst Sellin (1867–1946).

Sellin had arrived at Tell Balata with a deep scholarly interest in the Old Testament, especially the life of Moses and the events that had occurred during the Israelites' 40 years spent in the wilderness of Sinai, which, of course, included the construction of the Ark of the Covenant.[3] It was perhaps for this reason that Sellin wrote extensively about the ephod, the holy garment worn by the high priest when approaching the Ark.[4]

Sellin led excavations at Tell Balata from 1913 to 1914. World War I then interrupted his work there. He was only able to resume excavations in 1926, the year he discovered the massebah and stone altar. He continued to oversee work at the site in 1927 and 1928, with the excavations now being led by his colleague, fellow archaeologist Gabriel Welter. The Germans continued to work at the site through until 1934.

No doubt due to his strong interest in Old Testament studies Sellin identified the enormous standing stone and altar he found at the site as the one set up by Joshua when the Israelites first entered Shechem. It is a story told in the book of Joshua, which reads, "And he [Joshua] took a stone large and set it up there under the oak that [was] by the sanctuary of Yahweh."[5] This "oak," of course, was yet another allusion to the "oak" of Moreh, suggesting that either the original tree or a replacement still existed when Joshua reached this same spot with the children of Israel.

Sadly, Sellin's belief that the massebah and stone altar had been set up by Joshua was not taken seriously by his successors at Tell Balata, leading eventually to the standing stone being removed and thrown into a ditch, a vandalous act that caused it to break into separate fragments. Mercifully, the base was rescued and later resurrected and remains on display today.[6]

THE ARRIVAL OF THE ARK

From the site of the massebah stone's base, the visitor can gaze up at the peaks of Mount Gerizim to the south and Mount Ebal to the north (see plates 22 and 23). As Sellin knew full well, somewhere close to this spot, perhaps even on the stone altar he himself had discovered, the Ark of the Covenant was set down following the arrival in Shechem of Joshua and the children of Israel. With the twelve tribes positioned six apiece on the slopes of Mount Gerizim and Mount Ebal, "the priests and the Levites surrounded the ark over which hovered the 'shekina,' the presence of God" (English translation of the original Italian text).[7] What exactly was this "shekina"? Could it really be some kind of manifesting plasma, and was it really interpreted as the presence of God himself?

According to Samaritan tradition, following this ceremony of the curses and blessings, the Ark was carried to the summit of Mount Gerizim, where it would remain the central focus of the Israelite religion for the next 280 years. What became of it after this time is a story reserved for the final chapter of this book.

Having moved to the slopes of Mount Ebal, I was able to take some photos of Nablus and Mount Gerizim (see plate 24), after which a tire on Hasan's vehicle blew, resulting in the next hour or so being spent inside a car workshop, something I had not expected to do on this eventful day. (The tire change also revealed an even bigger problem: the brake pipe was leaking and had to be fixed, otherwise we were going nowhere.) I did find it weird that just two days earlier I had ended up sitting outside a small café attached to a car workshop in Tel Aviv after a tire on Ran Barkai's car had blown on our way out to the Qesem Cave.

CLIMBING MOUNT GERIZIM

Once the car was roadworthy again, we drove out to Mount Gerizim, which has to be approached from the mountain's southeastern limits. From there, we climbed a winding mountain track toward the modern Samaritan town of Luz, which lies close to the summit.

Our arrival, however, was badly timed for two reasons. First, it was a Saturday, meaning it was the Sabbath, the day of rest in both Jewish and Samaritan religious tradition. This meant that everything was closed, including the open-air ruins on the mountain's northern peak. Second, because it was the Sabbath, all the men—and only the men—were in the synagogue taking part in an afternoon service. There were plenty of women out on the streets, but no men, so if we wanted to speak to someone of religious authority among the Samaritan community, we would have to wait patiently in the vehicle.

My guide, who had visited the Samaritan settlement on various occasions, told me that when the men did finally emerge from the synagogue, I was not to do or say anything that might cause them to break the strict laws of the Sabbath. This, I was told, meant no photos and, unfortunately, no recordings of any kind.

After around 10 to 15 minutes of waiting, I started to see men in white robes wearing red-and-white headscarves disgorging from a somewhat modern-looking building I now realized was the synagogue.

We waited for the right person to appear, and then suddenly Hasan said, "There, he's the man you need to ask your questions," pointing at one of the last men to leave the building. "He is the next in line to become high priest," he added, realizing this was the best person for me to speak to on this occasion.

So without further ado, we got out of the vehicle and confronted the some-what startled holy man, who, from the look on his face, clearly thought he was about to be accosted in some manner. He seemed to be around 60 years of age and, with his full beard and traditional dress (see plate 25), looked as if he could have come straight out the pages of an old illustrated Bible. I later learned that his name is Father Hosni Wasef Al-Samri and that he is the founder and director of the town's Samaritan Museum.

GERIZIM ORIGINS AND LEGENDS

I started by asking him about Mount Gerizim, my words being conveyed by Hasan. Replying in Arabic (although Samaritans are bilingual and also speak fluent Hebrew), he told me that this was where God had created Adam. Indeed, he had apparently made him out of the very earth from the mountain. Only afterward was Adam placed in the Garden of Eden, which I knew from my own research was located in what is today eastern Turkey (and not in Lower Iraq, as most theologians and scholars are happy to assume).[8]

The Sacrifice of Isaac

The priest now told me about how Mount Gerizim was the only mountain that had remained above the water at the time of the Great Flood and how, afterward, Noah had built an altar on the mountain's summit. Gesturing with his hand, he made it clear that this was also where Abraham had come to sacrifice his son Isaac.

Even though I was unable to understand anything he was saying, the priest's insistence that it was on Mount Gerizim that Abraham had come to sacrifice Isaac almost seemed personal; he was clearly ready to argue the case with anyone who thought otherwise.

Jacob Slept Here

The priest then confirmed that it was here also, on this mountain, that Jacob had slept the night and dreamed of angels climbing up and down a ladder between heaven and earth. All that and more had occurred here, on Mount Gerizim, and not anywhere else.

Lights on the Mountain?

There were other things he said but which have been lost because I was unable to record the conversation. (I asked Hasan to recall everything the priest had said once we returned to the vehicle, and this *was* recorded.) There was, however, one pressing question that I needed to put to the priest: this being whether mysterious lights were seen on the mountain.

I asked Hasan to convey the question to the priest, who upon hearing it needed no time to answer. From his nods and the expression on his face as he spoke, I knew the answer was a positive one. Eager to know what had been said, I asked Hasan to repeat the priest's words. The guide looked toward me and said, "He says *yes*. They are many times seen on the mountain, and their color is mainly green. But they are not seen by Samaritans themselves, only when visitors come to the mountain."

This was a remarkable but also a highly unusual response from the priest, and one I had not really expected. However, before we closed (as I sensed the priest wanted to be elsewhere), I had one more question: What did the Samaritans believe these lights actually were?

The question was once again put to the priest, and even I understood the answer, for I clearly heard the word "*mal'akim*," the Samaritan word for "angels," from the singular form *mal'ak,* meaning "angel."[9] So the Samaritans saw the appearance of these lights on Mount Gerizim as evidence of the manifestations of angels, who were themselves expressions of God's presence on Earth.

This revelation was truly astonishing since it appeared to explain why the mountain had become so important to those who had inhabited the region from very earliest times through to the arrival of Joshua and the children of Israel following the 40 years spent in the wilderness of Sinai.

Clearly, the manifestation of mysterious lights, in all probability a plasma-based phenomenon generated by the Earth, had been important on Mount Gerizim across an extended period of time (although why the lights there are said to be mainly green in color is a complete mystery).

SEEING THE LIGHT

Were the Lower Paleolithic inhabitants of Jaljulia and the Qesem Cave really attracted to Mount Gerizim because it was seen to generate mysterious lights? Perhaps for them the presence of such phenomena was seen as tangible evidence of the power of the mountain, something that caused them to remove Eocene flint from its slopes since this was believed to contain the essence and potency of the mountain itself. I also now think it possible that the presence of the light phenomena on Mount Gerizim led the patriarchs of the Bible to see the mountain as quite literally divine in nature.

Locations that produce plasma manifestations on a regular basis are likely also to be subject to heightened EMFs generated by electrification in the underlying bedrock. Exposure to these occasionally quite intense energy fields can, as Greg Little pointed out in part 1 of this book, trigger transformative experiences in some people. These can lead to an individual believing that he or she has been contacted by supernatural entities such as spirits, angels, the Virgin Mary, and arguably even God himself. This is certainly a likely explanation for why the biblical patriarchs were able to so easily make contact with an intelligence they saw in terms of Yahweh and his angels on and around Mount Gerizim and why the location came to be seen as the dwelling place of God.

It is even possible that mystical teachings arose among the Israelite inhabitants of Shechem regarding Mount Gerizim's role as, quite literally, the Gate of Heaven. In other words, transformative experiences taking place on the mountain led to the belief that meditational, ritual, and perhaps even shamanistic practices could enable the practitioner to experience the true light of God. Jacob's dream vision on Mount Gerizim in which he saw angels going up and down the ladder between heaven and earth appears to be evidence of this mystical tradition, its deeper meaning having been lost in the narrative offered in the book of Genesis. Did mystics ascend Mount Gerizim to quite literally connect with what they saw as the light of God through transformative experiences?

THE LIGHT OF GOD ON MOUNT ATHOS

As speculative as all this might seem, it is a fact that on Mount Athos, a mountain in Greece's Chalkidiki peninsula (see plate 26), Orthodox monks, hermits, and aesthetics dedicate their lives to contemplating the light of God through meditational practices known as Hesychasm ("navel gazing"). They will retire to remote locations, often natural caves, cliff dwellings, or small cells (*kellia*), and hope to be able to experience manifestations of light that are seen as representative of the Holy Spirit.[10]

The significance of mentioning this tradition is that it is inspired by the fact that mysterious lights have been reported as manifesting on and around the mountain and peninsula for at least 1,000 years (see plate 27).[11] I have twice been to the Monastic Republic of Mount Athos, which is an all-male religious enclave on the Mount Athos peninsula, seeking evidence of the tradition of mysterious lights as spiritual manifestations, and I was able to speak to monks living there who were able to confirm its reality. So was something similar going on at Mount Gerizim in the Levant? There, however, the goal of the mystics was not to experience the Christian concept of the Holy Spirit, which had enveloped Jesus in light on Mount Tabor at the time of the Transfiguration, but communion and oneness with the Shekinah, Yahweh's presence on Earth, through mystical teachings such as the Holy Kabbala. Not only is the concept of Kabbala mentioned in the early writings of the Samaritans,[12] but it also teaches an understanding of the Shekinah.[13]

OTHERWORLDLY CONSCIOUSNESS

The question remains, however, of how exactly the earliest human beings at places like the Qesem Cave and Jaljulia might themselves have been affected by the presence of light phenomena on Mount Gerizim. Were these manifestations simply seen as evidence of the presence of the ancestors, perhaps the former *Homo erectus* population that had once inhabited the same region, or were they interpreted as evidence of a truly otherworldly intelligence that would occasionally intrude into the mundane world? Were their shamanistic practices, arguably involving the use of swan wing bones, designed to communicate with this force in the very basic knowledge that it was having a meaningful impact on their lives?

What also remains unanswered is whether or not the unusual behavior of plasma-based light-forms is merely something of our making, without any kind of basis in scientific reality or, as Greg Little has already suggested, they might play host to some form of sentient consciousness of unknown origin. However, to answer this question we will have to switch continents and head out to the remote rocky valleys of northeastern Utah in the American West.

34

ON THE EDGE OF REALITY

Four months before my arrival in Israel in December 2019, the search for clues as to whether or not plasma light-forms might harbor some kind of consciousness or intelligence had taken me to the northeastern corner of Utah's Uintah Basin (see fig. 34.1). There, at a remote location, hidden behind an entrance barrier and sentry box, was Skinwalker Ranch, one of the most paranormally active hotspots in the United States. Since the early 1990s, the multitude of strange happenings that have occurred in the area for centuries have received widespread notice, leading some to the conclusion that it is perhaps a perfect example of what might be described as a physical portal or point of contact— one connecting this world with somewhere we might call the Outside.

Contact with the Outside has come easy to the occupants of Skinwalker Ranch, initially to the Sherman family, who purchased the ranch in 1994, and after their departure just two years later, to the scientific study group put together by the new owner, businessman Robert Bigelow, the founder of Bigelow Aerospace. His team of experts, under the name National Institute for Discovery Science (NIDS), monitored the ranch 24/7, and once their investigations were wound down, the ranch was sold to Adamantium Holdings, owned by businessman Brandon Fugal. He remains the ranch's custodian to this day.

The bestselling 2005 book *Hunt for the Skinwalker* by NIDS team member and biochemist Colm A. Kelleher, Ph.D., and investigative journalist George Knapp adequately summarizes what occurred at Skinwalker Ranch during the Shermans' residency and later during the NIDS investigations.[1] Much of what the authors claim took place on the ranch was independently

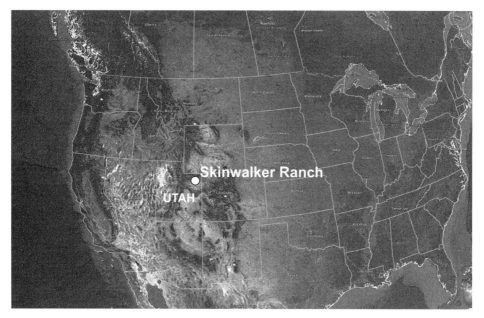

Fig. 34.1. Location of Skinwalker Ranch in Utah's Uintah Basin.

verified by the late Frank B. Salisbury, Ph.D., a plant physiologist and paranormal investigator.[2] His book *The Utah UFO Display* has a whole chapter addressing the Skinwalker Ranch phenomenon. Using the files of fellow UFO researcher Joseph Junior Hicks, Salisbury also makes it clear that sightings of strange lights and more structured craft have been reported in the Uintah Basin since the 1950s, with one historical account of a strange fireball witnessed by a Spanish missionary coming from as far back as 1776.[3]

What makes the Skinwalker Ranch story pertinent to this current work is that on various occasions, first the Shermans—Terry, Gwen, and their children—and afterward members of the NIDS team, witnessed aerial light-forms in the environment around the ranch. They would appear out of nowhere and interact with the witnesses in a seemingly intelligent manner, only to disappear from whence they'd come.[4] These radiant objects would come in different sizes and colors, and from the descriptions given, their appearances very clearly reflected the presence of a sentience that seemed to be watching the observers. On some occasions, the light-forms were considered nonintrusive, while on others, their actions were perceived as confrontational and sometimes even malevolent in nature. (Animal mutilations were taking place on the ranch at the time, and these were being linked to the presence of the lights.)

Having been asked to visit the ranch to investigate evidence of Native American activity in the area, I was provided with a rare opportunity to explore the local terrain and find out what might be triggering the manifestation of the strange phenomena seen there. While at the ranch, I was able to speak to various individuals who had been working there for some weeks. Even though they had no personal interest in UFOs or the paranormal themselves, several of them had witnessed balls of light appear during daylight hours.

NORTHERN MESA

Some of the objects seen were extremely high up, while others had made low passes over the mesa that forms the ranch's natural barrier on its northern side (see plate 28). Indeed, the more I learned about this mesa, the more I became convinced it was the main focus of the strange occurrences taking place not only on Skinwalker Ranch but also to its west on another ranch where similar phenomena occurs.[5] If this surmise is correct and the globes of light witnessed on both ranches *are* manifestations of plasma, then very likely the local geology should bear out this fact, and this indeed proved to be the case.

An inclined fault, aligned on an east-west axis, has been recorded at the western limits of the mesa (see fig. 34.2), showing that deformation of the

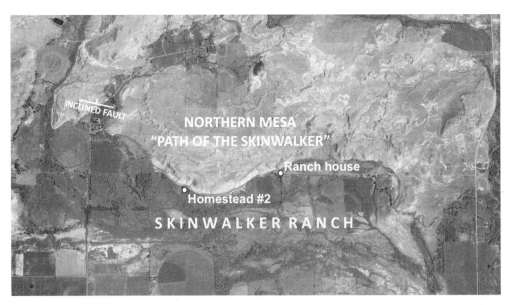

Fig. 34.2. Map of Skinwalker Ranch showing the position of the northern mesa and the inclined fault at its western termination.

underlying bedrock could be producing piezoelectric and triboelectric activity. This is made even more likely by the fact that the mesa's sandstone composition is high in quartz content, which through erosion becomes a fine dust-like powder that covers the entire area. This makes Skinwalker Ranch a perfect environment not only for the production of plasma lights but also for the generation of electromagnetic anomalies of the sort so frequently reported by visitors to the mesa in particular.[6]

After experiencing the ranch's eerie tranquility against a backdrop of high strangeness across a brief but eventful two days, I gained the overriding sense that the area was quite literally *"a paradise on the edge of reality,"* words that just kept going around my head when there (see plate 29). It was a truly unique feeling and is why perhaps Skinwalker Ranch is seen today as such an important location for the investigation of strange phenomena.

MARFA LIGHTS

This same sensation I have felt only on a few occasions, one of these being when at Marfa, Texas, home of the Marfa lights (see plates 30 and 31).[7] There mysterious lights and other more exotic objects have been reported since the first European colonists settled in the region during the mid-1800s.[8] My own researches at Marfa in the company of Greg and Lora Little in 2008 revealed that on various occasions witnesses have felt that the light phenomenon so frequently seen in the area is intelligent in nature.[9] For instance, one scientific survey of the Marfa lights conducted in 1973 by geologists Pat Kenney and Elwood Wright reported that when they would drive out into the Chihuahuan desert to observe manifesting lights, the lights would blink out as soon as the team began driving toward them. They would then reappear behind them, causing them to turn around and go in the opposite direction. Similar antics accompanied the appearance of lights on several nights, leading the investigators to conclude that the phenomenon "had intelligence, definitely. . . . It kind of looked like it was playing with us. It was a heck of a lot smarter than we were."[10]

LIGHT SENTIENCE

Greg Little in part 1 reported how the mysterious light phenomena seen in and around Piedmont, Missouri, and at Yakima in Washington State would act in a clearly sentient manner (see chapter 12). Members of Project Hessdalen, who since the early 1980s have monitored the strange lights and more exotic objects appearing in and around Hessdalen in Norway, came to similar conclusions. They said it was as if the lights could anticipate their every move and would often appear only when cameras were turned off.[11] On other occasions, the lights would gather together to form recognizable objects, such as "Christmas Trees," a traditional symbol of Norway.[12]

The intelligent nature of plasma-based light-forms is something that was first fully explored by Earth mysteries researcher and writer Paul Devereux and his colleagues in the 1980s.[13] However, the connection between the phenomena seen and the human mind had previously been noted by various pioneering UFO writers, including Carl Jung, Trevor James Constable, and John Keel (see plate 32) as Greg Little has already made clear. He has himself explored this same subject in groundbreaking books such as *The Archetype Experience* and *Grand Illusions,* as have I in the book *Lightquest.*

All this makes it seem undeniable that plasma light-forms as well as more exotic objects (I mean here larger constructs with apparent structural form and multiple lights) act and respond to a human presence, often transforming into what is more acceptable to the cultural and religious upbringing of those who see and interact with this phenomena, something I recognized as far back as 1979.[14]

So how exactly might this psychic connection between plasma constructs and the human mind work? The key as we see next is almost certainly the concept of quantum entanglement and its relationship to wormholes, extra dimensions, and the effect of the observer on the subatomic world.

35

THE ENTANGLEMENT OF ALL

Quantum entanglement is the ability of subatomic particles, most obviously electrons and photons, to communicate with each other across any distance in a manner that appears instantaneous. It was an idea first confirmed during the 1960s by physicist John Stewart Bell when exploring the so-called Einstein-Podolsky-Rosen (or EPR) paradox, this being a thought experiment proposed in 1935 by physicists Albert Einstein, Boris Podolsky, and Nathan Rosen to demonstrate the incomplete nature of the quantum information theory.[1]

What Bell and others such as American theoretical physicist David Bohm (see chapter 36) realized is that the EPR paradox was in fact real and that subatomic (that is, quantum) particles could indeed be linked together, or entangled, so that any action performed on one would produce what would seem like an instantaneous effect on the other. It is important to point out that when we say "instantaneous," in the world of physics this means at the speed of light, since it is considered that nothing can move faster than light. However, there is good reason to suggest that quantum entanglement does indeed occur more or less instantaneously as we shall see as this chapter proceeds.

Bell determined that for the EPR experiment to be real it would have to mean that the mechanical transfer of information between each entangled particle would have to take place outside the local medium of space. Instead, the entanglement of the two particles would be the result of a direct transfer of information through a previously unrecognized *nonlocal medium*.[2] Einstein found all this impossible to reconcile with his theory of relativity, which eloquently explained the mechanisms of the physical universe. This caused him to refer to the apparent entanglement of particles as "spooky action at a distance." However, since then the entanglement of subatomic particles has been repeatedly confirmed, showing that twin particles can indeed retain an apparently instantaneous connection between each other at any distance.[3]

The entanglement of electrons in particular tells us that when entire systems of entangled particles act in concert, dancing the same dance, there is every chance that their counterparts are taking part in the very same dance elsewhere, creating an instant transfer of information. This is a concept not unfamiliar to the scientific community. Quantum computers being developed right now will use an understanding of entangled particles to process data at hyperspeeds unimaginable today.[4] Moreover, the idea of whole systems of entangled particles dancing to the same dance has already been confirmed in experiments where the excitation of particles in one diamond caused a similar excitation of particles in a second diamond.[5]

ENTANGLEMENT ON A MACROSCOPIC SCALE

Recently, quantum entanglement has been directly observed and recorded on a macroscopic scale for the first time. It was a discovery made using two tiny aluminum drums that in size were no more than one-fifth the width of a human hair. Although this might still seem miniscule to the outsider, in quantum physics terms this is huge.

"If you analyze the position and momentum data for the two drums independently, they each simply look hot," said John Teufel, a physicist from the National Institute of Standards and Technology (NIST) in the USA. "But looking at them together, we can see that what looks like random motion of one drum is highly correlated with the other, in a way that is only possible through quantum entanglement."[6]

The implications of this finding are enormous since they tell us that entanglement can occur within macroscopic objects, something that prior to this time was thought impossible. The reason for this is because it was theorized that the actions of subatomic particles existing on a microscopic scale operate quite differently to those making up the macroscopic world. Now we know this is not the case and that both worlds, the microscopic and the macroscopic, are subject to the same laws of entanglement. In the tests researchers used microwave photons to vibrate the tiny membranes of the drums, keeping them both in a synchronized state with respect to their position and velocities. Outside interference was prevented by the drums being cooled, entangled, and measured in separate stages while inside a cryogenically chilled enclosure, the synchronized states of the drums were encoded in what is known as a reflected microwave field.

According to physicist Laure Mercier de Lepinay from Aalto University, in Finland, "The drums vibrate in an opposite phase to each other, such that when one of them is in an end position of the vibration cycle, the other is in the opposite position at the same time. In this situation, the quantum uncertainty of the drums' motion is canceled if the two drums are treated as one quantum-mechanical entity."[7]

It is hoped that these new findings can now enable the manipulation and entanglement of objects on a macroscopic scale in order to power next-generation communication networks.

TELEPATHY AND MIND OVER MATTER EXPLAINED?

An understanding of quantum entanglement occurring on a macroscopic scale can also now help provide a possible explanation for telepathy, the concept of information and sensation being shared between two brains.[8] This can come in the form of thoughts, feelings, and even mental images and impressions, the electrical circuits of one person being able to resonate with those of another through the shared entanglement of whole systems of subatomic particles in a manner similar to that of the tiny drums featured in the above experiment. If correct, then entanglement on a macroscopic scale might explain how one mind can influence another, making sense of everything from the success of magic spells to the power of prayer and positive thinking, and even synchronized dreaming between two people.

With this knowledge, the implications of quantum entanglement to the idea of interactions between the human mind and plasma-based light-forms are immense. Both plasma and human bodily systems rely on the same creation of positively charged ions and free electrons (negatively charged ions). Through entanglement, it thus becomes possible to create a direct link between electrons found in plasma environments and electrical activity in the brain.

OBSERVER EFFECT

An important example of the interaction between subatomic particles and human consciousness is what is known as the observer effect or the observer conundrum. This is the scientific notion that when an experiment is observed, or more correctly measured, on a quantum level, the simple act of observation causes a particle to "collapse" its function as a wave, changing its characteristics and forcing it to condense into a fixed momentum or position (this forming part of the so-called Copenhagen Interpretation of quantum mechanics devised by physicists Neils Bohr and Werner Heisenberg as far back as the 1920s).[9]

The consequences of the observer effect mean that simply by observing a subatomic particle we can affect its state of existence, and with the added addition of entanglement, this can result in outright manipulation. Even though this psychic interaction is occurring only on a quantum level, the fact that all atoms are made up of subatomic particles means that everything can be affected and changed on a fundamental level.

TWO-WAY COMMUNICATION

Yet the process is quite obviously not just one way; it is always two way, in that what we observe also has the opportunity to manipulate and affect human consciousness and human bodily systems since we are observing what is taking place. It is like a battle of wills, with the strongest one causing its counterpart to dance to the same rhythm. Even more bizarre is that for a telepathic empathy to exist between two entangled states, no direct line of sight is necessary. So in terms of mental telepathy, just thinking about something could conceivably affect the subatomic structure of an entangled system on a quantum level.

So entanglement can not only lead to plasma-based light-forms altering into what we expect to see and experience, but it can also allow the phenomena observed to interact with us and also change us. Of course, this supposition only becomes relevant if we assume that plasma can harbor its own independent intelligence. If it does, then this intelligence has the potential to convey information into our heads while at the same time subtly manipulating or controlling us in some manner. Instant information transfers resulting from entanglement could conceivably contain specific data, including sudden insights on the phenomena observed as well as some form of communication and empathy with the sentience associated with plasma light-forms and plasma environments in general.

NONLINEAR CAUSALITY

Something else to think about is the fact that linear time exists only as a mechanism of measuring movement in relativistic space-time. There is no reason therefore to assume that *all* entangled particles exist at the same moment in time.[10] One "twin" could exist in the present, while the other could be perceived to exist in the past or even in some linear projection of the future. Although this "future" has yet to exist for us, it must form the present for those already experiencing it. In short, quantum entanglement between subatomic particles might well take place outside of linear time. It is a theory that is now being taken seriously in the world of quantum physics under the name retrocausality,[11] or what might more appropriately be termed *nonlinear causality* (see chapter 37 for more on this subject).

The greater meaning and assumed consequences of a nonlinear interaction between two entangled states is that when we encounter plasma-based light-forms, we should remember that some part of their theorized intelligence could well exist outside normal space-time. In other words, at the same time these intelligences are interacting with us in the present, they might also have entangled links with the past and, conceivably, with the future.

All this might seem totally incredible, but in a three-dimensional reality like the one we live in, very little of what I've just said has any real-time meaning. However, there is now compelling evidence that plasma environments don't just constitute a new state of matter, they might additionally exist across four, and arguably even multiple, dimensions of space. It is a hypothesis that was first proposed by theoretical physicists at the beginning of the twenty-first century[12] and has more recently featured in *New Scientist* magazine.

FOUR-DIMENSIONAL BALLS OF LIGHT

An article published in the magazine in October 2020 focused on the ideas of Andrea Aiello, a theoretical physicist at the Max Planck Institute for the

Science of Light in Germany. He has proposed that ball lightning, a rare form of plasma manifestation that generally appears in association with thunderstorms and can move above the ground and even pass through walls, is composed of an exotic environment that exists in four-dimensional space.[13]

Interestingly, Aiello began taking an interest in ball lightning after one appeared to him at the age of ten at his childhood home outside of Rome during a thunderstorm one summer's day in the 1980s. Apparently, it was a glowing sphere the size of a soccer ball, which had appeared suddenly in the corner of the room. Without emitting any heat or smell, Aiello said it hovered about a meter (3.2 feet) distance from him and slightly above head height. He said it was dark yellow in color, completely opaque, and had "a wispy surface made from layered sheets of slowly rippling light."[14] It remained in view for about 10 seconds before disappearing back from whence it had come.

Very clearly this extraordinary incident affected Aiello, leaving his enquiring mind wanting to understand the mechanics behind the strange object seen. One of the oddest aspects about it, he said, was the fact that it was able to stand still, something that seemed impossible to him, since being composed of photons of light without mass, the laws of physics require that it should constantly be on the move. Yet this was not the case, leading him to come up with a novel solution. "My explanation is that this light moves, but in an additional dimension," he told *New Scientist* magazine. He believes that these balls of light are produced by four-dimensional lightning bolts, which "break into our space-time through a wormhole" and in the process can create "glowing, three-dimensional balls of light."[15]

In correspondence with the present author,[16] Aiello explained that to date he has not published on this topic, his main work at the Max Planck Institute involving the properties of quantum entanglement. However, he suspects that a mathematical explanation to this extra-dimensional process will be forthcoming. Although ball lightning might be created under quite different circumstances to the light-forms or plasmoids generated by electrical activity either within the earth or in the local environment, they are unquestionably related to each other in composition. If correct, then this increases the likelihood that other types of plasma-based light-forms not only contain additional dimensions of space, but could also act as sustainable portals into environments existing outside normal space-time.

EINSTEIN-ROSEN WORMHOLES AND
ENTANGLED SYSTEMS OF PARTICLES

Aiello's proposal that four-dimensional environments can manifest via wormholes is a unique idea that will need some explanation. The concept of a wormhole refers to the theoretical joining of two points in space-time by what is known as an Einstein-Rosen Bridge, a concept proposed originally by physicists Albert Einstein and Nathan Rosen in 1935.[17] Although the existence of physical wormholes remains unproven there is every reason to conclude they exist both in a microscopic sense and on a macroscopic scale. Theoretical physicist Juan Maldacena and physicist Leonard Susskind have taken the concept one step further by proposing that Einstein-Rosen Bridges, which are thought to join some black holes in space, are connected, end to end, by an entangled system of particles.[18]

So if entangled systems of particles do quite literally define the nature of wormholes then it means that an Einstein-Rosen Bridge is essentially the same as the EPR paradox, the original thought experiment that introduced the likelihood of the existence of entanglement to the world of physics. Both theories were published in 1935 and have in common Albert Einstein and Nathan Rosen. So as Maldacena, Susskind, and their colleagues now want to make clear: there is every reason to suppose that EP = EPR, in other words Einstein-Rosen Bridges (EP) or wormholes equal the entangled world of particles first envisaged in the Einstein-Podolsky-Rosen thought experiment (EPR).

THE REALM OF PRE-SPACE

One other highly important realization that has come out of this new research is that single entangled particles are also very likely connected by microscopic Einstein-Rosen wormholes.[19] In this manner everything from single entangled particles on a microscopic scale to wormholes and black holes on a macroscopic level are able to transfer information more or less instantaneously by using a nonlocal medium, a kind of "background timeless space,"[20] existing outside normal space-time.[21] This nonlocal medium has over the years been given various names, although the one perhaps most appropriate to what we are describing in this chapter is the term *pre-space,* coined in the 1980s by British quantum physicist Basil Hiley (for more on Hiley and his concept of pre-space see the next chapter).[22]

If this is correct, then what Aiello additionally proposes is that plasma constructs like ball lightning are able to emerge from Einstein-Rosen wormholes that appear during heightened electrical conditions such as those produced in lightning storms. The same then might be true of much larger plasma lightforms triggered into manifestation by electricity either in the earth or in the atmosphere. These are objects that, as Aiello has observed, are often able to remain stable in one spot in a seemingly impossible manner, and not be dispersed like clouds in the sky or smoke blown by the wind. What is more, and as we see next, entangled systems of particles existing at two different locations through the presence of plasma environments can effect the transfer not only of information, but also of mass and energy.

QUANTUM TUNNELING

During the late 2000s findings were published relating to the discovery of a unique phenomenon now known to science as quantum tunneling. This relates to the manner that when electrons are in an ionized (that is, plasma) state, upon encountering a barrier such as a helium atom, they do not go around it or over the top of it, they quite literally disappear and then reappear instantaneously on the other side of the obstacle, *almost as if they have teleported from one point in space-time to another* (see fig. 35.1).[23]

Very clearly this transfer of energy and mass (in the form of the particle itself) takes place through the same nonlocal medium that information is transferred between entangled systems of particles.[24] So by transferring from one measurable location to another in a medium of timeless space the particle utilizes spatial coordinates existing at two separate places at the same time. Since this is outside of the workings of a normal three-dimensional reality it suggests that quantum tunneling, as well as entangled systems of particles, adheres to extra-dimensional geometry. As wild as this all might seem it was the conclusion reached by Davide Fiscaletti of the SpaceLife Institute, San Lorenzo, Italy, and Amrit S. Sorli of the Scientific Research Centre BISTRA, in Ptuj, Slovenia, during their own work into the mechanisms behind quantum tunneling.[25]

Thus the transfer of mass, energy, and information from one point in space to another via the medium of pre-space requires not only entangled systems of particles and plasma environments, but also extra-dimensional geometry. It

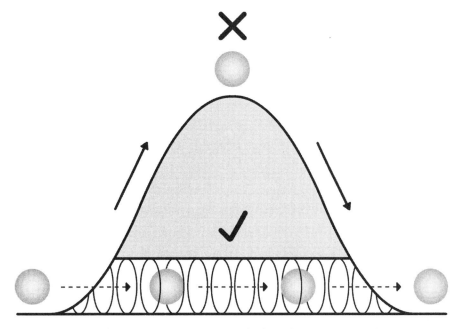

Fig. 35.1. Quantum tunneling is the finding that in an ionized state, electrons are able to jump instantly from one location in space-time to another to avoid barriers such as atoms, instead of navigating the obstacle by simply going around it, an action that would be subject to relativistic time and space. Illustration by Nick Burton.

is a process that begins with single pairs of entangled particles and gradually expands to embrace the concept of macroscopic wormholes and even some black holes; all are intrinsically linked together by the presence of entanglement.

QUANTUM ENTANGLEMENT AND THE MÖBIUS STRIP

The nature of the extra-dimensional geometry involved with entangled systems of particles needs some introduction. Two entangled particles will always have different axes, one up and the other down. When one of these particles is tweaked or spun, its partner will automatically spin in the equal and opposite direction, a finding first determined by physicist John Stewart Bell during the 1960s.[26] This kind of relationship between two entangled particles is very unique, and in the opinion of the present author can only be adequately explained if they are locked into the geometry of a mathematical construct known as the Möbius strip (see fig. 35.2, p. 264).[27]

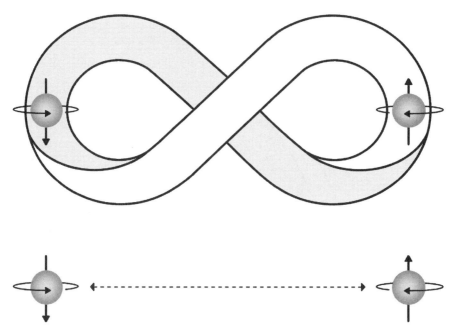

Fig. 35.2. Here we see two ways of depicting entanglement
(as drawn by artist Nick Burton). Below, the twin particles are linked in a
linear fashion, their spins and axes counter-opposed to each other. However,
the fact that the particles, when tweaked, spin in equal and opposite directions,
is seemingly impossible through a straight linear connection. Equal and opposite
axes and spins can, however, be achieved if the twin particles are linked,
as shown above, through the geometry of the Möbius strip.

ENTANGLEMENT AS AN EXTRA DIMENSION

The Möbius strip, band, or loop is a flat surface looped to form one continuous side with only one boundary curve. Shown either as a ring or, more importantly, as a looped figure eight (similar to the infinity symbol), it is named after German mathematician and theoretical astronomer August Ferdinand Möbius (1790–1868), one of two people to first describe it in 1858. It is generally considered a two-dimensional structure embedded in three-dimensional space, although it can be visualized also as a three-dimensional structure expressing a four-dimensional geometry.*

---

*This fourth-dimensional form is termed the Klein bottle, which was first described by German mathematician Felix Klein in 1882 (see "Klein Bottle," Impossible World website). This can be seen as a fourth-dimensional transformation of the Möbius strip.

SUMMARY

What all this tells us is that the permanent relationship existing between entangled particles across the medium of pre-space is defined by extra-dimensional geometry operating outside of normal space-time. The additional fact that entangled systems of particles must by their nature possess spatial coordinates at two different locations only adds weight to the idea that their synchronous actions constitute the presence of an additional dimension of space.

As extraordinary as these findings might seem, their importance is in the additional fact that electrons indulge in quantum tunneling when in an ionized state, in other words, *when they form part of a plasma environment.* So we can say with some certainty that if you are looking for clear evidence of an extra-dimensional state, then look no further than plasma. What all this implies is that buoyant plasma constructs or light-forms can act as conduits, interfaces, and even wormholes, allowing access to transdimensional realms existing beyond normal space-time. These realms constitute what we like to call the Outside, the posited place of origin of strange phenomena of the type that so frequently infests places like Skinwalker Ranch in Utah's Uintah Basin. Even if this is the case, what governs the manifestation of plasma-based light-forms? Is it simply some random process or is it the result of an intelligence, or intelligences, existing within the Outside? As we see next, the sentient actions of these light-forms appear to suggest the latter, but to understand why we must look more closely at the concept of multidimensionality.

36

MULTIDIMENSIONALITY

That plasma environments might host a form of consciousness or intelligence that operates outside of normal space-time was an idea first explored by David Bohm (1917–1992), a brilliant theoretical physicist and pioneer of quantum reality. Indeed, he was the first physicist to demonstrate how entangled particles communicate through a nonlocal medium after he devised a practical way to test the EPR paradox, the thought experiment proposed by Einstein, Podolsky, and Rosen in 1935. Yet Bohm's studies of quantum states went further since he noted that when electrons are introduced to a plasma environment, they cease to act individually and begin working together as part of a larger interconnected whole.[1]

Fig. 36.1. American scientist and theoretical physicist David Bohm (1917–1992).

Bohm (see fig. 36.1) observed that the more that electrons are introduced into the plasma mix, the more they seem to assume some kind of self-organization—behavior likened to life itself.[2] They not only worked together like cells in a body, but they could also regenerate themselves. In addition to this, they could also encase gas particles in a sheath or boundary wall similar to how a biological organism surrounds foreign bodies in a living system.

PLASMA PIONEERS

Earlier, in 1928, American chemist and physicist Irving Langmuir (1881–1957) had noted how fields of electrons in an ionized environment seemed to mimic the manner that *blood* plasma is able to carry red and white corpuscles inside the body.[3] It was from these observations that he applied the term *plasma*—from the Greek word πλασμα (plásma), meaning "to mold" or "to shape"[4]—to the ionization process.[5]

Langmuir, however, was not the discoverer of plasma. That prize goes to British physicist Sir William Crookes (1832–1919). He was able to observe luminous plasma created by using rarefied gases inside an electrical discharge tube made of glass and containing a partial vacuum (what became known as the Crookes tube).[6] He concluded that what he was seeing constituted proof of the existence of *radiant matter,* the imagined fourth state of matter after solids, liquids, and gases—something that had earlier been predicted as existing by Crookes's forerunner, the English scientist and electrical pioneer Michael Faraday (1791–1867).[7]

Crookes was thus the first person to properly identify plasma, his work being continued afterward by Langmuir and later by plasma physicists such as Bohm.

Bohm himself recognized that plasma was the key to understanding the mechanism behind the existence of order in the external world.[8] He saw this mechanism as stemming from an underlying self-organization going beyond physical matter—one that hinted at the handiwork of what he called a *proto-intelligence.* Incredibly, he conceived of this intelligence as ensuring that new evolutionary developments in the visible, tangible world were not generated in a random fashion but were part of an integrated whole coming from an external consciousness that exists as part of a deeper, implicate, or generative order of undivided wholeness.[9]

BOHM'S IMPLICATE ORDER

Bohm's proposed proto-intelligence formed part of what he came to refer to as the *implicate order*.[10] This was a concept similar in every way to the idea of a realm existing beyond normal space-time that Bohm's colleague and sometimes coauthor Basil Hiley had come to term the pre-space.[11] This, as we have seen, was the name given to the theorized nonlocal medium through which the instant transfer of energy and information takes place. As noted in chapter 35, the existence of pre-space enables not only the entanglement of subatomic particles to occur, it also becomes the means by which ionized electrons can quite literally teleport between spatial coordinates in the process known today as quantum tunneling.[12]

Bohm's concept of the implicate order and Hiley's ideas on the existence of the pre-space were clearly one and the same. Both, however, provide an answer to the potential whereabouts and point of origin of the so-called proto-intelligence that Bohm's research into quantum theory and plasma physics predicted was behind the evolution of order in the physical universe. As Bohm also made clear, this separate consciousness, should it exist, would be more readily accessible within manifesting plasma environments where access to the medium of pre-space was more freely available. What is more, since electrons are able to tunnel their way through barriers while in an ionized state, this tells us that we are probably dealing with an intelligence or intelligences functioning outside of normal space-time perhaps in a dimensional state not normally perceivable or accessible in a three-dimensional reality such as our own.

Plasmas and plasma-based light-forms are thus not intelligent life in their own right; they merely provide the environment by which other types of consciousness can emerge into normal space-time from a deeper level of existence. Once a manifesting plasma collapses, the inhabiting consciousness is forced to return from whence it came; that is, back into the state it existed beforehand.

When David Bohm used the term *proto-intelligence* for this other consciousness, he didn't necessarily mean it was a "proto-" or inferior form of life. Far from it, since there is every indication that it constitutes a type of intelligence that is able to use manifesting plasmas, such as glowing mists, spheres of light, anthropomorphic light beings, or even more exotic light-forms, to enter our own physical reality if only on a temporary basis.

These apparently transdimensional intelligences are likely also to be able to use entangled systems of particles manifesting in plasma environments to manipulate the local electromagnetic environment and interfere with nearby biological systems, most obviously those of nearby human beings. We function through the use of motor neurons that control whole series of electrons existing within the body. As indicated earlier, interactions with plasma-based intelligences might well result in what can only be described as a kind of two-way, telepathic communication, along with a very subtle form of mind control-style manipulation—both of the mind and of the body.

THE WORLD OF FLATLANDERS

So what exactly are these transdimensional intelligences, and what might they look like? Physical reality as already indicated is defined by dimensions of geometry: one-dimensional space is length alone (just lines and nothing else), two-dimensional space is composed of length and also breadth (allowing for the creation of a flat-plan reality), while three-dimensional space is composed of length, breadth, and height, creating physical reality as we know it. (Time is generally considered the fourth dimension, although this is arbitrary to the number of dimensions of space.)

A two-dimensional person (a Flatlander) living in a two-dimensional world we'll call Flatland—a term borrowed from the classic 1884 book *Flatland: A Romance of Many Dimensions* by Edwin A. Abbott (see fig. 36.2)—would see only flat shapes like squares, rectangles, and triangles in his or her flat

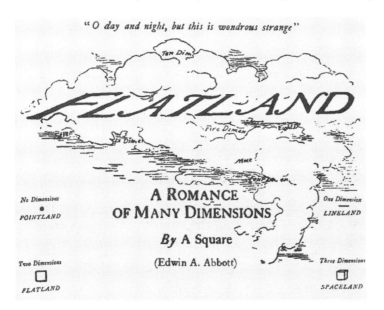

Fig. 36.2. Cover of *Flatland: A Romance of Many Dimensions* by Edwin A. Abbott, a classic work that helped popularize the concept of a fourth dimension.

Fig. 36.3. Showing what would happen if a three-dimensional structure passes through a two-dimensional "flatland." All that a Flatlander would see is a flat circle opening up and then closing again. Illustration by Nick Burton.

world. If a three-dimensional ball or balloon were to pass through Flatland, all the Flatlander would see is a circle that appears out of nowhere and gradually expands until it reaches the object's maximum width; thereafter the circle would reduce back down in size until it finally disappears completely (see fig. 36.3). That's all a Flatlander would perceive—nothing more. He or she would never be able to recognize the balloon's three-dimensional form since they do not possess the dimensional geometry to do so. Equally, a Flatlander could never be able to fully see or comprehend a three-dimensional being; they would perceive it only as a vague two-dimensional shape entering and exiting their own reality.

It is the same for us. We are three-dimensional creatures, and if a four-dimensional or multidimensional form—inanimate or otherwise—attempted to intrude into our world, we could only ever relate to it in three-dimensional terms, depriving us of knowing what it really looked like. We have no way of fully comprehending higher-dimensional reality. Shapes constructed using four-dimensional geometry are easily demonstrated, although they can only ever be displayed in three-dimensional terms (see fig. 36.4). Any perceived entity or being existing in this form would be virtually incomprehensible to us, leaving us to interpret it as both omnipresent and supernatural in nature.[13] Forced into this situation, quantum entanglement and the observer effect can cause our minds to mold manifesting plasmoids and the intelligence or intelligences inhabiting them into whatever we might expect to interact with under such circumstances. This could be an angel, a revered saint or ancestor, a creature

Fig. 36.4. Showing what happens when a four-dimensional structure, in this case, a four-dimensional cube known as a tesseract or hypercube, attempts to enter a three-dimensional reality. All that would be seen is a purely three-dimensional structure emerging out of nowhere, giving a false impression of its true nature. Illustration by Nick Burton.

from another planet, a spaceship, the Blessed Virgin Mary, or God himself. For some reason, it is a situation these intelligences seem to play along with, feeling perhaps that it is the only realistic way of responding to a human presence.

PASCAL'S TRIANGLE

Some might doubt the existence of higher dimensions, or even suggest that the three that form the basic coordinates of space are a human invention. However, the spatial coordinates of a cube in one-dimensional, two-dimensional, and three-dimensional form are clearly displayed in the number values making up rows two, three, and four of Pascal's triangle. This is a triangular array of numbers created using an ever-expanding series of binomial coefficients that can reveal everything from sequences of prime numbers to the Fibonacci series.

	1
1 DIMENSIONAL COORDINATES	1 1
2 DIMENSIONAL COORDINATES	1 2 1
3 DIMENSIONAL COORDINATES	1 3 3 1
4 DIMENSIONAL COORDINATES	1 4 6 4 1
5 DIMENSIONAL COORDINATES	1 5 10 10 5 1
6 DIMENSIONAL COORDINATES	1 6 15 20 15 6 1
7 DIMENSIONAL COORDINATES	1 7 21 35 35 21 7 1

Fig. 36.5. The first eight rows of Pascal's triangle (seen on the right), showing how the spatial coordinates of a cube in ever-increasing dimensions are revealed in each descending row.

The importance of mentioning this famous mathematical device—named after the French mathematician Blaise Pascal (1623–1662) but known much earlier to the Persians, Chinese, and Vedic sages of India—is that the numbers making up the *fifth* row of Pascal's triangle define the spatial coordinates of a *four*-dimensional cube known as a tesseract or hypercube (see fig. 36.5).*

Pascal's triangle thus confirms the mathematical existence of four-dimensional space. What is more, each additional row of Pascal's triangle must display even further dimensions of geometry showing the spatial coordinates of a fifth-, sixth-, seventh-, or more dimensional cube. It is a pattern that can continue ad infinitum, since there are no limits to the number of rows that can be added to Pascal's triangle.

N-DIMENSIONAL BEINGS

How many dimensions of space Bohm's proto-intelligence is able to exploit remains unclear. Quantum entanglement and quantum tunneling suggest four at least, although it could be as many as eleven, a figure that occurs in theories relating to strings, superstrings (in particular the so-called M-theory) and supergravity.[14] This same number of dimensions features also in connection with the

---

*If the reader wants to learn more about this subject, I recommend the PBS Infinite Series video *Dissecting Hypercubes with Pascal's Triangle,* which is available on YouTube.

operating mechanisms of the human brain. The Blue Brain Project of Switzerland, for instance, has determined that the human brain is "full of multi-dimensional geometrical structures operating in as many as 11 dimensions."[15] It is even possible that any intelligences existing primarily in Hiley's pre-space or Bohm's implicate order can use and move through any number of dimensions of space. It is for this reason that we refer to them as *n*-dimensional beings, or *n*-beings for short, with the letter *n* signifying *any* potential number of dimensions.

THE MIND OF GOD

N-beings, should they exist, are most likely identical to the concept of TIIME (*temporal intrusions of intelligent manifesting energy*), which was introduced to the reader by Greg Little in the first half of this book (see chapter 17). If so, they are the true source behind individual plasma intelligences, light beings, and manifesting entities of every kind.

How exactly an *n*-dimensional intelligence functioning across the medium of pre-space might be able to individualize its form as a single entity or being is currently beyond our understanding. It could be that there is just one single all-pervading consciousness manifesting in many forms, or there could be multiple intelligences, each with their own personalities. It could even be that this intelligence is of our own making, the product of all entangled thoughts—past, present, and future—creating a network of nonlinear consciousness I like to refer to as the Entanglement of All or, more enigmatically, the Mind of God (note that term—Mind of God, not God himself). This can be thought of as a constant field of universal thought similar perhaps to Jung's concept of the collective unconscious, Bohm's theory of the implicate order, and what John Keel called the supermind. This he saw as an omnipotent force that could emerge into visible manifestation, often in anthropomorphic form, from what he saw as a kind of "superspectrum" existing beyond the known regions of the electromagnetic spectrum.[16]

WHERE DO *N*-BEINGS COME FROM?

Should *n*-beings really exist, the question that must be asked is where do they come from? Where do they exist? And how exactly do they relate to the physical universe in which we live? As mind-bending as these thoughts might seem so-called string theory provides at least some tentative answers. Basic string theory is the idea that at its most microscopic scale the universe is made up of tiny one-dimensional vibrating strings, from which emerges all matter. For string theory to be real, however, it necessitates, as previously stated, the existence of additional dimensions of space.

One form of string theory known as M-theory has led to the development of a new model regarding the origins and structure of the physical universe. This, it is theorized, exists as a spatial environment of three dimensions known as a brane or brane world (from the word membrane), which is itself embedded within an infinite realm of four-dimensional hyperspace known as the bulk. Other three-dimensional brane worlds might exist within the bulk that could be either almost touching our own or perhaps even overlapping it in some manner. As many as six additional dimensions could exist within the bulk (making a total of eleven), although these are thought to be curled up or compacted to form tiny ball-like packets defined as Calabi-Yau manifolds.[17] How brane worlds form is still under debate although one theory posits that they could form matter and information emerging into three-dimensional reality from white holes. Instead of sucking in matter and information like black holes, white holes work in reverse, spewing out matter into the physical universe. Thus it becomes possible that white holes connected with the bulk were responsible for the birth and gradual expansion of our own brane world.[18]

So in the knowledge that the bulk operates on a minimum of four dimensions of space means that it exists in a state compatible with proposed four-dimensional plasma environments that, as we have seen, can act as points of contact between n-being consciousness and physical reality. Is it therefore possible that the true home of n-beings is the bulk, and that through the existence of Einstein-Rosen Bridges or wormholes, their two mouths connected by entangled systems of particles, these transdimensional intelligences are able to penetrate into the brane world we call the physical universe. One point in favor of this surmise is the prediction that activities in the bulk are likely to be able to cause effects in our brane world that go beyond any kind of normal causality associated with the standard model of physics. If correct, then this could very easily include the manifestation into our physical environment of strange phenomena associated with n-being consciousness. Whether or not the bulk is also identical to Basil Hiley's concept of pre-space or Bohm's implicate order, through which information, energy, and mass is able to pass instantaneously through the actions of quantum entanglement and quantum tunneling, remains to be seen. Since our brane world is itself embedded within the bulk then almost certainly the answer is going to be yes, and it is arguably through this dimensional step-down process that n-beings are able to emerge into and interact with the world in which we live.

These are extraordinary ideas that can be pursued more vigorously in the future. For the moment, however, we should just keep an open mind and continue to explore the possibility of the existence of n-dimensional beings and their relationship to four-dimensional plasma environments. Assuming, however, that they *do* exist means there is every chance they are able to more easily interact with humanity at locations of intense geological activity where the appearance of plasma-based light-forms and other types of strange phenomena can occur on a regular basis. This would include places where surface and underground faulting is present, along with important mineral deposits (quartz and tourmaline in particular) as well as sources of metal ores such as copper, iron, and mercury, all of which feature prominently in the electrification of rocks.[19] Such geological factors seem to aid and arguably even help trigger the manifestation of plasma-based light phenomena in the local environment, meaning it would be at such locations that interaction with n-beings is more likely to occur.

37

THE EGREGORE

Places where contact with the Outside can take place have been referred to as earth portals, window areas, and vortex sites. Through the electrification of rocks and the creation of plasma environments, each can become a point of contact with the hyperspace realm known as the bulk, the ultimate home of n-dimensional consciousness and thus transdimensional beings. Since these locations would also need to be able to affect human consciousness on a number of levels, the ancients would have seen them as liminal places where the veil between this world and the next was particularly thin.

Stone, wood, and earthen monuments would have been built to both mark the presence of these liminal spaces and enhance the connection with the intelligences manifesting out of them. (A strong correlation between the location of Late Neolithic and Early Bronze Age megalithic monuments in Britain, localized geological faults, and the manifestation of mysterious lights was determined by Paul Devereux and Paul McCartney in the book *Earth Lights,* published in 1982.)[1]

Such human activity presumably would have been undertaken to guarantee the occurrence of personal transformative experiences that would have been assured through the introduction of ritual practices, heightened and even encouraged by the presence of increased levels of electromagnetic activity. Examples of these disciplines perhaps included the mysticism of the Hebrew Kabbala, the Hesychasm of the Christian ascetics and anchorites of Mount Athos, and the Buddhist teachings regarding human interaction with bodhisattvas. These are in addition to the profound rites and deep ontological beliefs of the Native American peoples, which, as Greg Little made clear in part 1, existed to periodically reaffirm the link between the world of the living and the spiritual world that coexists with it.

PATH OF THE SKINWALKER

Paranormal hotspots like Skinwalker Ranch in Utah can be seen as obvious points of contact with the Outside. To the Ute and Navajo of the Uintah Basin, the location was a kind of hinterland existing between tribal boundaries. Due to the area's reputation, Ute tribal members are even today forbidden from stepping on the ranch's northern mesa, which they refer to as the "path of the skinwalker."[2]

The term *naagloshii*, "skinwalker," alludes to the supernatural creature that a Navajo "witch" shape-shifts into during rituals and ceremonies (see fig. 37.1). A common animistic form taken by a skinwalker is that of the wolf, called in

Fig. 37.1. Old postcard of a Navajo medicine man.

A NAVAJO MEDICINE MAN-
A DOCTOR, A RELIGIOUS LEADER AND HISTORIAN—
IN THE CHANTS HE SINGS, AND THE MYTHS WHICH HE RELATES
THERE IS PRESERVED. THE STORY OF HIS PEOPLE.

Fig. 37.2. An illustration of a Navajo skinwalker by Russell M. Hossain.

the Navajo language *ma'itso,* meaning the "Big Wanderer."[3] This supernatural being is known also as the First Angry or the Scolder and is connected with the trickster named Coyote.[4] Some Navajo say that *ma'itso* was responsible for the creation of witchcraft, in other words, what might be termed shamanism.[5] The Ute believe their tribe was cursed by Navajo witches as a revenge for siding against them following fierce intertribal wars during the 1800s. It is for this reason that the Ute believe skinwalkers, in other words Navajo witches in supernatural form (see fig. 37.2), have haunted the area around Skinwalker Ranch for "at least fifteen generations."[6]

WOLVES AND LYCAONS

Bizarrely, in addition to the mysterious globes and more exotic objects seen on the ranch, there have been sightings of out-of-place oversized wolves (which are not native to the region)[7] as well as canine-headed bipeds.[8] When identified in prehistoric art, these creatures are referred to as lycaons or lycaon men (from the Greek *lyco-* or *lyc-* meaning "wolflike").[9] Very clearly, the alleged supernatural manifestations of wolves and lycaons in and around Skinwalker Ranch echo the area's very real shamanistic past as a liminal realm existing between two worlds. Almost certainly, this is something that has helped configure the manner in which human interaction with the Outside is perceived to occur, even for nontribal members who come into the area.

HUMAN CONSCIOUSNESS INTERACTION

It might be asked what sightings of oversized wolves and terrifying lycaons have to do with the appearance of plasma light-forms. The answer could lie in the fact that the presence of such creatures is the by-product of human interactions with geological landscapes susceptible to plasma phenomena.[10] So if cryptids of these type are not simply sightings of out-of-place animals they might well be temporary physical manifestations resulting from the presence of plasma environments acting as mini Einstein-Rosen Bridges, that is, wormholes connecting two different locations in space and also, arguably, in time.

Having said this, very little out of the ordinary is likely to take place at such locations without what can only be termed *human consciousness interaction.* This can be described as the impact on the environment of the observer due both to quantum entanglement and the observer effect. Let me explain. Intelligences encountered within geologically active environments would seem to act in a manner that can best be described as like that of an egregore. This is a single, nonphysical entity, a kind of *genius loci,* or spirit of the place, that absorbs all human activity across an extended period of time. It is then able to externalize this past human activity as supernatural materializations and other types of strange phenomena. The effects of egregores can occur either in a confined environment, such as the interior of a building, thus creating what might be described as hauntings and poltergeist activity, or out in the open air at specific locations that act as points of contact with the supernatural—earth portals, window areas, vortex sites, and such.

Long-term investigators of portal locations have themselves sensed the presence of such egregore-like entities, which seem to act like puppet masters controlling the appearance of strange phenomena, whether this be materializing light-forms, the sudden existence of potential reality hoppers like cryptids, or strange effects on human beings and electrical apparatus. All are perhaps interrelated and the result of human consciousness interaction with a particular environment across an extended period of time.

THE OUTSIDE IN

At Skinwalker Ranch, for instance, its resident egregore has been dubbed the Host or the Other,[11] while at Bempton in northern England, Britain's own equivalent to Skinwalker Ranch, local investigator and writer Paul Sinclair has called it the Outside In.[12] Sinclair sees this omnipresent, invisible entity as the controller of all paranormal activity taking place at the locality, acting seemingly as if part of a hive mind.[13] This includes the manifestation of mysterious balls of lights, the appearance of fire fogs (electrically charged mists), and sightings of structured craft and reality hoppers such as canine-headed bipeds or lycaons like those seen also in the vicinity of Skinwalker Ranch.[14]

THE SHAMANS OF STAR CARR

The appearance in and around Bempton of lycaons is interesting and could be linked with the presence locally of Star Carr, Britain's most important ceremonial complex during the early Mesolithic age, circa 9000 BCE. Modified red deer skullcaps, still with the antlers attached (see plate 33), have been found here during excavations,[15] together with an almost complete wolf skull.[16] Their presence is a clear indication that shamanism took place at Star Carr and that modern-day sightings of lycaons are in some manner an echo of this activity reverberating across the ages. In many ways, it parallels the manner in which the Navajo and Ute witchcraft that has occurred in the Uintah Basin across an extended period of time continues to have an impact on the paranormal activity taking place at Skinwalker Ranch. All this becomes possible because quantum entanglement can affect the past, present, and future all at the same time, permitting nonlinear causality to have a subtle but noticeable impact on the physical world. This might include the actions of a shaman in some past setting having consequences in a far distant future, since in many ways what happened back then is still going on today.

THE FLIXTON WEREWOLF

A possible connection between Star Carr's shamanism and the frequent sightings locally of lycaons has been noted by Sinclair. He writes that "a traditional shaman can become one with the animal whose skin and bone they are wearing. If such things are true, then perhaps the Flixton Beast [or Flixton Werewolf, the name given to the lycaon creature seen in the Star Carr area;[17]

Fig. 37.3. Eighteenth-century woodcut showing a werewolf attacking a woman. A creature similar to this that has been seen in the vicinity of Star Carr, Britain's most important Mesolithic complex, is known today as the Flixton Werewolf.

see also fig. 37.3 on p. 281] *is* a remnant of an ancient knowledge, created by the shaman of Star Carr as they journeyed into other realities."[18] (emphasis in original)

These ideas are, in my opinion, getting close to the truth of the matter. Somehow the actions of the Star Carr shamans, and in particular their transformation into power animals such as wolves, is being projected onto the local landscape around Flixton and Bempton in the form of sightings of lycaons by the unfathomable actions of a quantum-based egregore fed by human consciousness interaction. This kind of high-strangeness activity is unquestionably being intensified due to the area's incredibly active geology. One of the biggest tectonic faults in Britain, the east-west trending Bempton fault, passes right through the area, which, with other lesser faults, corresponds very well to the positioning not only of Star Carr and Flixton but also several late Neolithic settlements, including the Rudston monolith, the tallest standing stone in Britain (see fig. 37.4). Were these created in full knowledge of the strange phenomena so strongly associated with the locality in more recent times? Has all this activity been going on ever since Star Carr was in full swing some 11,000 years ago? In the opinion of the current author the answer is almost certainly *yes*.

Nothing can be disconnected from a greater whole at places of contact like

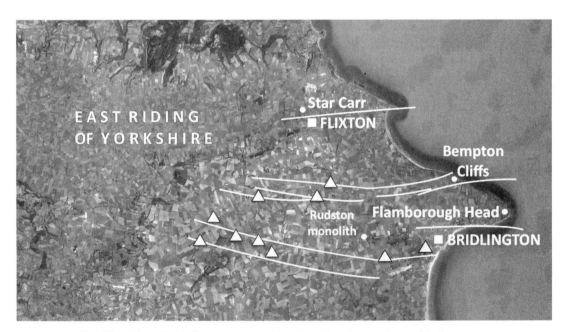

Fig. 37.4. Map of the Bempton area showing the close relationship between geological faulting and Neolithic settlements (shown as white triangles).

Bempton and Skinwalker Ranch, and this interrelationship helps to trigger the manifestation of everything from balls of light to the appearance of bizarre cryptids; all are the product of a nonlocal, entangled connection between the realm of pre-space and human consciousness interaction across many thousands of years. Behind all this is an inkling of the presence within the actions of the egregore of a powerful nonphysical entity, an *n*-dimensional being or consciousness, that is seen as omnipresent and able to make its presence known by whatever means it likes.

As the investigators of Skinwalker Ranch in Utah, Marfa in Texas, Hessdalen in Norway, and Bempton in England will tell you, these egregore-like entities appear to know you; they play with you and make their presence known *only if and when they want to do so.* They constitute the presence of Other, the collective intelligence of another reality that overlaps with ours most obviously at geologically active places of contact that almost certainly were known to the ancients.

THE LESSONS OF PROMETHEUS

We can only but speculate on how our most distant ancestors perceived such entities, the world's first trickster gods. However, I can't help but think of the story of Prometheus from the Greek myths. He was a Titan who is said to have stolen a lightning bolt from the gods, which he then gave to mortal kind, allowing our earliest ancestors to kindle fire for the first time. For this Prometheus—who was both a trickster and a hero—was punished terribly by the god Zeus. He was chained to a mountaintop, and every new moon, two vultures would come down and eat his liver, which would then grow anew so that the birds could come down and remove his liver again and again in a process that would continue his suffering for all eternity (see fig. 37.5 on p. 284).

Fire and lightning are likely to have been seen as part of the same otherworldly power by those who first learned how to make fire. Thus we can see in the story of Prometheus—whose name derives from the Greek *pro,* "before," and *methos* or *mathein,* "to learn," implying the name Forethinker. This reflects the manner in which the ancients felt they had to constantly appease the supernatural forces that were thought to produce not just lightning but indeed *all* forms of plasma-based manifestations, including, of course, fire itself.

Fig. 37.5. Copper engraving by French engraver Bernard Picart (1673–1734) showing Prometheus chained to a mountain and made to have his liver pecked out each new moon by vultures (from La Barre de Beaumarchais and Picart 1733).

DARK OF THE MOON

Did our earliest ancestors feel they had to appease localized egregores by feeding them in some manner, most obviously through leaving offerings? Very possibly, these offerings would have included blood sacrifices of some kind. Were the primal actions of such supernatural creatures compared with the manner that vultures, as eaters of carrion, swoop down to devour not only animal carcasses but also human cadavers? The fact that the vultures in the story of Prometheus are said to have arrived each month at the time of the new moon only emphasizes this connection with such appeasements. The new moon would have been seen as a time of darkness and uncertainty when egregore-like entities were at their most powerful. In contrast, the full moon might well have been a time of celebration through ritual and ceremony in which the presence of these same supernatural powers would be honored in some way.

If a localized egregore was seen in terms of a supernatural creature that had to be fed on a regular basis, making blood offerings would only have increased its potency. This we can see in the fact that human consciousness interaction across an extended period of time will only have intensified this symbiotic relationship with the phenomena observed, creating an inescapable cycle like the one in the story of how Prometheus's liver is forever destined to be plucked out and eaten each new moon by devouring vultures.

Something like this might well have been present among the Lower Paleolithic peoples of Israel's Qesem Cave, arguably one of the first proto–*Homo sapiens* communities in the world to habitually use fire. For them, I suspect, Mount Gerizim (and also most likely Mount Ebal), over which the full moon was seen to rise at certain times of the year, became a primary source of mysterious lights and other types of strange phenomena. These would have been seen as the result of an egregore-like intelligence similar to that identified at places of contact elsewhere in the world. If this is correct, its presence was likely viewed on the one hand as benevolent and helpful and on the other as bringing about ill omens and even death. Despite these risks, the possible gains from communing with such entities far outweighed the risks.

GLOBES OF EMBERS—GODS OF STORMS

I find it curious that the spheroids and polyhedrons found in the Qesem Cave match the most common appearance of plasma-based manifestations, in other words, shining, crystal-like spheres of light. As we have seen, the flint polyhedron found beneath the cave feature known as the Shelf would seem to have played a special role over and above that of its limestone counterparts. Flint is probably the most common form of "strike-a-light," this being a stone implement used since prehistoric times to ignite fires. Were flint polyhedrons in particular considered to be representations of the unearthly globes of, what would have been seen as, "fire" observed moving through the sky? Were these globes seen as extensions of lightning bolts and through them the power and potency of thunderstorms? Were such beliefs the genesis of much later deities who were

Fig. 37.6. Engraving by Dutch poet, illustrator, and engraver Jan Luyken (1649–1712) showing Mount Sinai alight with fire and lightning as the god Yahweh gives Moses the Divine Law (from Luyken, Covens, and Mortier 1729).

considered to have power and control over thunderstorms and lightning, like Zeus in the story of Prometheus? If the answer is *yes,* then even Yahweh, the god of the Israelites, comes to mind here (see fig. 37.6). Was his presence at Mount Gerizim simply a reflection of a very ancient belief in a local egregore that was able to create such powerful acts of the supernatural?

Very possibly, the spheroids and polyhedrons found in the Qesem Cave were used by its shamans as points of contact with their perceived great ancestors, that is, the former *Homo erectus* population of the Levant, but also with some kind of supernatural trickster seen to inhabit Mount Gerizim and its environs. It was this entity, I believe, that was seen as responsible for the appearance of manifesting light-forms, the occurrence of any allied strange phenomena, and the triggering within individuals and groups of transformative experiences.

THE PACE OF EVOLUTION

The spheroids and polyhedrons would, most obviously, have featured in rituals and ceremonies where the shaman would attain altered states of consciousness, arguably through the smoke produced when psychoactive plants were placed on the cave's communal fire. (See plate 35 for an artist's impression of Qesem's first shaman.) If this is correct, then these actions might have helped the community establish a nonlocal, entangled link with the intelligence or intelligences manifesting through the presence of any localized egregore. As we have seen, there is a good chance that nonphysical entities of this kind harbor some form of n-dimensional consciousness. By linking directly with such a consciousness through the process of quantum entanglement, the Qesem shamans were perhaps able to attune to and download otherworldly knowledge. This knowledge could then have been conveyed to the community as new insights and innovations, enabling its members to advance much faster than some of their neighbors. In doing so, they could well have accelerated their pace of evolution in a manner consistent with the discoveries being made at the Qesem Cave today.

All this is, of course, entirely speculation. Having said this, it seems the correct way forward as we try to bring together ancient beliefs in animism and panpsychism with our ever growing, and increasingly more bizarre, understanding of quantum realities, multidimensionality, and the effects of entangled systems on the mechanics of the physical universe. What is more, this new understanding of how our earliest ancestors might have interacted with n-dimensional beings can now throw new light on the way we think about the Israelites' most extraordinary technological achievement during the 40 years they spent in the wilderness of Sinai. I refer, of course, to the Ark of the Covenant.

38

WAS GOD AN *N*-BEING?

Shamanism involving communication with higher dimensional consciousness probably helped inspire the acceleration of human evolution from the Lower Paleolithic age at sites like the Qesem Cave in Israel through to the rise of civilization in multiple parts of the world. We have talked already about the Denisovans, whose Siberian population could well have links to the Levant's Acheulean-Yabrudian population (the AYCC). If introgression did take place between the Qesem people and the forerunners of the Siberian Denisovans, then it could explain the latter's incredible grasp of technology at places like the Denisova Cave as much as 45,000 to 50,000 years ago. This includes that incredible Denisovan bracelet, their manufacture of the earliest bone needles, the creation of the first musical instrument, their apparent knowledge of the cycles of the sun and the moon, and their sophisticated blade tool technology.

The last of the Siberian Denisovans would appear to have passed on their legacy to the earliest anatomically modern humans (*Homo sapiens*) to reach Siberia and Mongolia some 45,000 years ago. This kick-started the new technologies of the Upper Paleolithic age, which were then carried eastward into eastern and northeastern Asia and westward into Europe and southwestern Asia; this occurring between 45,000 to 11,600 years ago. What followed was the emergence of the Pre-Pottery Neolithic culture that inspired the creation of Göbekli Tepe in southeastern Turkey some 11,600 years ago. All this is the story told in the book *Denisovan Origins*, written by Greg Little and myself and published in 2019.

After the abandonment of Göbekli Tepe circa 8000 BCE, Anatolia's

Pre-Pottery Neolithic culture spread to new sites, including an occupational mound called Tell Idris (the "mound of Enoch") on the Harran plain, close to the border with Syria.[1] Its abandonment around 6000 BCE led to the flowering close by of a new occupational mound, which would eventually give birth to the Bronze Age city of Harran. It would be from there that Abraham would embark on his journey to the land of Canaan, the Promised Land of the Israelites.

As we have seen, Abraham made his way to Shechem, and there, beneath the gaze of Mount Gerizim and Mount Ebal, he erected the first altar in the Promised Land. So why did he go there in the first place? Why was Canaan considered God's Promised Land? The Samaritans would say it was because the Israelites were simply returning back to where the first patriarchs and Adam before them had either erected or repaired altars to the god Yahweh on Mount Gerizim, his earthly abode. Although such ideas might seem like groundless convictions, based on faith alone, there might well be something behind them.

A RETURN TO THE PLACE OF BEGINNING

Could it be possible that the earliest patriarchs, whether they be Enoch, Abraham, or Jacob, were in fact returning to a region where communication between the earliest humans and some kind of multidimensional consciousness had begun as much as 400,000 years earlier? (See fig. 38.1 for a map of this proposed migrational journey.) Did they *know* somehow that Mount Gerizim was the place of beginning, the first location where their own most distant ancestors had made contact with this same intelligent force? Was this why Mount Gerizim came to be seen as not only the dwelling place of God and the Gate of Heaven but also as the center of the world?

Whatever the answer to these questions, the intuitive manner in which these early patriarchs would seem to have connected with what might now be described as n-dimensional consciousness almost certainly helped create the concept of God himself, his presence really an updated form of the trickster-like egregore inherent to Mount Gerizim in particular. The existence of this deity, I suspect, helped inspire the true genesis of the Abrahamic faiths of Judaism, Samaritanism, Christianity, and Islam, all of which recognize the importance of the lives of the Hebrew patriarchs in their religious narratives. What these religions have always strived to achieve is an unerring belief in a divine presence that has been involved in the affairs of humankind since the creation of the

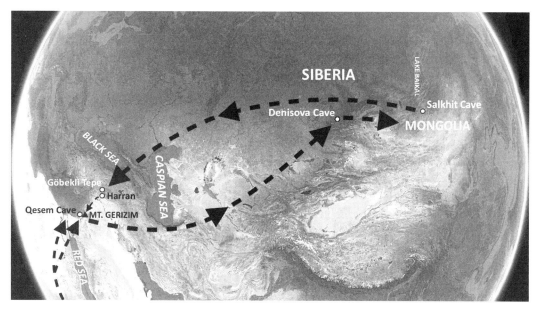

Fig. 38.1. Suggested migrational route from Africa via the Qesem Cave to Siberia and Mongolia, and then back again via Göbekli Tepe, Şanlıurfa (Ur of the Chaldees) and Harran to the area of Shechem (modern Nablus) and Mount Gerizim, this last part of the journey undertaken by the biblical patriarchs according to the Hebrew Bible.

world. This I now strongly suspect derives from communication with *n*-being consciousness in whatever form it has taken across the ages.

ORIGINS OF THE SPECIES

If all this started at Lower Paleolithic sites like the Qesem Cave as much as 400,000 years ago, then just maybe it occurred also much earlier still in the Great Rift Valley of East Africa, where one of the earliest members of the *Homo* species in the form of *Homo erectus* emerged for the first time around 1.95 million years ago. Known more correctly as the East African Rift System, it contains some of the most extreme geology in the world, including the meeting of highly active continental plates that have created literally thousands of faults and folds in the surrounding rock strata (see fig. 38.2 on p. 292). This makes Africa's Great Rift Valley one of the most electromagnetically active regions in the world, perfect for affecting human consciousness through transformative experiences.

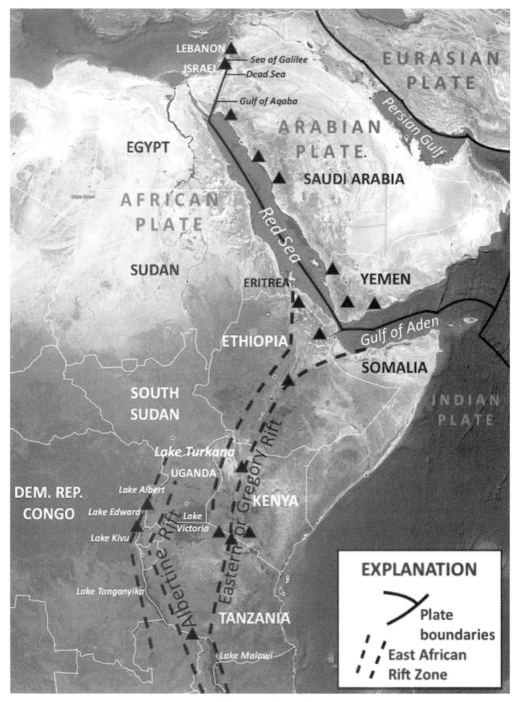

Fig. 38.2. Map showing the East African Rift System, on which many of the firsts for the forerunners of humanity took place. This included the manufacture of the first Acheulean handaxe at a site west of Lake Turkana in what is today Kenya some 1.76 million years ago (see plate 34).

Almost every site associated with the beginning of humanity's long climb toward civilization can be found in the vicinity of the East African Rift System. So the fact that the first major steps in human progress, including the creation of the first Acheulean handaxe by *Homo erectus* around 1.76 million years ago, occurred on what was arguably one of the most potent places of contact with multidimensional consciousness anywhere in the world leads to some powerful thoughts. Have *n*-beings and their plasma environments been the cause of human advances since the very beginning?

Could this connection with transdimensional consciousness have begun with the first intentional lighting of fires inside cave environments, which was certainly taking place by around 1.7 million years ago at places like South Africa's Wonderwerk Cave on the edge of the Kalahari Desert? (See chapter 20.) Almost certainly those who were using fire in this way at this early stage in the history of the *Homo* species were *Homo erectus*. So the fact that the creation of the first fires in confined spaces coincides pretty well with the invention of the Acheulean handaxe could indeed indicate that this is when contact with *n*-being consciousness first began to take place.

Just as might have been the case at the Qesem Cave in Israel around 400,000 years ago, it seems plausible that the accidental or purposeful burning of psychotropic plants on the earliest fires by *Homo erectus* caused them to fashion the first multifaceted Acheulean handaxes based perhaps on crystal-like geometric forms glimpsed during shifted states of consciousness in which they connected with higher-dimensional consciousness. It is important to point out that prior to this age, in Africa as in other parts of the world, stone tools, forming part of what is known as the Oldowan industry (2.7 million to 1.76 million years ago), were mostly made of large river-worn pebbles without any sustained form of design. Tools of this kind were incredibly crude in comparison to the more or less geometrically perfect Acheulean handaxe, which after its invention continued to be made by *Homo erectus* down to around 200,000 years ago.

So with the introduction of the Acheulean handaxe, and, of course, the first spheroids and polyhedrons, perhaps comes evidence of the *Homo* species first contact with Other, the collective term we can use for *n*-being consciousness, with all this occurring in the vicinity of Africa's Great Rift Valley, humanity's true Cradle of Life, as many as 1.76 million years ago.

THE ARK AS A PLASMA GENERATOR

We cannot, however, finish without exploring some of the more mystifying aspects of the Ark of the Covenant, which was made by following instructions given by Yahweh to Moses on Mount Sinai.[2] According to the book of Exodus, the Ark was built so that the presence of God could dwell above its mercy seat on which were two golden statues of winged cherubim facing each other.[3]

When the Israelites under the leadership of Joshua entered Canaan and came to rest in the valley between Mount Gerizim and Mount Ebal, God's presence, in the form of the Shekinah, is said to have shone forth from the Ark of the Covenant.[4] If this event occurred anywhere, it was most likely in the vicinity of the giant standing stone at the center of Tell Balata, ancient Shechem (see fig. 38.3).

If the Ark was truly able to generate such intense radiances, then can we see it as a form of plasma generator? Very clearly, under normal circumstances, a chest fashioned out of *shittim* wood (possibly the tree *Acacia seyal*) and overlaid with gold would not be able to produce plasma manifestations, so there has to be something else that was unique about the Ark's construction. Maybe

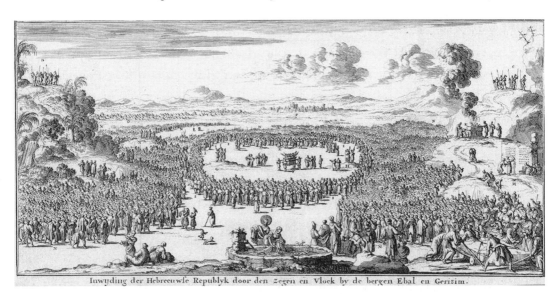

Inwyding der Hebreeuwſe Republyk door den zegen en Vloek by de bergen Ebal en Gerizim.

Fig. 38.3. Woodcut by Dutch poet, illustrator, and engraver Jan Luyken (1649–1712) showing the Ark of the Covenant center stage at Shechem during the Israelite ceremony of the curses and blessings carried out on Mount Ebal and Mount Gerizim (from Cunaeus 1683).

it was its dimensions (2½ × 1½ × 1½ cubits, roughly 52 × 31 × 31 inches, or 133 × 80 × 80 centimeters,). Maybe it was the box's internal volume, or just maybe it had something to do with what was inside it.

TABLETS OF THE LAW

The Ark is said to have contained the two Tablets of the Law, which were carved out by God himself when Moses was on Mount Sinai.[5] The fact that the tablets were made from stone taken from the mountain itself says something. It implies that through their transfer into the Ark, built specifically to house them, they acted as symbolic anchors ensuring the mountain god's constant presence immediately above the chest. Yet whatever the tablets were made of, there seems no logical reason why their composition might have contributed to the manifestation of plasma in connection with the Ark.

AN UNERRING BELIEF IN
THE SHEKINAH OF GOD

Very clearly, the production of plasma in connection with the Ark was the consequence of something that was in addition to the presence inside it of the Tablets of the Law. This X factor, I suspect, was the unerring belief of the Israelites in the Shekinah, the power of God to manifest as a shining radiance. This is something that had occurred both when Moses had encountered Yahweh as the burning bush on Mount Horeb and then afterward when he had received the Tablets of the Law on Mount Sinai. God's manifestation in the form of a blinding light was how the children of Israel recognized his presence, and this most assuredly originated with observations of these types of phenomena on geologically active mountains like Mount Gerizim and Mount Sinai.

So the Israelites' firm belief in Yahweh when in the wilderness of Sinai very possibly helped trigger plasma manifestations above the Ark, just in the same way that Egypt's Coptic Christians expected the appearance of the Virgin Mary on the roof of the Church of Saint Mary in Zeitoun, outside Cairo, to begin with a light or radiance. In many ways, God's Shekinah was something of their own making, aided no doubt by the power of quantum entanglement and the consequences of the observer effect.

THE ARK IS A COMMUNICATOR WITH GOD

The big difference between the Zeitoun apparitions of the 1960s and 1970s and the shining radiance that accompanied the Ark of the Covenant in the wilderness of Sinai is that in the latter case, the manifestations were portable. In other words, they could take place wherever the Ark came to rest each night. Yet it should be remembered also that the Ark was not only the focus of apparent manifestations of plasma in the form of a shining radiance (see fig. 38.4). It was also a communicator through which God was able to speak with Moses.[6]

Fig. 38.4. Engraving showing the high priest of the Israelites coming before the Ark of the Covenant (from Northrop 1894). Note the plasma-like radiance above the mercy seat.

This suggests that the Ark's plasma manifestations enabled a multidimensional intelligence that usually existed within the realm of pre-space to emerge temporarily into a three-dimensional spatial reality. A quantum-entangled link then allowed a state of communion to occur between this intelligence and the mind of Moses, something he perceived, rightly or wrongly, as instructions from God himself.

So in essence, the Ark might well have been a piece of *n*-being technology that enabled communication with an intelligence that the Israelites perceived as the voice of Yahweh. This is a quite extraordinary realization, and one made even more likely in the knowledge that the Ark's design specifications had come from God when he was manifesting as a "consuming fire."[7] The Israelites could see this divine radiance on the top of Mount Sinai even before Moses climbed the mountain to receive both the Tablets of the Law and the instructions on how to make the Ark and its accompanying Tabernacle.

So did knowledge of how to build the Ark of God come in fact from the same *n*-dimensional beings that I suspect have been behind the advancement of humanity since the beginning, from the creation of the first Acheulean handaxe on the East African Rift System 1.76 million years ago to the incredible technological achievements made by the Qesem people as much as 400,000 years ago? Was all this inspirational knowledge from the same higher source—a multidimensional consciousness usually existing outside of our own three-dimensional reality? Was God in fact not an astronaut, as some have speculated, but an *n*-being?

So if the Ark of the Covenant is our best example of multidimensional technology, what became of it? And where is it now? There are many roads one can take to answer these questions, the most popular being that the Ark made its way to Ethiopia, where it remains to this day (the conclusion of Graham Hancock in his excellent book *The Sign and the Seal,* published in 1992).[8] I, however, will take a somewhat different approach.

THE FATE OF THE ARK

Samaritan tradition tells the story of how in the 280th year after the arrival of the children of Israel in Canaan and the establishment of the Ark and the Tabernacle on Mount Gerizim, a priest named Eli, the son of Sephna, quarreled with the high priest of the Israelites, whose name was Aza, the son of

Bacha.[9] The dispute led to a schism developing between the different Israelite tribes, with Eli being forced to depart Mount Gerizim in the company of the tribes of Judah and Benjamin. Having traveled south some 53 miles (85 kilometers), Eli and his company came to settle at a place named Shiloh. There they made their encampment.[10]

According to Jewish tradition, however, the children of Israel reached Shiloh at a much earlier date, and it was from there and not Mount Gerizim that the twelve tribes dispersed to inhabit different parts of Canaan.[11] Very clearly, this discrepancy between what the Samaritans say and what the Jews say can be seen as yet another example of how the Levitical priests whitewashed the importance of Mount Gerizim in favor of Jerusalem when it came to the story behind the establishment of Israel in the Promised Land.

Of greater importance, however, is the Hebrew Bible's assertion that after reaching Shechem, the Ark of the Covenant was immediately transported to Shiloh, where it remained *until the age of Eli,* when, finally, it was captured by the Philistines.[12] It was afterward retrieved and taken to Jerusalem, where, eventually, it was placed in the holy of holies within Solomon's Temple.[13] There it remained until its disappearance sometime prior to the destruction of Jerusalem by King Nebuchadnezzar II of Babylon in 587 or 586 BCE. What happened to it after this time remains a mystery.

THE RETURN OF MOSES

Once again, the Samaritans tell an entirely different story. According to them, the Ark of the Covenant remained on Mount Gerizim following the departure of Eli, who after his arrival at Shiloh *constructed a replacement Ark,* complete with mercy seat and cherubim. It was therefore this Ark, *and not the original,* that eventually ended up in Solomon's Temple.[14]

As to the fate of the true Ark of the Covenant, the Samaritans say that the high priest Aza was instructed by Yahweh to hide it, along with the holy vessels used by the Israelites when in the wilderness of Sinai, in a cave located somewhere on Mount Gerizim.[15] God thereafter had the entrance to the cave removed from sight so that no one would be able to set eyes on the Ark again until the coming of a messianic figure called the Taheb. He will come from the house of Joseph, made up of the tribes of Ephraim and Manessah, from which the Samaritans have always claimed descent.[16]

The Taheb will continue the mission started by the prophet Moses; indeed, some Samaritans believe he will mark the return of Moses in corporeal form. This prophesized messiah will arrive at Mount Gerizim out of the east, rule the Israelites for 40 years (the duration the children of Israel spent in the wilderness of Sinai), and die when he is 110 years old. During his ministry, Yahweh will lay bare the entrance to the cave in which the Ark of the Covenant and the holy vessels of the Tabernacle lie hidden.[17] Thereafter the Ark and Tabernacle will be restored to their rightful place on Mount Gerizim, the true center of the world and the only true dwelling place of Yahweh on Earth. When this happens, the Shekinah will reappear on Mount Gerizim in all its glory.[18] (The Shekinah's considered absence since the schism that led to the departure of the tribes of Judah and Benjamin under the leadership of the priest named Eli is no doubt the reason why the current-day Samaritans interpret the lights seen on and around Mount Gerizim today as manifestations of mal'akim, that is, as angels, and *not* as evidence of the presence of the Shekinah.) This then is the revelation of the Samaritans. This is what they believe will take place when the end of the current world cycle is upon us.

Standing on top of Mount Gerizim, looking out over the Jordan valley with the city of Nablus down below, I wondered about the Ark of the Covenant. Was it here somewhere just waiting to be found? Was there a concealed entrance to a cave, or a crypt perhaps, located deep beneath the ruins of the Byzantine church complex that was built over the site of the first Samaritan temple? Has anyone in the past attempted to find it? (As Indiana Jones-like as this next statement might seem, there is every reason to suspect that German archaeologist Ernst Sellin, the excavator of Tell Balata in the 1910s and 1920s, and then later his successor at the site Gabriel Welter, were aware of Samaritan stories regarding the presence locally of the Ark of the Covenant and might even have been looking for clues as to it whereabouts themselves.)

So if the true Ark did indeed remain concealed in the darkness, ever awaiting the time that it would once again bring forth the Shekinah on Mount Gerizim as the Samaritans believe, what could we learn if it really was found? Would it reveal the divine technology given to humanity by a multidimensional intelligence, which was interpreted by the Israelites as God himself? Could the Ark's "divinely inspired" technology be back-engineered to give us a head start on how properly to communicate with *n*-beings?

The Ark of the Covenant now becomes a perfect symbol of the prizes on offer when and if we embrace the idea not only of the existence of n-dimensional intelligences but also of direct communication with them. Almost certainly, the technology behind the Ark's manufacture came from a plasma-based consciousness, and there seems little question now that what inspired Moses on Mount Sinai, Abraham on Mount Gerizim, and the advanced community that inhabited the Qesem Cave as much as 400,000 years ago is something that has almost certainly been in play since the invention of fire and the creation of the first Acheulean handaxe by Africa's *Homo erectus* population as many as 1.76 million years ago. If this is the case, then the same n-dimensional intelligences responsible for these sudden leaps in evolution are still guiding our destiny today, but we need to accept this fact to move forward. As my writing partner in this venture said on the closing page of his book *Grand Illusions* back in 1994:

> Shall you continue to sail along with the beliefs [in extraterrestrial visitations] that have failed for nearly 50 years, carried along by our unconscious fears and egos, or shall we ponder the deeper questions posed by the multitude of phenomena intruding into our world?[19]

For "50 years" read "75 years," or whatever it is since the start of the flying saucer era and the emergence of the UFO into modern pop culture. We need to wake up to the possibility that what has guided humanity since the beginning need not be looked for out there, in space. It is already here, on Earth, where contact with the Outside, contact with Other, begins.

NOTES

PREFACE.
RITE OF THE FIRST SHAMAN

1. Hershkovitz et al. 2011; Weber et al. 2016; Barkai et al. 2017.

CHAPTER 1.
SEEKING THE SOURCE OF THE PARANORMAL

1. Folsom and Folsom 1993.
2. Folsom and Folsom 1993.
3. Brandon 1983, 199.
4. See *Hellier* (2019) on the IMDb website.
5. Brandon 1983, 122.
6. Brandon 1983, 146.
7. See Wikipedia, s.v. "Starlink."
8. See Wikipedia, s.v. "Schumann resonances."
9. "What Is Schumann Resonance" 2021; Rusov et al. 2012.
10. Chevalier 1996.
11. Budden 1994; Budden 1998.
12. Milne 2016.
13. Budden 1994; Little 1994; Kirschvink, Kobayashi-Kirschvink, and Woodford 1992.
14. Little 2001a; Chevalier 1996.
15. "Radiation: Electromagnetic Fields." 2016. World Health Organization website, August 4.

16. Bandara and Carpenter 2018.

17. Rusov et al. 2012, 1.

CHAPTER 2.
UNDERSTANDING THE ANCIENT MINDSET:
A PSYCHOLOGICAL NEAR IMPOSSIBILITY

1. Little 2016, 301–6.

2. Hively and Horn 1982.

3. Kaiser 1987, 527.

4. Eastman 1911, 125.

CHAPTER 3.
CARL JUNG, TRICKSTERS, AND JOHN KEEL

1. Jung 1959.

2. Story 2001, 287.

3. Little 1984, 118.

4. Little 1984, 120.

5. Little 1984, 124.

6. Little 1994, 33.

7. Little 1984, 123–29.

8. Little 1984, 120–21.

9. Little 1984, 126.

10. Little 1984, 121.

11. Jung 1959, 120–23.

12. Little 1984, 127.

13. Little 1984, 127.

14. Jung 1969, paragraph 465.

15. Jung 1969, paragraph 465.

16. Radin, Jung, and Kerényi 1956.

17. Little 1990.

18. Little 1990, 61.

19. Little 1990, 61–62.

20. Keel 1975b.

21. Raynes 2019, 109.

22. Raynes 2019, 96.

23. Keel 1975a.

CHAPTER 4. THE LITTLE PEOPLE

1. Interview with the author, quoted in Raynes 2019, 182.
2. Hudson 1976, 171–72.
3. Dane 1973; Clark 1966; Kenyon 2015; Little 1990, 66–70.
4. McPherrer 2010, 189.
5. Erdoes and Ortiz 1984.
6. Lake 1993, 72.
7. Little 1990, 173.
8. Curtis 1919.
9. Grimm 1983.

CHAPTER 5.
THE CHEYENNE (TSISTSISTAS) MASSAUM CEREMONY

1. Schlesier 1985, ix.
2. Schlesier 1985, ix.
3. Schlesier 1985, xi, 43.
4. Schlesier 1985, 189.
5. Schlesier 1985, 45–89.
6. Schlesier 1985, 189.
7. Smith 2020, 51.
8. Smith 2020, 51–52.
9. Schlesier 1985, 7, 93, 190.
10. Schlesier 1985, 91.
11. Schlesier 1985, 91.
12. Schlesier 1985, 16.
13. Schlesier 1985, 90.
14. National Park Service: Jewel Cave National Park website. Accessed September 3, 2021.
15. Heller 2021.
16. National Park Service: Wind Cave National Park website. Accessed September 3, 2021.
17. Schlesier 1985, 8, 61, 190; Little 1990, 164–65.
18. Schlesier 1985, 83–87.
19. Eddy 1977.
20. Schlesier 1985, 78.
21. Schlesier 1985, 8; Little 1990, 164–65.
22. Brinton 1896, 330.

23. Gaddis 1977, 131.

24. Seton and Seton 1966, 42.

25. See Wikipedia, s.v. "Bloodletting."

26. Stevenson 1915, 37.

27. Stevenson 1915, 37.

28. Camazine and Bye 1980.

29. Hudson 1976, 63.

30. Spence 1914, 129.

31. Spence 1914, 130.

32. Little 2014b.

33. Spence 1914, 229.

34. Spence 1914, 247.

CHAPTER 6.
ANCIENT ANSWERS TO ETERNAL QUESTIONS

1. Steiger 1984, 24.

2. Barnes 2009, 17–19.

3. Barnes 2009, 17–19.

4. Brinton 1896, 330.

5. Hudson 1976, 121.

6. Hudson 1976, 120.

7. Lankford 2011, 50

8. Hall 1997, ix; Little 2014b.

9. Hall 1997, ix–x, 68–70; Little 2014b, 158–60.

10. Schlesier 1985, 7, 93, 190.

11. Cushing 1896, 379.

12. Hudson 1976, 123.

13. Also see Eastman 1911, x.

14. Hudson 1976, 123–24.

15. This Native American concept (creation and entropy) is incorporated into a self-help book: Little, Prachniak, and Prachniak 2019. Steiger relates that creation is the source of shamanistic power: Steiger 1984, 19.

16. Hudson 1976, 125–32; Schlesier 1985.

17. Hudson 1976, 156.

18. Hudson 1976.

19. Eastman 1911, 13.

20. Eastman 1911, 14.

21. Hudson 1976, 356–57.

22. Hudson 1976, 159.

23. Hudson 1976; Hall 1997.

24. Dye 2004, 196–97.

CHAPTER 7.
THE TWO SOULS AND THE DEATH JOURNEY

1. Hall 1997, 30, 54; Little 2014b, 140–42; Spence 1914, 129.

2. Little 2014b.

3. Little 2014b, 140–41.

4. Collins and Little 2019; Little 2014b; Little 2016.

5. Collins and Little 2019, 319–24.

6. Hall 1997, 163; Little 2014b. Hall cites a 1979 article relating that Orion is the Hand Constellation and that this has been known since 1900.

7. Hall 1997, 162.

8. See Collins and Little 2019, 315.

9. Collins 2006.

10. Little 2014b, 202–5.

11. Collins 2018, 270.

12. Collins and Little 2019, 326.

13. Collins and Little 2019, 325–26.

14. Collins 2018, 342.

15. Eliade 1951, 262; Krupp 2015.

16. Collins 2006; Collins 2018.

CHAPTER 8.
THE POLE HOLDING EVERYTHING TOGETHER:
A PSYCHOID REALITY

1. Spence 1914, 110.

2. Hall 1997, 102–8; Little 2014b, 161.

3. Hall 1997, 102–8; Raynes 2004, 11.

4. Lankford 2011, 54.

5. "What Is Gravity?" 2020.

CHAPTER 9. WHAT CAME FROM THE STARS?

1. Raynes 2004, 7.

2. Raynes 2004, 17.

3. Lankford 2011, 57.

4. Spence 1914, 218.

5. Spence 1914, 220–21.

6. Clark 1966, 125–27.

7. Clark 1966, 127.

8. Clarke 1962, 14.

9. Sagan 1963.

10. Krippner 2002.

11. Little 2014a.

12. Feder 2010, 15–16.

13. Sagan 1963.

14. Sagan 1963, 494.

15. Sagan 1963, 495.

16. Sagan 1963, 497.

17. Sagan 1963, 496.

18. Sagan and Page 1973.

19. Sagan and Page 1973.

20. Jung 1954; Jung 1955.

21. Jung 1960, 96.

22. Jung 1954.

CHAPTER 10. CONTACT WITH ALIENS

1. Little 1984, 21.

2. Story 2001, 57.

3. The material in the next section is a compilation from Kellogg 1902; Christian Spectator 1823, 617–25; Swedenborg 1890; and Swedenborg 1918.

4. Swedenborg 1758, 384.

5. Swedenborg 1758, 386.

6. Swedenborg 1758, 432.

7. Swedenborg 1890, 49.

8. White 1868.

9. Kripal 2011.

10. Little 1984, 32.

11. Newbrough 1882, 653.

12. Newbrough 1882, 11.

13. Newbrough 1882, 739.

14. Newbrough 1882, 750.

15. Newbrough 1882, 751.

16. Newbrough 1882, 751.
17. Newbrough 1882, 752.
18. Newbrough 1882, 420.
19. Newbrough 1882, 24.
20. Newbrough 1882, 13.
21. Newbrough 1882, 13.
22. Newbrough 1882, 23.
23. Little 1984, 32.
24. Newbrough 1882, 32.
25. Palmer 1960. Addendum to the reprint of Newbrough 1882, 907.
26. Abbott 2012; Little 1984, 33.
27. Story 1980, 89.
28. Lorenzen and Lorenzen 1976, 39.
29. Little 1984.
30. Bader 1995, 76.
31. Redfern 2010.
32. Angelucci 1955, 103.
33. Redfern 2010, 205, 208.
34. Story 1980, 13.
35. Story 1980, 14.
36. Raynes 2019, xiii.

CHAPTER 11.
THREE MYSTICAL, SPIRITUAL, LIFE-CHANGING EVENTS

1. Sackville-West 1936.
2. Sackville-West 1936, 34–35, 55–56.
3. Sackville-West 1936, 58, 109, 168, 255.
4. Sackville-West 1936.
5. Sackville-West 1936, 35, 55–58, 354.
6. Sackville-West 1936, 177.
7. Sackville-West 1936, 343–45.
8. Perhaps the most detailed and insightful biography of Cayce is Sidney Kirkpatrick's 2000 bestseller, *Edgar Cayce: An American Prophet*. A newer book by Sidney and Nancy Kirkpatrick, *True Tales from the Edgar Cayce Archives* (2015), provides even more astonishing details from Cayce's remarkable career and his influence. The A.R.E. (Association for Research and Enlightenment, the official Cayce organization) is an excellent source for the many biographies and analyses of Cayce. In contrast, it should be noted that skeptical website descriptions of Cayce are filled with

biased, demeaning, and often inaccurate depictions of Cayce. I have been astonished at the many out-and-out lies that academics have promoted. (Read more in Little, Van Auken, and Little 2001, 2–4.)

9. Kirkpatrick 2000, 24, 28.

10. Kirkpatrick 2000, 25–26.

11. Sugrue 2015, 65.

12. Kirkpatrick 2000, 40.

13. Kirkpatrick 2000, 36–37.

14. Kirkpatrick 2000, 50–51.

15. Kirkpatrick 2000, 90–91.

16. Kirkpatrick 2000, 95–96.

17. In an interview published on October 10, 1922, in the *Birmingham Age Herald,* Cayce related that he had helped over 8,056 people in an unspecified number of readings from 1901 to 1922. Wikipedia incorrectly states the article was in the *Birmingham Post-Herald,* which didn't exist until 1950. In private correspondence with the author, Kevin Todeschi, executive director of the A.R.E., related that Cayce had twenty-six different stenographers from Cayce's start until 1923. Some 400 of the early (pre-1923) readings are contained in A.R.E. files.

18. Kirkpatrick 2000, 144–45.

19. Edgar Cayce readings 5717-11 and 255-11. The Cayce reading numbers designate a number for a person followed by the particular reading given in a series for that person. The readings are at the A.R.E. (the Association for Research and Enlightenment) Library in Virginia Beach, Virginia, and are also online for association members. (All Edgar Cayce Readings © 1971, 1993–2007, the Edgar Cayce Foundation. Used with permission. All rights reserved.)

20. Edgar Cayce readings 1223-4 and 1226-1, among others.

21. Edgar Cayce reading 2828-4.

22. Kirkpatrick and Kirkpatrick 2015; Kirkpatrick 2000.

23. Little, Van Auken, and Little 2001, 11–12.

24. Edgar Cayce reading 5749-14.

25. Edgar Cayce reading 3744-5.

26. Edgar Cayce reading 541-1.

27. Edgar Cayce reading 5749-3.

28. Edgar Cayce reading 1776-1.

29. Edgar Cayce reading 3744-4.

30. Edgar Cayce reading 826-8.

31. Mullaney 2007.

32. Edgar Cayce reading 1616-1.

33. Edgar Cayce reading 1681-1.

34. Van Auken and Little 1999.
35. Tressoldi 2011.
36. Gayed 1985, 9.
37. Little 1990, 87; Pilichis 1975, 3.
38. Little 1990, 87–91; Little 2001c, 16–17; Pilichis 1975, 5.
39. Little 2001c, 17.
40. Little 2001c, 17.
41. Little 2001c, 17.
42. Derr and Persinger 1989, 127.
43. Musso 2017.
44. Nelson 1973, 11.

CHAPTER 12.
SCIENTISTS LOOK AT THE UFO PHENOMENON

1. Jackson 2019.
2. Chapman University 2018.
3. Saad 2019.
4. Little 1984, 82–83, 101.
5. Dahlgreen 2015.
6. Bartholomew, Basterfield, and Howard 1991, 215.
7. Little 1994, 65–66.
8. Raynes 2019.
9. Story 2001, 321.
10. Hernandez, Klimo, and Schild 2018.
11. Hernandez, Klimo, and Schild 2018, 12.
12. Redfern 2010, 205, 208.
13. In Andrew Collins's 2012 book *Lightquest,* I wrote the introduction, which summarized Rutledge's Project Identification.
14. Hewes 1976.
15. Rutledge 1981, 5.
16. Rutledge 1981, 5.
17. Hewes 1976; Rutledge 1981, 5–7.
18. Hewes 1976.
19. Hewes 1976.
20. Hewes 1976.
21. Rutledge 1981, 6–7.
22. Little 2010.
23. Rutledge 1981, 140–41.

24. Rutledge 1981, 232.

25. Rutledge 1981, 227.

26. Rutledge 1981, 232.

27. Rutledge 1981, 232–33.

28. Little 2010.

29. United Press International 1973.

30. Klass 1968.

31. Collins 2012, 17–18. See also Collins 1994.

32. Long 1982.

33. Long 1994.

34. Long 1994, 16–17, 22, 28–29.

35. Moody 1978.

36. Lamb 1978.

37. Long 1990, 31–37.

38. Long 1990.

39. Akers 2001. To read the reports, visit the the Willard J. Vogel Study website.

40. Private correspondence with David Akers, 2011.

41. Akers 2001.

42. Private correspondence with David Akers, 2011.

43. Story 2001, 87–89.

44. Project Sign 1949.

45. Story 2001, 576–77.

46. Story 2001, 576–77.

47. Story 2001, 577.

CHAPTER 13.
THE JIGSAW PUZZLE OF THE PARANORMAL

1. Little 1994, 1.

2. Story 1980, 17.

3. Personal notes, 1985.

4. Collins 2012, 3.

5. Little 1984, 105–17.

6. Vallee 1988, xvi–xvii.

CHAPTER 14. INTELLIGENT LIVING PLASMAS

1. Klass 1968, 94.

2. Emspak 2016.

3. Little 1994, 99–101, 128–29.

4. Defence Intelligence Analysis Staff 2000. Declassified in 2006.

5. Little 2006.

6. Chevalier 1996.

7. Hambling 2018.

8. Healey, Persinger, and Koren 1997.

9. Mizokami 2020.

10. Little 1994, 38–43.

11. Little 1994.

12. Mullins 1999.

13. Tsytovich et al. 2007.

14. Silverman 2007.

15. Little 2001b, 215–17.

16. Devereux et al. 1989, 15.

CHAPTER 15. JOHN KEEL'S ULTRATERRESTRIALS

1. Story 2001, 291.

2. Keel 1971, 92.

3. Keel 1971, 162.

4. Keel 1971, 170.

5. Keel 1971, 172.

6. Keel 1970, 35–36.

7. Keel 1970, 46–53.

8. Keel 1970, 63.

9. Butcher 2016.

10. Layne 1957.

11. Layne 1957, 4.

12. Keel 1970, 191–92.

13. Keel 1975a, 188.

14. Healey, Persinger, and Koren 1997.

15. Cook and Persinger 2001.

16. Little 2001a; Persinger and Lafreniere 1977, 201.

17. Devereux 1989, 23.

CHAPTER 16. ARCHETYPES AND SYNCHRONICITY

1. Little 1984, 106, 109.

2. Little 1984, 111.

3. Little 1984, 123–29.

4. Little 1984, 163.

CHAPTER 17. ALL THINGS ARE CONNECTED

1. Devereux 1989.

2. Little 1994, 100.

3. Wang et al. 2019.

CHAPTER 18. THE FIRST SHAMAN

1. Hurowitz 1992; Kiboko 2013, 137–39.

2. Kiboko 2013, 137–39.

3. Numbers 22–24.

4. Schuster 2019.

5. Blasco et al. 2019b.

6. Caricola et al. 2018.

7. Personal communication with Ran Barkai.

8. Barkai and Gopher 2016. Plus personal communication with Ran Barkai and Avi Gopher.

9. Personal communication with Ran Barkai.

10. Personal communication with Ran Barkai.

11. Caricola et al. 2018; Assaf et al. 2020.

12. Personal communication with Ran Barkai and Avi Gopher, as well as personal observation of the spheroids and polyhedrons at the Tel Aviv University.

13. Personal communication with Ran Barkai.

14. Personal communication with Ran Barkai.

15. Personal communication with Ran Barkai.

16. Schuster 2019.

17. Centro Nacional de Investigacio n sobre la Evolucio n Humana (CENIEH), Paseo Sierra de Atapuerca 3, 09002 Burgos, Spain, and the Department of Archaeology, Tel Aviv University, Institute of Archaeology, Tel Aviv, Israel.

18. Àrea de Prehistòria, Universitat Rovira i Virgili (URV), Tarragona, Spain, and IPHES, Institut Catala de Paleoecologia Humana i Evolucio Social, Tarragona, Spain.

19. Institut Catala de Paleontologia Miquel Crusafont, Barcelona, Spain.

20. Department of Archaeology and Ancient Near Eastern Cultures, Tel Aviv University, Israel.

21. Blasco et al. 2019b.

22. See Collins 2006.

CHAPTER 19.
FLY LIKE A BIRD

1. Finlayson et al. 2012; Finlayson 2019.
2. Finlayson 2019.
3. Mellaart 1967.
4. Uyanik 1974, 12.
5. Mannermaa, Panteleyev, and Sablin 2008, 6.
6. Mannermaa, Panteleyev, and Sablin 2008, 7–8.
7. Mannermaa, Panteleyev, and Sablin 2008, 8–9, 20, table 2.
8. Mannermaa, Panteleyev, and Sablin 2008, 21.
9. Mannermaa, Panteleyev, and Sablin 2008, 4.
10. Mannermaa, Panteleyev, and Sablin 2008, 19.
11. Lahelma 2012, 15–18; O'Shea and Zvelebil 1984, 6–7, 19, 27.
12. O'Shea and Zvelebil 1984, 6–7, 19, 27.
13. Noe-Nygaard 1974, 232.
14. Overton and Hamilakis 2013.
15. Medvedev 1998, 136.
16. Medvedev 1998, 136.
17. Medvedev 1998, 136.
18. Grosman, Munro, and Belfer-Cohen 2008.
19. Grosman, Munro, and Belfer-Cohen 2008, 17668.
20. Grosman, Munro, and Belfer-Cohen 2008, 17668.
21. Bodio 2012, 67–68; and among the Ket, see Jacobson-Tepfer 2015, 344–45.

CHAPTER 20.
QESEM AND THE GENESIS OF INNOVATION

1. Barkai et al. 2003; Gopher et al. 2005; Mercier et al. 2013.
2. Shimelmitz, Barkai, and Gopher 2011.
3. Garrod and Bate 1937; Rust 1950; Garrod 1955; Garrod and Kirkbride 1961; Jelinek 1977; Jelinek 1982; Solecki and Solecki, 1986.
4. Garrod and Kirkbride 1961.
5. Garrod and Kirkbride 1961.
6. Rust 1950.
7. Rust 1950.
8. Gopher et al. 2016; Venditti et al. 2019.
9. David 2017; Assaf, Barkai, and Gopher 2016.

10. Gopher et al. 2005. See also Verri 2004 for an analysis of flint tools from the Qesem Cave.

11. Gopher et al. 2005.

12. Barkai et al. 2009; Venditti et al. 2019.

13. Shahack-Gross et al. 2014; Barkai et al. 2017.

14. Beaumont 2011; Berna et al. 2012.

15. Shahack-Gross et al. 2014; Gowlett 2016.

16. Karkanas et al. 2007; Shahack-Gross et al. 2014; Barkai et al. 2017.

17. Agam et al. 2020; Schuster 2020.

18. Barkai et al. 2017; Blasco et al. 2019b.

19. Blasco et al. 2019a. See also "Prehistoric Humans Ate Bone," 2019.

20. Rabinovicha et al. 2012.

21. Rabinovicha et al. 2012.

22. David 2020; Lemorini et al. 2020.

23. Hershkovitz et al. 2011; Weber et al. 2016; Barkai et al. 2017.

24. Shea and Bar-Yosef 2005.

25. Bar-Yosef 1998.

26. Shea and Bar-Yosef 2005.

27. Gibbons 2017; Hublin et al. 2017; Richter et al. 2017.

28. Grün et al. 1996; Hublin et al. 2017.

29. "Fossil Reanalysis Pushes Back Origin of *Homo sapiens*" 2005.

30. Kalman 2010. See also the somewhat less sensational Siegel-Itzkovich 2010.

CHAPTER 21. COMETH THE HANDAXE

1. Lepre 2011.

2. Frere 1797.

3. Britton 1814, 226.

4. Sackett 2014.

5. Personal communication with Ran Barkai and Avi Gopher.

6. Personal communication with Ran Barkai.

7. Barkai 2021.

8. Dannaway 2010.

9. See Hancock 2007.

10. Kipling 1894.

11. Belmaker et al. 2002.

12. Barkai et al. 2018.

13. *Cambridge Dictionary* online, s.v. "crystal ball."

CHAPTER 22. PATH OF THE SWAN

1. Collins 2019b.
2. Reich et al. 2010; Meyer et al. 2012.
3. Reich 2018, 55.
4. Reich 2018, 55.
5. Meyer et al. 2012; Larena et al 2021.
6. Carlhoff et al. 2021.
7. Brumm et al. 2021.
8. Jacobs et al. 2019.
9. Derevianko, Shunkov, and Volkov 2008; "*Homo sapiens* or Denisovans? Who Made Stunning Cave Jewellery and Artefacts up to 48,000 Years Ago?" 2019.
10. On the discovery of the whistle/flute fragments, see Lbova, Kozhevnikov, and Volkov 2012, CD-1902; Lbova, 2010 11–12. On their attribution to Denisovans, see Collins 2018, 333–34.
11. "World's Oldest Needle Found in Siberian Cave That Stitches Together Human History" 2016.
12. Liesowska and Skarbo 2019.
13. Collins 2019a.
14. "Did Denisovans Usher in the Stone Age in Mongolia?" 2019; Collins 2018, 330–31.
15. Massilani and Pääbo 2020.
16. Massilani and Pääbo 2020.
17. Weber et al. 2016.
18. Chen et al. 2019.
19. Zhang et al. 2020.
20. Gibbons 2020.
21. Huerta-Sánchez et al. 2014.
22. Nebesky-Wojkowitz (1956) 1996, 15; Norbu 2013, 16–18.
23. Skarbo and Liesowska 2020.
24. Hatto 1961.
25. See Collins 2018, chs. 35 and 39, on swan ancestry and swan shamanism among the indigenous peoples of Siberia, Mongolia, and northern Asia as a whole.
26. "Jayrajc" n.d.
27. "Kailish Manasarovar—Home of God Shiva—Mount Kailish" 2013.
28. Leviton 2011, 543. See also "Hamsa, Hansa, Haṃsa, Haṃsā, Haṁsā, Hamsha: 47 Definitions" n.d.
29. For a full account of the discovery of the Dragon Man skull see MINNews 2021.
30. Ji et al. 2021; Ni et al 2021; Shao et al 2021.

31. Ji et al. 2021.
32. Ni et al. 2021.
33. Ni et al. 2021.
34. Ni et al. 2021.
35. Ni et al. 2021.
36. Ji et al. 2021.
37. Gibbons 2021; Smith 2021.
38. For more on the exceptional size of the Denisovans see Collins 2014b; Collins 2018, 326–28; and Collins and Little 2019, ch. 18.
39. Marshall 2021; Schuster 2021; Zaidner et al. 2021.
40. Schuster 2021.
41. Schuster 2021.
42. Li 2012.
43. Kidadl Team 2020.
44. MINNews 2021.

CHAPTER 23. MOON MAGIC

1. Wikipedia, s.v. "Qasim (name)."
2. David 2020.
3. Email from Rodney Hale to A. Collins, dated December 15, 2019.
4. Lacey 1975, 133.
5. Blackledge 2003, 242.
6. Blackledge 2003, 242–43.
7. Ellis and Abarbanel 1961, 593.
8. Ellis and Abarbanel 1961, 593.
9. See the various books by Stan Gooch that highlight this topic, such as Gooch 1977, Gooch (1979) 2006, Gooch (1989) 1995, and Gooch 2008.
10. Marshack 1972.
11. Shodoev 2012, 52, 56, 70, 76, 78, 87. "Seventy-two years" also reflects the approximate time it takes for the stellar background to shift one degree in a 360-degree precessional cycle of 25,920 years.
12. De Kay 1898, 189.
13. Lund University 2019; Norevik et al. 2019.

CHAPTER 24. WITHIN THE CAVE

1. Hardy et al. 2016.
2. Wikipedia s.v. "List of Acacia species known to contain psychoactive alkaloids."

CHAPTER 25. MOUNTAINS OF POWER

1. Israel Antiquities Authority 2018.
2. Personal communication with Ran Barkai.
3. Barkai and Gopher 2009.
4. Barkai and Gopher 2009.
5. Parker Pearson et al. 2015.
6. "Stonehenge 'Bluestone' Quarries Confirmed 140 Miles Away in Wales" 2015.
7. Parker Pearson et al. 2015 and the references therein.
8. Parker Pearson et al. 2015.
9. Collins and Little 2019, 188, 275–80.
10. See Saunders 2001.
11. Matthew 17:1–8; Mark 9:2–8; Luke 9:28–36.

CHAPTER 26. CENTER OF THE WORLD

1. 2 Samuel 5:6–10.
2. Conder 1878, vol. i, 55; Anderson 1980.
3. Judges 9:37.

CHAPTER 27.
AGE OF THE PATRIARCHS

1. Genesis 11:28, 11:31, 15:7 and Nehemiah 9:7. All Bible quotations are taken from the English transliteration as given by Biblehub online unless otherwise stated.
2. *Asatir,* ch. V, verses. 27–28; "Pitron or Commentary to the Asatir" ch. V, verses 27–28, see Gaster (1927) 2015, 225. This is also an oral tradition in Şanlıurfa still told today by guides.
3. See Collins (1996) 1998; Collins 2014a.
4. Genesis 12:6.
5. Genesis 12:6.
6. Genesis 12:6 (Young's Literal Translation).
7. Biblehub, s.v. "Moreh."
8. Bar 2012, 383.
9. Bar 2012, 383.
10. Genesis 12:7.
11. Genesis 12:7.
12. Rajki 2005, s.v. "Ballutt."

13. Rajki 2005, s.v. "Ballutt."

14. Rajki 2005, s.v. "Ballutt."

15. Geikie 1888, 208.

16. Genesis 22:2.

17. Genesis 22:8–9.

18. Genesis 22:10–12.

19. Genesis 22:13.

20. Genesis 22:15–18.

21. Cargill 2019, 47–48.

22. Cargill 2019, 49–50.

23. 2 Chronicles 3:1.

24. Cargill 2019, 49–50.

25. Genesis 28:10.

26. Genesis 28:11.

27. Genesis 28:12.

28. Genesis 28:12.

29. Genesis 28:13.

30. Genesis 28:15.

31. Genesis 28:17.

32. Genesis 28:18.

33. Genesis 28:19.

34. Mandeville 1900, 71.

35. Genesis 28:22.

36. Avner 2002.

37. Genesis 31:13.

38. Conder 1878, vol. i, 55.

39. Genesis 32:28.

40. Genesis 35:1.

41. Genesis 35:2.

42. Genesis 35:2 (Young's Literal Translation).

43. Genesis 35:3.

44. Genesis 35:4 (Young's Literal Translation).

45. Genesis 35:4.

46. Genesis 35:6–7.

47. Deuteronomy 27:4 (Young's Literal Translation).

48. Deuteronomy 27:4.

49. Deuteronomy 27:4 (Young's Literal Translation).

50. Deuteronomy 27:12–13.

51. Deuteronomy 27:15–26, Deuteronomy 28:1–20.

52. "Samaritan Story of the Death of Moses," Commentary, in Gaster (1927) 2015, 317, 319, 321.

53. See Cargill 2019, 47–48.

54. Ulrich 2015b, 54–57.

55. Ulrich 2015b, 55 and the references therein.

56. Charlesworth 2010.

57. Charlesworth 2010; Charlesworth 2012.

58. Ulrich 2015b.

59. Deuteronomy 27:4 translation as given in Charlesworth 2010.

60. Årstein 2020.

CHAPTER 28.
REALM OF THE MOUNTAIN GOD

1. Exodus 3:1–6.

2. Exodus 19–23.

3. Exodus 20–23.

4. Exodus 34:1–3.

5. Clifford (1972) 2010, 111, 130.

6. Collins and Ogilvie-Herald 2002, chs. 19–21.

CHAPTER 29. THE DIVINE SHEKINAH

1. Clifford (1972) 2010, 130, 130n36, 131.

2. Deuteronomy 27:12–13 translation as given in Petrozzi 1973, 196; Joshua 8:33.

3. Kohler and Blau (1906) 2012, s.v. "Shekinah."

4. Montgomery (1907) 1968, 209.

5. Kohler and Blau (1906) 2012, s.v. "Shekinah."

6. Kohler and Blau (1906) 2012, s.v. "Shekinah."

7. Costa 2010.

8. Kohler and Blau (1906) 2012, s.v. "Shekinah."

9. Exodus 3:1–2.

10. Exodus 24:17; Exodus 25:10–28.

11. Exodus 13:21.

12. Exodus 26:1–37.

13. Kohler and Blau (1906) 2012, s.v. "Shekinah."

14. Kohler and Blau (1906) 2012, s.v. "Shekinah."

15. "The Palestinian Targum on the Book Shemoth or Exodus," section 33, ch. 40, in Etheridge 1862, 579–80.

16. Joshua 3:3–8, 11–15, 17.

17. Jacob (1906) 2016, 20–21.

18. Jacob (1906) 2016, 10.

19. Deuteronomy 27:12–13 translation as given in Petrozzi 1973, 196; Joshua 8:33.

20. Noth 1962, 109.

21. Drake 1976, 126–128.

22. Jacob (1906) 2016, 20.

23. Jacob (1906) 2016, 20; Montgomery (1907) 1968, 233.

24. Montgomery (1907) 1968, 232.

25. Montgomery (1907) 1968, 232.

CHAPTER 30. LET THERE BE LIGHT

1. Genesis 1:1.

2. Genesis 1:2.

3. Genesis 1:3.

4. Genesis 1:4.

5. "Plasma, Plasma, Everywhere" 1999.

6. "An Enormous Number of UFO Sightings before Tsunami and Earthquake in South and Southeast Asia—Were They Trying to Warn?" 2004; Collins 2012, ch. 25.

7. For a full introduction to this subject, see Parkhomenko 1971.

8. Parkhomenko 1971; Thériault et al. 2014.

9. Curie and Curie 1880; Curie and Curie 1881.

10. Woodford 2019.

11. Parkhomenko 1971, 85, 111, 113

12. Parkhomenko 1971, 175, 186.

13. Parkhomenko 1971, 188, 190.

14. Parkhomenko 1971, 186, 189.

15. Parkhomenko 1971, 239–42, 244.

16. Parkhomenko 1971, 244–45.

17. Parkhomenko 1971, 248.

18. Parkhomenko 1971, 248.

19. O'Brien 1996; Ruleman and Machette 2007.

20. O'Brien, 1996.

CHAPTER 31. MOUNTAINS OF LIGHT

1. Blofeld 1972, 149–50.

2. Blofeld 1972, 150.

3. "Mount Taishan" (1987) 2011.

4. "Mount Taishan" (1987) 2011.

5. Lothian 2019, 62–63.

6. Devereux et al. 1989, 19–24.

CHAPTER 32. SAMARIAN LIGHTS

1. Shaw 1738, 363.

2. Shaw 1738, 363.

3. Shaw 1738, 363.

4. See also Joshua 21:21, which also talks about "Shechem with her suburbs in mount Ephraim."

5. Wilkins (1955) 1967, 248. Page number from the 1967 edition.

6. Milik 1976, 67, cf. *Kitāb al-Asātīr,* chs. 40–41.

7. Environmental Profile for the West Bank 1996, map 4:1.

CHAPTER 33. IN THE LAND OF ANGELS

1. Collins and Ogilvie-Herald 2002, chs. 23–24.

2. John 4:7–29.

3. Sellin 1922; Fohrer and Sellin 1969.

4. Sellin 1906.

5. Joshua 24:26.

6. Langfur 2019.

7. Deuteronomy 27:12–13 as translated by Petrozzi 1973, 196; Joshua 8:33.

8. See Collins (1996) 1998 and Collins 2014a.

9. Montgomery (1907) 1968, 216.

10. Collins (1987) 1988.

11. Collins (1987) 1988.

12. Montgomery (1907) 1968, 219, 223.

13. D'Este and Rankine 2011, 122–42.

CHAPTER 34. ON THE EDGE OF REALITY

1. Kelleher and Knapp 2005.

2. Salisbury (1974) 2010, ch. 8: "The Skinwalker Ranch."

3. Kelleher and Knapp 2005, 14, and see the book's Appendix Table 1 for a comprehensive list of sightings based on the files of Joseph Junior Hicks from 1956 to the present day.

4. Kelleher and Knapp 2005, especially chs. 11, 14, 18, and 22.

5. Personal communication with Erik Bard.

6. Personal communication Erik Bard; see also the TV series *The Secret of Skinwalker Ranch,* 2020.

7. For a full review of the Marfa lights, see Collins 2012, 65–73.

8. Thornsburg 2007, 5.

9. Collins 2012, 68–71.

10. Wright and Kenney 1973.

11. Devereux et al. 1989, 221.

12. Devereux et al. 1989, 220.

13. Devereux et al. 1989, 216–25.

14. Collins 1979.

CHAPTER 35.
THE ENTANGLEMENT OF ALL

1. Einstein, Podolsky, and Rosen 1935; Bell 1964.

2. Fiscaletti and Sorli 2010.

3. Popkin 2018; Riedinger et al. 2018.

4. Cartlidge 2019.

5. Ball 2011.

6. Nield 2021

7. Nield 2021.

8. Ball 2017.

9. Heisenberg 1949; Ball 2017; Brooks 2020, 36, 38–39.

10. Folger 2007.

11. Brown 2016; Brooks 2020, 30–33.

12. Rabinowitz 2001; Panigrahi and Chatterjee 2008.

13. Canan 2020.

14. Quoted in Canan 2020.

15. Quoted in Canan 2020.

16. Email correspondence between Andrea Aiello and the author on various dates between November 2020 and February 2021.

17. Einstein and Rosen 1935.

18. Gharibyan and Penna 2013; Maldacena and Susskind 2013; Susskind 2021.

19. Susskind 2021.

20. Fiscaletti and Sorli 2010.

21. Fiscaletti and Sorli 2010.

22. Bohm and Hiley 1984; Frescura and Hiley 1984; Bohm and Hiley 1993.

23. Chao 2008; Eckle et al. 2008; Fiscaletti and Sorli 2010.

24. Chao 2008.

25. Fiscaletti and Sorli 2010.

26. Bell 1964.

27. This topic is explored further in Ares et al. 2016.

CHAPTER 36. MULTIDIMENSIONALITY

1. Pratt 1993.

2. Peat 1996, 65–67.

3. Tonks 1967.

4. Pinheiro 2007.

5. Langmuir 1928. For more on Langmuir's plasma work, see Rajvanshi 2008.

6. Crookes 1879.

7. Crookes 1879. See also Pinheiro 2007.

8. Bohm and Hiley 1993.

9. Bohm 1980; Pratt 1993.

10. Bohm 1980; Pratt 1993.

11. Fiscaletti and Sorli 2010.

12. Fiscaletti and Sorli 2010.

13. Rucker (1984) 2014, 26–29, 52–53.

14. Becker, Becker, and Schwarz 2007.

15. Dean 2018.

16. Keel 1978, ch. 25 particularly.

17. For an introduction to brane world cosmology see Papantonopoulos 2002; Brax and van de Bruck 2003; Langlois 2003.

18. Pourhasan, Afshordi, and Mann 2014.

19. Parkhomenko 1971.

CHAPTER 37. THE EGREGORE

1. Devereux and McCartney 1982, 155–167, 187–204, 227.

2. Kelleher and Knapp 2005, 18, 44.

3. O'Bryan 1956, 33–34.

4. O'Bryan 1956, 3, 3n7, 8, 34, 34n84.

5. O'Bryan 1956, 3n7.

6. Kelleher and Knapp 2005, 44–45, 234.

7. Kelleher and Knapp 2005, 3–9, 26–28, 192.

8. Kelleher and Knapp 2005, 49.

9. "Sahara Prehistoric Rock Art" 2009; Lutz and Lutz 1995, 154–59, 161, figures 207–12, 215.

10. See Collins 2012.

11. Personal communication with Erik Bard.

12. Personal communication with Paul Sinclair.

13. Personal communication with Paul Sinclair.

14. See Sinclair 2016, Sinclair 2017, Sinclair 2019.

15. Clark (1971) 2009, 79–86, 91.

16. Clark (1971) 2009, 71–73, plate VI *A*.

17. Sinclair 2016, 194–96.

18. Sinclair 2016, 196.

CHAPTER 38. WAS GOD AN *N*-BEING?

1. Yardimci 2008, 362–64.

2. Exodus 25 and 35.

3. Kohler and Blau (1906) 2012, s.v. "Shekinah."

4. Petrozzi 1973, 196, cf. Deuteronomy 27:12–13; Joshua 8:33.

5. Deuteronomy 10:1–4.

6. Exodus 25:22; Leviticus 1:1; Numbers 7:89.

7. Exodus 24:17.

8. See, most obviously, Hancock 1992.

9. Jacob (1906) 2016, 14–15.

10. Jacob (1906) 2016, 17–18.

11. Joshua 18:1.

12. 1 Samuel 4:3–11.

13. 1 Kings 6:19.

14. Jacob (1906) 2016, 18.

15. Jacob (1906) 2016, 20–21.

16. Crane 1890, 178n109, for ch. 50.

17. Cowley 1895.

18. Cowley, Jacobs, Huxley (1906) 2012, s.v. "Samaritans."

19. Little 1994, 250.

BIBLIOGRAPHY

Abbreviations: n.d. = no date given; n.p.p. = no place of publication.

Abbott, Edwin A. 1884. *Flatland: A Romance of Many Dimensions*. London: Seeley & Co.

Abbott, Karen. 2012. "The Fox Sisters and the Rap on Spiritualism." *Smithsonian*, October 20.

Adams, Brian, and Brooke S. Blades, eds. 2009. *Lithic Materials and Paleolithic Societies*. Chichester, West Sussex, UK: Wiley-Blackwell.

Agam, Aviad, et al. 2020. "Estimating Temperatures of Heated Lower Palaeolithic Flint Artefacts." *Nature Human Behaviour* 5 (October 5): 221–28.

Akazawa, T., K. Aoki, and O. Bar-Yosef, eds. 1998. *Neandertals and Modern Humans in Western Asia*. New York: Plenum Press.

Akers, D. 2001. "Preliminary Report on Magnetic Field Measurements Recorded at Satus Fire Lookout." The Willard J. Vogel Study website, July 11.

Anderson, Robert T. 1980. "Mount Gerizim: Navel of the World." *The Biblical Archaeologist* 43, no. 4 (Autumn): 217–21.

Angelucci, Orfeo. 1955. *The Secret of the Saucers*. Stevens Point, Wisc.: Amherst Press.

Ares, F., et al. 2016. "Entanglement Entropy and Möbius Transformations for Critical Fermionic Chains." Cornell University's arXiv website, December 21.

Årstein, Justnes. 2020. "Fake Fragments, Flexible Provenances: Eight Aramaic 'Dead Sea Scrolls' from the 21st Century." In Bundvad et al. 2020, 242–72.

Assaf, Ella, et al. 2020. "Shaped Stone Balls Were Used for Bone Marrow Extraction at Lower Paleolithic Qesem Cave, Israel." *PLoS One* 15, no. 4 (April 9): 1–28.

Assaf, Ella, Ran Barkai, and Avi Gopher. 2016. "Knowledge Transmission and Apprentice Flint-Knappers in the Acheulo-Yabrudian: A Case Study from Qesem Cave, Israel." *Quaternary International* 398 (April 4): 70–85.

Aveni, Anthony, ed. 1977. *Native American Astronomy*. Austin: University of Texas Press.

Avner, Uzi. 2002. *Studies in the Material and Spiritual Culture of the Negev and Sinai Populations during the 6th–3rd Millennia BC.* Ph.D. diss., Hebrew University, Jerusalem, December.

Bader, Christopher. 1995. "The UFO Contact Movement from the 1950s to the Present." *Studies in Popular Culture* 17, no. 2: 73–90.

Ball, Phillip. 2011. "Entangled Diamonds Vibrate Together." *Nature,* December 1.

———. 2017. "The Strange Link between the Human Mind and Quantum Physics." BBC Earth website, February 16.

Bandara, Priyanka, and David O. Carpenter. 2018. "Planetary Electromagnetic Pollution: It Is Time to Assess Its Impact?" *The Lancet: Planetary Health* 2, no. 12 (December 1): ES12–ES14.

Bar, Abraham Omer. 2012. *Book of the Root of Tree of the Knowledge.* Scotts Valley, Calif.: Createspace Independent Publishing Platform.

Bar-Yosef, Ofer. 1998. "The Chronology of the Middle Paleolithic of the Levant." In Akazawa, Aoki, and Bar-Yosef 1998, 39–56.

Barkai, Ran. 2021. "The Elephant in the Handaxe: Lower Palaeolithic Ontologies and Representations." *Cambridge Archaeological Journal* 31, no. 2 (May): 349–61.

Barkai, Ran, and Avi Gopher. 2009. "Changing the Face of the Earth: At Sede Ilan, an Extensive Lower-Middle Paleolithic Quarry Site in Israel." In Adams and Blades 2009, 173–85.

———. 2016. "On Anachronism: The Curious Presence of Spheroids and Polyhedrons at Acheulo-Yabrudian Qesem Cave, Israel." *Quaternary International* 398, issue C (April 4): 118–28.

Barkai, Ran, et al. 2003. "Uranium Series Dates from Qesem Cave, Israel, and the End of the Lower Palaeolithic." *Nature* 423, no. 6943 (July): 977–79.

Barkai, Ran, et al. 2009. "A Blade for All Seasons? Making and Using Amudian Blades at Qesem Cave, Israel." *Human Evolution* 24, no. 1 (January): 57–75.

Barkai, Ran, et al. 2017. "Fire for a Reason: Barbecue at Middle Pleistocene Qesem Cave, Israel." *Current Anthropology* 58, no. S16 (August): S314–S324.

———. 2018. "A Land of Flint and Fallow Deer: Human Persistence at Middle Pleistocene Qesem Cave." In Pope, McNabb, and Gamble 2018, 60–82.

Barnes, Ian. 2009. *The Historical Atlas of Native Americans.* New York: Chartwell Books.

Bartholomew, Robert E., Keith Basterfield, and George S. Howard. 1991. "UFO Contactees and Abductees: Psychopathology or Fantasy Proneness?" *Professional Psychology: Research and Practice* 22, no. 3 (June): 215–22.

Beaumont, Peter B. 2011. "The Edge: More on Fire-Making by about 1.7 Million Years Ago at Wonderwerk Cave in South Africa." *Current Anthropology* 52, no. 4 (August): 585–95.

Becker, Katrin, Melanie Becker, and John Schwarz. 2007. *String Theory and M-Theory: A Modern Introduction*. Cambridge, UK: Cambridge University Press.

Bell, J. S. 1964. "On the Einstein Podolsky Rosen Paradox." *Physics Physique* 1, no. 3: 195–200.

Belmaker, Miriam, et al. 2002. "New Evidence for Hominid Presence in the Lower Pleistocene of the Southern Levant." *Journal of Human Evolution* 43, no. 1 (July): 43–56.

Berna, Francesco, et al. 2012. "Microstratigraphic Evidence of In Situ Fire in the Acheulean Strata of Wonderwerk Cave, Northern Cape Province, South Africa." *Proceedings of the National Academy of Sciences of the United States of America* 109, no. 20 (May 15): E1215–E1220.

Bezold, Carl, ed. 1906. *Orientalische Studien Theodor Nöldeke zum siebzigsten Geburtstag (2 März, 1906): Gewidmet von Freunden und Schülern*. 2 vols. Berlin, Germany: Alfred Töpelmann.

Blackledge, Catherine. 2003. *The Story of V: Opening Pandora's Box*. London: Weidenfeld & Nicolson.

Blasco, R. et al. 2019a. "Bone Marrow Storage and Delayed Consumption at Middle Pleistocene Qesem Cave, Israel (420 to 200 ka)." *Science Advances* 5, no. 10 (October 9): 1–12.

Blasco, Ruth, et al. 2019b. "Feathers and Food: Human-Bird Interactions at Middle Pleistocene Qesem Cave, Israel." *Journal of Human Evolution* 136 (November): 102653.

Blofeld, John. 1972. *The Wheel of Life: The Autobiography of a Western Buddhist*. Boulder, Colo.: Shambhala Publications.

Bodio, Stephen J. 2012. *Eternity of Eagles: The Human History of the Most Fascinating Bird in the World*. Lanham, Md.: Rowman & Littlefield.

Bohm, David. 1980. *Wholeness and the Implicate Order*. London: Routledge & Kegan Paul.

Bohm, David and Basil Hiley. 1984. "Generalisation of the Twistor to Clifford Algebras as a Basis for Geometry." *Revista Brasileira de Física, Volume Especial, os 70 Anos de Mario Schonberg:* 1–26.

———. 1993. *The Undivided Universe: An Ontological Interpretation of Quantum Theory*. London: Routledge.

Brandon, Jim. 1983. *The Rebirth of Pan: Hidden Faces of the American Earth Spirit*. Dunlap, Ill.: Firebird Press.

Brax, Philippe, and Carsten van de Bruck. 2003. "Cosmology and Brane Worlds: A Review." *Classical and Quantum Gravity* 20, no. 9: R201–R232. Cornell University's arXiv website, March 11.

Brinton, Daniel G. 1896. *The Myths of the New World*. Philadelphia: David McKay Publisher.

Britton, John. 1814. *The Beauties of England and Wales.* Vol. 15, *Wiltshire, Warwickshire, Westmoreland, and Worcestershire.* London: J. Harris, Longman and Co.

Brooks, Michael (ed.). 2020. *New Scientist Essential Guide No 5: Quantum Physics.* London: New Scientist Ltd.

Brown, Alan. 2016. "The Weird, But True, Evidence for 'Spooky Action' at Distance (Kavli Hangout)." Space.com website, January 8.

Brumm, Adam, et al. 2021. "Oldest Cave Art Found in Sulawesi." *Science Advances* 7, no. 3 (January 13): eabd4648.

Budden, Albert. 1994. *Allergies and Aliens.* New York: Sterling.

———. 1998. *Electric UFOs.* New York: Sterling.

Bundvad, Mette, et al. 2020. *Vision, Narrative, and Wisdom in the Aramaic Texts from Qumran: Essays from the Copenhagen Symposium, 14–15 August, 2017.* Leiden, the Netherlands: E. J. Brill.

Burkitt, M. C. 1921. *Prehistory.* Cambridge, UK: Cambridge University Press.

Butcher, Ginger. 2016. *Tour of the Electromagnetic Spectrum.* Washington: NASA.

Camazine, S., and R. A. Bye. 1980. "A Study of the Medicinal Ethnobotany of the Zuni Indians of New Mexico." *Journal of Ethnopharmacology* 2, no. 4: 365–88.

Canan, Eric. 2020. "Ball Lightning Is So Strange It Might Just Come from Another Dimension." *New Scientist* website, October 21.

Cargill, Robert R. 2019. *Melchizedek, King of Sodom: How Scribes Invented the Biblical Priest-King.* Oxford, UK: Oxford University Press.

Caricola, Isabella, et al. 2018. "Functional Analysis of Stone Balls (Spheroids/Polyhedron) from Middle Pleistocene Qesem Cave (Israel)." Paris, France: XVIIIe Congrès mondial UISPP, Paris, June 4–9.

Carlhoff, Selina, et al. 2021. "Genome of a Middle Holocene Hunter-Gatherer from Wallacea." *Nature* 596 (August 25): 543–47.

Cartlidge, Edwin. 2019. "Entanglement Lights the Way to Scalable Quantum Computers." PhysicsWorld website, November 30.

Chao, Wu Zhong. 2008. "The Imaginary Time in the Tunneling Process." Cornell University's arXiv website, April 1.

Chapman University. 2018. "Paranormal America 2018: Chapman University Survey of American Fears." The Voice of Wilkinson website, October 16.

Charlesworth, James H. 2010. "Announcing a Dead Sea Scrolls Fragment of Deuteronomy." *Maarav* 16 (March): 201–11.

———, ed. 1985. *The Old Testament Pseudepigrapha.* Vol. 2. Garden City, N.Y.: Doubleday.

Charlesworth, James Hamilton. 2012. "The Discovery of an Unknown Dead Sea Scroll: The Original Text of Deuteronomy 27?" *OWU Magazine,* Summer.

Chen, Fahu, et al. 2019. "A Late Middle Pleistocene Denisovan Mandible from the Tibetan Plateau." *Nature* 569 (May 1): 409–12.

Chevalier, Remy. 1996. "The Big Theories of Doctor Little." *Paranoia: The Conspiracy Reader* 13 (Summer): 36–40.

Christian Spectator. 1823. "Swedenborgianism." *Christian Spectator: Conducted by an Association of Gentlemen*, Vol. 5 (12), December 1, 1823, 614–26.

Clark, Ella. 1966. *Indian Legends from the Northern Rockies*. Norman: University of Oklahoma Press.

Clark, J. G. D. (1971) 2009. *Excavations at Star Carr: An Early Mesolithic Site at Seamer Near Scarborough, Yorkshire*. Cambridge, Cambridgeshire, UK: Cambridge University Press.

Clarke, Arthur C. 1962. *Profiles of the Future*. New York: Harper & Row.

Clifford, Richard J. (1972) 2010. *The Cosmic Mountain in Canaan and the Old Testament*. Harvard Semitic Monographs, vol. 4. Eugene, Oreg.: Wipf & Stock.

Clottes, J., dir. 2012. L'art pléistocène dans le monde/Pleistocene art of the world/Arte pleistoceno en el mundo Actes du Congrès IFRAO, Tarascon-sur-Ariège, Septembre 2010—Symposium "Datation et taphonomie de l'art pléistocène," LXV–LXVI, 2010–2011, CD and book. Tarascon-sur-Ariège, France: Société Préhistorique Ariège-Pyrénées.

Cochrane, Andrew, and Andy Jones. 2012. *Visualising the Neolithic: Abstraction, Figuration, Performance, Representation*. Oxford, UK: Oxbow Books.

Collins, Andrew. 1979. "UFOs and Psychic Abilities: What Is the Link?" Pts. 1 and 2. *Strange Phenomena* 1, no. 1: 8–9; 1, no. 2: 78.

———. (1987) 1988. "Mount Athos." *The Ley Hunter* 104: 15–23.

———. 1994. *Alien Energy*. Leigh-on-Sea, Essex, UK: ABC Books.

———. (1996) 1998. *From the Ashes of Angels*. Rochester, Vt.: Bear & Co.

———. 2004. *Twenty-first Century Grail*. London: Virgin Books.

———. 2006. *The Cygnus Mystery*. Rochester, Vt.: Bear & Co.

———. 2009. *The New Circlemakers*. Virginia Beach, Va.: Fourth Dimension Press.

———. 2012. *LightQuest: Your Guide to Seeing and Interacting with UFOs, Mystery Lights, and Plasma Intelligences*. Memphis, Tenn.: Eagle Wing Books.

———. 2014a. *Göbekli Tepe: Genesis of the Gods*. Rochester, Vt.: Bear & Co.

———. 2014b. "The Coming of the Giants: Rise of the Human Hybrids." In Little 2014b, 227–39.

———. 2018. *The Cygnus Key*. Rochester, Vt.: Bear & Co.

———. 2019a. "New Shocking Clues Into Human Origins From Qesem Cave." Ancient Origins website, October 14.

———. 2019b. "45,000-Year-Old Cave Lion Figurine Uncovered At Denisova Cave." Ancient Origins website, November 20.

Collins, Andrew, and Gregory L. Little. 2019. *Denisovan Origins*. Rochester, Vt.: Bear & Co.

Collins, Andrew, and Chris Ogilvie-Herald. 2002. *Tutankhamun: The Exodus Conspiracy.* London: Virgin Books.

Conder, Claude Reignier. 1878. *Tent Work in Palestine: A Record of Discovery and Adventure.* Vol. 1. London: R. Bentley & Son.

Condign Report. 2000. "Flying Saucery Presents . . . The Real UFO Report." Declassified in 2006. UK-UFO.org website.

Cook, C. M., and M. A. Persinger. 2001. "Geophysical Variables and Behavior: XCII. Experimental Elicitation of the Experience of a Sentient Being by Right Hemispheric, Weak Magnetic Fields: Interaction with Temporal Lobe Sensitivity." *Perceptual and Motor Skills* 92, no. 2 (April): 447–48.

Costa, José. 2010. "The Body of God in Ancient Rabbinic Judaism: Problems of Interpretation." *Revue de l'histoire des religions* 227, no. 3 (July): 283–316.

Cowley, A. 1895. "The Samaritan Doctrine of the Messiah." *The Expositor* I, 5th series (March): 161–74.

Cowley, A., Joseph Jacobs, and Henry Minor Huxley. (1906) 2012. *Jewish Encyclopedia,* s.v. "Samaritans."

Crane, Oliver Turnbull. 1890. *The Samaritan Chronicle or the Book of Joshua, the Son of Nun.* New York: John B. Alden.

Crookes, William. 1879. *On Radiant Matter: A Lecture Delivered to the British Association for the Advancement of Science, at Sheffield, Friday, August 22, 1879.* London: E. J. Davey.

Cunaeus, Petrus. 1683. *De republyk der Hebreen, of Gemeenebest der Joden.* Vol. 3. Amsterdam: Wilhelmus Goeree.

Curie, Jacques, and Pierre Curie. 1880. "Development, via Compression, of Electric Polarization in Hemihedral Crystals with Inclined Faces." *Bulletin de la Societe de Minerologique de France* 3: 90–93.

———. 1881. "Contractions and Expansions Produced by Voltages in Hemihedral Crystals with Inclined Faces." *Comptes Rendus* 93: 1137–40.

Curtis, E. S. 1919. *The North American Indian.* 20 vols. Seattle, Wash.: E. S. Curtis; Cambridge, Mass.: The University Press.

Cushing, Frank. 1896. "Outlines of Zuñi Creation Myths." In *Thirteenth Annual Report of the Bureau of Ethnology,* edited by J. Powell, 325–447. Washington: Smithsonian Institution.

Dahlgreen, Will. 2015. "Majorities across Britain, Germany, and the USA Believe That Extra-terrestrial Life Exists." YouGov website, September 24.

Dane, C. 1973. *The American Indian and the Occult.* New York: Popular Library.

Däniken, Erich von. (1968) 1969. *Chariots of the Gods.* Translated by Michael Heron. London: Souvenir Press.

Dannaway, Frederick R. 2010. "Strange Fires, Weird Smokes, and Psychoactive

Combustibles: Entheogens and Incense in Ancient Traditions." *Journal of Psychoactive Drugs* 42, no. 4 (December): 485–97.

David, Aerial. 2017. "400,000-Year-Old 'School of Rock' Found in Prehistoric Cave in Israel." *Haaretz* newspaper website, November 22.

———. 2020. "Early Humans in Today's Israel Used Ash as Their 'Freezer.'" *Haaretz* newspaper website, October 13.

Davidson, David. 1862. *The Comprehensive Family Bible Containing the Old and New Testaments with Copious Notes and Practical Reflections, Introduction, Parallel Passages and Index.* Glasgow, Edinburgh, and London: Blackie & Son.

De Kay, Charles. 1898. *Bird Gods.* New York: A. S. Barnes.

Dean, Signe. 2018. "The Human Brain Can Create Structures in up to 11 Dimensions." ScienceAlert website, April 21.

Defence Intelligence Analysis Staff. 2000. *Unidentified Aerial Phenomena in the UK Air Defence Region.* London: Ministry of Defence.

Derev'anko, Anatoliy, Demitri B. Shimkin, and W. Roger Powers. 1998. *The Paleolithic of Siberia: New Discoveries and Interpretations.* Translated by Inna P. Laricheva. Urbana and Chicago: University of Illinois Press.

Derevianko, Anatoliy, M. V. Shunkov, and P. V. Volkov. 2008. "A Paleolithic Bracelet from Denisova Cave." *Archaeology Ethnology and Anthropology of Eurasia* 34, no. 2 (June): 13–25.

Derr, John. S., and Michael A. Persinger. 1989. "Geophysical Variables and Behavior: LIV. Zeitoun (Egypt) Apparitions of the Virgin Mary and Tectonic Strain-Induced Luminosities." *Perceptual and Motor Skills* 68 (February 1): 123–28.

D'Este, Sorita, and David Rankine. 2011. *The Cosmic Shekinah.* London: Avalonia.

Devereux, Paul, et al. 1989. *Earth Lights Revelation.* London: Blandford Press.

Devereux, Paul, and Paul McCartney. 1982. *Earth Lights.* Wellingborough, Northamptonshire, UK: Turnstone Press.

"Did Denisovans Usher in the Stone Age in Mongolia?" 2019. *Siberian Times,* August 19.

Dow, James R., Roger L. Welsch, and Susan D. Dow, eds. 2010. *Wyoming Folklore: Reminiscences, Folktales, Beliefs, Customs, and Folk Speech.* Lincoln: University of Nebraska Press/Federal Writers Project.

Drake, W. Raymond. 1976. *Gods and Spacemen in Ancient Israel.* London: Sphere Books.

Dye, David. 2004. "Art, Ritual, and Chiefly Warfare in the Mississippian World." In Townsend and Sharp 2004, 191–205.

Eastman, Charles A. [Ohiyesa]. 1911. *The Soul of the Indian.* Lincoln: University of Nebraska Press.

Eckle, P., et al. 2008. "Attosecond Ionization and Tunneling Delay Time Measurements in Helium." *Science* 322, no. 5907 (December 5): 1525–29.

Eddy, John A. 1977. "Medicine Wheels and Plains Indian Astronomy." In Aveni 1977, 147–69.

Einstein, A., B. Podolsky, and N. Rosen. 1935. "Can Quantum-Mechanical Description of Physical Reality Be Considered Complete?" *Physical Review* 47 (May 15): 777–80.

Einstein, A., and N. Rosen. 1935. "The Particle Problem in the General Theory of Relativity." *Physical Review* 48, no. 73 (July 1935): 73–77.

Eliade, Mircea. 1951. *Shamanism*. Princeton, N.J.: Princeton University Press.

Ellis, Albert, and Albert Abarbanel, eds. 1961. *The Encyclopædia of Sexual Behaviour*. Vol. 2. New York: Hawthorn Books.

Emspak, Jesse. 2016. "States of Matter: Plasmas." LiveScience website, May 5.

"An Enormous Number of UFO Sightings before Tsunami and Earthquake in South and Southeast Asia—Were They Trying to Warn?" 2004. *India Daily,* December 31.

Environmental Profile for The West Bank, Volume 5—Nablus District. 1996. Jerusalem: Applied Research Institute.

Erdoes, R., and A. Ortiz. 1984. *American Indian Myths and Legends*. New York: Random House.

Estebaranz-Sánchez, Ferran, Laura M. Martínez, and Paulo Pereira. 2019. "The Sedimentary Record: The Very Early Acquisition of Fire by Hominins." In Pereira et al. 2019, 3–14.

Etheridge, J. W. 1862. *The Targums of Onkelos and Jonathan ben Uzziel on the Pentateuch: With the Fragments of the Jerusalem Targum: From the Chaldee—Genesis and Exodus*. London: Longman, Green, Longman, and Roberts.

Feder, Ken. 2010. *The Encyclopedia of Dubious Archaeology*. Santa Barbara, Calif.: Greenwood.

[Fell, Herbert Granville.] 1896. *The Art Bible, Comprising the Old and New Testaments: With Numerous Illustrations*. London: George Newnes.

Finlayson, Clive. 2019. *The Smart Neanderthal: Bird Catching, Cave Art, and the Cognitive Revolution*. Oxford, UK: Oxford University Press.

Finlayson, Clive, et al. 2012. "Birds of a Feather: Neanderthal Exploitation of Raptors and Corvids." *PLoS One* 7, no. 9 (September): e45927, 1–8.

Fiscaletti, Davide, and Amrit S. Sorli. 2010. "Perspectives towards the Interpretation of Physical Space as a Medium of Immediate Quantum Information Transfer." *Prespacetime Journal* 1, no. 6 (September): 883–98.

Fohrer, Georg, and Ernst Sellin. 1969. *Einleitung in das Alte Testament*. Heidelberg, Germany: Quelle & Meyer.

Folger, Tim. 2007. "Newsflash: Time May Not Exit." *Discover,* December 20.

Folsom, F., and M. E. Folsom. 1993. *America's Ancient Treasures*. Albuquerque: University of New Mexico Press.

"Fossil Reanalysis Pushes Back Origin of *Homo sapiens*." 2005. *Scientific American,* February 17.

Foster, Charles. 1897. *Bible Pictures and What They Teach Us: Containing 400 Illustrations from the Old and New Testaments with Brief Descriptions.* Philadelphia: Foster Publishing Company.

Frere, John. 1797. "Hoxne Brick Pit Letter." Hoxne, Norfolk: Sites of Special Scientific Interest. Natural England website. No longer available, but retrievable using Wayback Machine.

Frescura, F. A. M., and B. J. Hiley. 1984. "Algebras, Quantum Theory, and Pre-Space." *Revista Brasilera de Fisica, Volume Especial, os 70 anos de Mario Schonberg:* 49–86.

Furst, Jill L. M. 1997. *The Natural History of the Soul in Mexico.* New Haven, Conn.: Yale University Press.

Gaddis, Vincent. 1977. *American Indian Myths and Mysteries.* New York: Indian Head Books.

Gargaud, Muriel, et al., eds. 2015. PDF of *Encyclopedia of Astrobiology.* Berlin: Springer.

Garrod, D. A. E. 1955. "The Mugharet El-Emireh in Lower Galilee: Type-Station of the Emiran Industry." *Journal of the Royal Anthropological Institute of Great Britain and Ireland* 85, no. 1/2: 141–62.

Garrod, D. A. E., and D. M. A. Bate. 1937. *The Stone Age of Mount Carmel.* Vol. 1. Oxford, UK: Oxford University Press/Clarendon Press.

Garrod, D. A. E., and D. Kirkbride. 1961. "Excavation of the Abri Zumoffen, a Paleolithic rock-shelter near Adlun, South Lebanon." *Bulletin du Musée de Beyrouth* 16: 7–46.

Gaster, Moses. (1927) 2015. *The Asatir: The Samaritan Book of the Secret of Moses.* Eugene, Oreg.: Wipf & Stock.

———. (1927) 2015. "Pitron or Commentary to the Asatir." In Gaster (1927) 2015, 185–301 (odd numbers only).

———. (1927) 2015. "Samaritan Story of the Death of Moses," In Gaster (1927) 2015, 303–21 (complete with original commentary).

Gayed H. B. 1985. *The Apparition of Virgin Mary at El-Zeitoun Church.* Zeitoun, Egypt: St. Mary Coptic Church.

Geikie, John Cunningham. 1888. *The Holy Land and the Bible: A Book of Scripture Illustrations Gathered in Palestine.* New York: James Potts & Co.

Gharibyan, Hrant, and Robert F. Penna. 2013. "Are Entangled Particles Connected by Wormholes? Support for the ER = EPR Conjecture from Entropy Inequalities." *Physical Review* D 89, no. 6: 1–10.

Gibbons, Ann. 2017. "World's Oldest *Homo sapiens* Fossils Found in Morocco." *Science,* June 7.

———. 2020. "DNA Tracks Mysterious Denisovans to Chinese Cave, Just before Modern Humans Arrived Nearby." *Science,* October 29.

———. 2021. "Stunning 'Dragon Man' Skull May be an Elusive Denisovan—or A New Species of Human." *Science,* June 25.

Gooch, Stan. 1977. *The Neanderthal Question.* London: Wildwood House.

———. (1979) 2006. *The Dream Culture of the Neanderthals.* Formerly *Guardians of the Ancient Wisdom.* Rochester, Vt.: Inner Traditions.

———. (1989) 1995. *Cities of Dreams: When Women Ruled the Earth.* London: Aulis Books.

———. 2008. *The Neanderthal Legacy.* Rochester, Vt.: Inner Traditions.

Gopher, Avi, et al. 2005. "Qesem Cave: An Amudian Site in Central Israel." *Journal of the Israel Prehistoric Society* 35 (January): 69–92.

Gopher, Avi, et al. 2016. "Spatial Aspects as Seen from a Density Analysis of Lithics at Middle Pleistocene Qesem Cave: Preliminary Results and Observations." *Quaternary International* 398 (April 4): 103–17.

Gowlett, J. A. J. 2016. "The Discovery of Fire by Humans: A Long and Convoluted Process." *Philosophical Transactions of the Royal Society B* 371, no. 1696 (June 5).

Grimm, J. A. 1983. *The Shaman.* Norman: University of Oklahoma Press.

Grosman, Leore, Natalie D. Munro, and Anna Belfer-Cohen. 2008. "A 12,000-Year-Old Shaman Burial from the Southern Levant (Israel)." *Proceedings of the National Academy of Sciences of the United States of America* 105, no. 46 (November 18): 17665–69.

Grün, Rainer, et al. 1996. "Direct Dating of Florisbad hominid." *Nature* 382 (August 8): 500–501.

Hall, Robert L. 1997. *An Archaeology of the Soul.* Urbana: University of Illinois Press.

Hambling, D. 2018. "The Secret History of Plasma Weapons." *Popular Mechanics,* November 14.

"Hamsa, Hansa, Haṃsa, Haṃsā, Hamsā, Hamsha: 47 Definitions." n.d. Wisdom Library website.

Hancock, Graham. 1992. *The Sign and the Seal.* London: Heinemann.

———. 2007. *Supernatural: Meetings with the Ancient Teachers of Mankind.* New York: The Disinformation Company.

Hardy, Karen, et al. 2016. "Dental Calculus Reveals Potential Respiratory Irritants and Ingestion of Essential Plant-Based Nutrients at Lower Palaeolithic Qesem Cave Israel." *Quaternary International* 398 (April 4): 129–35.

Hatto, A. T. 1961. "The Swan Maiden: A Folk-Tale of North Eurasian Origin?" *Bulletin of the School of Oriental and African Studies* 24, no. 2: 326–52.

Healey, Faye, M. Persinger, and S. A. Koren. 1997. "Control of 'Choice' by Application of the Electromagnetic Field Equivalents of Spoken Words: Mediation by Emotional

Meaning Rather Than Linguistic Dimensions?" *Perceptual and Motor Skills* 85, no. 3 (December 1): 1411–18.

Heisenberg, Werner. (1930) 1949. *The Physical Principles of the Quantum Theory.* Translated by Carl Eckart and Frank C. Hoyt. Mineola, N.Y.: Dover Publications.

Heller, Dave. 2021. "Old, Old News: A Cave in Bear Buttes." Redheaded Blackbelt website.

Hernandez, Rey, Jon Klimo, and Rudy Schild, eds. 2018. *Beyond UFOs: The Science of Consciousness and Contact with Non Human Intelligence "Volume 1."* n.p.p: Experiencer.org.

Herries, Andy I. R. 2011. "A Chronological Perspective on the Acheulian and Its Transition to the Middle Stone Age in Southern Africa: The Question of the Fauresmith." *International Journal of Evolutionary Biology:* 1–25.

Hershkovitz, Israel, et al. 2011. "Middle Pleistocene Dental Remains from Qesem Cave (Israel)." *American Journal of Physical Anthropology* 144, no. 4 (April): 575–92.

Hewes, Hayden. 1976. "Piedmont, Missouri, UFOs." *TRUE Flying Saucers & UFOs Quarterly,* nos. 2 and 3.

Hively, Ray, and Robert Horn. 1982. "Geometry and Astronomy in Prehistoric Ohio." *Journal for the History of Astronomy* 13, no. 4 (February 1): 1–20.

Hodder, Ian. *The Leopard's Tale: Revealing the Mysteries of Çatalhöyük.* London: Thames and Hudson, 2006.

Holmes, William Henry, Walter E. Roth, and Matilda Coxe Stevenson. 1915. *Thirtieth Annual Report of the Bureau of American Ethnology to the Secretary of the Smithsonian Institution, 1908–1909.* Washington, D.C.: Government Printing Office.

"*Homo sapiens* or Denisovans? Who Made Stunning Cave Jewellery and Artefacts up to 48,000 Years Ago?" 2019. *Siberian Times,* February 4.

Hublin, Jean-Jacques, et al. 2017. "New Fossils from Jebel Irhoud, Morocco and the Pan-African Origin of *Homo sapiens.*" *Nature* 546, no. 7657 (June 8): 289–92.

Hudson, Charles. 1976. *The Southeastern Indians.* Knoxville: The University of Tennessee Press.

Huerta-Sánchez, Emilia, et al. 2014. "Altitude Adaptation in Tibetans Caused by Introgression of Denisovan-Like DNA." *Nature* 512, no. 7513 (July 2): 194–97.

Hurowitz, Victor. 1992. "The Expression ûqsāmîm beyâdâm (Numbers 22:7) in Light of Divinatory Practices from Mari." *Hebrew Studies Journal* 33, annual 1992: 5–15.

Hutton, Ronald. 2001. *Shamans: Siberian Spirituality and the Western Imagination.* London: Hambledon Continuum.

Israel Antiquities Authority. 2018. "An Important and Rare Prehistoric Site Uncovered in Israel." Israel Ministry of Foreign Affairs website, January 7.

Jackson, Chris. 2019. "A Quarter of Americans Believe That Crashed UFO Spacecrafts Are Held at Area 51 in Southern Nevada." IPSOS website, August 29.

Jacob (forename only). (1906) 2016. *History and Religions of the Samaritans.* Edited and introduction by William Eleazar Barton, and translated by Abdullah Ben Kori. Delhi, India: Facsimile Publisher.

Jacobs, G. S. et al. 2019. "Multiple Deeply Divergent Denisovan Ancestries in Papuans." *Cell* 177 (May 2): 1010–21.

Jacobson-Tepfer, Esther. 2015. *The Hunter, the Stag, and the Mother of Animals: Image, Monument, and Landscape in Ancient North Asia.* Oxford, UK: Oxford University Press.

Jayrajc. n.d. "Kailash Mansarovar Is Literally Heaven on Earth." Thomas Cook blog website.

Jelinek. A. J. 1977. "A Preliminary Study of Flakes from the Tabun Cave, Mount Carmel." *Eretz Israel* 13: 87–96.

———. 1982. "The Tabun Cave and Paleolithic Man in the Levant." *Science* 216, no. 4553 (June 25): 1369–75.

Ji, Qiang et al. 2021. "Late Middle Pleistocene Harbin Cranium Represents a New Homo Species." The Innovation online, June 25.

Jung, Carl. 1954. "Interview with Carl Jung by Georg Gerster." *Weltwoche* 22, no. 1078: 7.

———. 1955. "Dr. Carl Jung Himself on Unidentified Flying Objects." *Flying Saucer Review* 1, no. 2.

———. 1959. *Flying Saucers: A Modern Myth of Things Seen in the Sky.* New York: Harcourt, Brace, & World.

———. 1960. *Answer to Job.* New York: Meridian Books.

———. 1969. *The Collected Works: Archetypes and the Collective Unconscious.* Vol. 9. Princeton, N.J.: Princeton University Press.

"Kailish Manasarovar—Home of God Shiva—Mount Kailish." 2013. The Hindu Portal website, December 31.

Kaiser, R. 1987. "Chief Seattle's Speech(es)." In Swann and Krupat 1987, 497–536.

Kalman, Matthew. 2010. "Did First Humans Come Out of Middle East and Not Africa? Israeli Discovery Forces Scientists to Re-examine Evolution of Modern Man." *Daily Mail* website, December 28.

Karkanas, Panagiotis, et al. 2007. "Evidence for Habitual Use of Fire at the End of the Lower Paleolithic: Site-Formation Processes at Qesem Cave, Israel." *Journal of Human Evolution* 53, no. 2 (August): 197–212.

Keel, John. 1970. *Operation Trojan Horse.* New York: G. P. Putnam & Sons.

———. 1971. *Our Haunted Planet.* Greenwich, Conn.: Fawcett Publ., Inc.

———. 1975a. *The Eighth Tower.* New York: Dutton.

———. 1975b. *The Mothman Prophecies.* New York: Dutton.

———. 1978. *The Cosmic Question.* UK edition of *The Eighth Tower.* St. Albans, Hertfordshire, UK: Granada Publishing.

Kelleher, Colm, and George Knapp. 2005. *Hunt for the Skinwalker: Science Confronts the Unexplained at a Remote Ranch in Utah.* New York: Paraview Pocket Books.

Kellogg, D. O., ed. 1902. *The Encyclopedia Britannica.* New York: Werner.

Kenyon, D. 2015. *Forgotten Origins.* Livingston, Mont.: Atlantis Rising Books.

Kiboko, J. Kabamba. 2013. *Divining the Woman of Endor: African Culture, Postcolonial Hermeneutics, and the Politics of Biblical Translation.* London: Bloomsbury.

Kidadl Team. 2020. "All of the Chinese Dragon Names from Mythology to Inspire You." Kidadl website.

Kipling, Rudyard. 1894. *The Jungle Book.* London: Macmillan & Co.

Kirkpatrick, Sidney. 2000. *Edgar Cayce: An American Prophet.* New York: Riverhead Books.

Kirkpatrick, Sidney, and Nancy Kirkpatrick. 2015. *True Tales from the Edgar Cayce Archives.* Virginia Beach, Va.: A.R.E Press.

Kirschvink, J. L., A. Kobayashi-Kirschvink, and B. J. Woodford. 1992. "Magnetite Biomineralization in the Human Brain." *Proceedings of the National Academy of Sciences of the United States of America* 89, no. 16 (August 15): 7683–87.

Klass, Philip J. 1968. *UFOs—Identified.* New York: Random House.

Kohler, Kaufmann, and Ludwig Blau. (1906) 2012. *Jewish Encyclopedia,* s.v. "Shekinah." Jewish Encyclopedia website.

Kripal, J. J. 2011. *Mutants and Mystics.* Chicago, Ill.: University of Chicago Press.

Krippner, Stanley C. 2002. "Conflicting Perspectives on Shamans and Shamanism: Points and Counterpoints." *American Psychology* 57, no. 11 (November): 962–78.

Krupp, Edwin C. 2015. "Native American Cosmology and Other Worlds." In Gargaud et al. PDF.

La Barre de Beaumarchais, Mr. de [Antoine], and Bernard Picart. 1733. *The Temple of the Muses; or, the Principal Histories of Fabulous Antiquity, Represented in Sixty Sculptures.* Amsterdam: Zachariah Chatelain.

Lacey, Louise. 1975. *Lunaception: A Feminine Odyssey into Fertility and Contraception.* New York: Coward, McCann & Geoghegan.

Lahelma, Antti. 2012. "Strange Swans and Odd Ducks: Interpreting the Ambiguous Waterfowl Imagery of Lake Onega." In Cochrane and Jones 2012, 15–33.

Lake, Medicine Grizzlybear. 1993. *Native Healer.* New York: Harper.

Lamb, C. 1978. "Close Encounters: Reservation UFO Sightings So Common They're Legendary." *Yakima* (Wash.) *Herald-Republic,* January 29, 3A.

Lambrecht, Kálmán. 1933. *Handbuch der Palaeornithologie.* Berlin: Gebrüder Borntraeger.

Langfur, Stephen. 2019. "Ancient Shechem (Tell Balata)." NET/Near East Tourist Agency website.

Langlois, David. 2003. "Brane Cosmology: An Introduction." *Progress of Theoretical Physics Supplement* 148: 181–212. Cornell University's arXiv website, September 30.

Langmuir, Irving. 1928. "Oscillations in Ionized Gases." *Proceedings of the National Academy of Sciences of the United States of America* 14, no. 8 (August 1): 627–37.

Lankford, G. E. 2011. *Native American Legends of the Southeast.* Tuscaloosa: University of Alabama Press.

Larena, Maximilian et al. 2021. "Philippine Ayta Possess the Highest Level of Denisovan Ancestry in the World." *Current Biology,* August 12.

Layne, Meade. 1957. *The Coming of the Guardians.* San Diego, Calif.: Borderland Sciences Research Associates.

Lbova, Liudmila. 2010. "Evidence of Modern Human Behavior in the Baikal Zone during the Early Upper Paleolithic Period." *Bulletin of the Indo-Pacific Prehistory Association* 30: 9–13.

Lbova, Liudmila, Darya Kozhevnikov, and Pavel Volkov. 2012. "Musical Instruments in Siberia (Early Stage of the Upper Paleolithic)." In Clottes 2012, CD-1900–CD-1904.

Lemorini, C., et al. 2020. "The Use of Ash at Late Lower Paleolithic Qesem Cave, Israel—An Integrated Study of Use-Wear and Residue Analysis." *PLoS One* 15, no. 9 (September 21): e0237502.

Lepre, Christopher J. 2011. "An Earlier Origin for the Acheulian." *Nature* 477, no. 7362 (August 31): 82–85.

Leviton, Richard. 2011. *Hierophantic Landscapes.* Bloomington, Ind.: iUniverse.

Li, Rowena (uploader). 2012. "How the Heilongjiang (Amur River) Got Its Name." Vimeo video, July 12.

Liesowska, Anna, and Svetlana Skarbo. 2019. "Cave Lion Figurine Made of Woolly Mammoth Tusk Found at Denisova Cave." *Siberian Times,* November 20.

Little, Gregory L. 1984. *The Archetype Experience: Resolving the UFO Mystery and the Riddle of Biblical Prophecy Using C. G. Jung's Concept of Synchronicity.* Moore Haven, Fla.: Rainbow Books.

———. 1990. *People of the Web.* Memphis, Tenn.: Eagle Wing Books.

———. 1994. *Grand Illusions: The Spectral Reality Underlying Sexual UFO Abductions, Crashed Saucers, Afterlife Experiences, Sacred Ancient Sites, and Other Enigmas.* Memphis, Tenn.: White Buffalo Books.

———. 2001a. "Geomagnetic Explanations of UFOs." In Story 2001, 214–15.

———. 2001b. "Geomagnetic Intelligent Energy Theory of UFOs." In Story 2001, 215–17.

———. 2001c. "Science at the Frontier: A Merging of Ancient and Modern Science." *Journal of Religion and Psychical Research* 24, no. 1: 2–25.

———. 2006. "UK Ministry of Defence Confirms UFOs as Plasmas." *Alternate Perceptions Magazine* 102 (June).

———. 2010. "Why Do Ufologists Largely Ignore the Most Scientific Field Study of UFOs Ever Conducted?" *Alternate Perceptions Magazine* 146 (March).

———. 2014a. "The Origin of the Ancient Astronaut Idea." *Alternate Perceptions Magazine* 201 (December).

———. 2014b. *Path of Souls.* Memphis, Tenn.: Archetype Books.

———. 2016. *The Illustrated Encyclopedia of Native American Indian Mounds & Earthworks.* Memphis, Tenn.: Eagle Wing Books, Inc.

Little, G. L., K. Prachniak, and S. Prachniak. 2019. *Freedom to Change.* Memphis, Tenn.: Freedom 2 Change.

Little, G. L., J. Van Auken, and L. Little. 2001. *Mound Builders: Edgar Cayce's Forgotten Record of Ancient America.* Memphis, Tenn.: Eagle Wing Books, Inc.

Long, G. 1982. "Memories of a Lookout: UFOs on the Yakima Indian Reservation." *MUFON Journal* (April): 7–11.

———. 1990. *Examining the Earthlight Theory: The Yakima UFO Microcosm.* Chicago, Ill.: Center for UFO Studies.

———. 1994. "Strangeness at Yakima." *International UFO Reporter* 19, no. 4.

Lorenzen, Coral, and Jim Lorenzen. 1976. *Encounters and UFO Occupants.* New York: Berkley Publishing Corporation.

Lothian, Brett. 2019. "The Denisovans at the Gates of Dawn." *New Dawn,* November/ December, 54–64.

Lund University. 2019. "The Moon Determines When Migratory Birds Head South." ScienceDaily website, October 16.

Lutz, Rüdiger, and Gabriele Lutz. 1995. *Das Geheimnis der Wüste: Die Felskunst des Messak Sattafet und Messak Mellet-Libyen.* Innsbruck, Austria: Universitätsbuchhandlung/ Golf Verlag.

Luyken, Jan, Johannes Covens, and Cornelis Mortier. 1729. *Afbeeldingen der merkwaardigste geschiedenissen van het Oude en Nieuwe Testament.* Amsterdam: Johannes Covens and Cornelius Mortier.

Machette, M. N., M. M. Coates, and M. L. Johnson, eds. 2007. *2007 Rocky Mountain Section Friends of the Pleistocene Field Trip—Quaternary Geology of the San Luis Basin of Colorado and New Mexico, September 7–9, 2007.* U.S. Geological Survey Open-File Report 2007–1193. Reston, Va.: U.S. Geological Survey.

Maldacena, Juan, and Leonard Susskind. 2013. "Cool Horizons for Entangled Black Holes." *Fortschritte der Physik* 61, no. 9: 781–811.

Mandeville, John de. 1900. *The Travels of John de Mandeville: The Version of the Cotton Manuscript in Modern Spelling.* London: Macmillan.

Mannermaa, Kristiina, Andrei Panteleyev, and Mikhail Sablin. 2008. "Birds in Late Mesolithic Burials at Yuzhniy Oleniy Ostrov (Lake Onega, Western Russia)—What Do They Tell About Humans and the Environment?" *Fennoscandia Archaeologica* 25: 3–25.

Marshack, Alexander. 1972. *The Roots of Civilization: The Cognitive Beginning of Man's First Art, Symbol, and Notation.* New York: McGraw-Hill.

Marshall, Michael. 2021. "Newly Identified Ancestor of Neanderthals Complicates the Human Story." *New Scientist* website, June 24.

Massilani, Diyendo, and Svante Pääbo. 2020. "Denisovan DNA in the Genome of Early East Asians: Scientists Identify 34,000-Year-Old Early East Asian of Mixed Eurasian Descent." Max-Planck-Gesellschaft website, October 29.

McDougall, Ian, Francis H. Brown, and John G. Fleagle. 2005. "Stratigraphic Placement and Age of Modern Humans from Kibish, Ethiopia." *Nature* 433, no. 7027 (February 17): 733–36.

McPherrer, Ida. 2010. "Medicine Wheel Legends." In Dow, Welsch, and Dow 2010, 187–192.

McPherron, Shannon P., et al. 2010. "Evidence for Stone-Tool-Assisted Consumption of Animal Tissues before 3.39 Million Years Ago at Dikika, Ethiopia." *Nature* 466, no. 7308 (August 12): 857–60.

Medvedev, G. 1998. "Art from Central Siberian Paleolithic Sites." In Derev'anko, Shimkin, and Powers 1998, 132–37.

Mellaart, James. 1967. *Çatal Hüyük: A Neolithic Town in Anatolia.* London: Thames and Hudson.

Mercier, Norbert, et al. 2013. "New Datings of Amudian Layers at Qesem Cave (Israel): Results of TL Applied to Burnt Flints and ESR/U-series to Teeth." *Journal of Archaeological Science* 40, no. 7 (July): 3011–20.

Meyer, Matthias, et al. 2012. "A High-Coverage Genome Sequence from an Archaic Denisovan Individual." *Science* 338, no. 6104 (October 12): 222–26.

Milik, J. T., ed. 1976. *The Books of Enoch: Aramaic Fragments of Qumrân Cave 4, with the Collaboration of Matthew Black.* Oxford, UK: Oxford University Press/Clarendon Press.

Milne, A. 2016. *Sky Critters.* Cambridge, Cambridgeshire, UK: Empiricus Books.

MINNews. 2021. "Chinese Scientists Discovered a New Race: 'Dragon Man.'" MINNews website, accessed July 1, 2021.

Mizokami, K. 2020. "Does the Navy's Missile-Fooling Plasma Tech Explain Recent UFO Sightings?" *Popular Mechanics,* May 13.

Montgomery, James Alan. (1907) 1968. *The Samaritans, the Earliest Jewish Sect: Their History, Theology, and Literature.* New York: Ktav Publishing House.

Moody, D. 1978. "Yakima Valley Prime for UFO Sightings." *Tri-City Herald* (Kennwick, Wash.), November 5, Section 2, 1.

"Mount Taishan" (1987) 2011. World Heritage Datasheet website.

Mullaney, James. 2007. *Edgar Cayce and the Cosmos.* Virginia Beach, Va.: A.R.E. Press.

Mullins, Justin. 1999, "And the Voice Said." *New Scientist* website, December 25.

Musso, Valeria Céspedes. 2017. "Marian Apparitions in Cultural Contexts: Applying Jungian Depth Psychological Principles to Mass Visions of the Virgin Mary at Zeitoun." *International Journal of Jungian Studies* 9, no. 3 (February): 183–96.

Nebesky-Wojkowitz, René de. (1956) 1996. *Oracles and Demons of Tibet.* Delhi, India: Book Faith India.

Nelson, Cynthia. 1973. "The Virgin of Zeitoun." *Worldview* 16, no. 9 (September): 5–11.

Newbrough, John Ballou. 1882. *Oahspe.* New York: Oahspe Publishing Associates.

Ni, Xijun et al. 2021. "Massive Cranium from Harbin in Northeastern China Establishes a New Middle Pleistocene Human Lineage." The Innovation online, June 25.

Nield, David. 2021. "Quantum Entanglement Has Now Been Directly Observed at a Larger Macroscopic Scale." ScienceAlert website, May 8.

Noe-Nygaard, Nanna. 1974. "Mesolithic Hunting in Denmark Illustrated by Bone Injuries Caused by Human Weapons." *Journal of Archaeological Science* 1, no. 3 (September): 217–48.

Norbu, Chögyal Namkhai. 2013. *A History of Zhang Zhung and Tibet.* Vol. 1, *The Early Period.* Translated by Donatella Rossi. Berkeley, Calif.: North Atlantic Books; Arcidosso, Italy: Shang Shung Publications.

Norevik, Gabriel, et al. 2019. "The Lunar Cycle Drives Migration of a Nocturnal Bird." *PLoS Biology* 17, no. 10 (October 15): e3000456.

Northrop, Henry Davenport. 1894. *Treasures of the Bible.* Philadelphia Pa and Chicago, Ill.: International Publishing Co.

Noth, Martin. 1962. *Exodus: A Commentary.* Philadelphia: Westminster Press.

Obermaier, Hugo. 1925. *Fossil Man in Spain.* New Haven, Conn.: Hispanic Society of America; London: Oxford University Press.

O'Brien, Christopher. 1996. *The Mysterious Valley.* New York: St. Martin's Press.

O'Bryan, Aileen. 1956. *The Dine: Origin Myths of the Navaho Indians.* Smithsonian Institution/Bureau of American Ethnology. Bulletin of the Bureau of American Ethnology, vol. 163. Washington D.C.: United States Government Printing Office.

O'Callaghan, Jonathan. 2014. "Is It Really Just a 'Shiny Rock?' NASA Claims to Have Solved Mystery of the Light on Mars." *Daily Mail,* April 10.

O'Shea, John, and Marek Zvelebil. 1984. "Oleneostrovski Mogilnik: Reconstructing the Social and Economic Organization of Prehistoric Foragers in Northern Russia." *Journal of Anthropological Archaeology* 3, no. 1 (March): 1–40.

Overton, Nick J., and Yannis Hamilakis. 2013. "A Manifesto for a Social Zooarchaeology. Swans and Other Beings in the Mesolithic." *Archaeological Dialogues* 20, no. 2 (November 8): 111–36.

Palmer, Ray. 1960. "Addendum." In Newbrough 1882, 907–10.

Panigrahi, D., and S. Chatterjee. 2008. "General Relativistic Plasma in Higher Dimensional Space Time." Cornell University's arXiv website, August 8.

Papantonopoulos, E. 2002. "Brane Cosmology." *Cosmological Crossroads. Lecture Notes in Physics* 592: 458–77. Cornell University's arXiv website, February 7, revised February 22.

Parker Pearson, Mike, et al. 2015. "Craig Rhos-y-felin: A Welsh Bluestone Megalith Quarry for Stonehenge." *Antiquity* 89, no. 348 (December 7): 1331–52.

Parkhomenko, Eleonora I. 1971. *Electrification Phenomena in Rocks.* Monographs in Geoscience. Translated from the Russian by George V. Keller. New York and London: Plenum Press.

Peat, F. David. 1996. *Infinite Potential: The Life and Times of David Bohm.* New York: Basic Books.

Pereira, Paulo, et al., eds. 2019. *Fire Effects on Soil Properties.* Clayton South, Victoria, Australia: CSIRO Publishing.

Persinger, Michael, and Gyslaine Lafreniere. 1977. *Space-Time Transients and Unusual Events.* Chicago, Ill.: Nelson-Hall Co.

Petrozzi, Maria Teresa. 1973. *Samaria.* Jerusalem, Israel: Franciscan Printing Press.

Pilichis, Dennis. 1975. *Apparition Phenomenon in Zeitoun, Egypt 1968–1969–1970: A Page Research Library Newsletter Special Report.* Cleveland, Ohio: Page Research Library.

Pinheiro, Mario J. 2007. "Plasma: The Genesis of the Word." Cornell University's arXiv website, March 27.

"Plasma, Plasma, Everywhere." 1999. NASA Science: Share the Science website, September 7.

Polehampton, Rev. Edward, and John M. Good. 1818. *The Gallery of Nature and Art: Or, a Tour through Creation and Science.* London: R. Wilks.

Pope, Matthew, John McNabb, and Clive Gamble. 2018. *Crossing the Human Threshold: Dynamic Transformation and Persistent Places during the Middle Pleistocene.* Abingdon, UK: Oxon; New York: Routledge.

Popkin, Gabriel. 2018. "Einstein's 'Spooky Action at a Distance' Spotted in Objects Almost Big Enough to See." *Science* magazine website, April 25.

Pourhasan, Razieh, Niayesh Afshordi, and Robert B. Mann. 2014. "Out of the White Hole: A Holographic Origin for the Big Bang." *Journal of Cosmology and Astroparticle Physics,* no. 4: 1–16.

Pratt, David. 1993. "David Bohm and the Implicate Order." *Sunrise* magazine, February/March.

"Prehistoric Humans Ate Bone Marrow like Canned Soup 400,000 Years Ago." 2019. ScienceDaily website, October 9.

Project Sign. 1949. Wright-Patterson Air Force Base, Ohio: Air Materiel Command.

Rabinovicha, R., et al. 2012. "Elephants at the Middle Pleistocene Acheulian Open-Air Site of Revadim Quarry, Israel." *Quaternary International* 276–77 (October): 183–97.

Rabinowitz, Mario. 2001. "*n*-Dimensional Gravity: Little Black Holes, Dark Matter, and Ball Lightning." *International Journal of Theoretical Physics* 40, no. 4 (January): 875–901.

Radin, Paul, C. G. Jung, and Karl Kerényi. 1956. *The Trickster: A Study in American Indian Mythology.* New York: Bell Publishing Company.

Rajki, András. 2005. *Arabic Etymological Dictionary.* Download available at Academia website.

Rajvanshi, Anil K. 2008. "Irving Langmuir: A Pioneering Industrial Physical Chemist." *Resonance* 13, no. 7 (July): 619–26.

Raynes, Brent. 2004. *Visitors from Hidden Realms.* Memphis, Tenn.: Eagle Wing Books, Inc.

———. 2019. *John A. Keel: The Man, the Myths, and the Ongoing Mysteries.* n.p.p.: Create Space, Amazon.

Redfern, Nick. 2010. *Contactees.* Franklin Lakes, N.J.: New Page Books.

Reich, David. 2018. *Who We Are and How We Got Here.* New York: Pantheon.

Reich, David, et al. 2010. "Genetic History of an Archaic Hominin Group from Denisova Cave in Siberia." *Nature* 468, no. 7327 (December 22): 1053–60.

Richter, Daniel, et al. 2017. "The Age of the Hominin Fossils from Jebel Irhoud, Morocco, and the Origins of the Middle Stone Age." *Nature* 546 (June 8): 293–96.

Riedinger, R., et al. 2018. "Remote Quantum Entanglement between Two Micromechanical Oscillators." *Nature* 556 (April 25): 473–77.

Rucker, Rudy. (1984) 2014. *The Fourth Dimension: Toward a Geometry of Higher Reality.* Mineola, N.Y.: Dover Publications, Inc.

Ruleman, C., and M. N. Machette. 2007. "An Overview of the Sangre de Cristo Fault System and New Insights to Interactions between Quaternary Faults in the Northern Rio Grande Rift." In Machette, Coates, and Johnson 2007, 187–97.

Rusov, V. D., et al. 2012. "Can Resonant Oscillations of the Earth Ionosphere Influence the Human Brain Biorhythm?" *Physics-General-Biology* 23 (August): 1–13.

Rust, Alfred. 1950. *Die Höhlenfunde von Jabrud (Syrien).* Neumünster, Germany: Wachholtz.

Rutledge, Harley. 1981. *Project Identification.* Englewood Cliffs, N.J.: Prentice-Hall.

Saad, L. 2019. "Americans Skeptical of UFOs, but Say Government Knows More." Gallup website, September 6.

Sackett, J. 2014. "Boucher de Perthes and the Discovery of Human Antiquity." *Bulletin of the History of Archaeology* 24, pt. 2 (January 6): 1–11.

Sackville-West, V. 1936. *Saint Joan of Arc.* Garden City, N.Y.: Doubleday Doran Co.

Sagan, Carl. 1963. "Direct Contact among Galactic Civilizations by Relativistic Interstellar Flight." *Planetary and Space Science* 11, no. 5, 485–98.

Sagan, C., and T. Page. 1973. *UFO's: A Scientific Debate.* AAAS Symposium, Boston, December 1969. Ithaca, N.Y.: Cornell University Press.

"Sahara Prehistoric Rock Art." 2009. Temehu website.

Salisbury, Frank B. (1974) 2010. *The Utah UFO Display.* Springville, Utah: Bonneville.

Saunders, Nicholas J. 2001. "A Dark Light: Reflections on Obsidian in Mesoamerica." *World Archaeology* 33, no. 2 (November 5): 220–36.

Schlesier, Karl H. 1985. *The Wolves of Heaven*. Norman: University of Oklahoma Press.

Schuster. 2021. "Israeli Archaeologists Think New Chinese Hominin 'Dragon Man' May Be Homo Nesher." *Haaretz* newspaper website, June 27.

———. 2020. "'Galilean Man' Invented Pyrotechnology over 300,000 Years Ago, Team Suggests." *Haaretz* newspaper website, October 7.

———. 2019. "Why Archaic Humans in Israel Collected Feathers 420,000 Years Ago." *Haaretz* newspaper website, September 23.

The Secret of Skinwalker Ranch. History Channel TV series.

Sellin, Ernst. 1906. "Das israelitische Ephod." In Bezold 1906, vol. 2, 699–717.

———. 1922. *Mose und seine Bedeutung für die israelitisch-jüdische Religionsgeschichte.* Leipzig, Germany: A. Deichertsche Verlagsbuchhandlung.

Seton, Ernest, and Seton, Julia. 1966. *The Gospel of the Redman*. Santa Fe, N.Mex.: Seton Village.

Shahack-Gross, Ruth, et al. 2014. "Evidence for the Repeated Use of a Central Hearth at Middle Pleistocene (300 ky ago) Qesem Cave, Israel." *Journal of Archaeological Science* 44, no. 1 (April): 12–21.

Shao, Qingfeng, et al. 2021. "Geochemical Provenancing and Direct Dating of the Harbin Archaic Human Cranium." The Innovation online, June 25.

Shaw, Thomas. 1738. *Travels or Observations Relating to Several Parts of Barbary and the Levant*. Oxford, UK: Steph. Niblett.

Shea, John J., and Ofer Bar-Yosef. 2005. "Who Were the Skhul/Qafzeh People? An Archaeological Perspective on Eurasia's Oldest Modern Humans." *Mitekufat Haeven: Journal of the Israel Prehistoric Society* 35: 451–68.

Shimelmitz, Ron, Ran Barkai, and Avi Gopher. 2011. "Systematic Blade Production at Late Lower Paleolithic (400-200 kyr) Qesem Cave, Israel." *Journal of Human Evolution* 64, no. 4 (August): 458–79.

Shimelmitz, R., et al. 2014. "'Fire at Will': The Emergence of Habitual Fire Use 350,000 Years Ago." *Journal of Human Evolution* 77 (October): 196–203.

Shodoev, Nikolai. 2012. *Spiritual Wisdom from the Altai Mountains*. Alresford, Hampshire, UK: John Hunt Publishing.

Siegel-Itzkovich, Judy. 2010. "*Homo sapiens* Lived in Eretz Yisrael 400,000 Years Ago." *The Jerusalem Post,* December 26.

Silverman, Jacob. 2007. "Are We Looking for Aliens in the Wrong Places?" Science: How Stuff Works website.

Sinclair, Paul. 2016. *Truth-Proof: The Truth That Leaves No Proof.* Bridlington, East Riding, Yorkshire, UK: PBC Publishing.

———. 2017. *Truth-Proof 2: Beyond the Thinking Mind.* Bridlington, East Riding, Yorkshire, UK: PBC Publishing.

———. 2019. *Truth-Proof 3: Bringing Down the Light.* Bridlington, East Riding, Yorkshire, UK: PBC Publishing.

Skarbo, Svetlana, and Anna Liesowska. 2020. "Sensational Discovery of a 250,000 Year Old Milk Tooth Found inside the Denisova Cave in Siberia." *Siberian Times,* October 1.

Smith, Julian. 2020. "The Power of Secret Societies." *Archaeology* 73, no. 4 (July–August): 50–55.

Smith, Kiona N. 2021. "Is the 'Dragon Man' Skull Actually from a New Hominin Species?" Ars Technica website, July 4.

Solecki R. L., and R. S. Solecki. 1986. "A Reappraisal of Rust's Cultural Stratigraphy of Yabroud Shelter I." *Paléorient* 12, no. 1: 53–59.

Solodenko, Natalya. et al. 2015. "Fat Residue and Use-Wear Found on Acheulian Biface and Scraper Associated with Butchered Elephant Remains at the Site of Revadim, Israel." *PLoS One* 10, no. 3 (March 18): e0118572.

Sparrow, W. Shaw. 1905. *The Old Testament in Art.* London: Hodder & Stoughton.

Spence, Lewis. 1914. *Myths of the North American Indians.* London: Harrap & Co.

Squier, E. G., and E. H. Davis. 1848. *Ancient Monuments of the Mississippi Valley.* Washington, D.C.: Smithsonian Institution.

Steiger, Brad. 1984. *Indian Medicine Power.* Atglen, Pa.: Whitford Press.

Stevenson, Matilda Coxe. 1915. "Ethnobotany of the Zuñi Indians." In Holmes, Roth, and Stevenson 1915, 35–100.

"Stonehenge 'Bluestone' Quarries Confirmed 140 Miles Away in Wales." 2015. UCL News website, December 7.

Story, Ron. 1980. *The Encyclopedia of UFOs.* New York: Doubleday.

———, ed. 2001. *The Encyclopedia of Extraterrestrial Encounters.* New York: New American Library.

Stringer, Chris B., and Ian Barnes. 2015. "Deciphering the Denisovans." *Proceedings of the National Academy of Sciences of the United States of America* 112, no. 51 (December 22): 15542–43.

Sugrue, T. 2015. *There Is a River.* Virginia Beach, Va.: Tarcher/Penguin/A.R.E. Press.

Susskind, Leonard. 2021. "Copenhagen vs Everett, Teleportation, and ER=EPR." arXiv:1604.02589v2 [hep-th].

Swann, B., and A. Krupat, eds. 1987. *Recovering the Word: Essays on Native American Literature.* Berkeley: University of California Press.

Swedenborg, E. 1758. *Earths in the Universe: Renamed Earths in Our Solar System.* London: Swedenborg Society.

———. 1890. *Heaven and Its Wonders and Hell.* Philadelphia: Lippincott.

———. 1918. *Journal of Dreams.* Bryn Athyn, Pa.: The Academy Book Room.

Thériault, Robert, et al. 2014. "Prevalence of Earthquake Lights Associated with Rift Environments." *Seismological Research Letters* 85, no. 1 (January/February): 159–78.

Thornsburg, William K. 2007. *The Marfa Lights: A Close Encounter.* Victoria, Tex.: privately printed.

Tonks, Lewi. 1967. "The Birth of Plasma." *American Journal of Physics* 35: 857–58.

Townsend, Richard F., and Robert V. Sharp, eds. 2004. *Hero, Hawk, and Open Hand.* Chicago, Ill.: Art Institute of Chicago.

Tressoldi, Patrizio E. 2011. "Extraordinary Claims Require Extraordinary Evidence: The Case of Non-local Perception, a Classical and Bayesian Review of Evidences." *Frontiers in Psychology* 2 (June 10): 117.

Tsytovich, V. N., et al. 2007. "From Plasma Crystals and Helical Structures towards Inorganic Living Matter." *New Journal of Physics* 9, no. 8 (August): 263.

Ulrich, Eugene. 2015a. *The Dead Sea Scrolls and the Developmental Composition of the Bible.* Vetus Testamentum, Suppl, vol. 169. Leiden, the Netherlands: E. J. Brill.

———. 2015b. "Joshua's First Altar in the Promised Land." In Ulrich 2015a, 47–65.

United Press International. "UFO Reports in Ozarks Discounted." 1973. United Press International (UPI), April 26.

Uyanik, Muvaffak. 1974. *Petroglyphs of South-eastern Anatolia.* Graz, Austria: Akademishe Druck-u. Verlagsanstalt.

Vallee, Jacques. 1988. *Dimensions: A Casebook of Alien Contact.* London: Souvenir Press.

Van Auken, John, and Lora Little. 1999. *The Lost Hall of Records.* Memphis, Tenn.: Eagle Wing Books.

Venditti, Flavia, et al. 2019. "Recycling for a Purpose in the Late Lower Paleolithic Levant: Use-wear and Residue Analyses of Small Sharp Flint Items Indicate a Planned and Integrated Subsistence Behavior at Qesem Cave (Israel)" *Journal of Human Evolution* 131 (June): 109–28.

Verri, G., et al. 2004. "Flint Mining in Prehistory Recorded by *In Situ*–Produced Cosmogenic ^{10}Be." *Proceedings of the National Academy of Sciences of the United States of America* 101, no. 21 (May 25): 7880–84.

Wang, Connie X., et al. 2019. "Transduction of the Geomagnetic Field as Evidenced from alpha-Band Activity in the Human Brain." *eNuero* 6, no. 2.

Weber, Gerhard W., et al. 2016. "The Qesem Cave Hominin Material (Part 1): A Morphometric Analysis of the Mandibular Premolars and Molar." *Quaternary International* 398 (April 4): 159–74.

"What Is Gravity?" 2020. NASA Science: Space Place website, December 17.

"What Is Schumann Resonance and Why Is It Important for Your Health." 2021. Radiance Wellness Spa: Diana Ralys Skin Health website.

White, William. 1868. *Emanuel Swedenborg: His Life and Writings.* London: Simpkin, Marshall, Co.

Wilkins, Harold T. (1955) 1967. *Flying Saucers Uncensored*. New York: Pyramid Books.

Wilkins, Jayne, and Michael Chazan. 2012. "Blade production ~500 thousand years ago at Kathu Pan 1, South Africa: support for a multiple origins hypothesis for early Middle Pleistocene blade technologies." *Journal of Archaeological Science* 39: 1883–1900.

Woodford, Chris. 2019. "Piezoelectricity." ExplainThatStuff! website.

"World's Oldest Needle Found in Siberian Cave That Stitches Together Human History." 2016. *Siberian Times,* August 23.

Wright, Elwood, and Pat Kenney. 1973. "The Marfa Lights: The Enigma Lights of Marfa—An Unexplained Phenomena." Internet Archive: Wayback Machine website, March 14–June 16.

Yardimci, Nurettin. 2008. *Mezopotamya'ya açilan kapi Harran*. Istanbul: Ege Yayın.

Young's Literal Translation. "Genesis." Bible Hub website.

Zaidner, Yossi, et al. 2021. "Middle Pleistocene Homo Behavior and Culture at 140,000 to 120,000 Years Ago and Interactions with Homo sapiens." *Science* 372, no. 6549 (June 25), 1429–33.

Zhang, Dongju, et al. 2020. "Denisovan DNA in Late Pleistocene Sediments from Baishiya Karst Cave on the Tibetan Plateau." *Science* 370, no. 6516 (October 30): 584–87.

INDEX

Numbers in *italics* preceded by *pl.* refer to color insert plate numbers.